Why the Axis Lost

# Why the Axis Lost

*An Analysis
of Strategic Errors*

JOHN ARQUILLA

*Foreword by* Victor Davis Hanson

McFarland & Company, Inc., Publishers
*Jefferson, North Carolina*

LIBRARY OF CONGRESS CATALOGUING-IN-PUBLICATION DATA

Names: Arquilla, John, author. | Hanson, Victor Davis, writer of foreword.
Title: Why the Axis lost : an analysis of strategic errors / John Arquilla ;
foreword by Victor Davis Hanson.
Description: Jefferson, North Carolina : McFarland & Company, Inc.,
Publishers, 2020 | Includes bibliographical references and index.
Identifiers: LCCN 2020004658 | ISBN 9781476674520 (paperback) ∞
ISBN 9781476639529 (ebook)
Subjects: LCSH: Strategy. | World War, 1939–1945—Equipment and supplies. |
World War, 1939–1945—Campaigns. | World War, 1939–1945—Germany. |
World War, 1939–1945—Japan. | World War, 1939–1945—Italy.
Classification: LCC D743 .A723 2020 | DDC 940.54—dc23
LC record available at https://lccn.loc.gov/2020004658

BRITISH LIBRARY CATALOGUING DATA ARE AVAILABLE

ISBN (print) 978-1-4766-7452-0
ISBN (ebook)978-1-4766-3952-9

Front cover images: Emperor Hirohito delivering a message
to Lt. General Hideki Tojo (National Archives); Mussolini and Hitler
in Munich, June 18, 1940 (© 2020 Everett Historical/Shutterstock)

Printed in the United States of America

*McFarland & Company, Inc., Publishers
Box 611, Jefferson, North Carolina 28640
www.mcfarlandpub.com*

For Mike Murray

*The war had two outstanding characteristics: It was a war of remarkable mobility and of unrivalled inhumanity.*
—Major General J.F.C. Fuller

# Contents

# *Acknowledgments*

PROFESSORS COMMONLY AVOW that they learn a great deal from their students. This is especially true when one teaches at a military school for more than a quarter-century. As my signature course examines professional military responses to technological change, World War II features in a most prominent way; and so, for many years I have been the fortunate beneficiary of the fresh perspectives offered up by soldiers, sailors, airmen and marines about this greatest of all conflicts. To my students, too numerous to mention by name, I give my very sincerest thanks for your many insights—and for the sheer privilege of working with you.

My dear colleagues at the Naval Postgraduate School have, through countless discussions, made their own profound contributions. Indeed, it is thirty years since Wayne Hughes and I had our first (of many) conversations about naval operations and strategy in the Second World War. Kalev Sepp has an inexhaustible storehouse of detailed operational knowledge—and a most remarkable knack for locating just the right maps and pictures. Nancy Roberts awakened me to the possibility of looking at military affairs through the lens of "design"—an epiphany that has, in recent years, completely re-energized me as a scholar.

In terms of support, the staff of the Dudley Knox Library have gone out of their way to track down many of the key sources required for this study—going so far at one point as to hunt down pages that had been torn out of a critically important document from the 1940s that were thought lost forever. Patricia Hamilton has done superb work with the manuscript's format, maps, and pictures. At McFarland & Company, Rhonda Herman embraced this project warmly from the outset, and Dylan Lightfoot has probed, prodded and guided in the manner of all great editors.

Last, there are two other important influences, felt early in my life, and which continue to this day. The first is Katharine Savage's *Story of the Second World War.* I came upon it as a schoolboy in the 1960s—she wrote for younger readers—and have read and reread it many times since. Her ability to grasp larger themes, and at the same time to seize upon crucial moments and key individuals, captured my imagination and set me on a lifelong course of inquiry into World War II. Since the 1970s, my friend Mike Murray, to whom this book is dedicated, has played a big role as well, often coming up with the odd detail, or the precisely correct question, that has lighted the way ahead at just the right time.

For all the debts of gratitude owed, this book represents my sincerest effort to provide worthy recompense.

# *Foreword*
## by Victor Davis Hanson

WHY DID THE ALLIES WIN WORLD WAR II? In this engaging analytical dissection of the Second World War, John Arquilla takes on the determinist view that wars are won by those with the most guns and people. Thus, by early 1943 the fully mobilized British Empire, Soviet Union and United States were supposedly foreordained to defeat the Axis powers.

Arquilla does not deny the logic of that consensus view. Instead, he offers a subtler, alternate explanation about World War II, and indeed, of armed conflicts in general, especially those of the 20th century. In his view, there are myriad factors that determine how material advantages are expressed—or sometimes not utilized fully at all. And such criteria range from weapon design, and operational and strategic doctrine, to supreme command, economic mobilization, and national will and spirit—all beyond just matters of manpower and matériel potential.

Germany, Italy and Japan certainly suffered a narrower margin of error than what became by 1942 an alliance of convenience of more powerful enemies. But such disadvantages did not preclude the reality that better decisions might have reversed the course of the war—or at least prevented an unconditional Axis surrender, resulting in an annihilating and humiliating defeat and occupation.

Arquilla offers a number of fascinating vignettes that illustrate his thesis. Germany had the right idea of focusing on fleets of U-boats, given its past expertise in submarine warfare and its inability to match the Royal Navy's fleet of surface ships. And the *Kriegsmarine*'s ill-fated, prewar Plan Z demonstrated that it had the potential to build expensive, first-class capital ships. Yet had Admiral Raeder forgone building super and pocket battleships and heavy cruisers, and instead focused on mass production of late-model U-boats—in the fashion of the American submarine fleet of 1943–45—then an effective blockade of Britain, even destruction of allied shipping lanes in the Mediterranean, might have been feasible.

Germany also never fully calibrated aerial attack in terms of the cost, human and fiscal, to deliver a pound of high explosives or incendiaries to the target. Had it been more pragmatic, it might have used its traditions of aeronautical engineering excellence to send out large fleets of four-engine heavy bombers over Britain and the Soviet Union.

What good did Italy's sometimes excellent vehicles, ships, and planes matter if they were not produced in number, or were never married to realistic strategic ends? Or put another way, why was an anemic Italy soon simultaneously fighting a desert war across East and North Africa, invading the Balkans and occupying Greece, fighting a Mediterranean naval war, and sending tens of thousands of Italians to their deaths on the Russian front?

In the case of Japan, Arquilla notes that Midway did not quite change the entire course of the Pacific theater, as so often thought. After all, the U.S. was subsequently down to a single viable fleet carrier after a series of murderous sea battles off Guadalcanal by late 1942, in the years before the arrival of dozens of *Essex* fleet carriers, and far more light and escort carriers.

Unlike Japan, America knew that it had the wherewithal to wage land, sea, and air war against Japan in a way that played to its strengths and utilized American expertise in mass production, pragmatic weapon design, and a structure of civilian and military command that often precluded foolhardy military adventurism. In contrast, by 1944 Japan did not have the oil to fuel all its marooned superships. And it certainly had no business scattering its land and naval forces from the Mongolian border to Wake Island, and from the Aleutians to the Indian Ocean.

Japan built the war's best torpedo, first-class destroyers, and the finest first-generation fighter of the conflict—but neither in the numbers nor with the wisdom required to utilize these assets to nullify the innate advantages of the Allies. There was no need for the massive "Hotel Yamato" and Mushasi super battleships that gobbled up Japanese finite resources without sinking a single fleet carrier or battleship. Japan's generals should have known from their ill-fated late summer 1939 war with Marshal Zhukov on the Mongolian-Manchurian border that famed Japanese discipline and bravery were no substitutes for superior fire support and armor.

In matters of geostrategy, many of the Axis' inspired decisions might have turned out disastrously for the Allies had they just been supported and focused. Had Rommel been given ten divisions and secure supply lines, he well might have driven the British and Commonwealth troops out of Africa entirely. And had the Germans and Italians coordinated in taking Malta (the far more strategically important island than Crete), and cut access to the Suez Canal, the supply lines of the British Empire would have become disastrously fragmented.

The invasion of the Soviet Union, like the Athenian invasion of Sicily in the Peloponnesian War, was a quite bad idea, given an unconquered Britain at Germany's rear, inexact German information about Soviet industrial potential and armor, and the danger of a freelancing Japan bringing the Americans into the conflict at exactly the wrong time. But bad ideas sometimes work. So, the Germans might well have concentrated on two rather than three prongs of advance, and thus taken both Leningrad and Moscow, and then cut off and slowly strangled a southern rump state without having to send almost a million men into the Stalingrad grinder and hundreds of thousands more on a one-way drive toward the Caspian Sea.

Arquilla also points out that, often, the course and events of World War II still influence contemporary military operations, tactics and strategy. He points as an example to the innovative methods of improved or ad hoc "repurposed" defense—such as the emergence of the German 88mm flak gun as the best anti-tank weapon of the war—quite in contrast to the white elephant Tiger I and Tiger II tanks. In the European theater, the side that built heavy four-engine bombers, aircraft carriers, and tens of thousands of transport planes won; those who did not lost. In a larger sense, the nations that failed to focus their strength on a clear strategic target—whether the vast, dispersed 1,800-mile German line of advance into Russia or the scattershot plans of the Japanese at Midway—likewise lost.

No one in ascendant Japan in 1941 dreamed of using kamikazes. But by late 1944 hundreds of Japan's conventional pilots were being slaughtered on virtual suicide missions without getting anywhere near their targeted American carriers and battleships, given the many layered air cover defenses of American fleets.

One-way kamikazes, in contrast, doubled the range of fighter aircraft. They turned Zeros, obsolete fighter planes by 1944, into sophisticated cruise missiles doing more damage to the American fleet off Okinawa than in any other single naval battle of the war. One shudders to think what might have happened if such macabrely brilliant, low-tech weapons had been employed in early 1942.

The kamikaze cruise missile seems the antithesis of one of the most sophisticated and costly weapons of the war—the German V-2 ballistic missile—whose inaccuracy and cost in delivering 2,000 lbs. of explosive made it little more than a frightening, but strategically irrelevant terror weapon of a few months' duration.

Had Hitler far earlier allowed the punishing defensive tactics of Walter Model and Erich von Manstein to be universalized, the Eastern Front in theory might have been held well into 1946. In a wider sense, had the Nazis or the Japanese adopted a strategy of "national liberation"—that is, of winning hearts and minds in occupied Russia and China—they might have created chaos among Stalin's beleaguered apparat, and exacerbated existing tensions between Chinese Nationalists and communists.

Arquilla reminds us that we unfortunately forget the low-tech lessons of World War II: Italy's frogmen in torpedo boats did far more damage to the British Mediterranean fleet than did its elegant and costly battleships. German rail guns were a waste of time and money that might have been better spent on more support trucks and transport planes. What good was it to produce the jet-powered ME-262—the signature fighter of the war—if there was neither the fuel to train its pilots adequately, the materials to build it en masse, nor the insight into how to best use such a potentially devastating weapon?

Thus, many of Arquilla's theses transcend World War II, and remain cogent today— if often ignored—providing insight into how *not* to fight a war. When fighting begins, it is stunning how often supreme leaders do not ask themselves where—and with what— do they wish to end up, and whether they have the likely means to pursue those ends. How often in Vietnam, Korea, and Iraq did the high command ignore the battlefield acumen of seasoned captains, majors, and lieutenant colonels who might have warned them that blowing stuff up, or taking and temporarily occupying strategic hills did not necessary translate into lasting strategic success? Did the Vietnamese or Iraqis have to have a monopoly on asymmetrical warfare?

In World War II, the conflict that Germany, Italy, and Japan had planned for in their massive rearmament programs of the 1930s was exactly the opposite of the war that all three found themselves fighting by 1942. In other words, nations that could easily surprise and defeat their unprepared neighbors had neither the power nor the insight to fight a global conflict across continents by land, sea, and air—a caveat that the Axis ironically seemed to have once accepted in 1939.

Arquilla concludes by reminding us that the causes of these serial Axis flaws in operations, armament and strategy were not simply the result of bad luck. Nor were they haphazard. And they are not the stuff of exaggeration in contemporary histories that tend to see the war from the viewpoint of the winners.

Rather, Germany, Italy, and Japan as authoritarian countries were headed by leaders who had little experience abroad and did not welcome criticism from subordinates. The winning political gymnastics of the 1930s, coupled with the initial military successes prior to 1942, had convinced the Axis leadership that their own genius and the weakness and timidity of their enemies explained such spectacular results. Consequently, they never grasped that their often wrong-headed decision-making and modus operandi had been good enough only to defeat surprised and unprepared neighbors.

Such "victory disease" amplified their disadvantages when they finally found themselves in a global war against an alliance of enemies that they had never imagined and who brought with them advantages completely unforeseen.

John Arquilla's history of World War II turns out to be a philosophical tract, not just about how and how not to wage war, but also why wisdom is ignored and ignorance is embraced, then and now.

*Victor Davis Hanson is the author or editor of more than 20 books and many articles and public commentaries. An advisor to President George W. Bush, who awarded him the National Humanities Medal in 2007, Dr. Hanson is the Martin and Illie Anderson Senior Fellow in classics and military history at Stanford University's Hoover Institution. The* New York Times *described his* The Second World Wars: How the First Global Conflict Was Fought and Won *as* "full of the kind of novel perceptions that can make a familiar subject interesting again."

# *Preface*

AT SOME POINT EACH DAY, World War II intrudes upon my thoughts. Occasionally, fresh insight into a long-familiar sequence of events emerges. Which is most useful for the course I have taught for many years at the U.S. Naval Postgraduate School about how military organizations respond to technological change. The war still provides the most fertile ground for this sort of study. I am especially drawn to the puzzle posed by the three main Axis Powers, the aggressive architects of the greatest conflict in human history. Germany, Italy, and Japan chose to go to war at a time of intense social ferment and revolutionary advances in all manner of weapons systems. Given that the global conflagration they caused ended in their utter defeat at the hands of dozens of nations joined in alliance against them, why would they have started such a conflict? Was complete disaster inevitable? Were the Axis Powers not so much outfought as gang tackled?

For my parents, both of whom worked in a tank factory in Chicago during the war, Axis defeat was easy to explain: the sheer scale of American production guaranteed Allied victory. However, for a couple of my uncles, both infantrymen, the story was very different. They seldom talked about their experiences in the war; but at our annual family gatherings at Crystal Lake each summer, they reminisced. I listened.

Uncle Frank had landed first in North Africa, then Sicily, Salerno and, finally, Anzio where he was gravely wounded. Uncle Mondo fought from Normandy to Germany. The common thread in each of their stories was about how they and their comrades-in-arms *improved*, eventually being able to defeat the Germans tactically. Uncle Frank always pointed out that the Italian units he encountered fought hard, too. For my uncles, victory was not about numbers, or even superior strategy, but rather about sheer, hard soldiering. The same was true of the Marine veterans I came to know later on, from the neighbor decorated for bravery on Guadalcanal to the office co-worker who had survived Tarawa. Each had great respect for their Japanese foes; each affirmed that victory was hardly assured. From their perspectives, the Marines—and by extension men of the other services and our allies who deployed to the Pacific—had to learn how to outfight the enemy.

Which view is correct? Greater numbers or improved soldiering? No doubt each catches a partial glimpse of the truth. Sheer productive capacity was important. But production of what? Which technologies were to be emphasized, in what proportions? In some cases, as with the aircraft carrier whose reach and lethality were far greater than that of the battleship, the answer was obvious. So, the U.S. Navy, which began the war with just seven, ended in 1945 having launched 150—more than two dozen of the major "fleet" types, the rest "jeep carriers" that were, despite their smaller size and lesser air complements, highly effective. With regard to particular types of tanks, planes, guns, torpedoes, and other weaponry, the correct developmental path quite often proved more difficult to discern, posing many daunting design challenges. Yet most were mastered in the end.

As to effectiveness in battle, design mattered here, too—largely in terms of identifying the correct organizational structure and empowering it by the adoption of a well-aligned concept of operations. Here the Axis Powers did the Allies the unintended favor of showing the way ahead in terms of military organization and doctrine. For it was the German army, alone among the major powers, that pioneered the notion of concentrating armor in purpose-built panzer divisions and relying upon attack aircraft to act like flying artillery to provide close support to their mobile operations. As to the Imperial Japanese Navy, its understanding of the revolutionary nature of naval aviation led to the creation of the carriers of the *Kido Butai*. In both cases the Allies, after initial reverses, showed themselves quite able to imitate, even to improve upon, Axis war-fighting designs. Indeed, it is more than a little ironic that the innovations introduced by the Axis Powers provided the blueprints the Allies followed in building the forces that would ultimately bring about the fall of the Fascist regimes.

The crucial insight here is that, while numbers and fighting skill do indeed matter, the greater issue of the causes of victory or defeat is tightly coupled to notions of *design* that speak to what will be produced and how operations will be conducted. This strategic perspective on design goes much deeper than the surface-level design aesthetics commonly associated with the Axis Powers: logos like the Nazi hooked-cross swastika, Japan's "rising sun" flag, Italy's Roman-style *fasces* and other oddments, such as the Viking *runes* of the SS and the master-crafted samurai swords that Japanese officers carried into machine-age battles. Rather, the aspect of design that I emphasize in this book goes to the heart of the matter of victory or defeat in war. How will the units of action be organized? What weapons will they wield? Does military doctrine align with organizational structure and the technology of arms to optimize performance in battle? These are questions that must be explored if a true design perspective is to emerge and guide a fresh analytic approach to understanding the outcome of World War II.

To be sure, the strategies chosen during the course of a war matter as well; but it must be remembered that, particularly in the greatest of wars, both sides make their share of blunders, and luck can break both ways. No major conflict is conducted with "perfect play" that drives the outcome to some predetermined result. Even here, however, the notion of design plays an important role. For a blunder in the field can be retrieved, a point best made with reference to the huge Russian losses from June to October 1941—about 4,000,000 troops killed, wounded, or captured—in the wake of which the German drives on Leningrad and Moscow were still somehow stopped over the next few weeks, thanks to the generalship of Georgi Zhukov and the indomitable fighting spirit of Red Army soldiers. But a design blunder is more lasting than a defeat, even several defeats, in the field. If the wrong technology is emphasized, outdated concepts of organization and operations adopted, then the path to disaster looms ahead, ever more difficult to avoid.

In the case of the Axis Powers, many flaws become evident when one employs a design perspective. At sea, for example, ponder why the German Navy invested heavily in building surface warships during the 1930s, even after Hitler repudiated the Versailles-imposed ban on U-boats. *Graf Spee, Hipper, Lützow, Scharnhorst, Gneisenau, Bismarck* and *Tirpitz* were all beautifully designed, but did little to affect the naval balance of power that so heavily favored Britain and the United States. Why wasn't the primary German focus on U-boats, which nearly won the war? And with regard to the Imperial Japanese Navy and submarines, a similar design-blindness seems to have arisen. Japan's battleships and cruisers dwarfed their I-boats, and the latter's efforts were directed to focus on attacking American naval combatants rather than to prey upon Allied supply ships traversing long, vulnerable sea lines of communication. An even greater Japanese naval strategic design blunder was the failure to build adequate escort vessels, in anticipation of a possible American commerce-raiding submarine strategy. Needless to say, there are other naval concerns to consider, and many more strategic design issues to explore as well when it comes to the Axis Powers' varied approaches to the development and operation of air and land forces.

If Axis defeat in World War II is best explained in terms of flawed strategic designs—the argument advanced in this book—I must admit that this insight, which helps to solve one puzzle, prompts another. That is, the German, Japanese, and even some of the Italian designers—in and outside of their respective militaries—were often quite brilliant, especially in terms of aligning emerging technologies with effective concepts of operations. Heinz Guderian and Erwin Rommel played leading roles in formulating Germany's *Blitzkrieg* doctrine. Japan's Isoroku Yamamoto pioneered the development of carrier-based naval warfare, and demonstrated its potential in a series of swift conquests in the several months after the attack on Pearl Harbor. Each of these "designers" was hard at work, from the 1920s on, right into the war years during which they strove to adjust their designs to meet the demands of changing strategic circumstances. Yet each somehow failed. Why?

Yamamoto was killed in 1943, his plane intercepted while he was on an inspection tour. Rommel was given the option of suicide late in 1944—he took it—as Hitler suspected him of involvement in the July 20 plot against the Nazi regime. Guderian lived and rose to high command; yet his most innovative initiatives were thwarted at key moments, not only by Hitler but by the weight of common opinions held by most senior German military leaders. These three, and others who played roles in the Axis designs for war, will be followed, from the years after the Treaty of Versailles went into effect, to and through the war. Beyond tracking careers of "lone geniuses" in the Axis militaries, some attention will also be given to lead designers at the major companies engaged in weapons development, from Messerschmitt to Mitsubishi—and others. How and why they all failed is indeed a puzzle.

As much as I owe to my parents and uncles for sparking what became my lifelong interest in World War II, I must confess that the very idea of exploring this conflict from a design perspective comes mostly from having watched the classic 1952 documentary, *Victory at Sea*. It was already in syndication when I first saw it in 1960 and was immediately hooked. I re-watched it religiously whenever it aired, drawn in always by the very first episode, "Design for War" which, despite the naval-oriented title of the series, looked at innovations in land and aerial warfare as well. Throughout the series there is a design sensibility that still remains somewhat under-examined in the vast literature on World War II. I was very pleased when videocassettes and DVDs came along; now I could get a *Victory at Sea* fix whenever needed. I still go back to watch it; the strategic design perspective developed in this book owes much of its inspiration to that fine series.

This "design approach" is especially valuable, I believe, for purposes of analyzing the behavior of aggressors. They plot and plan for years before launching their wars, often giving them an important early edge in terms of military innovation. The Axis Powers had exactly this sort of advantage as they prepared for what was to become history's greatest armed conflict, and had sufficient time to adjust their approaches, even after swift victory proved elusive. Which makes them and their designers interesting subjects of study.

My hope is that, by developing a deeper understanding of the beliefs and actions—the mistakes and misperceptions, too—of the key "thought leaders" of the Axis Powers, it may be possible to illuminate some useful principles of strategic design. In doing so, it might also prove of practical value in gaining insights into the thoughts and actions of those who imperil our world today, and who may be plotting and planning, even now, for the next war.

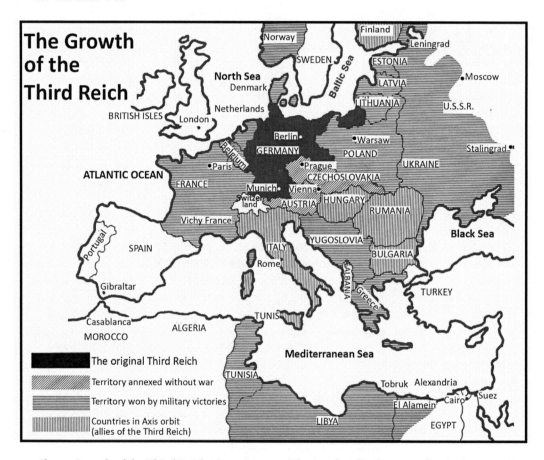

*Above:* **Growth of the Third Reich.** *Opposite page:* **The Pacific Island Groups (both photographs public domain, edits courtesy Patricia Hamilton).**

# The Pacific Island Groups

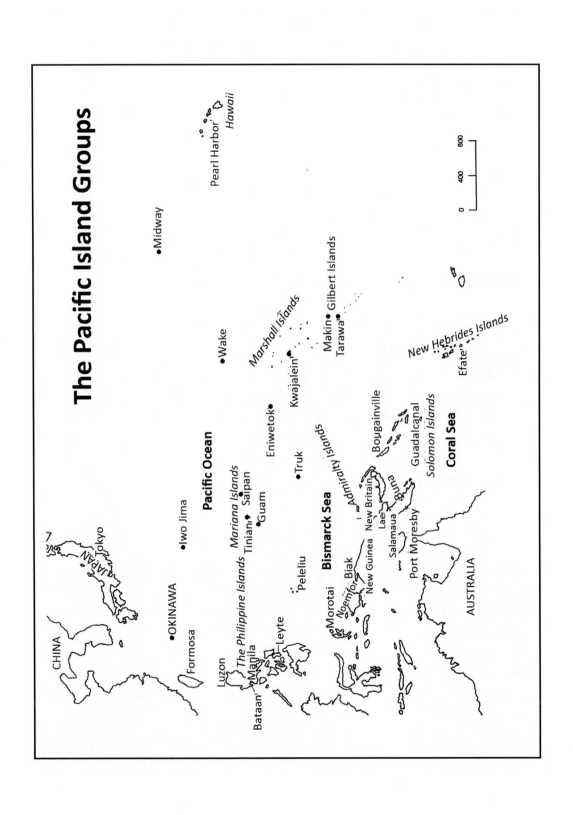

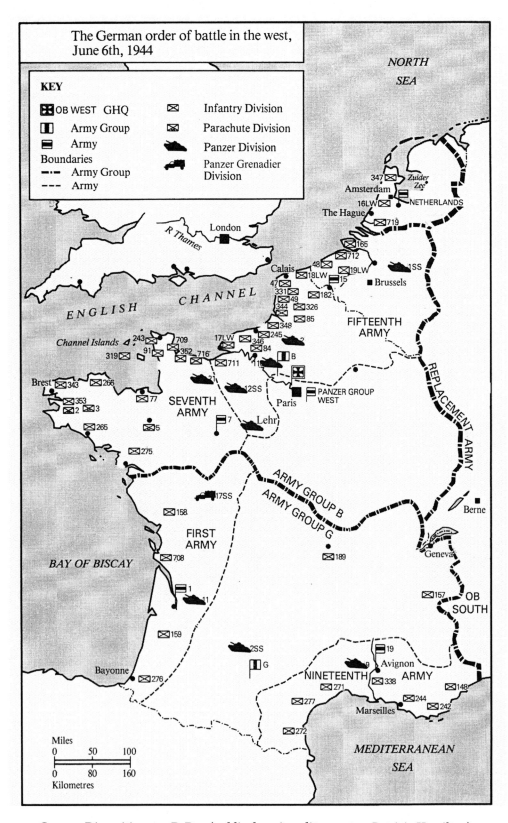

**German Dispositions on D-Day (public domain, edits courtesy Patricia Hamilton).**

# 1. Paths to Victory (or Defeat)

THE COURSE OF HISTORY, since ancient times, has been profoundly shaped and repeatedly redirected by major wars, putting a premium on understanding how they have been won or lost. A special importance has attached to the extensive efforts to explain why those large-scale conflicts of the modern industrial age—especially the Civil War and the world wars—turned out as they did, fueling the rise of a widely agreed upon set of what might be called "principles of war outcomes." One prominent line of argument holds that great wars are essentially "numbers games," material advantages proving decisive with metronomic regularity. Another view sees advances in war-related technologies as crucially important to victory. Indeed, the soldier-scholar Major General J.F.C. Fuller went so far as to state that "weapons, if only the right ones can be discovered, form ninety-nine percent of victory."[1] Along with these varied material and technological matters, sheer chance and human factors are generally included, too, among efforts to explain war outcomes. These "luck and pluck" points of view consider victory or defeat as, at heart, "contingent"—that is, as products either of happenstance or of the complex interactions of the combatants' relative skill levels and their battle choices in the moment.

The contingency-based perspective has generated all manner of "What if?" hypotheticals—an approach that has grown into something of a cottage industry since publication of Robert Cowley's creative, deeply thoughtful anthology of speculative essays by leading military historians.[2] But the Cowley undertaking was long preceded by what still stands as one of the most famous exercises in hypothetical military historical analysis: a strategic meditation by MacKinlay Kantor about the Civil War. Kantor chose to keep his approach simple, conjuring visions of Union defeats at Vicksburg and Gettysburg as, respectively, the products of U.S. Grant's untimely accidental death and Robert E. Lee's more forceful handling of his corps commanders.[3] An interesting variant of this hypothetical approach looks at *actual* military campaigns on the brink of disaster to gauge the importance of having an able "savior general"—historian Victor Davis Hanson's, term—in charge at just the right moment.[4] This "reverse method," fully steeped in real events as they occurred, is perhaps an even more powerful way to make a point about the importance of contingency to war outcomes.

Beyond Kantor's and others' hypothetical analyses of the Civil War, there are plenty of additional reasons to re-examine this conflict as a basis for evaluating theories of war outcomes. The Civil War, in which rifles, railroads, ironclads, and the electric telegraph first came into wide use, has been subjected to very close scrutiny. And the outcome of this first truly modern war has been explained in a manner consistent with *all* of the major theories of war outcomes. But if there is a view that should be seen as first among equals, it is certainly the material dimension. Southern generalship and the high quality of the Confederacy's soldiers have commonly been seen as better than the North's—at least during the first two years of the war. Yet these factors, it has been argued, were eventually overcome by the North's massive advantages in materials, finances, and manpower. The late Shelby Foote put the matter succinctly, and quite starkly, in a comment he made on filmmaker Ken Burns' famous PBS documentary about the Civil War: "The North fought that war with one hand behind its back ... [and if necessary] simply would have brought that other arm out.... I don't think the South ever had a chance to win that war."[5]

The pre-eminence of a "materialist mindset" is also evident in choices made by senior political and military leaders during World War I—and by historians of that conflict ever since. Sadly, given the massive increase in the destructive power of weaponry in the half-century following the Civil War, the failure to improve generalship or to innovate doctrinally led, for most of World War I, to year after year of indecisive, bloody slaughter of the brave soldiers on both sides who were worthy of far better leaders. Eminent historian Correlli Barnett observed that the high levels of command in World War I were held by "those born and bred in the last age ... men locked in struggle with events greater than themselves."[6] Thus mindless attrition went on for far too long, ended only by the fresh material resources and the huge increases in manpower that accompanied American entry into the war and made decisive Allied victory at last possible.

Then along came World War II—offering a fresh explanation of its outcome is the purpose of this book—in which the potential of advancing technologies overturned more popular notions about the importance of sheer numbers of troops and weapons. Increases in engine power made tanks and planes far more potent than they had been in their embryonic stages during World War I. Radio enabled command and control of large campaigns over greater distances than ever before. Radar made possible detection of enemy forces when still well out of visual range. Technology ruled, briefly; but its diffusion to all combatants brought numbers to the fore again. So much so, it is thought that, as John Ellis summed up the situation the Germans faced: "Once Hitler arrayed himself against the material might of both Russia and the USA his battle, even for mere survival, was hopeless."[7] Similar views of Japan's fate abound.

The strongest countervailing arguments to quantitative analyses of World War II's outcome fall into two categories: contingency and human factors. Contingent arguments are further subdivided into views of the merits or demerits of choices made in battle and critiques of the broader strategies chosen. In the European theater, perhaps the best-known battle contingency has to do with the controversial halting of German armor for just long enough near Dunkirk to allow more than 300,000 Allied troops to evacuate the Continent in late May and early June 1940. In the Pacific, the "contingent moment" came at the Battle of Midway in June 1942, when American dive bombers arrived on target just at the moment when Japanese fighter aircraft were distracted dealing with a low-level torpedo plane attack. Three Imperial Navy carriers were lost in this action, a fourth soon after.[8]

At the grand strategic level, much has been made of the disastrous consequences of the German decision to invade Russia in June 1941 rather than first finishing off the British in the Mediterranean and North Africa. Indeed, just a small fraction of the German resources employed against Russia would have been needed to advance from Italian-held Libya to Suez, then link up with the 40,000 Vichy French forces that controlled Lebanon and Syria until June 1941. In short, Britain's war effort would have been crippled. Given that the Germans *did* invade Russia, historians have also critiqued Japan's ultimately disastrous choice to pursue the Imperial Navy's preferred "southern program"—that entailed going to war with the United States—instead of attacking the Russians in the Far East while Hitler's forces were at the gates of Moscow. Had Japan coordinated with its Axis ally against Russia—the preference of the Imperial Army—it is hard to see how Stalin could have spared sufficient forces from Siberia to come to the rescue of his forces that were being so badly battered by the Nazi invasion.

Then there was the apparently outsized influence of Hitler, focus upon which sharpened the discourse about the highest levels of command decision-making. Defeated German generals formed something of a Greek chorus, extolling their own skills while cataloguing Hitler's strategic misjudgments and gross blunders. On the Eastern Front they concentrated their criticisms on his decision to turn south to the Ukraine—instead of sticking with the drive on Moscow—in the opening campaign in Russia in 1941, and then on Hitler's refusal to allow the encircled 6th Army to break out of Stalingrad the following year. In the West, beyond the early Dunkirk debacle, the principal counts in the indictment against Hitler-as-strategist have focused on his reluctance to send the powerful, nearby 15th Army to join the bitter fight in Normandy in the summer of 1944, then soon after on the suicidal counter-offensive at Mortain that was intended to cut off Patton's Third Army and other Allied formations that were just then starting to fan out across France.[9]

However, there have been more balanced historical assessments, too, that credit Hitler when due. For example, his "hold on" order during the winter of 1941-42 averted the sure catastrophe that would have ensued had he listened to his generals and attempted a retreat on the Eastern Front. As Alan Clark summed up the situation in December 1941, "[a]ny attempt to withdraw from its positions … to retreat across the drifting snow fields … would have resulted in the whole German Army being cut to pieces." Clark went on to describe this time as "Hitler's finest hour." But more generally, in his view, "occasions when Hitler was right and the General Staff wrong are far more numerous than the apologists of the German Army allow."[10]

The critique of Japan is more subtle at the level of human factors, keying on organizational pulling and hauling for control over strategy and policy between the Imperial Japanese Army and Navy as having sowed the seeds of defeat. The Navy, hungry for oil and entranced with its ideas about creating a barrier-chain of island fortresses, won out with its call for a sea war that meant confronting the United States. The Army, it has been argued, remained reluctant to embrace—and ultimately shortchanged—the Navy's strategy, preferring to use most of its large forces in extended campaigns in China and Southeast Asia because, in senior generals' eyes, "war with the United States and Britain was regarded as primarily a naval problem."[11] The matter of human and organizational factors aside, the sheer material and numerical inferiority of Japan—whose only potentially useful allies were half a world away—has generally been viewed as foreordaining defeat. Indeed, the basic materialist argument against Japan having war-winning chances seems convincing, mooting any discussion of why it lost.

The same is seen as the case with Italy, the third member of the Axis Tripartite Pact. Though in addition to Italy's material deficiencies there is evidence of technological backwardness, too—especially regarding tanks and aircraft. The Italian Navy's lack of even a single aircraft carrier (the *Aquila* was never completed) made its battleship fleet, which *was* reasonably modern, all too vulnerable. Shore-based aircraft proved insufficient to meet the needs of modern sea warfare, either in fleet actions or in combating the British submarines and attack aircraft that preyed mercilessly on the supply ships needed to sustain the campaign in North Africa. As an excellent Italian account put the matter, it was the "consequent lack of fuel oil and air cover that had paralyzed the Italian fleet."[12]

Then there is the huge role of mismanagement at the very top, with Mussolini's missteps in the Balkans and the Western Desert coming under the same kind of critical scrutiny as Hitler did for his strategic blunders. As to the reason for the Allied invasion of Italy and the long, bloody march north to Rome—and beyond—this had little to do with the need to deal directly with *Italian* power, which was deemed negligible. Instead, as Robert Leckie has argued: "The chief reason for the invasion of Italy was the Allied desire to draw *German* divisions away from the Eastern Front and to keep them preoccupied when the invasion of France began in the spring of 1944."[13]

Other German allies have been viewed in similarly dismissive fashion. The Finns, though outstanding fighters and well led, were far too few and refused to pursue operations that would take them beyond the limits of the territories they lost in the Winter War against the Soviets (1939-40). And when the tide turned, they quickly switched sides and joined the fight against Germany. There were somewhat more Romanians and Hungarians fighting on the Axis side; but their forces were of much lesser quality than the Finns'.[14]

The defeat of the Axis thus seems well explained by existing theories ranging from material matters to human factors. Even the technology-based arguments favor the Allies, at least during the latter years of the war when advances in submarine detection won the Battle of the Atlantic, and long-range fighter aircraft enabled the devastating daylight bombing of Germany. As to generalship and the combat-savvy of frontline soldiers, there was also a clear leveling effect that emerged over the course of the war. In terms of outstanding field commanders, the U.S. Army's George Patton and the Red Army's Georgi Zhukov proved quite equal to—perhaps even better than—Germany's Field Marshals Gerd von Rundstedt and Erwin Rommel. At sea, the U.S. Navy Admirals Raymond Spruance and "Bull" Halsey outdid the Imperial Navy's Isoroku Yamamoto and Chuichi Nagumo. As to the Allied soldiers, sailors, and airman, they too fought with every bit as much of the courage, skill, and determination shown by their Axis counterparts.

With the foregoing in mind, one might well doubt whether there is any need to continue to think about why the Axis lost. Indeed, the evidence of all sorts seems overwhelming. Germany, Japan, and their allies simply could not match the material resources and manpower of their opponents. If they had any sort of technological edge, empowered by innovative concepts of operations like *Blitzkrieg* on land, or wolf-pack tactics and carrier-based warfare at sea, such advantages were blunted, countered, and even exceeded by the Allied responses to them. In addition to all this are the many strategic blunders made by senior Axis leaders at crucial moments in the war, and the plain good luck that broke for the Allies at critical moments.

Yet in the early years of the war the Axis Powers *were* able to redress their material deficiencies by means of conquest. Their weaponry and battle doctrines did dominate on land, at sea and, at least tactically, in the air. And in terms of blundering, the Allies made their share of grave errors—see, for example, poor Russian performance from June to October 1941, when losses suffered in killed, wounded, and captured amounted to roughly *four million*. As to luck, things had to break right for the Germans in the battle of France in 1940, and for the Japanese on their approach to and attack upon Pearl Harbor in December 1941. With regard to the fall of France, the eminent historian Ernest May summed the matter up thus: "If leaders in the Allied governments had anticipated the German offensive through the Ardennes, even as a worrisome contingency, it is almost inconceivable that France would have been defeated."[15] The tragedy of errors that led to an American disaster at Pearl Harbor has been widely and thoughtfully chronicled as well, nowhere better than in Gordon Prange's luminous *At Dawn We Slept*.[16]

Given the operational skills of the German and Japanese armed forces, and the conquests they made that added substantially to their resources, at least the material aspects of the conventional wisdom about the outcome of World War II can be questioned. As to the matters of strategic blundering and sheer chance, it seems that here, too, both the Axis and the Allies made their share of mistakes in roughly equal proportion. Lady Luck broke for one side or the other with alarming indifference. German and Japanese soldiers, sailors, and airmen fought tenaciously to the very end of the war, despite having lost all hope of victory—or even of some sort of acceptable peace. Nor did their civilian populations break under Allied bombing, so a psychology-based argument about why the Axis lost is unpersuasive as well.

On balance, and especially with the first three years of the war in mind, the overall situation was such that historian Richard Overy judged the conflict's ultimate outcome in favor of the Allies to reflect "a remarkable reversal of fortunes." As to contingencies, human foibles, and "What ifs?" arising out of choices made at critical moments during the war, Overy went on to argue the point that "chances of a single battle or decision seriously explaining its outcome are remote." And while he accepted the fundamental importance of material and numerical factors, Overy blended them together with the many technological innovations so necessary to improving their effectiveness, noting that victory in the Second World War "can only be explained by incorporating the role of production *and* invention."[17]

For J.F.C. Fuller, the particular area of technological invention that mattered most to the outcome of the war had to do with improvements to the speed, range, and firepower of tanks and aircraft, which made them far more potent than either had been in their early days during World War I. The key was, he believed, that increased motive power made World War II a conflict of "remarkable mobility … in the main due to the [widespread] adoption of the internal combustion engine." Further, Fuller drew from this insight the conclusion that "the highest profitable mobility was attained when air power was integrated with land or sea power."[18]

It seems that, even on the basis of the brief reflections set forth above, a far more complex picture begins to emerge about how victory is achieved or defeat is suffered in a major war. In the specific case of World War II, the Axis Powers used their innovations—principally German *Blitzkrieg* on land and Japanese carrier-based warfare at sea— to run up a string of early victories that largely erased their material deficiencies relative to the Allies. But the latter were able to hold on long enough and improve their fighting methods sufficiently to inflict ultimately crushing blows on the Axis. The Allies won because, in the end, they were able to *outfight* both the Germans and the Japanese.

Just how these Allied improvements were achieved is a subject that has been studied, in bits and pieces, by many. High-frequency direction-finding technology has been given much credit for winning the war against the U-boats in the Atlantic, for example. Drop tanks that increased the range of Mustang fighter planes so that they could escort B-17s and other aircraft all the way to Germany vastly increased the potency of strategic bombing.[19] The humble landing craft played a key role in the island-hopping campaign in the Pacific, as well as in Allied amphibious operations in the European theater, the latter greatly aided by a range of other technological innovations, not least the "mulberry" artificial harbors that created on-the-spot ports.

Technology aside, credit should also be given to crucially important battle experience. For the British in North Africa, learning took time; but they did eventually become habituated to concentrating their armor—as Rommel routinely did with his *Afrika Korps*—rather than wasting their tanks in piecemeal attacks.[20] American GIs did poorly in their initial encounter with Rommel at Kasserine Pass, but soon improved and played an effective role in bagging over 200,000 Axis prisoners in Tunisia—less than three months after that stinging defeat. This gave them, as General Eisenhower, the Allied commander noted, "a great *élan* for the sterner tests to come."[21]

A similar pattern of learning from hard experiences in battle can be seen in the campaigns against Japan. In Burma, for example, an initial drubbing, followed by the repulse of an Allied counter-offensive, led to improvements that ultimately transformed, in Field-Marshal Viscount Slim's words, "defeat into victory." And when it came to assaulting Japan's chain of island fortresses, the high human cost of the invasion of Tarawa—over 3,000 casualties were suffered in the three-day battle—generated lessons learned that vastly improved performance in subsequent attacks.[22]

These notions about World War II's outcome having been determined by the development of technological solutions to operational challenges and by tactical improvements resulting from battle experience, suggest that the path to victory is blazed by cultivating a problem-solving mindset aimed at improving "tools and practices." Such a perspective enjoys considerable explanatory power; for it allows us to understand how the Axis Powers' innovative concepts of operations enjoyed initial runs of success, but were ultimately thwarted by Allied invention, production, and military doctrinal innovations. Most histories have touched upon these themes, at least in part, but there has been only one study that focuses in detail on the Allies' main problem-solving efforts: Paul Kennedy's magisterial *Engineers of Victory.* From the outset, Kennedy makes clear he "resists all efforts at reductionism, such as that the winning of the war can be explained solely by brute force, or by some wonder weapon, or by some magical decrypting system." Instead, he undertakes a thorough "analysis of how grand strategy is achieved in practice, and makes the claim that victories cannot be understood without a recognition of how those successes were engineered, and by whom."[23]

The notion of engineering solutions to military operational and tactical problems implies a connection with the concept of *strategic design,* a process that, if applied to military affairs, can help to imagine the things that engineers might build, how they might be put to use, and what sorts of organizational forms and innovative battle doctrines the new tools might empower. "Design" is most often associated with the engineering aspects of industry and commerce, but also with more aesthetic undertakings that speak to form and function, as in architecture. Needless to say both art and fashion rely heavily upon aesthetic aspects of design as well, and often loop back to commercial appeal, among other things.[24] Strategic design has, to date, been closely associated with organizational structure and business management choices aimed at, as one leading scholar asserted, "conferring to social and market bodies a system of rules, beliefs, values, and tools to deal with the external environment."[25] These factors can all be applied to military affairs.

Indeed, my precise intent in this book is to employ the strategic design concept as a lens through which to re-examine the course and outcome of the Second World War. I do so because it is an approach not yet systematically taken, and I believe that it will lead to fresh insights into the defeat of the Axis. Doing so may well lead to a conclusion that the outcome of this great conflict was shaped far more by design than by any other factors.

Paul Kennedy has begun the process of engaging in a design-based analysis with his examinations of how the U-boat threat was mastered, the *Blitzkrieg* blunted, long-range bombers successfully escorted, and the tough problem of landing on hostile shores solved. He has also reflected on the overall system that enabled the projection and sustenance of power over great distances in a global-scale conflict. All these challenges had to be overcome if the Allies were to win against the Axis; and the case Kennedy makes is compelling.

Still, some issues remain to be explored further, prompted by the *de facto* "design approach" itself that Paul Kennedy has so skillfully employed. First among all the design-related issues at hand is the need to extend the analysis by thinking about strategic design from the Axis point of view. As Germany, Italy, and Japan had many years during which to contemplate their future aggressions, this puts a premium on undertaking a searching analysis of their chosen strategies, their preferred organizational structures, and the choices about weapons development they made during the so-called interwar period of the 1920s–1930s. While all three countries that would one day form the Axis were affected in different ways by World War I, all three of them experienced deep internal turmoil but little or no external conflict during the first decade after that conflict ended.

But the second decade of this period was a time when all three acted in increasingly hostile ways externally. From 1931 on, Japan was openly engaged in fighting in China, which spread later into Southeast Asia, and the Imperial Army even waged (and lost) the brief Nomonhan War on the Mongolian-Manchurian border against the Russians in 1939. As to the Germans, many of their soldiers, sailors, and airmen—manning the panzers, U-boats, and attack aircraft—saw combat during the bitter Spanish Civil War (1936–1939) in which nearly a million soldiers and civilians died. As Nazi leader Hermann Goering put it at his war crimes trial at Nuremberg, Spain was the Wehrmacht's "testing ground."[26] Italy was very actively involved in this conflict as well, and even before its intervention in Spain had invaded Ethiopia, where Mussolini's forces experimented with aerial bombardment using chemical weapons—as recommended by one of the fathers of air power theory, Italian General Giulio Douhet.[27] Thus the "interwar period" was actually a time of much involvement in conflict for the three powers that would form the core of the Axis and shake the world just a few years later. It was a time of design, field experimentation, and redesign that profoundly shaped the conduct and course of World War II.

The years before the German invasion of Poland in September 1939 and the Japanese attack on Pearl Harbor in December 1941—the two events by which we measure the start of the war and then its transition to a truly global conflict—afforded the aggressors opportunities both to engage in analytic design thinking and to benefit from combat experiences. It was a time when they could ponder deeply the operational and strategic problems likely to be posed in the way of their expansionist aims, giving them the chance to develop solutions to looming operational challenges beforehand.

Yet such processes do not stop when the firing and the bombing starts; and so my examination of Axis design efforts ranges throughout the long course of the conflict. Even as the Axis Powers began to lose the initiative in 1942–1943, it can be seen that they strove mightily to find design-based, problem-solving solutions to fresh strategic dilemmas that were emerging. Since the Allies were working on their own designs at the same time, World War II might usefully be seen as a kind of a "strategic design competition." Explaining why and how the Axis lost this competition is the specific goal of this book.

How should one think about warfare designs? Paul Kennedy has made a clear case for "engineering"—in the broadest sense of the word, incorporating whole systems inclusive of technologies and human operators—as a means by which to observe and analyze the design process. This is a quite excellent foundation upon which to build, as Kennedy's approach relates very closely to more general views of design's role in engineering.[28] But there is more to say and study in order to understand strategic design. With Paul Kennedy's problem-solving approach in mind, and building upon it, I see strategic design as comprised of a range of elements. Technology is of crucial importance, and for purposes of design-based analysis it should be divided into the three basic sub-component areas that range across the land, sea, and air warfare domains: weaponry, transportation, and information systems. In World War II the design challenge, technologically, was to envision the future landscape of conflict and build the kinds of forces most likely to thrive in what would inevitably become a very harsh environment.

Typical strategic design issues Axis leaders had to address included whether to emphasize one domain—land, sea, or air—over the others, or to prepare broadly and equally to compete in each. Either way, good, robust designs called for the *alignment* of weapons, transports and information systems with each other and across the land, sea, and air domains. And with the need to keep enemy arsenals and other military-related developments well in mind, along with questions about whether to imitate others or to go off separately in search of fresh innovations.

Beyond pure technology, there are several other significant elements of general strategic design to consider. One has to do with choices made about force structure. Should combat units be comprised of relatively few, large formations, or of many small ones? How might the answer to this question vary across ground forces, air wings, or navies? The notion of few-large versus many-small has played out across history, going back to the massed phalanxes of Alexander the Great and Hannibal in ancient times, the latter being ultimately defeated by the Roman general Scipio whose legions, comprised of countless maniples ("handfuls") of infantry were much more flexible, ultimately carrying the day at the Battle of Zama (202 B.C.E.), and laying the foundation for centuries of Roman military successes.

Two millennia later the similarly small German stormtroop units of World War I, which in their March 1918 offensive came so close to winning the war against larger, balkier Allied field formations, rekindled a classical organizational structure debate. As historian Lynn Montross put the matter, "the armies of 1918 were bringing up to date the ancient tactical duel between the legion and phalanx!"[29] In more recent times, the great war between nations and terrorist networks, under way since September 2001, has featured the same sort of tactical dual between large national forces organized in relatively few, large units versus networked enemies who fight in countless, widely dispersed "handfuls."

Yet a third design element, in addition to technology and organization—and in some respects growing out of them—has to do with battle doctrine. That is, how will the tools of war be used by the military formations that have been developed? Here, too, there are common design fundamentals to consider. Should the approach to battle be focused upon seeking decisive clashes that will conclude wars swiftly? Or should one's armed forces be optimized for attrition, for the wearing-down of the enemy? To some extent, land powers—like Germany, for example—have tended toward preferring short, sharp wars in the style of those waged under the skillful guidance of the 19th century "Iron Chancellor," Otto von Bismarck. Sea powers such as Britain have recognized that decisive naval battles, like Trafalgar, can only achieve command of the sea. But naval mastery gained does allow for a gradual massing of greater resources that helps to wear down land powers over time, and conveys an ability to strike them at points of the maritime power's choosing.

Early air power theorists thought that strategic aerial bombardment would achieve swift results, yet in practice—particularly during World War II, but in other conflicts since as well—it has turned out that such campaigns are at heart attritional. And even then, success has proved elusive. Still, it must be noted, air power used in close support of ground operations, as at the zenith of the German *Blitzkrieg* in 1940–41, or half a century later in the American-led Operation Desert Storm in 1991, has repeatedly shown its profound value in enabling swift and decisive battle results to be achieved.

Overall, though, the strategic designer will benefit most by keeping in mind the foregoing point that there are just two approaches to warfighting. Historian Hans Delbrück described this phenomenon best by dividing wars, in his classic *History of the Art of War,* either into those of swift, decisive "annihilation" (*Niederwerfungsstrategie*) or of slower-acting, attritional "exhaustion" (*Ermattungsstrategie*).[30] He saw Alexander and Napoleon as examples of the former, Pericles and Frederick the Great of the latter.

When it comes to designing military doctrines, such factors as the material balance and technological superiority or inferiority, while not being decisive, remain salient. A nation confronted by numerous foes may strive for early decisive victory, to avoid being worn down by attrition. This was certainly a German consideration during the 1930s, as it was the earlier hope of General Staff planners charged with making the sweeping Schlieffen Plan work at the outset of World War I.[31] Sometimes—though more rarely than one might think in light of crushing defeats of tribal peoples in the colonial wars of the 19th century—technological inferiority can be offset by numbers. And when inferior in both numbers and weaponry, an attritional approach based on hit-and-run guerrilla operations may prove to be the key to victory. The point is that strategic design must include a warfighting doctrine to go along well with its technological and organizational elements.

Perhaps the most important insight required for informing and guiding the process of doctrinal development—and of strategic design overall—has to do with whether, in a particular era, there is some inherent advantage to being either on the offensive or the defensive. This is a deceptively simple matter. In his classic *On War,* the German philosopher of conflict Carl von Clausewitz concluded, based on his experiences in and reflections on the Napoleonic Wars, that the defensive was stronger. Yet the Baron Antoine Jomini, who served with Napoleon's forces and wrote his *Art of War* from a similar analytic foundation, made the offensive his preeminent principle of war. A century after Napoleon's end at Waterloo in 1815, all the combatants in World War I seemed to have misread Clausewitz and embraced Jomini by striving doggedly to be on the offensive—

despite the many changes wrought by industrialization and the new weapons that slaughtered the serried ranks of their armies. And when World War II came just a generation later, all too many believed—no doubt based on the experience of World War I—that the defensive was dominant when in fact technical advances greatly improved the attacker's chances. Getting the offense-defense balance right is hard. Very hard. But failure to do so dooms any strategic design to costly defeat, the Maginot Line being perhaps the emblematic instance of such a failure.

Mention of the French focus on fortification as a linchpin of strategic design in an era in which defense was thought (by so many) to be dominant serves to remind that this area too falls within the rubric of design. Indeed, it seems clear that attempts to fortify against threats have been undertaken at least as far back as Neolithic times. Among the earliest known examples is a sizeable log fort with palisades surrounding a major settlement in Britain that dates back over 6,000 years. There is abundant evidence of walled settlements in later prehistory as well.[32]

And from very early on in historic times, fortifications that had profound strategic importance emerged. The Long Walls of Athens assured access to the sea. China's Great Wall did much to shield settled lands from nomadic raiders. Hadrian's Wall set the limits of imperial control in ancient Roman Britain. Perhaps the greatest expression of design by means of fortification—that spanned the strategic and the aesthetic—was the triple-walled defensive design that protected Constantinople for so many centuries after the fall of Rome. Needless to say, the castles of the Middle Ages were fortified points that had profound social and political impact, shoring up the decentralized power structure and economics of feudalism. Their prevalence in Europe may also have helped thwart the 13th century Mongol invasions.

But the invention of heavy artillery soon followed, and finally brought down the Byzantine Empire in 1453. Shortly after, heavy guns were fielded by French armies in destructive campaigns against previously secure Italian city-states. Yet even this seeming cataclysm failed to bring an end to the use of above-ground fortifications. Indeed, a very steady stream of fortification designs emerged to restore the viability of the defense. A key element of design being creation of sharp angles and slopes that made direct hits with artillery less likely and glancing blows more the norm—and allowed for secure bastions from which to pour enfilading fire on attacking forces.

Thus the *trace italienne* came along, a beautiful design whose effect on the offense-defense balance, some have argued, constituted a "military revolution." Indeed, as Geoffrey Parker noted, this design was so successful that "the capture of a stronghold defended by the *trace italienne* required months, if not years."[33] Further refinements followed, with the 17th and 18th century fortresses of the renowned Sébastian le Prestre de Vauban—who knew both how to build *and* besiege such structures—standing proudly as works of "practical art." Thus, fortification proved to be that aspect of military-related design in which the strategic and the aesthetic were most skillfully blended.

Eventually, in the modern era, advances in sheer firepower and the rise of more mobile operations—fortresses do not move—drove design in the direction of low-silhouetted field fortifications. Extensive trench lines first appeared in the American Civil War, for example, and by World War I dominated the battlefields. Even more fixed fortified structures—like the Maginot Line and the German Siegfried Line—grew squatter and had more underground aspects. Fortresses remained a significant presence in the strategic design scheme during World War II, especially in what Hitler and his propagandists came to call the "Atlantic Wall," whose aim was to deter or defeat an Allied amphibious assault in northwest Europe. Physical terrain, too, was often neatly incorporated into a fortification scheme, as was the case with the Gustav Line and other German defensive designs employed in the bitter, two-year-long battle for Italy.

The usefulness of fortifications like the Atlantic Wall—not to mention other aspects of design—for propaganda purposes touches upon yet another important domain to consider in any examination of strategic design: the realm of psychology and influence. These factors, like the ancient Roman dual god Janus, face in two opposite directions. One looks inward, the other to the outside. The best strategic influence designs can radiate in both directions.

A good example of an effectively designed "influence weapon" was provided by issuance of Abraham Lincoln's Emancipation Proclamation during the Civil War, which made it quite clear that the conflict was not just about restoring the Union, but also about ending slavery. The Proclamation helped to shore up the North's will to fight, raised serious concerns in the Confederacy, and also played a role in helping convince the British, who had outlawed slavery decades earlier, to remain neutral rather than intervene militarily on the South's behalf. That President Lincoln waited for just the right moment to make his announcement—in the wake of his Union forces having thwarted Robert E. Lee's first invasion of the North at Antietam—is a sign of his very deft touch at the influence aspect of strategic design, and his understanding that such informational means should be closely aligned with conditions "on the ground."

The psychology of influence will quite often draw upon the aesthetic aspects of design as well. For example, the massive buildings, torch-lit stadium rallies and parades of the Nazis, as well as the near-ubiquitous presence of hooked-cross swastika flags, and even the foreboding black uniforms of the SS "asphalt soldiers," all fed the Nazi mystique. Adolf Hitler, who saw himself as an artist, was very deeply attuned to the potential of such imagery to influence others. It is hardly surprising, then, that he drew the young architect Albert Speer so closely to him. And aside from the way in which these designs restored the spirits of a defeated, depressed, and resentful German people, the images of rekindled strength and vitality had profound effects internationally, striking admiration in some abroad and fear in others. The great American aviator hero Charles Lindbergh expressed an open admiration for the German recovery; and the French, the British, and others stood idly by in the face of Hitler's increasingly aggressive moves, from the Rhineland to the rape of Austria—and beyond. The deterrent psychological effect of the Nazi strategic design was so great that it took six years from Hitler's accession to power before Britain and France at last decided to stand and fight. Almost too late.

The other leading Axis Powers also showed a keen awareness of this "strategic aesthetic." In Benito Mussolini's Italy it came in the form of hearkening to the grandeur of the Roman Empire—including use of the ancient symbol of the *fasces*—and conjuring a vision of its rebirth. In Japan militarists combined past and present in their aesthetic as well, connecting the noble samurai tradition to a future in which the "rising sun" symbolized triumphs to come. Both these design efforts resonated externally as well, intimidating the world community into quiescence when Mussolini's forces invaded Abyssinia and the Japanese did the same to China.

Clearly, leaders in Berlin, Rome, and Tokyo were able to employ the aesthetic in service to the strategic. There seemed to be implicit awareness among them that this aspect of design conveyed a powerful sense of identity internally, one that radiated outward, shaping others' perceptions in useful ways. Current design experts emphasize this point, and note the far-reaching effects that are possible. As John Heskett has observed:

> construction of identity, however, goes much further than an expression of who someone is; it can be a deliberate attempt by individuals and organizations, even nations, to create a particular image and meaning intended to shape, even pre-empt, what others perceive and understand.[34]

The Axis Powers proved quite adept at this. And it should be noted that those terrorist organizations—al Qaeda and ISIS, for example—that have sometimes been labeled as Islamo-Fascist have gone well out of their way to cultivate a similar strategic design aesthetic. Their powerful call to identity has been to remind jihadis that the ultimate goal is restoration of a medieval caliphate. In some respects, though, today's Muslim terrorists are hampered in trying to build a design-based sense of identity, given religious strictures against graven images. So, no swastikas or *fasces* for them. Worse, their fighters are even called upon to destroy ancient carvings and sculptures—depriving humanity of some of its most treasured cultural heritage, and prompting a question about whether there is such a thing as "anti-design."

But the design aspect of terrorism is a matter for another time. The key point here is to recognize the complexity, the many dimensions, and the continuing relevance of strategic design. And there is no better historical example than World War II in which to view all aspects of design. In that greatest of all conflicts strategic design was put to the sternest of tests. It is my contention that the Axis Powers ultimately failed these tests, and that it was their shortcomings in the design realm—rather than material inferiority, operational blundering, or sheer bad luck—that led to their defeat. Needless to say, looking through the lens of the Axis Powers' strategies from a design perspective will also allow for fresh insights to emerge that can improve our understanding of the Allies' ultimate success as well.

When testifying before the influential Nye-Vandenberg Committee over five years prior to Pearl Harbor, K.K. Casey, a director of the DuPont Corporation, observed: "Wars frequently begin ten years before the shooting starts."[35] When one thinks like a designer, that timeline should probably be doubled. With this in mind, our story begins almost exactly twenty years before the invasion of Poland, in the immediate aftermath of the signing of the Treaty of Versailles that ended World War I. From a design perspective, this peace provided just the right environment to prepare for the next war.

But just who did the preparing during this interlude? A handful of geniuses? Was there a Thomas-Edison–like figure in the field of strategic design? To be sure, there were key individuals who played important roles during this period. *Blitzkrieg* concepts were profoundly shaped by the ideas of Heinz Guderian and Erwin Rommel. Both wrote insightful books on modern warfare,[36] then played key parts in the conquest of France in 1940—not to mention their contributions across a range of later campaigns. The development of Japanese carrier-based naval warfare owed much to Isoroku Yamamoto who, as early as 1924, made clear that he saw the end of the battleship era coming by changing his specialty from heavy gunnery to naval aviation. These are just some of the key individuals who played important "designer roles" in the Axis militaries. In Germany, one would have to add Erich von Manstein as a leader in planning and battle doctrine, and Karl Doenitz as the father of the U-boat wolfpack swarms. In Japan, Tomoyuki Yamashita was the most creative of the Imperial Army's field commanders. Italy's Italo Balbo designed its Air Force, while J. Valerio Borghese, "the Black Prince," pioneered a form of guerrilla warfare at sea that, for a time, had a virtually crippling effect on the Royal Navy in the Mediterranean.

Each of these "designers"—and several others—will be followed, from the years after the Great War to and through World War II. Needless to say, Hitler, Mussolini, and Tojo all had an impact on processes of strategic design—but these senior leaders deferred to their militaries far more than is commonly thought. As to the aforementioned designers, it is important to note that they hardly worked alone or absent other influences. Militaries, like other large organizations, should be examined as complex systems of interaction. Ideas flow across teams, service branches, and from one country to another. Liddell Hart may not have provided all the inspiration that the Germans needed to light the way to *Blitzkrieg,* but Guderian, Rommel, and others were well aware of his works. They also read Charles de Gaulle's *Le fil de l'épée* (*The Edge of the Sword*), a deeply thoughtful rumination on the potential of tank-heavy formations operating *en masse.* As to the design of the Pearl Harbor attack in December 1941, Yamamoto and his planners drew insight from the Royal Navy's air strike—with biplanes!—against the Italian fleet at Taranto in November 1940. Design at the strategic level is very system-oriented, well integrated, and influenced by the broad diffusion of ideas, much like design processes in commerce, industry—even the arts.[37]

With this in mind, it is also important to consider design contributions by leaders from industry, along with the scientists and other academics from the various universities and research institutes attuned to issues in military and security affairs. While they worked with significant inputs from those in uniform, the imprint of the industrialist and the scientist on Axis strategic designs was nevertheless quite strong. Interestingly, in the important area of aircraft design, both the German Messerschmitt and Japanese Mitsubishi firms came up with fighters that were swift and maneuverable, but much less rugged than British Spitfires or American Corsairs. And as the war dragged on, Allied fighter aircraft designs improved while the Axis stayed with their original designs—for the most part, that is. An important exception was the German effort to produce jet fighters, but these came into use too late in the war, and too small in number, to have a significant effect.

Beyond aircraft, the area of design and production of armored fighting vehicles is revelatory as well. While the Japanese and Italians did little if anything to improve their tanks, German industrialists worked hard in this realm. The resulting Tigers, Panthers, even the "Ferdinand"—a massive armored fighting vehicle named after Ferdinand Porsche—were remarkable weapons that had significant tactical impact. But again, they came into wide use too late in the war, had many "bugs," and their production inflicted huge opportunity costs on the German Army, in that overall tank output fell substantially below the level that could have been achieved had earlier, still-adequate tank designs been emphasized.

Incorporation of inputs from industry and academe into the "design mix" deepens awareness of the trade-offs that businesses deal with every day—but which have profound and deadly effects in the crucible of combat. Product experimentation may be a useful idea in business; but in war it comes with high risks. Arthur C. Clarke's classic short story, "Superiority," describes an interstellar war in which one side loses because its scientists successfully lobbied their military leaders to allow production of the most cutting-edge weaponry they could dream up. Needless to say, this came with opportunity costs and teething and training problems that, eventually, had fatal effects.

Clarke's cautionary tale shouldn't be taken too much to heart, though. For the design process—whether technological, organizational, or doctrinal—must continue well beyond a major war's outset, informing and guiding the fighting force. Sometimes by learning from the enemy, as was the case with the Allies' adoption of concepts of operations where the Axis had the initial lead—for example, with armored maneuver operations on land and carrier warfare at sea. Sometimes by technological advances and designs aimed at offsetting enemy capabilities, as in the case of the radar systems that helped defeat the *Luftwaffe* in the Battle of Britain, the code-breaking capability of American Magic that enabled the U.S. Navy to surprise the Japanese at Midway, and the high-frequency direction-finding equipment that did so much to thwart the U-boat menace. Needless to say, strategic design also sometimes extends to critically important arms races. It was a great blessing that the Manhattan Project team built an atomic weapon while the Axis floundered—the latter's failure being in part due to Allied special operations aimed at derailing German proliferation processes in particular.[38]

Perhaps the sheer complexity of strategic design processes explains why there hasn't yet been a full study of World War II from this perspective. But, as noted above, this approach has already been applied with success to explorations of business organizations replete with their own complexities. Analyzing the largest conflict in human history through the lens of design is undoubtedly a more daunting task; but doing so offers fresh opportunities for structuring and *simplifying* the process of shedding light on why the Axis Powers, that had so many advantages for so long, were ultimately defeated. As we shall see, the fault lay not "in their stars," but rather in their designs.

# 2. From Versailles to the Vistula

ON 28 JUNE 1919, five years to the day since Gavrilo Princip assassinated Austrian Archduke Franz Ferdinand and his wife in Sarajevo sparking World War I, the peace treaty ending that conflict was signed. It was a retributive document that imposed territorial losses and staggering reparations on the defeated, a reflection of the bitterness of the victors who had finally prevailed, but at ruinous cost to some. The three major Western Allies who had suffered mightily, France, Britain, and Italy, had seen a combined three million soldiers, sailors and airmen killed in battle—with an additional seven million wounded. In the East, Russia, knocked out of the war by the Germans and excluded from Versailles by the Allies, had lost two million dead, five million wounded, and control of Poland and the Baltic countries. The United States came in late, engaging fully only in the last year of the war, and had suffered just over 100,000 battle deaths, double that number wounded. Japan entered the war three weeks after it began in 1914 and quickly attacked German territories in China. Next in line were the Kaiser's holdings in the Marianas, Carolines, and Marshalls. Japan claimed those islands *in perpetuo* at Versailles and was granted mandates over them by the League of Nations. All this for a loss of 300 killed in action, 1,000 wounded. Having suffered least in the war, Japan gained the most from it.

Leaders in Tokyo, from the Emperor to the politicians and the military, were quick to seize upon the strategic opportunity afforded by these easy gains. Among their first acts was the building of strong fortifications on the formerly German-held islands in the Pacific. Here was an early glimpse of the island-chain "shield" idea that would one day form a central element of Japan's strategic design for the future. The basic concept was that, if the islands came under attack, their strong garrisons would hold out in the sun-hardened pillboxes that primarily comprised these fortifications until relief came from naval and air forces that were to engage the enemy at sea and then deliver reinforcements for the fight on land.

A key question that arose from the outset was: What kind of naval and air forces should Japan develop to support such a strategy? For the most part, thinking focused upon capital ships—battleships and the less well-armored, but faster and still heavy-hitting, battle cruisers. Eventually, the battleship advocates embraced an "8-8 Plan" (eight very modern vessels of each type) that would give Japan a battle fleet a little over two-thirds the size of its American counterpart. But this was an aspirational goal, both costly to achieve and at variance with the Washington Naval Treaty negotiated during 1921–22, by the terms of which Japan agreed to build a force of capital ships no more than 60 percent the size of either the British or American battle fleets.

Battleships aside, these were years in which spirited debates about the role of attack aircraft in naval warfare were beginning to emerge, sparked in part by Billy Mitchell's sinking of the *Ostfriesland*—a German dreadnought that had been ceded to the United States as part of war reparations—by aerial bombing in July 1921. Mitchell's action and his subsequent strong advocacy of the air arm sparked a bitter controversy in American military circles, and led finally to his court-martial.[1] The humbling of Mitchell was hardly the only reason why air power was under-appreciated by most of the leading navalists at the time; there was also the simple fact that battleships were the preferred instruments of influence of *all* the leading navies of the world. Oliver Cromwell's sturdy maxim that "a man-of-war is the best ambassador" was borne out by what psychologists call "social proof," the affirmation of what is acceptable by observation of its acceptance by others. The battleship ruled the seas because so many *believed* that it did.

However, Billy Mitchell was not alone, and American mavericks were not the only ones to appreciate the importance of air power in naval affairs. Perhaps the most important convert to Billy Mitchell's point of view was a Japanese naval officer, Isoroku Yamamoto, who was studying at Harvard during 1919–1921. His biographers all make clear that he did some high living while in the United States at this time. But he also traveled widely in the States and did some close observing and deep thinking that changed his views about sea power. As a very junior officer, having graduated from the Imperial Naval Academy with a gunnery specialty in 1904, Sub-lieutenant Takano—he wasn't adopted into the Yamamoto family until 1916[2]—served in the Russo-Japanese War and was wounded at the battle of Tsushima in 1905. It was the most decisive naval engagement since Lord Nelson's victory at Trafalgar in 1805. This formative experience affirmed young Takano's devotion to and belief in the gun power of the Imperial Japanese Navy's battle fleet. But fifteen years later, now as Yamamoto, he followed the American debate closely and was swayed by it. As his biographer Hiroyuki Agawa observed: "By the time he returned to Japan in 1921 … Yamamoto already seems to have been quite firmly convinced of the future importance of air armament."[3] In 1924 he went so far as to switch branches from the surface fleet to the naval air arm and, at forty, learned to fly.

Yamamoto's enthusiasm for naval air power was fairly easy to accommodate as Japan, after taming some war-caused inflation, had seen its manufacturing production double from the last pre-war year, 1913, to 1923. By 1929, the year the Great Depression hit, production had tripled. And the 1930s, so hard on most nations economically, saw further gains. Indeed, by 1938, Japanese manufacturing had increased nearly six-fold from its 1913 level. This while British production had barely increased, and even the United States had seen only 40 percent growth over those same 35 years.[4] Thus Japan had the capability to build a strong carrier strike force, and the Washington Treaty limitation set for its capital ship tonnage (315,000 tons) meant that production of a few battleships underway would have to stop. But instead of being scrapped, they were converted into carriers. Japan's edge in naval aviation, the result of its robust economic climate as well as of Yamamoto's advocacy during his rise to the head of the Imperial Navy's Aeronautics Department— and in 1939 to the command of the Combined Fleet—resulted in Japan having a 10:7 advantage in carriers over the U.S. Navy by December 1941. American economic sanctions put in place in response to Japanese aggression on the East Asian mainland cast a pall over all this progress, though, and stoked the appetites of Japan's "war party."

As to the American attempt to apply economic pressure as a means of getting Japan to cease its expansionary war in China—a conflict that began in earnest in 1931, becoming full-blown by 1937—it backfired very badly. Japan's growing population (now over sixty million) and paucity of natural resources of its own put the Empire in the position of being, as Ambassador Edwin Reischauer described the situation, "dangerously dependent on the good will and tolerance of foreign powers."[5] Economic sanctions only fanned the flames the war party had been stoking, giving them the edge over the businessmen who preferred peaceful development and trade, had been the principal sources of Japan's post–World War I boom, and supported the more liberal democratic politics that proved all too briefly ascendant.

The businessmen of the *zaibatsu* commercial class were not alone in preferring peace. Yamamoto, well aware of the inherent size and strength of the United States, firmly believed that no war should be fought against the Americans, as it could not in the end be won. In this view he was not alone. Tomoyuki Yamashita, a rising Imperial Army officer just a year younger than Yamamoto, came to the same conclusion. Beyond avoiding open war with the Americans, he even went so far as to call for ending the conflict in China—which put him in bad odor with the radicals of the military faction.

Yamashita had spent some years abroad in Europe soon after the end of World War I as a military attaché, first in Switzerland and then in Austria. But he also traveled widely in Germany, sometimes in close company with a fellow officer, Hideki Tojo, who later became a principal proponent of an aggressive foreign policy and who rose to the position of prime minister just seven weeks before the attack on Pearl Harbor. Over the years, Tojo and Yamashita grew further apart in their views. But in these early days, they enjoyed each other's company, perfected their German-language skills, and learned much from their travels. Yamashita in particular came away with a sense of the growing importance of tanks—in which the Imperial Army was deficient—and of the absolute need for close coordination of ground forces with close-support attack aircraft.

Much as Yamashita became an advocate for highly innovative mobile mechanized operations on land, Yamamoto had radical ideas about naval warfare, too. His key insight was the notion of concentrating many aircraft carriers in an overwhelming striking force (*Kido Butai*) that would have a reach out-ranging the guns of the Imperial Fleet's battleships more than fifteen-fold. Until Yamamoto came along, carriers were parceled out one each to battleship-heavy squadrons—to act largely in a scouting capacity for them. Yamamoto sought to change this with his new design for sea power.

But one lone voice, however articulate and insightful, seldom changes the course set by large military organizations. This is true of virtually all major powers; and it was certainly the case with Japan in the 1930s. By the end of 1934, the Japanese were becoming more embroiled in their war in China, their relations with the West more strained. And so, at this point Tokyo renounced the Washington Naval Treaty and began an aggressive expansion plan for the Imperial Navy. But instead of fully embracing Yamamoto's vision of carrier-based naval warfare, a policy of what might be called "broad preparation" was pursued instead. That is, both carriers *and* battleships were emphasized, the design of the latter being driven by giantism, as the *Yamato* and *Musashi* were 72,000-ton behemoths. With their nine 18-inch guns, the idea was that, though Japan could never keep up with American production, these mega-ships—twice the size of the 36,000-ton USS *Washington,* for example, which had only 16-inch guns—would be superior enough in quality to offset the enemy's numerical advantages. As was quickly demonstrated during the Pacific War, carriers were more useful and effective than battleships. Japan's "broad preparation" was a mistake.

And what of the aircraft themselves? Japanese designers did amazing work with the various types throughout the 1930s, developing outstanding torpedo- and dive-bombers. In 1935, the Mitsubishi *zaibatsu,* a diversified group of firms that had formed in 1870 and helped propel the modernization of Japan, developed the world's first monoplane fighter able to take off from a carrier, the A5M "Claude." But it was Mitsubishi's elegant design of its successor, the A6M "Zero," that would do so much to enable the victorious campaigns that Japan enjoyed early in the war. As Ronald Spector put it, the Zero "was the first carrier-based fighter to equal or surpass the performance of the best contemporary land-based fighters; it was superior to *any* fighter in the United States Army or Navy at the outbreak of the war."[6]

Introduced in 1940, the Zero was used on land and at sea. In skilled hands it was an instrument of deadly efficiency. Heavily armed with two machine guns and two 20mm cannons, its great speed and climb capabilities made the Zero highly maneuverable, too. Saburo Sakai, who would become Japan's most honored fighter pilot, described the plane when it first came to his squadron on Formosa—from which he and his colleagues sortied against the Chinese—as "a dream to fly. The airplane was the most sensitive I had ever flown, and even slight finger pressure brought instant response. We could hardly wait to meet enemy planes in this remarkable new aircraft."[7] For all its strengths, though, the Zero suffered from some serious design flaws. To achieve its speed and maneuverability, the Mitsubishi engineers chose to forgo armoring the plane. Coupled with the lack of self-sealing fuel tanks, this made the Zero vulnerable even to light battle damage—and prone to turn into a fireball when hit. In the years to come, as veteran pilots were lost to attrition and better armed and armored American planes came on line, the Zero's design vulnerabilities were to have grave consequences.

But that day was still far off. In the late 1930s, Japan enjoyed local air superiority and its pilots gained extremely useful experience in the fighting over the skies of China. Its growing advantage in aircraft carriers was further augmented by the development of the Type 93 "Long Lance" torpedo designed by the Navy and put in service in 1933 for use by surface ships. The idea being that even light vessels like destroyers could threaten cruisers and battleships with a torpedo whose range was over 12 miles, ran at nearly 50mph, and delivered a half-ton warhead. Driven by compressed pure oxygen, the Type 93 had roughly five times the propulsive power and greater range than its compressed-air-powered (20 percent oxygen) American counterpart.

The tactical concept behind the Type 93—it was American historian Samuel Eliot Morison who later named it the Long Lance—was to engage the likely enemy, the U.S. Navy, at night by detecting and attacking enemy warships before they could come within effective gun range. Imperial Navy ship crews trained relentlessly for night fighting, with special emphasis on improving operations under very low visibility conditions. It was a practice that would pay dividends in several naval battles, especially early on in the Pacific War. But there was a curious design flaw: a de-emphasis on making radar a key element in this surface fighting doctrine. To some extent this was the result of radar's being in an early phase of development. There was also, however, a *Bushido*-esque belief in the superiority of highly developed human skill and senses over and against electronic detection. That said, when Yamashita led a delegation to Germany more than a year prior to Pearl Harbor, he made sure to send part of his team to one of the Nazis' radar stations where "[t]he Germans turned out everything for them and the Japanese took copious notes."[8] Even so, the Imperial Navy was slow to develop and improve radar capabilities—the very effective Type 11 and 12 equipment did not come into significant operational use until mid–1943 and 1944, respectively—a crucial error as future combat results were to prove.

This dilatoriness about adopting advanced surface and air detection equipment on Imperial Navy ships did not apply, however, to sonar—or "asdic" as it was generally called then. This technology was indeed fully embraced by senior naval leaders during the interwar period, and at the war's start, American submarine skippers were to learn, to their surprise, that the enemy already had sonar. As to effectiveness, Clay Blair put it this way about the Imperial Navy's sonar capabilities: "They not only had it, they knew how to use it."[9]

But there was a difference between having sonar and designing an effective anti-submarine warfare campaign plan. For a nation so dependent upon imports from overseas, it is stunning that the Imperial Navy did so little during the 1930s to prepare for the defense of merchant shipping against commerce raiding by submarines. This despite the fact that many Japanese sailors had the opportunity to serve in European waters during World War I on Imperial Navy destroyers deployed to that theater of operations to help in the campaign against the deadly German U-boats. Even though the U-boat menace in World War I was finally tamed by the employment of escorted convoys, the lesson was lost on the Japanese, who generally preferred a doctrine of unescorted sailings of merchant ships.

Perhaps the most compelling explanation for Japan's poor preparation for antisubmarine warfare is that the Imperial Navy was "mirror imaging" its own preferred use of submarines, believing that the Americans would also use theirs as scouts and skirmishers in support of surface battle fleet actions. Atsushi Oi, who rose to become head operations officer of the Grand Escort Command Headquarters that was established far too late—at the end of 1943—described the problem this way: "Our navy … estimated that the U.S. Navy had no intention of waging any extensive warfare against merchant marines. The Japanese navy took it for granted that the role to be played by American submarines would be the same as that of Japan's own submarine forces, and slighted their role as raiders of commercial shipping."[10] It was a fatal assumption that set Japan on the path toward catastrophic, irretrievable losses in the war to come.

Another area of concern for Japan grew out of the rising availability of radio-electronic communications. This improving technology made possible the command and control of land, sea, and air forces over vast distances, but also made this form of messaging vulnerable to interception. Code-making to ensure the secrecy of communications became an important military function—diplomatic, too—for virtually all nations during this period. Japan initially relied upon hiring European experts, and came up with a *kata kana* code based upon seventy-three syllables rendered in Latin letters. This turned out to be breakable by straightforward cryptanalysis based on frequency distributions, with some additional clues derived from common words—for example, *owari* (stop) at the ends of sections or messages, or *doitsu* for frequent correspondent Germany.[11] Later, more sophisticated Imperial codes, labeled by the Americans Red and Blue—the colors of the folders U.S. intelligence kept the intercepts in—were also broken despite the shift from Latin to a pure *kana* script with nearly 100,000 distinct foundational symbols. The success of American code-breakers was due in part to the large number of messages intercepted by the network of outposts and carefully positioned ships that were always listening. These provided large amounts of data that greatly aided the cryptana-lysts' work.

In the spring of 1931 any doubt about the vulnerability of Japan's codes was dispelled by the publication of an American code-breaker's memoirs. H.O. Yardley's *The American Black Chamber*, written in the wake of his firing by Secretary of State Henry Stimson, who famously said that "gentlemen do not read other gentlemen's mail," made clear among its many other revelations that Japanese codes had been broken. This caused quite a stir in Tokyo and throughout the Empire's military and diplomatic services. The Navy in particular worked hard to improve its code-making capabilities, augmenting them with disinformation campaigns. For example, historian John Prados has observed that, in its annual funding requests to the legislature, "the data the Imperial Navy presented were deliberately askew—ships were slightly faster, displaced more, and were armed somewhat differently than the Diet was told."[12] While better codes and deceptions, coupled with American diffidence about this form of spying—which lasted for some years—improved Japanese information security temporarily, growing tensions in the 1930s sparked renewed U.S. intelligence efforts that led to the "Magic" code-breaking capability that was to play an important role in the Pacific War.

Much of the rising U.S.-Japan tension in the late 1930s was caused by the expand-ing Japanese land campaign in China, which had ramped up significantly, beginning in 1937. This was when the terrible Rape of Nanking occurred that resulted in as many as 250,000 innocent Chinese being murdered, and when the deliberate Japanese attack on the American gunboat *Panay* took place. In response to the latter incident, Yamamoto hurried to the U.S. embassy to explain the "mistake," and later issued a profound, eloquent public apology that helped to ease the tensions that could easily have led to war right then.[13]

Around this time Yamashita, now a general officer, held command of an elite army division that saw much action in northern China. Aside from pitched battles, he also had to deal with the irregular tactics of the Chinese guerrillas, gaining insight into the potential of even quite small units to have significant impacts on the course of campaigns. While this was a useful time for Yamashita, other senior colleagues in the Kwantung Army were not so fortunate. Their over-aggressive actions toward Mongolia, at the time a country enjoying Soviet protection, sparked a brief war in the summer of 1939 in which a young Russian general, Georgi Zhukov, used three armored brigades and supporting infantry with exceptional skill to rout the invading Japanese.[14] The result bore out Yamashita's earlier recommendations about mobile mechanized warfare—a concept about which most senior leaders of the Imperial Army were generally dismissive. The validation of his ideas, and the hard experience of the so-called Nomonhan War, helped to revive Yamashita's career, which had been stalled because of his opposition to the war party—which was now led by his old colleague Hideki Tojo.

*    *    *

Soon after Zhukov's victory over the Japanese, Germany invaded Poland. The conflict that erupted in Europe in September 1939 came precisely on the timetable that France's Marshal Ferdinand Foch had set when he dismissed the terms of the Versailles Treaty as too lenient, declaring, "This is not a peace. It is an armistice for twenty years."[15] However, his was a minority view. The general assessment at the time was that the Treaty of Ver-sailles, by dismantling the Ottoman, Austro-Hungarian, and German Empires—along with the heavy reparations imposed, especially on the Germans[16]—punished the defeated appropriately and effectively. But over the course of the interwar years, and to a great degree in the decades after, there was a growing popular view that it was the excessive *vengefulness* of Versailles that fueled German resentment, helped the Nazis rise to power, and paved the way for the next world war.

The eminent historian A.J.P. Taylor articulated the most compelling critique of the Treaty as being too retributive, and reserved his highest praise for those so-called "appeasers" who had, during and before the Munich crisis, "courageously denounced the harshness and short-sightedness of Versailles."[17] Taylor's view is at one end of the spectrum of opinion; but the majority of historians still fall into the category of seeing Versailles as quite reasonable and appeasement as a great blunder. And on the other end of the spectrum, Victor Davis Hanson has defended Foch's view—acting as a kind of "anti–Taylor"—affirming the argument that the Treaty should have done much more to disable Germany and slow its recovery.[18]

Some also critiqued the Treaty on ethical grounds, warning that its overreach would lead to troubles. The economist John Maynard Keynes, who served as representative of the British Treasury at Versailles—until he resigned in protest—advanced the argument that a "policy of reducing Germany to servitude for a generation, of degrading the lives of millions of human beings, and of depriving a whole nation of happiness should be abhorrent and detestable.... [N]ations are not authorized, by religion or by natural morals, to visit on the children of their enemies the misdoings of parents or of rulers."[19] Thus it seems that, whether the Treaty of Versailles was too harsh, too lenient, or unethical, all assessments were to lead to the same future—one that was to feature the onset of a disastrous, cataclysmic new war in Europe.

Aside from reparations, Germany suffered from military occupation of the Rhineland as well—to which the industrial Ruhr was added in 1923 when payments to the Allies were not kept up—and was forbidden any sort of military aircraft or submarines. The army (*Reichswehr*) was limited to 100,000 service members—including just 4,000 officers—and the navy to 15,000 sailors and but a handful of ships. There was no air force. It is easy to see why Marshal Foch's dire prediction about Germany's return was not treated with too deep a concern; the defeated foe had been prostrated. In addition to these military restrictions, there were social humiliations as well, sometimes taking the form of outrages committed by Allied soldiers against German women in the occupied zones. French colonial troops from Senegal figured in many rape cases, which especially enraged the German people. Along with the pain of hyperinflation and other ills, this fed a deep well of social resentment that helped pave the way for the Nazis' eventual rise.

The German army was the first service to begin throwing off the yoke imposed by Versailles. Not in any material sense early on, but rather in the realm of concepts of operations. General Hans von Seeckt, who had served with great success on the Eastern Front in World War I and was the military adviser to the German delegation at Versailles, was named commander of the *Reichswehr* in 1920, a position he held until retirement in 1926. During these years, von Seeckt drew upon his own combat experience in the East, as well as insights from the Allies' armored operations on the Western Front in 1917 and 1918, to begin preaching what Liddell Hart called "a gospel of mobility, based on the view that a quick-moving, quick-hitting army of picked troops could, under modern conditions, make rings around an old-fashioned mass army."[20] Among his many gifts as a leader, von Seeckt was also a keen-eyed talent-spotter who nurtured the careers, even under the tight limits of the Versailles Treaty, of many who would become outstanding field commanders during World War II.

Perhaps the most influential innovator to emerge during this period was a young signals officer who came from a Prussian military family, Heinz Guderian, who had seen and learned much on the Western Front during World War I, and now sought to bring von Seeckt's vision of a swift, supple mobile force to life. Denied the ability to work with actual tanks, he was assigned to a command role in the "motor transport" branch of the *Reichswehr*, from which he began to conduct exercises that simulated armored operations using mock-ups. The results of these experiments, and his reading of the works of Liddell Hart[21] and J.F.C. Fuller, led Guderian to assert, "It would be wrong to include tanks in infantry divisions: what was needed were armored divisions which would include all the supporting arms needed to allow the tanks to fight with full effect."[22]

This insight implied a radical organizational redesign, shifting tanks from their primary role supporting infantry—the dominant view of French and British generals throughout the 1920s and 1930s, and on into the early part of World War II—to become the core of army field forces in future conflicts. After von Seeckt's retirement, Guderian found that most senior German generals, like their Anglo-French counterparts, were opposed to creating such concentrated armored (panzer) divisions. At the end of one of Guderian's exercises, his superior Gerd von Rundstedt—who would later win some remarkable victories using these very methods—turned to him and said, "All nonsense, my dear Guderian, all nonsense." Williamson Murray has summed up the situation facing Guderian and his small but devoted band of believers this way: "In truth, there was considerable skepticism about the potential of panzer units up to the 1939 Polish campaign."[23] But this kind of stiff-necked opposition had not been able to prevent the formation of at least a few panzer divisions, which soon had a doctrine that energized them.

If Guderian effectively championed organizational redesign of the *Reichswehr*, the emerging concept of mobile exploitation of breakthroughs made by concentrated armored formations was powerfully developed by the son of a Swabian schoolteacher, Erwin Rommel, another innovator whose career was nurtured by von Seeckt. As a junior officer during World War I—three years younger than Guderian, Rommel was just twenty-two when he fought in the 1914 Battle of the Marne—he later on served with distinction in the Balkans and played a critical role in the great victory over Italian forces at Caporetto. In each of his actions in the field, Rommel showed an aptitude for infiltrating defenses, disrupting rear areas, and then returning to help disrupt the enemy's main forces. While his approach was similar to the "stormtroop" doctrine—also known as von Hutier tactics, so called after another brilliant officer—that debuted on the Western Front in the failed March 1918 Ludendorff offensive, Rommel brought a new concept to command that was to shape *Blitzkrieg* profoundly: the notion of "leading from the front." This idea was central to Rommel's successes in both of the world wars, and he was to become the archetype of this mode of command, the kind of leader who was, as his British biographer Desmond Young described him, "cunning, ruthless, untiring, quick of decision, [and] incredibly brave."[24]

Guderian and Rommel had to deal with strong institutional opposition to their ideas. Neither made much progress in realizing their dreams for the *Reichswehr* until Adolf Hitler came to power in 1933. The Nazi dictator's grand strategy for expansion called for developing an ability to fight and win short, sharp wars. Guderian's vision of panzer divisions and Rommel's ideas about swift infiltration operations appealed to him greatly. In fairness, it should be noted that Hitler had also been thinking about mobile maneuver warfare for at least a decade before he first met Guderian in 1934. In *Mein Kampf*, for example, Hitler wrote of the "general motorization of the world, which in the next war will manifest itself overwhelmingly and decisively."[25] But even advocacy by Germany's *Führer* proved insufficient for purposes of moving the army decisively in the direction of mechanization.

While it had expanded significantly once Hitler threw off the shackles of Versailles and enacted a new law that called for universal conscription, the *Heer* (army) portion of the newly named *Wehrmacht* was still comprised overwhelmingly of infantry. So much so that by the time of the September 1939 invasion of Poland with over fifty divisions, only six of that total were armored. Even so, this thin layer of panzers performed so well that it proved the validity of the ideas Guderian had expressed in his *Achtung Panzer!* and that Rommel had elucidated in his *Infanterie Greift An* (*Infantry Attacks*). Both books appeared in 1937 and were well received. Rommel's eventually sold nearly 400,000 copies. *Blitzkrieg,* had a wide popular audience.

Close air support was a key element in the lop-sided victory over the Poles, especially as manifested in the form of the dive-bombing capability of Germany's new *Luftwaffe*. Though the Versailles Treaty forbade rebuilding an air force, the Germans maintained some capacity for aircraft production in support of civilian aviation. Lufthansa grew into a vibrant airline during this time, and its chief executive Erhard Milch would go on to become one of the senior leaders of the *Luftwaffe*. And even well before the rise of the Nazis to power in 1933, flying clubs had become popular in Germany, with much emphasis on gliders—which were to play an important role in airborne operations during World War II.

Also, in circumvention of Treaty limitations, the secret training of combat pilots began at Lipetsk in the Soviet Union in 1925, and continued there for over eight years. The Russians were willing to host this activity largely because they shared Germany's resentment of and antipathy toward the newly formed Polish state—one of the creations that resulted from the Versailles process. The Poles had defeated invading Red Army forces in 1920,[26] a humiliation that Moscow long remembered and sought finally to avenge by joining with the Germans in attacking Poland in 1939.

The important role the *Luftwaffe* was to play in the emergence of mobile maneuver warfare in 1939 seemed foreordained, given that so many of its senior officers had long-standing Army backgrounds. Field-Marshal Albert Kesselring, for example, began as an artillery officer early on in his career during World War I, but rose to broader duties and responsibilities on both Western and Eastern fronts later in that conflict. He was also one of those officers chosen by von Seeckt during the 1920s to reshape the German Army into a more mobile, mechanized force. Later, after Hitler came to power in 1933 and decided to create an air force as an independent service two years later, Kesselring was picked by Hermann Goering to become its second chief of staff—the first having been killed in an aviation accident.

Goering, an ardent Nazi and close associate of Hitler's, was also a World War I ace with twenty-five kills who rose to command the "Flying Circus"—so named because of the varied colors in which its aircraft were painted—after the death of its first leader, Baron Manfred von Richtofen, in April 1918. The top fighter pilot under Goering's command was Ernst Udet, a young aero club enthusiast from Munich who was credited with sixty-two kills by war's end—when he was just twenty-two. Udet and Goering became good friends, and both did more than their share of aerial barnstorming and high living during the 1920s.

Over time, Udet became more and more interested in the close-support capabilities of combat aircraft. His memory of how the enemy had begun to engage in ground attacks late in the Great War remained keen, and he wrote painfully in his memoir about how German forces were "strafed daily by swarms of close support aircraft."[27] In ensuing years at air shows—some in the United States, where he met and befriended American ace Eddie Rickenbacker and Charles Lindbergh—Udet's signature move was a deep dive from which he would pull out at the very last moment. This maneuver led him eventually to his insight that dive-bombing would prove far more accurate and effective than level-bombing.

Udet was particularly impressed with the design of the Hawk, a remarkable American biplane he first tried out at the factory airfield of the Curtiss-Wright Company in Buffalo, New York, in 1933. While he lacked the resources to purchase the plane, his old comrade Goering, now serving as Hitler's Commissioner of Aviation, wired enough funds so that he could acquire *two* of them. With just one Hawk as a foundation—Udet crashed the other early on—German aircraft manufacturers set to work designing dive-bombers of their own. Several firms were involved, but eventually the competition came down to the Heinkel 118 and the Junkers 87 *Stuka* (*Sturzkampfflugzeug,* or "dive-bomber"). Junkers won out, and the inverted gull-wing aircraft soon after showed its capabilities when pilots of the German Condor Legion served on Francisco Franco's Fascist side in the Spanish Civil War (1936–1939). The *Stuka* became operational with the Legion only in the last year of that war, but quickly outperformed level bombers in terms of accuracy and effect. So much so that Wolfram von Richtofen—Condor's commanding general and a cousin of the late Red Baron—an early skeptic about the potential of the *Stuka,* "had all of his doubts concerning the value of dive-bombing removed while in Spain."[28]

A key part of the successful *Stuka* design was the installation of automatic pull-up air brakes that would work even if g-forces caused pilots to black out during dives. In Poland and beyond, as Cajus Bekker noted in one official history, "it was the *Stuka* that cleared the way for the German armour and infantry, and made rapid victory possible."[29] More than any other single technology, the swift, highly accurate "flying artillery" that the *Stuka* represented, and the unnerving psychological effect of its wailing "Jericho Trumpet" siren, made this plane a critically important element of *Blitzkrieg.* Ironically, this term for the new concept of operations was popularized by a German refugee from the Nazi regime, Fritz Sternberg,[30] picked up by the British press, then widely adopted— if just briefly before defeats began to pile up—by the Nazis themselves.

Spain was not only a proving ground for dive-bombers. Fighter planes were tested out there, too; the most successful was the Bf109 designed by Willy Messerschmitt. It was a sleek, swift fighter that packed a lot of firepower as well. The 109 virtually swept Spanish skies, challenged only by the nearly 500 Soviet I-16 low-wing monoplanes Moscow sent the Leftist government that, for their small size and great maneuverability, were called *Moscas* (Flies). Until the war in Spain, the 109 had faced much opposition from senior *Luftwaffe* leaders, largely because, as fighter pilot Adolf Galland—a Condor Legion veteran who in World War II rose to command all German fighter squadrons—summed the matter up: "They were stuck on the idea that maneuverability in banking was primarily the determining factor in air combat…. [T]his was proved false in practice."[31] The 109 made the case for the superiority of speed and firepower.

All that the *Luftwaffe* lacked during this period was a long-range attack aircraft that would give it a strategic bombing capability. Various plans were being drawn up by several competing aircraft manufacturers as what came to be called the "Ural Bomber" project proceeded, inspired by the ideas of General Walther Wever, a career Army officer who nevertheless had keen insight into the potential of strategic long-range bombing and used his position as *Luftwaffe* chief of staff skillfully to advance this cause.[32] But fate intervened in June 1936 when Wever, piloting his own Heinkel 70 *Blitz,* crashed on takeoff, the fuel-laden plane exploding in a great fireball. This led to his replacement by Kesselring, who was much more interested in the close-support mission of the *Luftwaffe.* The Chief of the Technical Office, Wilhelm Wimmer, whose views were closely in line with Wever's, was replaced a week after the latter's death by ... Ernst Udet.

At that time, Udet was happily serving as Inspector of Fighters and Dive-Bombers; and though he absolutely loathed the idea of leading a day-to-day office life, he also saw the opportunity to advance the cause of dive-bombing decisively from this new perch. Cajus Bekker described Udet's new position this way: "As chief of the Technical Office, he virtually directed what was then the biggest armaments concern on earth."[33] Ten months later the Ural Bomber program was closed down in favor of a focus on dive-bombing and shorter-range, level-delivery "fast bombers." It was a strategic design choice that was to prove beneficial in supporting the early campaigns of the Army; but the consequences of the lack of a long-range bombing capability were to prove quite grave later in the war, during the Battle of Britain and in the protracted conflict that loomed beyond.

As to the mid-range fast bombers, they were to have the unintended consequence of slowing fighter production, because it was believed that, due to their speed and defensive armament, they could operate without the need for fighter escort. This led to a de-emphasis on fighter aircraft, which were allotted less than a third of total production (450 out of 1,490) in 1939—a ratio that fell to just over one-fourth (1,700 out of 6,600) in 1940.[34] Peak production of fighters came only under the guidance of the brilliant Albert Speer—in 1944, quite late in the war. Far too late.

While Hitler's gaze was cast primarily eastward, where *Lebensraum* was to be found—hence the naming of the "Ural" bomber—it eventually became clear that the British were growing more openly opposed to German expansion and would have to be deterred or otherwise dealt with. And as much as Grand Admiral Alfred von Tirpitz a generation earlier had come up with the idea of building a "risk fleet" designed to discourage Royal Navy participation in any continental war,[35] so the German navy under Hitler was assigned a very similar task. Hitler gave his admirals an excellent boost by negotiating a separate bilateral naval agreement with Britain in 1935 that effectively put an end to constraints imposed by Versailles. Now Germany could build battle cruisers, "pocket battleships," and one key clause in the agreement even allowed creation of a U-boat fleet equal to the Royal Navy's submarine forces in size.[36] Winston Churchill, still mired in his "wilderness years," rose in Parliament to condemn the agreement, arguing that the rise of a powerful German navy would soon prove a grave threat to British sea power, the consequence being that "very soon one of the deterrents of a European war will gradually fade away."[37] Churchill was right.

Britain's saving grace was to come at the hands of the German naval leaders themselves. Most flag officers of the *Kriegsmarine* were devoted battleship sailors, not least Erich Raeder, who had fought heroically at the Battle of Jutland in 1916 and whose fifteen years as navy chief (1928–1943) spanned the Versailles era, the period of the Anglo-German naval treaty, and the opening and middle phases of World War II. Raeder and those of like mind—a dominant majority—believed the key to designing the navy was the ideal of a "balanced fleet" comprised of *all* the various types of warships. As Rear Admiral Hans Meyer recalled, this was "a view that was agreed to by all but a few officers (among whom was Doenitz, later *Grossadmiral*)."[38]

Karl Doenitz, like Rommel born in 1891, was the son of an engineer. Decades before his dissent from Raeder's views, he served on the *Breslau,* companion ship to the famous *Goeben* in the opening days of World War I. The successful flight of these vessels across much of the Mediterranean to Constantinople—eluding far superior Royal Navy forces—contributed to the Ottoman Empire's decision to ally with Germany and Austria-Hungary. Later on in the war, Doenitz switched to the submarine service, and was captured in October 1918 when his U-boat was forced to the surface in an engagement. But by then he had had enough experience to form his ideas about how to wage war at sea with submarines operating in large, controlled "packs" rather than as lone wolves. The swarming *Rudeltaktik* concept that grew from his early experience and thinking stayed with Doenitz throughout the interwar period—just waiting for the time when the binding shackles of Versailles were to be thrown off.

It was a moment repeatedly postponed, even after the Anglo-German naval agreement of 1935. Despite growing evidence that the aircraft carrier and the submarine were indeed revolutionizing naval warfare, neither of these newer vessel types was aggressively pursued. Instead, the battleship sailors had their day, which led to the laying down in 1936 of the *Bismarck* and *Tirpitz,* each of more than 40,000 tons and carrying eight fifteen-inch guns. Raeder and his minions even went so far as to convince Hitler of the need for an additional six "super battleships" of more than 55,000 tons and carrying eight sixteen-inch guns—though the projected timeline for delivery of these unrealistically ran out to 1948.[39] Nevertheless, even as tensions rose, war approached and revisions to the *Kriegsmarine's* strategic design became unavoidable, the priorities of its "Z-Plan" presented to Hitler in February 1939 remained largely unchanged from earlier fleet-building concepts. Two aircraft carriers were still in the Plan for delivery some time in 1941—an initiative never properly funded or carried forward—and the super-battleship concept was dropped. But the *Bismarck* and *Tirpitz* stayed top priorities, as did heavy and light cruisers.[40]

Raeder's concept of operations for the employment of this World War I–style battle fleet was to use these heavy units as raiders, preying on British commerce and forcing the Royal Navy to disperse its own warships in order to protect the convoys of merchant ships upon which Britain's survival in wartime would depend. Needless to say, when war came in September of 1939, Raeder noted fatalistically in his diary that the conflict had come five years too soon, and that all the *Kriegsmarine* could do now was fight and "show that they know how to die gallantly."[41] This was hardly a strategy for victory. The Z-Plan was a bust.

Thus, as the Poles were being overwhelmed by the Germans' radically new designs for warfare—defeated in four weeks by the handful of panzer divisions for whose creation Guderian had advocated, and by Udet's *Stukas*—Doenitz's stock in submarines was rising. It would not be very long before naval production was to shift emphasis toward his U-boats. Germany had only fifty-seven at the outset of the war in September 1939, just over a third of them with sufficient range to operate in the Atlantic, making Doenitz's *Rudeltaktik* concept hard to carry off given the sheer size of the area of operations. And even as commander of submarines, he still had dissenters of his own to deal with. Many of his subordinates were concerned that his notion of trying to control wolfpacks from a distance by radio command—in Doenitz's view the only efficient and effective way to concentrate the U-boats for decisive attacks on convoys—would imperil them. So much so that "some naval staff officers even wished to eliminate the submarines' radios, contending that they were of more danger than value."[42]

Doenitz and many other high-level commanders throughout the *Kriegsmarine* believed that this concern was unwarranted because of their three-rotor Enigma coding machine—later versions had four rotors—that had been developed, a typewriter-like device invented by German engineer Arthur Scherbius that had hundreds of thousands of possible substitutions for any letter or number keystroke. Each tap of a letter caused the rotors, or cipher wheels, to whir and end up with a substitution, advancing the position of each rotor so that whole new alphabets were created with each keystroke. With three rotors, the possibilities per stroke were 17, 576 ($26 \times 26 \times 26$). Later, when a fourth rotor was added, the possibilities rose exponentially, to 456, 976 ($26 \times 26 \times 26 \times 26$).[43]

What Doenitz and his minions in the *Kriegsmarine* failed to reckon with was the code-breaking effort the Allies were to mount at Bletchley Park in Britain where "Ultra" was born, and in the American "Magic" that built upon capabilities already used to penetrate deep Japanese secrets. It helped during the war that Enigma material sometimes fell into British hands, windfalls from, in one case, a raid on the Norwegian coast that yielded cipher wheels taken from a German patrol vessel and, in another instance, the capture of the *U-570* off Iceland in 1941.[44] But the real breakthrough came from the creation, by Alan Turing and his colleagues at Bletchley Park, of the world's first high-performance computer that could grapple with the great number of ever-shifting possible substitutions of the Enigma codes.

All the reverses the Germans would suffer from having their codes broken were yet to come. For now, at the war's start, their communications were secure enough—on land, at sea, and in the air—to enable and help coordinate a series of striking victories. The *Blitzkrieg* on Poland was only the beginning, a preliminary field test of Guderian's organizational idea about concentrating tanks in armored divisions and Rommel's notion of emphasizing infiltration and exploitation operations. Both these officers performed ably in this short, sharp campaign against a weaker adversary. Udet's *Stukas* had created absolute havoc from the skies as well, screaming down with their sirens blaring to make pinpoint attacks. Warsaw was struck hard from the air by the *Luftwaffe's* other types of bombers as well, heralds of the grim new kind of warfare that H.G. Wells had foreseen as far back as 1908 in his novel *The War in the Air*. The panzers arrived all too soon at the Vistula, completely outmaneuvering Polish forces while at the same time outrunning their own infantry. Yet it must not be forgotten that, at the very height of the fighting, the Red Army struck Poland from the east—"in the back," so to speak. For just nine days before the invasion, the Soviet Union had entered into a formal alliance with Nazi Germany.

\*   \*   \*

The Russo-German alliance was destined to fray, given Soviet leader Josef Stalin's continual territorial nibbling and Adolf Hitler's absolute fixation on expansion to the East. But Germany had another ally at this time in Italy, which as early as 1936 had seen the Fascist dictator Benito Mussolini join with Hitler in announcing a "Rome-Berlin axis." Their alliance was strengthened in May of 1939 with the declaration of the so-called

"Pact of Steel," though Italy stayed out of the fighting when France and Britain declared war on Germany in the wake of the invasion of Poland in September of that year. But Italy did choose to enter the conflict in June 1940 as France was falling, and signed the Tripartite Pact with Germany and Japan in September 1940. Italians, who had fought hard against Germany and Austria in World War I, were to fight just as determinedly alongside the Germans in World War II. First as a united country, until serious military reverses caused the fall and detention of Mussolini in 1943, after which there were Italians fighting on *both* sides. Some joined the Allies. Others were to remain loyal to Mussolini after he was rescued in a quite daring German commando raid led by Otto Skorzeny, then set up as head of a fascist rump state, the Salò Republic, that continued as a German ally until the bitter end.

How had the Italians ended up in the Axis? Probably because Italy had suffered greatly in World War I—its armed forces too often dealt the most punishing, humiliating blows, its economy wracked by runaway inflation—and received too little from Versailles. When the Italians signed the Treaty of London that joined them to the Allies in 1915,[45] the terms of the agreement included the promise of major territorial gains. Rome was to rule over significant portions of a carved-up Austro-Hungarian Empire, hold a protectorate over Albania, and be granted portions of German overseas holdings and a "fair share" of the liberated territories of the Ottoman Empire to be divided up with Britain and France. But at Versailles the Italians came away with far less: some territory in the Austrian Tyrol, a small percentage of reparations payments, and an invitation to join the League of Nations.

Benito Mussolini, one of Italy's relatively few war heroes and a well-known, popular journalist, skillfully fanned the flames of resentment via his newspaper, *Il Popolo d'Italia*. In its pages, and in his speeches and dramatic public events, Mussolini inveighed against the injustice of Versailles and began to sketch the vision of a renewed Italy whose strength was to be kindled by reaching back to its Roman roots. Indeed, even to the point of rebuilding the empire—though on a smaller scale. The ancient symbol of the *fasces* that united all together in one great national purpose became the logo of the new Italy.

Among the leaders of the Italian fascist movement was another hero of the Great War, Italo Balbo. Just twenty when Italy entered the war, Balbo aspired to become a pilot. But as reverses in the field piled up for Italian forces, Balbo found himself swept up—along with so many others—into the army. He fought bravely, survived the war, and found an outlet for his own discontent about Italy's postwar condition by earning a law degree, with which he hoped to effect change. But the slow, steady kind of change that came via the law proved less attractive to Balbo than the prospect of swifter and more radical change. Balbo had made a close study of the 19th century Italian revolutionary, Giuseppe Mazzini, and above all came to value *action*. Thus, he soon joined up with Mussolini and the Blackshirt organization. Their march on Rome in October 1922 led to the triumph of the Fascists, as King Victor Emmanuel III felt compelled, in light of their wide popular support, to hand the reins of government over to them peacefully.

Balbo, still an aviation enthusiast, held various positions in the fascist government until 1926, when at last he was made Minister for Air. Finally, he became a pilot, and led air expeditions himself—the most famous of which flew from Italy to the Century of Progress exposition in Chicago in 1933. Later that year, Balbo was made Governor-General of Libya, which had been an Italian colony since 1911 when it was wrested from the control of the Ottoman Empire—and which was one of the first places in which aerial bombing of civilians was practiced, in this instance against recalcitrant Arab tribes. Balbo, fully familiar with the air power theories of General Giulio Douhet, was tasked with expanding Italian colonial control to new territories in Africa, with a special eye on very remote areas with uncertain borders. Aircraft were well suited to fill the need to reconnoiter these areas; but Balbo's vision was even broader, his gaze cast directly eastward with the notion of eventually overthrowing British rule in Egypt.

One step in this direction took the form of a kind of grand strategic flanking movement. In October 1935, ten months after a border incident with Abyssinia—the name then for the combined territory of Ethiopia and Eritrea in East Africa—at an Italian outpost set up just beyond the territorial limits of their Somaliland colony, the Fascists invaded. Abyssinian forces were numerous, but the Italians had better weaponry—and a powerful air force whose creation Balbo had overseen. In accordance with ideas Douhet had advanced in his treatise, *Command of the Air,* civilians were targeted and chemical weapons were widely used. Needless to say, this created international outrage—but little action beyond a few economic sanctions.

The war was popular with Italians, not only because it was going well, but because it was also revenge, nearly forty years after an Abyssinian army had crushed Italian forces at Adowa during the previous colonial conflict in this area. Balbo continued to lobby for an invasion of Egypt, as he saw the risk to Italians in East Africa, given continuing British control of the Suez Canal. Winston Churchill, still a backbencher in Parliament at this time but active in the discourse during the crisis, gave a public speech just days prior to the invasion in which he did his best to point out to the Fascists the grave risk that they were taking: "To cast an army of nearly a quarter of a million men, embodying the flower of Italian manhood, upon a barren shore two thousand miles from home ... is to give hostages to fortune unparalleled in all history."[46] Mussolini, confident that Britain would not act forcefully, went ahead with the attack on Abyssinia. He also wisely tabled Balbo's suggestion of expanding into Egypt. For the present.

Having gotten away with aggression against Haile Selassie—emperor of Ethiopia and, more popularly, "The Lion of Judah"—Mussolini next turned to providing support to the Fascist rebels who had risen up against the Republican government of Spain. The Germans, as mentioned above, sent the Condor Legion to support Franco's forces; but the Italians were even more involved. Over 60,000 troops of various sorts were sent to join the fighting, including the elite "Black Flames" Division that, along with Italian attack aircraft, were also pioneering, as Hugh Thomas observed, "those tactics later celebrated as *Blitzkrieg*."[47] But the Italians suffered some sharp reverses as well, particularly at Guadalajara where they were beaten, in part by a unit of their fellow countrymen who were fighting for the Republic—the "Garibaldi Battalion." In that battle, the vulnerability of Italy's light tank designs—the products of a joint venture between the FIAT and Ansaldo firms—was seriously exposed, both to anti-tank guns and to the heavier Russian armor (the T-26) that Moscow had sent to support the struggle against the Fascists. Further, while the FIAT CR-32 fighter aircraft performed well in Spain, its operational results misled the Italians into believing that a biplane of this sort would do well in the next war—largely because of its maneuverability—even against the much faster, better-armed monoplanes then being developed. Thus, Italy was fated to enter World War II with inadequate armored vehicles and fighter aircraft. These deficiencies were to have grave consequences. But for the present, Italian forces had proved themselves capable in campaigns ranging from East Africa to Spain.

The Italian Navy was also active during the Spanish Civil War, most notably in the attacks mounted by its submarines against merchant ships bringing supplies and arms to the Loyalist Republicans. The losses inflicted by these subs became so worrisome that an international conference was called at Nyon, Switzerland, in September 1937 to address the threat. Italy was not directly accused, the attacks instead being labeled "piracy by unnamed parties." A resolution was drawn stating that any patrolling naval power was now authorized to pursue and attack pirate submarines; and it was backed by the deployment of a joint Anglo-French force of some eighty destroyers and even more aircraft. Mussolini's "pirates" disappeared. As Winston Churchill summed the matter up, "the outrages stopped at once."[48] But more was to be heard from the Italian submarine forces in the war to come. Italian naval leaders were leery of Doenitz's wolfpack concept, preferring instead to have their submarines operate as lone wolves. Even so, they performed quite well in World War II with these methods, with average tonnage-sunk-per-boat on a par with the U-boats of their German ally. The Italians went even one step further in undersea warfare during the 1930s, continuing the development of "manned torpedoes"—begun during World War I—that were destined to wreak absolute havoc upon the Royal Navy.

The guiding spirit of Italian "naval special warfare" forces was a young Tuscan noble—and ardent Fascist—*Don* Junio Valerio Borghese, who was just thirty-four and had already conducted two patrols as a submarine commander by the time Italy went to war against France in the summer of 1940. But he was destined to focus his energies on sabotage operations mounted by small teams of frogmen who either steered manned torpedoes and stealthily emplaced their detachable warheads or swam in covertly by themselves to attach explosives to British warships. As commander of the Tenth Light Flotilla, he would also one day lead the main Italian motor-torpedo-boat operations, including the explosive speedboats whose lone pilots were expected to jump overboard shortly before impact. Borghese was a believer in the growing power of small units armed with the most advanced munitions. His successes during the war were to bear out his faith in this mode of naval warfare fully.

But just as Doenitz was the lone champion of U-boat-centric wolfpack naval operations among senior German naval officers, so too Borghese was overshadowed for years by the more conventional-minded Italian admirals. To be sure, the emphasis they placed on battleships had its merits—and the latest Italian dreadnoughts were elegantly designed to maximize speed, firepower, and defensive armor—but the decision to rely on land-based aircraft rather than on carriers was to prove a major design error. In fairness, some naval leaders understood the importance of carriers, and construction of the *Aquila* (Eagle) was indeed begun. But it was never completed.

Even so, the Italian navy had good chances of doing well against the British in the Mediterranean—despite its backwardness in radar technology—partly due to the occasional strong support received from the *Luftwaffe,* but also because Italy's own naval code-breakers of the *Servizio Informazione Segreto* were quite good, often learning the where and when of Royal Navy movements in advance of them. Given the complex interplay of sea, air, and land operations in the Mediterranean theater, the Italian army's *Servizio Informazione Militare* often provided information useful to the navy as well.

Together, the *SIS* and *SIM* were so good that David Kahn praised them for having provided "undoubtedly the broadest and clearest picture of enemy forces and intentions available to any Axis commander throughout the whole war."[49] Kahn made this statement in the specific context of the intelligence support given by the Italians to Erwin Rommel's

*Afrika Korps*—but this particular case simply serves to highlight the overall excellence of the *SIS* and *SIM,* both of which made masterful use of radio intercepts and proved adept at codebreaking, even without possession of an advanced machine computing capacity of their own.

By the late 1930s, all was going quite well for Italy. The situation in East Africa was relatively settled—despite annoyances created by Ethiopian insurgents. Italo Balbo was doing wonderful things in Libya, improving infrastructure and agriculture, even attracting Italian colonists. In the fall of 1938 Mussolini played a significant role at Munich in achieving a peaceful resolution of the Sudeten Crisis—which had erupted just a few months after Hitler's bloodless annexation of Austria. Indeed, as Telford Taylor put it, Mussolini's intervention with Hitler had "clinched the postponement of hostilities."[50] But it was only a postponement, as Hitler moved beyond the Sudetenland in March 1939 to absorb the rest of Czechoslovakia. In the wake of this action, Britain and France finally determined to resist any further German expansion. However, they initially neglected to aim their deterrent policy toward Italy, and in April Fascist forces invaded Albania. King Zog quickly fled to Greece, and the popular resistance to the invasion dissipated when it became known that the monarch had taken the country's gold reserves with him. The Albanian legislature, in response, voted to embrace the Italian take-over.

With this move, Mussolini was not simply emulating or trying to keep up with Hitler. Italy's strategic interest in Albania was of long standing—that is, since before World War I—given that naval bases there would allow the Italians to maintain an iron grip on the Adriatic Sea. Also, Albania had some oil resources that proved of interest to the Italian military. Not to mention that this territory had been promised decades earlier, most Italians believed, in return for Italy's having joined the Allies' side in World War I. Whatever the intricate web of motivations that led to the invasion, Winston Churchill was quick to see the strategic implications of this Italian foothold in the Balkans. In a letter to Prime Minister Neville Chamberlain on April 9, 1939, Churchill said, "What is now at stake is nothing less than the whole of the Balkan Peninsula."[51] A clear British "guaranty" of Greek and Romanian security soon followed, a strong foreshadowing of the rising importance of the Eastern Mediterranean.

\* \* \*

In sum, by the fall of 1939 Japan, Germany, and Italy were all on the march, with many successes and but a few reverses—for Japan in the Nomonhan War, and for some Italian forces in the Spanish Civil War. But far more importantly, for all their successes the three countries that would form the core of the Axis Powers had each made major errors in their strategic designs. Japan, so dependent on maritime trade, had made virtually no preparations for dealing with the submarine threat to its merchant shipping. For its part, Germany had spent very heavily on building a surface-ship navy when it should have been emphasizing U-boats, neglected development of a long-range bombing capability, and had only "thinly mechanized" its ground forces. Italy's strategic design flaws were just as grave, as its reliance on a biplane fighter plane, the lack of an aircraft carrier, and a wildly insufficient approach to tanks made quite evident.

Weighed against these flaws, however, the principal Axis Powers introduced many successful innovations. Japan's carrier strike force, the *Kido Butai,* was the greatest in the world. Germany's panzer divisions and close-support dive-bombers made *Blitzkrieg* possible. And Italian interest in "naval special warfare" was soon to demonstrate its profound power. In the coming few years, 1939–1942, the careers of most of the strategic designers mentioned in this chapter were to reach their peak. But even in the years of their greatest triumphs, their countries' design flaws and strategic errors were to become ever more apparent, ever more damaging.

Not enough by themselves to be the ultimate causes of catastrophic defeat, but more than enough to require radical changes in battle doctrine and overall strategy as the Allies adapted to—and sometimes adopted—the innovations the Axis designers had introduced. As will grow clear in the following chapters, World War II can probably be best viewed and most clearly understood as a protracted "strategic design competition."

# 3. Rising Tide, Early Reverses

SWIFT VICTORY IN POLAND was a great relief to the Germans, as it allowed for significant forces to be redeployed in the West. Of the hundred divisions in the *Heer* at the time, only forty had been left to deal with potential Anglo-French intervention during the Polish campaign. But the Allies declined to go on the offensive against the "Westwall"—also known as the Siegfried Line—the string of pillboxes and anti-tank traps the Germans had begun building in 1938 opposite the French Maginot Line. And as panzer and other divisions made their way west, the Allies became ever less inclined to attack. Instead, they waited, initiating a period known as the "Phony War," or even more derisively, the *Sitzkrieg*. But for all the inaction on land, the war at sea began immediately. Indeed, on September 3, the very day France and Britain went formally to war with Germany, the *U-30* mistook the passenger liner *Athenia* for an auxiliary cruiser and sank her. Most of those on board were rescued by other ships in the vicinity, but over 100 lives were lost and an international incident arose over this violation of the Hague Convention, which required submarines to surface and provide warning when attacking a civilian vessel. Needless to say, the *Athenia* incident foreshadowed the bitterness of the sea war that was to flout all conventions and continue unabated over the next six years.

Two weeks after the *Athenia* went down, the *U-29* torpedoed and sank the British aircraft carrier *Courageous*. Over 500 officers and men lost their lives in this sinking. Then in October, Günther Prien, skipper of the *U-47*, threaded his 218-foot Type VIIB submarine through the defenses of the main Royal Navy base at Scapa Flow in the Orkney Islands and sank the 33,000-ton battleship *Royal Oak*. Prien made good his escape, and over the next few months accounted for tens of thousands more tons of shipping. By the end of the year, he and his colleagues, serving in a *Kriegsmarine* that could average just fourteen oceangoing U-boats at sea at any one time, sank over a hundred Allied vessels. And this for a cost of just nine U-boats lost during this period. The rate of ship sinkings was to rise sharply in 1940, and repeatedly rose further through the first quarter of 1943, after which Allied countermeasures—escort carriers, high-frequency direction-finding radar, and code-breaking—began to take a heavy toll. But this response to the submarine campaign required nearly four years to develop. Imagine how high Allied losses would have been had Hitler and Raeder heeded Doenitz's recommendations in the years before the war's outbreak, and emphasized U-boat construction rather than persisting with the Z-Plan's call for prioritizing the building of battleships.

As to German naval surface combatants, the three "pocket battleships" built before the war—so named by the Allies for their significant gun power, despite being less than half the tonnage of a typical dreadnought—were used as commerce raiders. These *Panzerschiffe* were the products of a design developed by Raeder's predecessor, Admiral Hans Zenker, whose vision was that they should be able to "outrun all heavier-gunned war vessels and outshoot all faster ships."[1] While this was generally true, what the design could not deal with was the risk to these ships that radio messages sent by their victims would give away their location. This was the fate of the *Graf Spee* when, in December of 1939, its position was detected and a British squadron with one heavy and two light cruisers caught up with it off the South American coast near the Rio de la Plata. Captain Hans Langsdorff outfought the three Royal Navy ships, severely damaging the heavy cruiser *Exeter*.[2] But *Graf Spee* had suffered some injury as well, expended much fuel and over half its ammunition. So Langsdorff retreated to Montevideo harbor in neutral Uruguay, but was given only seventy-two hours to make repairs and be on his way. He knew that the British bulldog tenacity would ensure that his movements would be opposed, and that *Graf Spee* would be hunted down relentlessly should he decide to make a run for it. Instead, he disembarked the crew, scuttled the ship, went ashore and committed suicide.

*Graf Spee* had, by its end, sunk eight ships, totaling about 50,000 tons. One of three *Panzerschiffe*, its sister ship *Deutschland*—renamed *Lützow* to avoid having ever to report the loss of a ship bearing the country's name—sank only two ships as a raider. The *Admiral Scheer*, however, accounted for over 100,000 tons, making it the most successful pocket battleship. The Germans complemented these raiders with deployment of nine merchant cruisers (*Hilfskreuzer*), all of which were lightly armed and heavily reliant on deceptive appearance for survival. They and the *Panzerschiffe* were supported by supply ships that arranged, via coded radio messages, various rendezvous points for refueling and revictualing. Overall, the *Hilfskreuzer* accounted for about 800,000 tons of shipping. Seven were sunk; the other two made it back to ports in occupied France after one cruise. Adding in the vessels accounted for by the *Panzerschiffe*, about one million tons of enemy shipping was sunk by the raiders. U-boats, on the other hand, exceeded this amount even before the average number on station reached twenty-five in the summer of 1941. By war's end, they had sunk almost *15,000,000 tons*.[3]

Clearly, Doenitz should have been listened to during the pre-war debates about the strategic design of the *Kriegsmarine*. Surface raiders were far too vulnerable to detection and tracking-down, given the radio warnings sent out by their victims. And the radio traffic required to coordinate link-ups with supply ships was sometimes intercepted and decoded, leading to unhappy endings for many of the "milch cows"—and sometimes for the raiders themselves. For example, code-breaking brought about the end of the famous *Atlantis* that, during its lengthy cruise, sank twenty-two vessels, amounting to nearly 150,000 tons of merchant shipping. We have already noted Raeder's fatalistic memo of September 3, 1939, with its wording about knowing how to die gallantly. Another German admiral, Friedrich Ruge, about whom more will be heard later, put the matter more clinically in his memoirs: "In this struggle the German surface ships clearly had no chance of achieving any decisive success."[4]

But even if the case in favor of emphasizing submarines over surface combatants is compelling, is it necessarily true that the surface fleet had "no chance" of achieving success? Hardly, as was soon to be demonstrated in an amazing sea-air-land campaign for Norway in the spring of 1940. This was a time when Hitler had grown distrustful of Oslo because the Norwegians had not opposed a British raid in the Jossing Fjord to free 300 prisoners held on the *Altmark*—*Graf Spee's* supply ship, which had taken on the crews of the raider's victims and seemingly escaped the Royal Navy in a sea chase that captured world attention.[5] Hitler also worried that the Allies were about to invade Norway to interdict iron ore flows coming overland from northern Sweden, then down the Norwegian coast. To pre-empt this—it was indeed an act of pre-emption, as the British were readying an assault force even as the Germans gathered for their attack—Hitler moved decisively in April, just a day ahead of the Allies. Landings by small German forces, including the pioneering use of paratroops to seize airfields, were made at several points on Norway's long coast. The take-over was swift, with little bloodshed at the outset, save for the fate of the German heavy cruiser *Blücher*, which was sunk in Oslo Fjord by the torpedo battery of the Oscarsborg fortress. Of the ship's crew, 600 died, 1,000 were taken prisoner. The opening phase of the German invasion was not otherwise blemished, though, nor did it depend—despite popular belief to the contrary—on collaboration with the pro–Nazi traitor Vidkun Quisling. Nonetheless, the operation's success was not going to be allowed to stand without being vigorously contested.

The Allied response came first at sea with British submarines leading the attack on supply vessels, and Royal Navy warships mounting fierce shore bombardments of German positions. These actions were followed by troop landings at Namsos and Andalsnes—both of which failed—and then another much farther north at Narvik that led to a highly critical situation for the Germans. Overall, the naval fighting was most difficult, with each side suffering serious losses. The British carrier *Glorious* and its two escorting destroyers came under the guns of the German battle cruisers *Scharnhorst* and *Gneisenau* and were sunk with heavy loss of life.[6] Allied naval losses also included a cruiser, ten destroyers and six submarines. For its part, the *Kriegsmarine* saw three cruisers, ten destroyers and six U-boats sunk—the latter hampered by defective torpedoes. The *Luftwaffe* engaged deeply as well. As Telford Taylor put it, in this campaign "the decisive factor was air power."[7] But the cost in aircraft was substantial. Of the thousand *Luftwaffe* planes deployed, 240 were lost—about a third of them transports. And at Narvik, the one place where fighting continued unabated, the Germans' situation remained tenuous. But they held on, barely, until the enemy withdrew in June. France was falling, and Allied leaders reasoned that continuation of the campaign in Norway now entailed too great a risk.

Unfolding events in France aside, what is clear about this campaign is that the *Kriegsmarine* held its own against the toughest possible opposition. Royal Navy Captain Donald Macintyre, DSO, DSC and commander of a destroyer that fought at Narvik, gave this assessment: "The German Navy, displaying the skill, resolution and ruthlessness demanded of it, secured for Hitler a strategic success of immense significance in the prosecution of the naval war, one which was to cost the Allies dear when the business of supplying Russia by the Arctic route came into being."[8] The point here is that, given the significant German investment in surface combatant ships, employing them—with proper air support—against enemy warships was almost surely the best way to use the fleet. Yet, as we shall see, the major units of the *Kriegsmarine* would, over the course of the coming year, be (mis)used for primary purposes of supporting an oceanic "trade war" against Allied merchant shipping. The lesson to be drawn is that crafting the right strategic design demands vision that extends beyond the technological level, to encompass doctrine—that is, how the technology will be used in war—as well as the most effective organizational structure. The *Kriegsmarine* was to stray, fatefully and ultimately fatally, from the optimal use of the fleet that had been designed and built with such care, and at such great cost.

In the Battle of France, which began on May 10, 1940, right in the middle of the Norwegian campaign, the *Heer* came to the fore, with the concentrated panzer divisions that Guderian had done so much to design being the key organizational innovation. In terms of the battle doctrine employed, Rommel's infiltration and exploitation tactics proved to be the key to success. Needless to say, Udet's *Stukas*—which had done well in Norway—played an essential role in supporting the panzer breakthroughs that virtually won the campaign in its first ten days. How did this happen?

Perhaps the most trenchant analysis of Allied defeat in the Battle of France came from the scholar-soldier Marc Bloch, who wrote his *Strange Defeat* shortly after the fighting ended. Unsparing about French culpability, he noted that "[w]hatever the deep-seated causes of the disaster may have been, the immediate occasion … was the utter incompetence of the High Command." Bloch also gave credit to the enemy's new logic of armed conflict: "The ruling idea of the Germans in the conduct of this war was speed." Finally, he made an organizational point about the importance of massing forces, criticizing the French army's violation of this principle: "Small groups of reinforcements were continually dribbled into every breach as it occurred, with the inevitable result that they were cut to pieces."[9]

Bloch's analysis—that of a professional academic serving in the French Army—was fully affirmed by General André Beaufre, who served on the Army General Staff during the 1940 campaign. In his account of these events, the influence of World War I looms large in the form of an unwavering faith in the superiority of defensive firepower against any attacking force. The fact that France was on the winning side in the Great War led to what Beaufre called a "narrow conquerors' dogmatism," while the devotion to the defensive contributed to idleness during the Phony War. Instead, Beaufre argued, "If we had really assaulted the Siegfried Line we would have trained our troops, rejuvenated the high command, tried out our methods of combat and put new life into the war effort."[10] Alistair Horne's account of the fall of France also critiques Allied inactivity in the months after the Polish campaign, noting that the French "Saar offensive" saw just nine divisions marching up to, but not attacking, the Siegfried Line, and the occupation of twenty villages the Germans had preemptively evacuated.[11]

For all these deficiencies of preparation, mindset, and offensive spirit, Anglo-French forces did have many strengths. The Maginot Line was a formidable, well-designed fortification that would force the Germans to mount some kind of general flanking movement if they were to attack with hope of success. Thus, the bulk of French forces were deployed beyond the formal Line, in the areas where a lesser version of it had been extended. But the key to Anglo-French strategy, which anticipated a sweeping "right hook" by the Germans—as in their 1914 Schlieffen Plan—was to advance quickly into Belgium to throw the attack off balance from the outset. Did such an approach make sense, given the correlation of forces on the opposing sides? Harvard historian Ernest R. May thought so, expressing his view of the issue clearly and convincingly: "Overall, France and its allies turn out to have been better equipped for war than was Germany, with more trained men, more guns, more and better tanks, more bombers and fighters." This assessment provided the foundation for May's view—contrapuntal but also complementary to Bloch's—that the German triumph was indeed a "strange victory."[12]

German generals certainly did not overestimate their chances of success, and argued forcefully against the early offensive in the West that Hitler was eager to launch in the fall of 1939. Their original concept for the campaign was, as the Allies presumed, a replay of the 1914 Schlieffen Plan—a Channel-brushing flanking movement. But a copy of the plan fell into the hands of the Belgians, who quickly shared it around, and Hitler and his military minions felt the need to pursue a different course. General Erich von Manstein, who later in the war emerged as one of the best German field commanders, came up with the idea of striking at a hinge point in the Allied line that would present itself once the Anglo-French forces deployed to the north to meet the noisy—and showy, with the spectacular use of paratroops and glider-borne assault forces—but basically diversionary German attacks on the Netherlands and Belgium. The leading edge of the offensive, its *Schwerpunkt,* was to be through the Ardennes, the hilly, forested terrain thought to be very unsuitable ground for a tank offensive, thus increasing the likelihood of achieving surprise.

Guderian further refined the idea and championed it in wargames held early in February 1940, emphasizing the need for massed armor, speed, and exploitation of the breakthrough he envisioned making at Sedan. General Franz Halder, the Army Chief of Staff, considered Guderian's addition to Manstein's concept "senseless," in particular the narrow concentration of armored forces and the notion of then pushing deeply with these tank formations after the crossing of the Meuse. Instead, Halder wanted the armor to race to that river, create several bridgeheads, then wait for the infantry—the *Heer* was still 90 percent non-mechanized—so that a "properly marshaled attack in mass" (*einen yangierten Gesamtangriff*) might be mounted.[13] Guderian persisted, was supported by Hitler, and placed in charge of a panzer corps. For his part, Rommel was given command of the 7th Panzer Division—which was to become known for its daring, lightning advances as the "Ghost Division." As to Udet's *Stukas,* they worked in very close cooperation with the panzers. But not *en masse;* instead they came in a steady stream of small attack groups. Cajus Bekker summed up their effects on the battle for the Meuse River crossing at Sedan: "Continuous air attacks held down the enemy artillery fire and prevented the arrival of reinforcements."[14] Another important aspect of the air campaign was the systematic targeting of Allied forward air bases, which were largely put out of commission in the first days of the campaign.

For all the cleverness of the German battle plan, the concentration of the armor, and the close support of the attack aircraft, the Allies still had many strengths. Their 3,000 tanks included over 300 Matildas of the British Expeditionary Force and nearly the same number of French Char B heavies; with their thicker armor and heavier guns, both types were far superior to German Panzer I and II models, and better than the medium Panzer III and IV models. Of the 2,500 German tanks, about 600 were evenly split between their two medium types, the Panzer IIIs and IVs, and augmented by another 300 Czech medium tanks that had been incorporated into the *Heer.* Thus, somewhat more than a third of German armor was comprised of medium tanks. The rest were light. As to the Allies, in addition to their absolute edge in heavies, they fielded twice the number of mediums as their enemy, being somewhat outnumbered only in the category of light armored fighting vehicles. The saving grace for the Germans was that the Allies had sprinkled their tanks about roughly evenly among their more than 150 divisions. Guderian, having won the day in terms of organizational design, had ensured that German armored forces would be far more concentrated. He had also lobbied hard to make sure that German tanks would be able to communicate by radio—an area in which the Allies were deficient—which gave the panzers the capacity to work in teams tactically, and to give their higher commands excellent "topsight" as to their positions in the field and ability to exploit gaps. Their radio communications, sometimes encrypted, were often transmitted *en clair;* for in a fast-moving tank battle, there was hardly ever time for the enemy to exploit intercepts.

Concentration of armor and better communications made all the difference at the Meuse; but even in the wake of this engagement there were obstacles to success, notably in the Allied counterattack at Arras. Rommel was hard pressed there, coming under furious armored assault. He described the fighting as "violent and costly," noting further that even the "anti-tank guns which we quickly deployed showed themselves to be far too light to be effective against the heavily armored British tanks." It was only the re-purposed anti-aircraft guns, the soon-to-be famous "88s," that saved the day. First used in this manner briefly during the Polish campaign, their flat trajectory and high velocity—designed against high-flying aircraft, they had the power to shoot projectiles far up, swiftly—made them very effective as anti-tank weapons. Rommel's presence added to their effectiveness at Arras. Writing of the battle, he recalled "I personally gave each gun its target."[15] Thus we see his designer's instinct for re-purposing technology.

More will be heard from the 88mm anti-aircraft "flak" gun (short for *Flugzeugab-*

"Fast Heinz" Guderian (Creative Commons, courtesy Bundesarchiv, Bild 101I-769-0229-10A / Borchert, Erich (Eric) / CC-BY-SA 3.0, May 1940).

*wehrkanone)* that became the premier field artillery piece of the Second World War. *Stukas,* too, were to be re-enlivened later in the conflict, gun-modified to enhance their anti-tank function. For now, in the Battle of France, both 88s and *Stukas* played key roles in the breakthrough at Sedan and the advance to the English Channel. But the *Luftwaffe* soon suffered a serious reverse in the skies over Dunkirk, failing to interdict the evacuation of more than 300,000 Allied troops. As to why the panzers were ordered to halt for a few days outside Dunkirk, before resuming their drive on the worn-out, beleaguered Allied troops, Hitler has been seen, generally, as bearing the primary responsibility for this apparent blunder. But as Ernest May noted, "it is more clear that the order originated with General Rundstedt. He took alarm from the British counteroffensive at Arras." Also, General Hans-Günther von Kluge, the German Fourth Army commander—and Rommel's boss—was well aware that over half his tanks were out of commission, and so "suggested that the Panzer commanders be told to let supporting forces catch up before they moved forward."[16]

A premature, hard fight at Dunkirk might well have damaged German armor to the point of allowing French forces in the south to rally and mount a renewed, sustained defense. Indeed, German forces ran into very stubborn resistance when they got moving again toward Dunkirk after their brief halt and, had the decision not been taken to conserve them for the upcoming operations in the south, the enemy might well have recovered. As matters unfolded, the French did try to benefit from the time the Germans were losing by continuing the fight up north. As General Beaufre recounted, "the next phase of the battle was prepared during the breathing-space which the agony of Dunkirk allowed us."[17]

Aside from concern about the wearing-out of the panzers and the recuperation of French forces in the south, another very real worry that had preyed on General von Rundstedt's mind ever since the initial breakthrough was the possibility of an Allied pincer attack being mounted on his advanced—and increasingly vulnerable—armored forces undertaken simultaneously from *both* north and south. The Allies certainly had sufficient formations remaining to do this, and so, as May put it, the halt orders "were issued in part because General Rundstedt, unlike Tippelskirch [the army chief of intelligence], feared the Allies would do what they seemed capable of doing."[18] Indeed, the Allies were very much of a mind to cut off the leading edge of the German mobile forces. Winston Churchill, put the matter evocatively, noting in a communication with the French commander, General Maxime Weygand—his predecessor, General Maurice Gamelin, had been sacked in the middle of the battle—that "the beast has stuck his head out of his shell." Beaufre elaborated on this vivid metaphor, noting "the neck constituted a few divisions strung out with very long flanks. Could we not draw back the two halves of our severed Armies and cut through this weakly held neck, thus encircling the enemy's armored forces?"[19]

As the endgame played out, the Allied attempt to counter-attack and continue the campaign failed, partly due to Rommel's effective defense at Arras and partly because the dynamic French General Gaston Billotte, who was to lead the counterattack, was killed in a German air raid immediately after meeting with Weygand to go over final details. But a big part of the success of the Germans in the final phase of this campaign was due to the fact that the panzers' edge had not been blunted in Flanders.

Hitler was soon faced with the need to decide about what to do next. He mused about a cross–Channel invasion, but the Germans had done virtually no training for such a complex operation. As Andrew Roberts has observed, those German generals like Paul von Kleist, who criticized the panzer halt order at Dunkirk and thought "that after the capture of the BEF 'an invasion of England would have been a simple affair,'" had got it wrong, "as the RAF and the Royal Navy were still undefeated."[20]

Indeed, in the skies over Dunkirk the Royal Air Force had given the *Luftwaffe* its first taste of strong, capable opposition—foreshadowing a hard future fight. As to the *Kriegsmarine*, Winston Churchill found a way to redeem the costly defeat of the Royal Navy in Norway by noting, of the German naval losses in that campaign: "From all this wreckage and confusion there emerged one fact of major importance potentially affecting the whole future of the war. In their desperate grapple with the British Navy, the Germans ruined their own…. The German Navy was no factor in the supreme issue of the invasion of Britain."[21] Churchill may have engaged in a bit of hyperbole there, as the *Kriegsmarine* would continue to deliver stinging blows. The German surface fleet, when used properly, gravely imperiled the Arctic convoys that helped keep the Russians in the fight later in the war. And the U-boats were soon to enjoy their first "happy time," thanks to the availability of French ports—usable just a month after the fall of France in June 1940, saving about a week of transit time from each patrol—and the recall of most Royal Navy destroyers and escorts to the Channel against the prospect of a German invasion attempt. It also helped that, for the moment, *Kriegsmarine* intelligence was decoding a very significant amount of British maritime radio traffic.

The biggest factor affecting the naval war, though, was redeployment of the Royal Navy's lighter combatant ships away from convoy duty to the English Channel. As historian Correlli Barnett has observed, this shift "committed virtually half of Britain's remaining destroyer strength to a defensive screen widely spread around England's southeastern shores, so inevitably denuding Western Approaches Command (responsible for the Atlantic convoys)."[22] The consequences were almost immediately felt, with a loss of over seventy ships totaling more than 320,000 tons in August—fifty-six ships and over a quarter-million tons to U-boats, fifteen more ships and the rest of the tonnage to air attacks from new *Luftwaffe* bases along the French coast.[23] All this was achieved with lone-wolf U-boat attacks; the situation worsened when Doenitz began to form and unleash his "wolfpacks" in September. Smaller convoys began to experience extremely heavy losses, sometimes as high as three-fourths of all vessels sailing together. But the opportunity cost of the German Z-Plan—which had emphasized building large warships along with its call for building more submarines—was now sharply felt, as U-boat strength in September 1940 was the same as a year earlier, fifty-seven. New production had only covered losses to date.

Even worse, though, operational boats in commission had dropped from thirty-nine to twenty-seven, due to the need to put new boats and crews through sea trials and shakedowns.[24] One needs little imagination to envision how much more severe the U-boat menace would have been had Raeder and the other senior German admirals heeded Doenitz's arguments in favor of much greater U-boat production during the years before the war.

After the fall of France, Hitler had an enhanced but still too limited capacity for waging the war against commerce at sea. Though he considered an invasion of Britain, his surface warships were too few, his army generals (a dozen of them were now field-marshals, promoted to this rank in the wake of victory over France) too reluctant to risk their forces. The *Luftwaffe*, which had been unable to dominate the skies over Dunkirk, was hardly likely to achieve total control over the Channel and possible landing zones along the southern British coast. In the end, as Peter Fleming so aptly summed up the issue, Hitler had "to admit that invasion was a strategical necessity ... [but also] a tactical impossibility."[25] This left only one apparent option for bringing Britain to heel, if a peace agreement were not reached in the immediate wake of the fall of France: strategic bombing.

In a series of rousing speeches delivered by Winston Churchill in May and June of 1940, he made it quite clear ("We shall never surrender!") that the British people would fight on. Soon after, what has come to be known as the Battle of Britain began, the first effort in the young aeronautical age to win a war primarily by means of strategic bombing. After a brief period of attacks on Channel shipping—ports had to be left intact while the convenient fiction of invasion was maintained, as German expeditionary forces would have urgent need of resupply and reinforcement through them—the targets shifted to British airfields and, eventually, cities. But the bombing capacity of the *Luftwaffe* was light;

this was an air force designed for close support of field forces. The workhorse Dornier 17, "the Flying Pencil," carried a bomb load of just over a ton—which was cut in half when the plane was fueled to the maximum. The Heinkel 111, another mainstay in the battle, had double the bomb load of the Dornier— halved once again when fully fueled— but was, like the Dornier, highly vulnerable to fighter attack. The other medium bomber employed was the Junkers 88, with a payload like the Heinkel's, and the same degree of vulnerability as the other aircraft that spearheaded this campaign.[26]

As to Udet's beloved *Stuka*, "the prime weapon in the *Luftwaffe* armoury until the summer of 1940,"[27] it proved utterly unable to function in a strategic capacity. With a light half-ton payload, slow cruising speed of 175 mph, and little self-defense capacity, the *Stukas* were slaughtered. They didn't benefit much from fighter escorts, as Messerschmitts, due to structural limitations,

Ernst Udet favored close air support over strategic bombing (Creative Commons, courtesy Bundesarchiv Bild 146–1984–112–13/ CC-BY-SA 3.0, ca. 1940/1941).

could not accompany them on dives. Pilots feared that the 109's wings would tear off. So, RAF Spitfires and Hurricanes waited for *Stukas* until they were alone, then made mincemeat of them. They were quickly withdrawn from the fight, an admission that the design emphasis of the *Luftwaffe* under Udet's guidance was so focused on close support aircraft that the German air service was unable to conduct strategic bombing against any but the most helpless adversaries. Walther Wever's death, Udet's rise, and the shutdown of the "Ural Bomber" initiative were the factors that led to the *Luftwaffe* being designed for short *Blitzkrieg* campaigns, not the sort of protracted, attritional air attacks for which the Allies' air forces prepared and at which they proved so adept later in the war. Indeed, the Halifax of the RAF and the American Flying Fortress were heavy bombers *par excellence,* compared to the *Luftwaffe,* with payloads of six and five tons, respectively.[28]

Curiously, German pilots suffered from poor communications. Where the panzers had benefited greatly from their radio links during the Battle of France, *Luftwaffe* formations had less of this sort of connectivity between bombers and fighters during the Battle of Britain. Thus, plans formed prior to a day of raiding were followed rigidly by air crews, while RAF squadrons benefited from the Chain Home radar stations that provided early warning, the Observer Corps that kept track of enemy formations from over a thousand ground stations, and Fighter Command, the nerve center of the defense. Air Chief Marshal Hugh Dowding made skillful, ruthless use of all this information, vectoring his initially outnumbered interceptors to where they were most needed. The information edge the RAF enjoyed proved particularly vexing for *Luftwaffe* fighter escort aircraft. As the highly decorated pilot, Werner Baumbach, summed up the situation, "German fighters, which could not be directed from the ground, literally had their hands tied."[29] The great fighter ace, Adolf Galland, added that the limited range of the German fighter escorts meant "that our offensive could only be directed against a small and extraordinarily well-defended sector of the British Isles."[30]

The end result: during the critical months of the battle, while the RAF saw a bit over 900 aircraft shot down, the *Luftwaffe* lost nearly double that number, counting both bombers and fighters.[31] Fighter losses were roughly equal on both sides, but the balance of serviceable single-engine fighters available changed radically in just a few months. On the 1st of July 1940, serviceable *Luftwaffe* fighters totaled 725, the RAF's just under 600. But by the 1st of October, the number for the Germans had fallen to 275 (!) while RAF fighter strength had risen to over 700.[32] The cause of this profound shift in the correlation of forces was the fighter production level on each side. During these three months, the British produced nearly 1,500 new fighters, the Germans slightly over 600.[33]

None of this bean-counting is intended to diminish the importance of Dowding's generalship; but the relative production figures do serve as something of an indictment of the German approach to air warfare. Over-emphasis on close-support light and medium ground attack aircraft led not only to the complete neglect of heavy bombers, but also to a dangerous de-emphasis on production of fighter aircraft—the fault of Udet, who also bore responsibility for failure to champion the more rapid development of jets. Which was to have grave consequences.

In this way the plan for invading Britain, "Sea Lion," died a quiet death. Continuing air attacks were soon relegated largely to night raids. Late in the fall, and over the winter of 1940-41, Hitler's restless gaze turned to Russia. The over-arching concept of pursuing *Lebensraum* in the East, as William L. Shirer put the matter, "lay like a bedrock in Hitler's mind."[34] So plans for Operation Barbarossa began to form. But hardly unopposed. In September 1940 Admiral Raeder made a strong case for focusing on the Mediterranean instead, and briefly captured Hitler's interest in what came to be called the "peripheral strategy."[35] Hermann Goering echoed Raeder's views, arguing long and hard for continuing the fight against the British in that theater of operations, with emphasis on seizing Gibraltar and Suez. His biographer Leonard Mosley noted "Goering had been working on the Mediterranean Plan ever since he had realized, in the summer of 1940, that the Fuehrer was serious about his intention of attacking Russia. The idea of waging a war with the Red colossus in the East before Britain was disposed of in the West appalled him."[36]

In an interview given in captivity shortly after the war, Field Marshal Wilhelm Keitel—once head of the *Wehrmacht*—concurred with Goering: "Instead of attacking Russia, we should have strangled the British Empire by closing the Mediterranean."[37] But Hitler, deeply distrustful of Josef Stalin, who was now making seemingly threatening moves in the direction of the Romanian oilfields upon which the *Wehrmacht* so heavily relied, was having none of this and drew support from many of his generals who preferred a fight on land against the Russians to a series of campaigns reliant upon air-sea and amphibious operations. Also, many thought war with Russia was inevitable. As German Foreign Minister Joachim von Ribbentrop put the matter to doubters, "The Fuehrer has information that Stalin has built up his forces against us in order to strike at us at a favorable moment."[38] He went on to argue that war should be waged before the enemy grew any stronger. Besides, success in the Mediterranean would depend upon the Italians, who inspired little confidence. German concerns were soon borne out, as Italian reverses in the Balkans and North Africa would, by spring 1941, force a diversion of German attention and manpower, with the time taken to restore the situation imposing a possibly damaging delay on the start of Barbarossa.

\* \* \*

Italy entered the war opportunistically on June 10, 1940, as France was falling—and yet got a bit of a bloody nose for its troubles. Twenty-eight Italian divisions invaded the Riviera, opposed by just four French divisions. Despite these odds, and with the full knowledge that their comrades up north were collapsing, these outnumbered Frenchmen, as John Keegan observed, "held their ground without difficulty, yielding nowhere more than two kilometers of front, losing only eight men killed against Italian casualties of nearly 5,000." Indeed, to show that they had achieved at least some kind of success, the Italians used borrowed German transports to airlift a battalion behind the French defenses, "as a token of success."[39]

Results elsewhere were hardly more encouraging. In Africa, Italo Balbo's strategic design for driving

Italo Balbo was a much-decorated Italian hero of World War I (Newberry Collection. Courtesy Archival Collection Grant Schmalgemeier Century of Progress Collection, 1930/1939, https://collections.carli.illinois.edu/cdm/singleitem/collection/nby_teich/id/414995).

the British from Egypt seemed on the verge of becoming a reality, for he commanded a field army of more than 200,000. His counterpart in East Africa, the Duke of Aosta, had a force of equal size. Against this, British General Archibald Wavell had just 36,000 troops in Egypt, some 7,000 facing the Italians in East Africa, and a kind of central reserve of just under 30,000 in Palestine. This placed the numerical odds in favor of the Italians at better than 5:1. As J.F.C. Fuller summed up Wavell's dire situation, "On paper, his strategical position was an all but impossible one."[40] Yet Wavell chose to preempt Balbo, who had served in Libya as a marvelous colonial governor but proved a slow campaigner. In June, soon after Italy joined the war, Wavell *attacked*. But not in the usual way, with massed forces. Instead, he pursued an irregular approach, his standing order enjoining his forces to "make a raid look like an advance."[41] And before the Italians could regain their footing, they lost Balbo, who was killed when his plane was shot down by his own troops as he was coming in for a landing at Tobruk. They had just fought off a British air raid, and were expecting more hostile action. The Axis Powers had lost the first of the key "strategic designers" who animated their efforts. In his diary entry for June 29, 1940, Italian Foreign Minister Galeazzo Ciano noted, "Balbo is dead…. He did not desire war, and opposed it to the last…. But once it had been decided … he was preparing to act with decision and daring."[42] The same cannot be said of his successor, Marshal Rodolfo Graziani, who was soon to preside over an absolute military debacle.

But before the situations in North and East Africa deteriorated—that is, while the Italians were still ostensibly on the offensive in both areas—some hard naval fighting was already getting under way. The day after Italy's entry into the war an Italian submarine sank the British light cruiser *Calypso.* This auspicious beginning was followed in July by some fierce surface fleet actions. The Italians held their own in the battleship duel at Punta Stilo, but the Royal Navy got the better of it in the naval engagement off Cape Spada. In these sea fights, the growing role of attack aircraft became more and more apparent—and very revealing of Balbo's design flaw when he had been in charge of Italian aviation. He and his successors in the air ministry had chosen to emphasize attacking naval ships with high-level bombers rather than with aircraft from carriers, or even land-based torpedo- or dive-bombers. As to the high-level bombers, they were strictly con-trolled by the Air Force, not the Navy. The end result: high-level bombers soon proved to be quite ineffective against naval targets, and poor inter-service cooperation meant that *Regia Marina* ships too often had to fight without adequate air cover. Indeed, at Punta Stilo, as naval officer/historian Marc' Antonio Bragadin noted, "Not even one Italian fighter plane had appeared in the skies over the scene."[43]

The British edge in radar and, increasingly, intelligence gained by intercepting and decrypting enemy message traffic, were also to play an important role in the war at sea in the Mediterranean. And the lack of an aircraft carrier not only diminished *Regia Marina* capability, it also seemed to limit the Italian imagination regarding what the enemy might do. Thus, in November a surprise attack on the Italian naval base at Taranto, by twenty Swordfish biplanes launched from the carrier *Illustrious,* resulted in serious damage to three battleships—half of the principal striking power of the *Regia Marina.* Correlli Barnett summed up the importance of this action as an event that "marked the dethronement of the battleship as the arbiter of seapower after four centuries, and the opening of a new era of naval warfare."[44] Admiral Yamamoto certainly understood this, as he and his staff closely studied the Taranto attack, especially the British use of torpedoes that ran at less than six fathoms' depth—a point that would be of great importance if the *Kido Butai* were ever to attack Pearl Harbor.

Whatever the difficulties of the Italian surface fleet, *Don* Junio Borghese was making progress during these months in the development of the manned torpedoes with which he intended to strike at British capital ships at both ends of the Mediterranean. By October 1940, Italian submarines had brought the so-called "pigs"—which had been lashed to their decks during transport—within close striking range of Royal Navy battleships at both Gibraltar and Alexandria. But in both cases the British sortied before the Italian frogmen could ride their "pigs" into these harbors, plant explosive charges, and exfiltrate. Bad luck. But Borghese's fortunes were eventually to turn for the better, and he and his "flotilla" were destined to play a major role in the Mediterranean theater at a critical moment in the war. Italy may have been backward-looking when it came to preparing for major naval action; yet when it came to understanding the potential of small units to create great damage, the *Regia Marina* wisely chose to nurture and support the innovative designs of Borghese and his "sea devils."

But for the moment the main action in the Italian war effort shifted from the sea to operations on land. Marshal Graziani, Balbo's successor, was getting on the move, if ponderously, with an advance into Egypt. The Duke of Aosta was becoming somewhat active in East Africa, overtaking British Somaliland and making minor advances in Kenya and the Sudan—then, mystifyingly, going over to the defensive. The major development, though, came late in October 1940 when Mussolini invaded Greece, on the surface in response to Greek obstinacy in a territorial dispute over Ciamuria. In reality, because of "the importance of Greece within the framework of the Mediterranean war against England," as Mussolini told German Foreign Minister Ribbentrop in a September 1940 meeting. Possible British moves aimed at using Greece as a bulwark against the Italians, as well as a base for bombing the Romanian oilfields at Ploesti, had to be pre-empted. Much as, Mussolini also pointed out, Germany had been obliged to occupy Norway before the British were able to do so. As Martin van Creveld assessed the matter, "Ribbentrop could not possibly object."[45] Nor did Hitler, in his subsequent meeting with Mussolini at the Brenner Pass.

For all this agreement among aggressors about the intended fate of Greece, there was the fundamental problem that Italian forces did poorly in this operation. They attacked Greece in an area replete with rough terrain in worsening weather. Compounding these problems, the outnumbered Greeks fought well, had the edge in artillery, and enjoyed some air support from the RAF. Italian generalship proved poor. As Gerhard Weinberg summed up the matter of Italian military (in)competence at command levels, it was "an army where intelligence and rank were distributed in inverse proportions."[46] The Italians were soon driven back into Albania, and barely held on there.

Now the Germans had to consider what to do about the possibility of having British ground and air forces in Greece—posing a threat to their strategic right flank as the *Wehrmacht* prepared for and was on the brink of its massive invasion of Soviet Russia. Plans had to be laid for intervening in Greece before a British foothold there could become a stronghold. But even as contingency planning proceeded, disaster upon disaster unfolded in Africa that soon demanded a further diversion of German forces away from their focus on preparing for war with Russia. In December 1940, Wavell and his brilliant field leader, Major General Richard O'Connor, launched a stunning offensive with just 30,000 troops—but with nearly 300 tanks, many of them Matildas, the type that had given Rommel such a thin time at Arras—driving the Italians from western Egypt and eastern Libya in short order.

Aside from skillful generalship and superior armor, the British also benefited from the dominance of the RAF over the Italians' very outdated fighters; the Royal Navy contributed significantly as well, with timely shore bombardments of Italian forces along the coast. But in the end, as Alan Moorehead noted in his eyewitness account of the campaign, "It was largely a victory of the infantry tanks and scarcely one of these had been lost."[47] The tank was to play a crucial role in the complex campaigns that were to unfold in North Africa over the next few years.

While Marshal Graziani was in full retreat across Libya, the Duke of Aosta was still sitting passively on the defensive in East Africa. That is, until February 1941 when British forces mounted a three-pronged offensive: overland from Kenya; with vigorous amphibious landings to reclaim British Somaliland and invade Italian-held Eritrea; and with irregular troops led by the eccentric but innovative Orde Wingate coming from the Sudan. Soon the Duke's forces were marching off into captivity and Haile Selassie, the Ethiopian emperor and "Lion of Judah" who had been driven out by the Italian invasion several years earlier, was restored to his throne in Addis Ababa.

This was a string of disasters on land and sea to try the patience of even the staunchest of allies; but Hitler remained tactful with Mussolini and realized that he was going to have to retrieve the situation. Plans were put in motion to have the *Luftwaffe* help contest for control of the Mediterranean; and Rommel was chosen to take a small force to North Africa and stabilize the front in Libya. In the event, Rommel was to do much more. As to the Balkans, a solution there would require more resources, given the pluckiness of the Greeks and increasing British involvement. But this diversion was necessary lest the RAF, operating from Greek bases, begin to strike at the Romanian oilfields so necessary to keep the *Heer* moving once Barbarossa—codename for the upcoming Russian campaign—got under way.

For all this diversion of resources in shoring-up activities—which also cost some time—the German high command had no second thoughts at this point about coming back to the earlier "peripheral strategy" against Britain that made the Mediterranean the focus of operations. The invasion of Russia remained at the center of their attention. Hitler, and many around him—for the most part generals, not admirals—had finally given up on the idea of emphasizing the Mediterranean. A key turning point had come when Hitler traveled to meet Generalissimo Francisco Franco, the Spanish dictator, at Hendaye in October 1940. At this session, the latter revealed his reluctance to enter the war on the Axis' side. But in fact, Franco had been grasping for gains at the same time he was being evasive. He had requested the cession of Vichy French North African holdings to Spain, in return for allowing German forces into his country on their way to capturing Gibraltar. Hitler feared an agreement of this sort would drive Vichy forces in North Africa to side with Charles de Gaulle's Free French—a geostrategic loss to the Axis. As matters stood, bad blood flowed between Vichy and Britain, because after the fall of France the Royal Navy attacked the French fleet at its North African bases—to keep these ships from falling into German hands. Hitler, seeking to exploit Anglo-French animus, had to reject Franco's terms.[48]

So, the Germans remained fixated on the upcoming campaign against the Russians— the "turn to the East"—all the while knowing they had to bail out the Italians before they could march on Moscow. The need to rescue Mussolini from his seemingly self-inflicted misfortunes led to widespread resentment of Italy among the Germans, not only in military circles but in civilian society as well—at all levels. The American journalist Joseph C. Harsch, posted in Berlin at this time before the United States entered the war, recounted a joke about Italian tanks that he overheard some German office secretaries in Joseph Goebbels' Propaganda Ministry laughing about as they did their typing:

> "I hear they have three gears for reverse and one for going forward."
> "Why do they want the one for going forward?"
> "Oh, that's in case they are attacked from the rear."[49]

*   *   *

The Germans had much more respect for the Japanese, and sought eagerly to bring them into the Axis. After the swift German victory over the French, the Japanese grew more interested in aligning with the Nazis. In September 1940, at a meeting in Berlin, their ambassador, Saburo Kurusu, signed on to the Tripartite Pact that bound Japan to Germany and Italy. Kurusu was later sent to the United States as Japan's "special envoy," and strove to find a peaceful solution to Japanese-American tensions in the last days before the Pearl Harbor attack. He failed in Washington in 1941; but at Berlin in 1940 he engineered what his government thought was a great diplomatic triumph. For the signal German victory over Anglo-French forces just a few months earlier had given heart to Japan's war party, whose stock had been falling as their campaign in China dragged on, indecisively and interminably. Japan's Prime Minister Prince Fumimaro Konoye felt "that with all the conquest of vast areas, the Japanese were no nearer to victory but were sinking more deeply into a quagmire."[50] But at this low moment the German *Blitzkrieg* victory in France gave Japanese militarists a glimpse of what might be; and they further shored up popular support by linking Japan's current situation to the traditional concept of *kodo*, the Imperial Way. Formerly associated with a more insular perspective, the term "was twisted now into signifying world order and peace to be achieved by Japanese control of East Asia."[51]

A key early move was to base Japanese forces in French Indochina (now ruled by the pliant, collaborationist Vichy regime) in September 1940, a two-pronged initiative that allowed for air attacks on more of China and created a jumping-off point for an invasion of Malaya and points south. But even this strategic flanking movement couldn't solve the most fundamental problem that Imperial Japanese forces faced: China was simply too big to conquer and occupy. Saburo Sakai, the ace fighter pilot who was serving in this theater of operations, recounted the emerging stalemate as one in which "our troops occupied key walled towns at strategic areas.... But outside the protection of these major walled towns death awaited all.... Chiang's [Kai-Shek's] guerrillas, as well as those of the Chinese communists, waited in savage ambush.... It was, indeed, a strange war."[52] Just as galling, the move into Indochina had created great concern in Washington, leading President Franklin Delano Roosevelt's administration to impose an embargo on the shipment of scrap iron and steel to Japan. This action only deepened the Japanese-American tensions that had been rising for some time, as the United States strongly opposed Japanese aggression in China and had grown increasingly worried about Tokyo making additional moves against tempting targets further south.

Before Japan could seriously consider undertaking what became their "southern program" of expansion, however, they had to deal with the grave vulnerability on their northern flank. The Russians had already shown their capabilities during the brief Nomonhan War, when General Zhukov had made such skillful use of his mobile armored forces. This was a mode of war in which the Imperial Army was, and remained throughout the coming conflict with the Allies, utterly deficient, despite Yamashita's fervent urging to learn from both the Germans and the Russians. Japan's Mitsubishi firms did produce large numbers of tanks—over 2,000 in 1939 alone—but these were all light Type 95 Ha-Go and medium Type 97 Chi-Ha armored fighting vehicles at a time when heavy tanks were destined to dominate battlefields. As Ronald Spector summed up Japan's design approach, "their tanks were decidedly inferior."[53] This deficiency contributed to the case against going to war with Russia, which was likely to fight hard and well, and whose vast resources were less accessible than those of the vulnerable British and Dutch holdings in Southeast Asia. Thus, very soon after Japan joined the Axis in September 1940, Russo-Japanese diplomatic talks opened up in Moscow, in the hope that a durable peace could be crafted between the two great powers.

Interestingly, the Germans initially supported these talks, and even hoped that, through the Japanese, the Russians might be convinced to join the Axis formally—going well beyond their simple non-aggression pact with the Nazis. As the historian G.A. Lensen put it, German Foreign Minister Ribbentrop sought "a totalitarian front against the democracies … and the extrication of Japan from the China embroilment in order to permit Japanese support of Germany and Italy in the war against Great Britain."[54] The talks that unfolded in Moscow went on for months, ending in April 1941 in a very "strange neutrality" two months prior to Germany's invasion of Russia, eight months before Japan struck Pearl Harbor. In the bitter war that ensued, the Japanese never attacked the Soviet Union, and the Russians stayed out of the war with Japan until after Germany's final defeat. Strange neutrality indeed.

For the Germans it was an especially frustrating neutrality. While they were entertaining—and sharing ideas and technologies with—the Japanese delegation led by General Yamashita in the fall of 1940, they were frustrated and puzzled by Japan's reluctance to strike at the British and Dutch holdings in Southeast Asia. Admiral Ruge summed the matter up incisively, concluding that, had Japan entered the war actively at this point,

> Great Britain would have been subjected to severe and continuous pressure at a time when she was least able to stand it. She would have been forced to reduce her naval forces at home and in the Mediterranean in order to maintain her position in Southeast Asia. Italy would at once have felt relief in the Mediterranean. New Zealand and Australia would have been unable to send troops to Egypt and East Africa. Any troops that could be spared from Great Britain would have had to be rushed to Malaya, not Egypt…. Had all this happened, it is highly probable that Spain and [Vichy] France would have been sufficiently impressed to throw in their lot with Germany.[55]

But this future was not to be. At least it was not going to unfold in the autumn of 1940, when a Japanese move into Malaya and points south would have had a profound impact on the course of the war against Britain. For the Japanese were not ready then to risk an action that would bring on American intervention. By the time Japan *did* decide to strike south a year later, the Italian position in East Africa had collapsed, the *Afrika Korps* was in retreat in North Africa, and German attention and resources were almost completely diverted to what had become a desperate winter fight against the Russians.

Admiral Yamamoto had much to do with Japan's grand strategic design during the period from Tokyo's embrace of the Axis to the attack on Pearl Harbor. While he had overseen and provided naval cover for the move into Indochina, Yamamoto remained deeply opposed to taking any action that might result in open war with the United States— a country he knew so well and whose capabilities he respected. Yet Japan's war party was now committed to moving against the British in Malaya, and pushing on to the Dutch colonies in the East Indies. Here were to be found rubber, tin, and oil in abundance. Faced with the implacable logic of the search for resources, Yamamoto came up with the only solution that made sense to him: to mount a preventive strike against the United States Navy. And he intended to carry out such an attack by massing Japan's aircraft carriers for a raid on Pearl Harbor—much as Guderian had been the advocate of concentrating German panzers in a relative handful of divisions and massing them for a thrust through the Ardennes.

As Edwin Hoyt observed, Yamamoto's design for war was seen by his colleagues as far too radical an approach: "In 1940 the army and navy high commands opposed it … [and were] aghast at the idea of sending a striking force halfway across the Pacific to get at the American Pacific fleet in Pearl Harbor."[56] How Yamamoto eventually overcame institutional reluctance and oversaw the brief, brilliant period of Japanese victories that ensued will be related in the following chapter. But on the day Japan joined the Axis, Count Ciano noted, skeptically and presciently, "Japan is far away. Its help is doubtful."[57]

*　　*　　*

The opening phase of the war in Europe had by now concluded, and bit of a pause ensued. As of February 1941, Germany had conquered Denmark and Norway, France and the Low Countries. The *Kriegsmarine* had shown an ability to slug it out on even terms with the Royal Navy during the campaign in far northern seas—thanks to the close support offered by the *Luftwaffe* in waters near enough to be covered by land-based aircraft. But the wide-ranging surface raiders had been less effective, with the loss of *Graf Spee* foreshadowing the tragic end of this naval strategy. As to Doenitz's U-boats, they were just beginning to show their great potential; but the failure to make them the top priority in German naval construction meant that far too few were available, even after a year-and-a-half of open warfare. The *Luftwaffe* was critically important to the success of the *Blitzkrieg* doctrine—and had proved highly effective, thanks to Ernst Udet's having championed the development of the *Stuka*. But this slow dive-bomber fell easy prey to RAF fighters during the Battle of Britain, as did Germany's light and medium bombers. Indeed, that campaign, the first aimed at bringing an opponent to its knees by air attack alone, was ill suited to the *Luftwaffe's* strengths. The German Air Force had been created fundamentally for close support of field forces, not strategic bombardment. It was not designed for the heavy, repeated air raiding of important targets necessary in order to win in the absence of an invasion.

The one unalloyed design success of the Germans was organizational. Heinz Guderian's refinement of the innovative idea of concentrating armor in "panzer divisions"[58]— at a time when the other great powers were simply sprinkling their tanks about evenly, with the idea they would provide support to the infantry—paid off handsomely in the campaign against France and the Low Countries in 1940. Erwin Rommel's notion of creating and exploiting narrow gaps that could be opened up breathed further life into the *Blitzkrieg* design, as he and others demonstrated later in the war. F.O. Miksche, an insightful contemporary observer of these events, noted this was a radically new mode of warfare whose "basic principle is infiltration, but of infiltration carried to new levels by the use of new material—infiltration motorized."[59] Major General F.W. von Mellenthin, who served in several key campaigns during the war, clarified that "infiltration" called for close cooperation with infantry—a point counter to the thinking of the early tank enthusiasts, who believed armor could do much on its own. He noted, "From Sedan onwards armor and infantry were used in mixed battlegroups (*kampfgruppen*)."[60]

For all this early success by means of innovative organizational design, though, there was also growing evidence of the onset of institutional pathology in the form of the rapid growth of the *Waffen SS*—the military arm of the *Schutzstaffel* (literally, "Protection Squadron"). From its humble beginnings as "hall guards" at Nazi meetings in the 1920s, the SS grew to include elements that handled general policing, intelligence, operation of the concentration camps, and the wide-ranging activities of the Gestapo. In the Polish campaign, the first four regiments of *Waffen SS* were deployed. By the time of the Battle of France the following year, this organization had expanded significantly—now to four divisions. And in their behavior they foreshadowed the war crimes that were committed with such abandon later on in the East. As Andrew Roberts noted of their early excesses in France, late in May 1940 nearly 100 men of the British Royal Norfolk Regiment "were massacred in cold blood" by the *Waffen SS*. The next day 90 more captured soldiers, this time from the Royal Warwickshires, were executed by the SS. Roberts concludes, "These despicable, cold-blooded massacres give the lie to the myth that it was desperation and fear of defeat ... [that led to these acts]; in fact such inhumanity was there all along, even when Germany was on the eve of her greatest victory."[61]

As to the Italians, this was a period in which their significant strategic design flaws were fully exposed. Italo Balbo's incomprehensible belief in the continuing value of biplane fighter aircraft resulted in the British gaining air superiority quite easily in East and North Africa and achieving signal victories over larger Italian forces in both areas. British advantages in land battles were not only the result of RAF close support; their heavy tanks won out swiftly against Italian armor, which was just a mix of light and medium tanks.

At sea, the lack of an aircraft carrier, along with poor coordination with the Italian Air Force's land-based fighters and bombers, was already giving the Royal Navy a powerful edge—manifested only in part by the deadly strike against Italian battleships at Taranto. The British also enjoyed the advantage of having radar, an area in which the Italians were lagging. For all these deficiencies, though, the Italians did have one remarkable new capability in Borghese's "manned torpedoes"—which were soon to show their considerable hitting power. This design was to prove of inestimable worth, altering the naval balance of power in the Mediterranean.

If German strategic designs were strongest at the organizational and doctrinal levels, and Italian design flaws were largely technological, Japan's challenge at this point—i.e., in the two years leading up to Pearl Harbor—was for the most part diplomatic. One key problem had to do with the need to continue expanding in a manner that wouldn't necessarily mean war with the United States. Given the general Japanese disinclination to engage in a renewed conflict with Soviet Russia—for the many abovementioned reasons—this meant arranging what Lensen called "the strange neutrality" with Moscow to cover this flank while continuing step-by-step aggression in Southeast Asia. Yamamoto was the first to understand that this would inevitably draw Japan into conflict with the United States; reluctant as he was to engage in such a war, his design for carrier-centered naval operations gave his country a fighting chance to achieve an acceptable outcome. At the same time, Yamashita had learned a great deal from his inspection trip to Germany, bringing back with him fresh ideas about how Japanese armies could engage in "infiltration" operations. He would soon show how much he had gleaned from observing the Germans—and how much he added of his own thinking to craft a distinct Japanese doctrinal design.

The stage was now set for operations in the spring of 1941. The Axis enjoyed most of the advantages, their design innovations outweighing design flaws. And, over the course of the coming year, they would force the Allies—a grand alliance ironically formed by the German decision to attack Russia and the Japanese carrier strike at Pearl Harbor—to the very brink of defeat.

# 4. At the Flood

FOR ITALY, THE SPRING OF 1941 brought fresh hope of a favorable reversal of the fortunes of war. Rommel and most of one panzer division arrived safely in Libya in March, thanks to the *Luftwaffe's* Tenth Air Corps, which quickly put great pressure Malta and made trans–Mediterranean passage perilous for the Royal Navy. By early April Rommel was pursuing a full-on offensive featuring his usual wily tank maneuvers, augmented now by the traps he set for British armor with his deadly 88s. Italian ground forces were energized anew by this German leavening, and began to perform at much higher levels. Soon the British were driven back to the Egyptian frontier, the only Libyan territory still in their hands the besieged fortress of Tobruk.

Rommel's offensive was aided by the diversion of some of the British forces from North Africa to Greece—to help the Greeks face an expected German invasion of the Balkans. The British also aided the successful plot to overthrow a Nazi-friendly regime in Yugoslavia, creating a fresh concern for Hitler. In response, early in April the Germans launched simultaneous armored assaults on Yugoslavia and Greece—the latter invasion jumping off from Bulgaria. The result: yet further affirmations of the effectiveness of the *Blitzkrieg* doctrine—despite the need to campaign in terrain far more difficult for tanks than the Ardennes had proved the previous year.

Indeed, the million-man Yugoslav army collapsed in just ten days, as it was designed for positional warfare, not rapid mobile operations. For the Germans the campaign entailed a negligible cost in casualties. For example, as John Keegan noted, "XLI Panzer Corps lost a single soldier dead, though it was in the forefront of the advance to Belgrade."[1] The fighting in Greece took only a few weeks more, though it was harder, and German casualties rose to about 5,000—Greco-British forces suffered losses many times higher than this, and over a quarter-million Greek soldiers were taken prisoner. For their part, the Italians had pushed at the Greeks from Albania, making little headway on their own but tying down considerable forces. In the wake of this victory Hitler was generous to Mussolini, granting the Italians control of Bosnia, Dalmatia, and Montenegro. These territories would, in the years to come, turn out to be "poison pills," as Yugoslav partisans were to pose great difficulties for the Italians—for German forces in the area, too.

At sea, the *Regia Marina* was still having troubles during this period, not least when its battleships tried to interdict the British "Operation Lustre," which was in the process of moving expeditionary forces to Greece in late March. Italian security for the interception force was breached by British codebreakers at Bletchley Park, and the *Regia Marina* squadron was soon sighted by enemy patrol aircraft—well in advance of the naval engagement that took place off Cape Matapan, one of the fingers of land that protrude from the southern end of the Peloponnesus. Aside from loss of surprise, the Italians also suffered from very poor coordination with the *Luftwaffe*, which failed to turn up to provide air cover as planned and when needed. This resulted in a major disaster when British attack aircraft arrived on the scene. Admiral Franco Maugeri, who fought in this battle, recalled, "The air was thick with British planes. Not only those from the *Formidable*, but land-based fighters from Crete had also joined the attack. Except for our anti-aircraft guns, we were helpless against their onslaughts."[2] A night surface action followed, in which the Royal Navy's edge in radar again enabled its warships to inflict further damage, with two Italian destroyers sunk in the opening minutes. As to their heavy ships, the Italians lost three cruisers sunk in this action, though the battleship *Vittorio Veneto* escaped, despite suffering some battle damage. Thus, British sea lines of communication with Greece remained open, enabling evacuation of their defeated forces at the end of the campaign there.

After Matapan, the Italian battle fleet was largely limited to operating in coastal waters under fighter aircraft protection. "Mussolini and the Air Force were at last convinced that the Navy could obtain proper air support only by having some aircraft carriers," Commander Marc' Antonio Bragadin noted.[3] The strategic design that Italo Balbo had championed—relying on land-based air cover for naval forces—had been shown up as deeply flawed. So, the decision was taken to develop two aircraft carriers. But by 1941 it was already too late. Neither the *Aquila* nor the *Sparviero* were completed by the time Italy surrendered to the Allies in September 1943. To be sure, after Italy's early naval defeats the *Luftwaffe* provided better air coverage than the *Regia Aeronautica* had ever been able to; but operating from land was still a limitation and, as the painful experience at Matapan showed, coordination between the Axis partners at sea was less than smooth.

Whatever the limitations of the larger elements of the *Regia Marina*, *Don* Borghese and his colleagues in the Tenth Light Flotilla were now at a point where they were able to demonstrate the very considerable punch they packed. In a series of actions—of the sort that we call today "naval special warfare"—Italian explosive motorboats and manned torpedoes began to do serious damage to the Royal Navy in the Mediterranean. For example, on the night of March 26, 1941—the eve of the Matapan debacle—the Tenth mounted a motorboat raid on Souda Bay in Crete, gravely damaging the cruiser *York* and three merchant ships serving the British, "amounting to 32,000 tons … sunk or put out of commission for the duration of the war," per Borghese's account.[4] Just a few days later the Italian submarine *Ambra* sank another British cruiser, the *Bonaventure*. These actions book-ended the losses at Matapan with some stinging Italian blows of their own.

The naval war in the Mediterranean continued in this fashion through the rest of 1941. Italian submarines, reinforced by some U-boats, proved the worthiness of their design for far more than just commerce raids on convoys. But the British held up under this attrition, confident in the dominance of their battleships and carriers over the Italian surface fleet and the security of their bases at Gibraltar, Malta—despite its being besieged— and Alexandria. Yet in December 1941, just a week before Christmas, a remarkable reversal of fortunes arose, thanks to Borghese's attack on Alexandria with manned torpedoes that put the *Queen Elizabeth* and *Valiant* out of commission for many months. Admiral Friedrich Ruge assessed the situation as one in which the balance in the Mediterranean had shifted sharply in the wake of Borghese's raid on Alexandria, because "about this

The *maiale* ("pig") manned torpedo, Italy's deadly naval weapon (Wikimedia Commons, Open-source Ticket Request System [OTRS], ticket #2010033010023591).

time, too, the British battleship *Malaya* was seriously damaged by a torpedo from the *U-81*."[5]

These losses proved disastrous, as they came on the heels of serious reverses that had occurred the previous month, when the carrier *Ark Royal* was torpedoed—an earlier victim of the *U-81*—and the battleship *Barham* was sunk by the *U-331*.[6] *Ark Royal* lived on for a day before sinking, with almost its entire complement saved. The *Barham* crew were not so lucky, nearly 900 of them perishing. Around the same time, grave damage was done to a British cruiser squadron when it ran into an Italian minefield off Tripoli. One cruiser, the *Neptune*, sank. The *Aurora* and *Penelope* suffered severe damage and barely limped back to port. These losses to submarines and mines gave proof of the superiority—given Italy's lack of carriers—of what can be best described as an "irregular warfare" approach to the fight at sea. A point emphasized by Borghese's devastating raid at year's end. As Correlli Barnett summed up the effect of this assault by manned torpedoes, "Thanks to this final attack by six brave and bold Italian sailors the [British] Mediterranean Fleet entirely ceased to exist."[7] Barnett was being slightly hyperbolic—there were still three light cruisers remaining—but his main point, that the naval balance had shifted profoundly, still rings true.

These naval developments gave heart to the Italians and reinvigorated Admiral Raeder's desire to see Germany and Italy re-focus their energies on the great potential of a more active Mediterranean strategy that would drive the British from Suez, open up the Middle East—and win the war. But the pre-requisite for all of this was to draw the sting from Malta, the formidable British base in the heart of the Mediterranean. As T.V.

Tuleja summed up Raeder's argument, "The success of this plan depended on the capture of Malta—*Malta delenda est*."[8] Raeder took his plan to Hitler, but the Fuehrer was reluctant to assault this fortress, as it would require a major airborne operation, and the costly assault on Crete at the end of the Greek campaign had taken him aback. On May 20, 1941, the Germans launched the first of the four great airborne operations of World War II—the Allies undertook the other three at Sicily, Normandy, and Arnhem—and in just days lost 4,000 elite troops killed in action. Almost as many as had been lost in the entire campaign in the Balkans. Part of the story behind this high casualty rate has to do with the "boffins" of Bletchley Park once again, who had broken the *Luftwaffe's* Red Code and passed on details of Operation Mercury so that the defending forces were well prepared and lying in wait.

But the truly essential problem was with the designers of airborne warfare—General Kurt Student in particular—who believed that assault from the air *en masse* against a hard target was feasible. Student and others were bolstered in this belief by the success of the small German airborne detachment that took the Belgian fortress at Eben-Emael the previous year. However, that action had the advantage of total surprise, shaped charges that could blow open the handful of casemates on the small attack site, and air superiority that enabled close support to fend off enemy reinforcements coming to the rescue of the fortress and the nearby bridges. Crete was a much larger target area, bristling with fore-warned defenders whose anti-aircraft and other fire capabilities were so great that over a third of the 600 German transports flying in the troops were destroyed. Overall, "Mercury" was a bloodbath.[9] German reluctance to repeat this risky undertaking—an attitude shared by Mussolini and his minions—was justified. John Keegan put it well, noting "Hitler's appreciation of Operation *Merkur* was correct: parachuting to war is essentially a dicing with death, in which the odds are loaded against the soldier who entrusts his life to silk and static line."[10]

For all the terrible cost of Crete—as Baron von der Heydte concluded, "it seemed almost a miracle that our great and hazardous enterprise had succeeded"[11]—it was now in Axis hands and had the potential to support occupation of other Eastern Mediterranean islands. A task to which some Italian and German forces were quickly devoted. Crete was also ideally positioned as an "unsinkable aircraft carrier" at a very strategic location. But its potential in this capacity was never actualized. The month after the fall of Crete, Hitler launched three million of his German soldiers into Russia—along with nearly a million more allies, many of them Romanians and Finns—supported by the vast majority of *Luftwaffe* combat aircraft.

The Battle of the Atlantic was now in full swing as well, yet another distraction and draining of air and naval resources from the Mediterranean. *Scharnhorst* and *Gneisenau,* now based in France at Brest, scored a success in their March 1941 raid on a convoy. They sank thirteen merchant ships and captured another three. But the Royal Navy soon adjusted to the threat, bombed Brest relentlessly, and made another such sortie by these German warships too risky. Proof that battleships should not be used as raiders came just a few months later, in May while the battle for Crete was raging. The *Bismarck* and its companion, the cruiser *Prinz Eugen,* broke out into the North Atlantic and sank the great Royal Navy battleship *Hood* in a brief action—seriously damaging the *Prince of Wales* as well. But *Bismarck* was quickly hunted down and sunk in turn. *Prinz Eugen* escaped and survived the war, only to be destroyed in a post-war nuclear test at Kwajalein.

Ludovic Kennedy, who wrote perhaps the best study of the chase of the *Bismarck*—

and whose father commanded an armed merchant-cruiser and was killed in an action against the *Scharnhorst* in November 1939—summed up the situation succinctly: "British air power was growing in strength daily. The combination of aircraft carriers, long-range flying boats and radar meant that once a German warship was picked up in the mid–Atlantic, she would be unlikely to get away; carrier planes by day and radar by night would maintain contact until superior forces could be brought up."[12] Admiral Raeder was devastated by loss of the *Bismarck;* and Hitler understood that his warships shouldn't be squandered on Atlantic raids. He quickly forbade them to sortie far from shore in search of convoys.

Instead, U-boats were now to be relied on as the principal tool in the Battle of the Atlantic. Even when their numbers had been very small, they had dealt harsh blows—augmented by the magnetic mines they laid just off British ports, sinking nearly half a million tons of merchant shipping, as Cajus Bekker noted, "in sight of their own coast and almost within reach of harbour."[13] German destroyers also helped plant these stealthy "influence" mines, which were able to detect the magnetic signature of a surface ship and detonate, even when laid several fathoms' deep. *Luftwaffe* aircraft deployed a small number as well, unwittingly contributing to the British understanding of the threat when one airdropped mine fell in too shallow water and was recovered when the tide went out. The British soon learned to de-magnetize, or "degauss" their ships and this serious danger waned.

But the growing number of U-boats on station at any given time had by May 1941 nearly doubled, from the average of fourteen in the opening months of the war, to twenty-five. And the pace of submarine construction had increased five-fold over the same period, from just over two per month to more than ten per month. Thus, in April 1941 alone nearly 700,000 tons of shipping were sunk by Doenitz's U-boats, which he vectored to the target convoys by radio after receiving an initial report of a sighting. It was a system that worked well for the next few years, but which was to suffer mightily due to German overconfidence in their Enigma coding machines. Doenitz's American counterpart, Admiral Chester Nimitz—a submarine officer as well—chose to keep his "lone wolves" radio silent out of concern that such communications might be intercepted and decrypted. When the "Ultra" capability at Bletchley Park finally broke Enigma—and air cover and radar detection improved—the consequences were dire for Germany's sea wolves.

For now, though, the Battle of the Atlantic raged with the Germans holding the advantage in what they saw as their best chance to keep hurting the British. Also, the looming war with Russia was soon to dominate land and air operations, sucking men and material into its maw, ravenously and unceasingly. These were the reasons why, from a shifting grand strategic perspective, the Mediterranean became a theater of operations characterized by holding actions and an economy of force. For Italy—and ultimately for Germany, too—primary emphasis on the war with Russia meant that a great, but fleeting, opportunity in the Middle Sea was missed.

\*    \*    \*

At the outset of the invasion of the Soviet Union in June 1941 the *Luftwaffe* was still suffering from what Victor Davis Hanson has called the "crippling blow" suffered in the Battle of Britain. So much so that "[d]espite the enormous resources arrayed for Operation Barbarossa and the stepped-up plane production, the Luftwaffe started the campaign markedly weakened, with at least two hundred fewer bombers than it had at the beginning of May 1940."[14] Attrition in the Mediterranean—not least during *Merkur*—contributed as well, but so did the production problems that could be, and increasingly were, blamed on Ernst Udet. World War I ace and visionary about close-support attack aircraft like the *Stuka,* Udet had great design instincts but was a poor administrator. He was self-aware enough to tell Goering from the outset that he shouldn't be made chief of the Technical Office. But Goering had persuaded his old comrade from the Flying Circus to take the job, saying, "Do you think *I* understand all the things I've got to deal with? But they get done all the same. You, too, will have qualified specialists who will do the work for you."[15] By the spring of 1941, though, it became clear that Udet's poor management caused overall aircraft production to decrease precipitously. This was due in part to teething problems with new aircraft designs, particularly the Me 210, that couldn't make tight turns—sparking a bitter acrimony between Udet and Willy Messerschmitt. So, on June 20, 1941, just two days before the invasion of Russia, Goering finally stepped in and made Field-Marshal Erhard Milch head of production. Udet's star was fading.

For all these difficulties, the *Luftwaffe* performed magnificently in the opening phase of Barbarossa. Its 800 serviceable bombers and 400 fighters destroyed 1,500 Soviet aircraft on the ground, another 300 in the air—about three-fourths of the Russian total on their Western frontiers—*on the first day of the campaign.* This gave the Germans air supremacy from the outset, enabling the bold panzer thrusts that unfolded in the following weeks. The *Blitzkrieg* design still worked well and Guderian, now commanding a panzer group, was in the forefront of the action. His concepts had diffused widely among his colleagues commanding other armored groups—still not much more than 10 percent of total ground forces—and over the course of the summer they launched one pincer move after another, capturing staggering numbers of Russians. Some three million were taken before winter, with advances of well over a thousand kilometers deep on a front running from the outskirts of Leningrad in the north to Rostov in the south. Such swift, startling results had not been since the sweeping offensives of the Mongols seven centuries earlier. David Downing summed up this performance: "German generals were the finest thinking and fighting soldiers of modern history."[16]

Soldiering aside—for the moment—it is also important to note that German successes in the great ground campaigns of the early years of the war were also due to the remarkable contributions of the Krupp firm, an arms manufacturer that had been operating since the late 16th century. It was an exceptionally diversified, well-coordinated enterprise that had tied together the many threads of technological advances to the organizational and doctrinal implications of modern warfare. William Manchester put the matter this way: "[N]o one weapon accounted for the stunning success of the blitzkrieg. Krupp had fashioned an incredibly sophisticated arsenal…. To an extent unprecedented in the history of industry, a corporation had become an integral part of a warlord's apparatus."[17] If Udet had bollixed up aircraft production, the Krupp firm more than made up for this deficiency by its fine work with tanks like the Panzer IV, guns like the 88—the company made heavy naval guns as well—and with the steel that it provided in great quantities to other German industrial firms involved in the war effort.

But even this fine Krupp weaponry, further empowered by near-complete mastery of the air, couldn't alter the fundamental strategic calculus of time, space, and force. The Russians could trade their ample space for time, time in which to bring up vast reserves of material and manpower. Time that would see winter slowing, even halting, the German advance. For the Germans, the further they pushed into Russia the more tautly and thinly stretched their forces were. The fact that the invaders suffered very nearly a million casualties of their own in the first five months of the war exacerbated the force-to-space issues, making it impossible to continue the offensive by all three army groups simultaneously.

A major debate arose in August 1941—and raged on for a fortnight—about whether to emphasize a central thrust against Moscow or to divert most of the panzers to help out in the south, where Field-Marshal von Rundstedt faced massive Russian forces and tough sledding. Guderian, whose panzers had been driving Army Group Center forward, ever forward, argued vehemently for focusing on a direct blow against Moscow. Hitler and many of his senior generals preferred a massive enveloping move to trap Russian forces in and around Kiev in the south. In the end, the Fuehrer's preferred course of action was chosen.

For all his reservations, Guderian nevertheless threw himself wholeheartedly into the task at hand, and contributed to one of history's most decisive military victories. In the "cauldron battle" that ensued, the Russians were decisively defeated, with over 600,000 troops captured. The victory was so swift that Guderian was able to take his armor back to the central front and *still* conduct his drive on Moscow. It was by now late in September and Guderian had a growing sense of urgency, worrying that when "the autumn rains came … [they] would turn the trackless countryside into a morass, and the movement of motorized formations would be paralyzed."[18] Indeed, the mud of the fall months was a dire threat to the *Heer* since the vast majority of its vehicles, other than tanks, ran on *tires* rather than tracks. The poor Russian road system—most of it unpaved—became an absolute quagmire until the winter's first freeze. The design flaw in the German system of mechanized warfare was that, while tires worked quite well in Western Europe, and even throughout much of the Balkans where the road infrastructure was good, Russia's very backwardness made it essential for any invader to rely on tracked vehicles for mobility, especially in the fall and spring when rains turned the roads into rivers of mud.

Hitler's choice to redirect the offensive in the East on a strike to the south early in September 1941 has had more than its share of critics—not unlike the criticism of his decision to halt his panzers the year before instead of driving them straight at the Anglo-Allied forces trapped at Dunkirk. In that earlier instance, there were several good reasons for the halt, discussed in the previous chapter. In this situation in the East, there was an equally valid, even compelling, rationale for focusing on defeating and destroying the massive Russian forces in the south before driving on Moscow.

Aside from the economic arguments about the value of the Ukraine that Hitler made to Guderian—and others—there was the problem that the Red Army in the south could drive north, imperiling a central drive on the Soviet capital. This dilemma, Gerhard Weinberg has observed, "gave the arguments over what to do next a particular twist for the Germans. If they pushed ahead in the center toward Moscow, they risked very serious dangers on the southern flank of such a thrust, dangers which they lacked the reserves to meet."[19]

Germany did not lose the war with Russia because of its turn south—where it won a great strategic victory. But even in this early moment of triumph the fundamental design flaw in the *Heer* was growing ever more apparent: the army was just over one-sixth mechanized (i.e., 34 of the 180 divisions, 19 panzer, 15 motorized); and just one-tenth of the vehicles in *those* divisions were tracked. Given the exceptional breadth and depth of the Eastern theater of operations, and the primitive nature of the Russian road system, this very basic design deficiency played a key role in the ultimate German defeat. The failure to mechanize a larger proportion of the army—as von Seeckt envisioned in the 1920s—may well have been the decisive factor in determining the outcome of history's largest, bloodiest campaign.

While the *Luftwaffe* continued to provide outstanding close support to German ground troops in the East during the fall of 1941, its inability to act in an effective strategic manner—for example, against very limited Russian rail infrastructure that was bringing massive reinforcements from the Far East—was a grave deficiency. The Soviets benefited from their "strange neutrality" with Japan, as well as from reassurance given by their master spy Richard Sorge that the Japanese were not going to double-cross Josef Stalin by joining with the Germans in attacking Russia. The consequences of the earlier decision to cancel the "Ural Bomber" program were now clear to be seen. Making matters even worse, Ernst Udet and Erhard Milch were now waging bitter bureaucratic warfare against each other, with Milch getting much the better of it and enjoying growing support from Goering.

So much so that the *Reichsmarschall* ordered Udet to go on sick leave, which the old fighter ace did for a month from late August to late September. When he returned, much of his management team was gone, replaced by Milch's own people. Udet despaired, was drinking heavily, but did his best to stay on and contribute. In mid–November, though, he heard from a trusted friend the most disturbing news about horrible atrocities being committed in Russia. Two days later, Ernst Udet shot himself in the head. Depression caused by loss of Goering's support and relationship problems with his girlfriend may have been contributing factors—but the timing of his death so soon after learning of Nazi war crimes suggests another stressor was in play as well. Whatever the ultimate cause or causes of his death, one more of the Axis' key designers was now gone—another aviator, like Balbo.

And what of the news Udet heard about the killings of the innocent in the East? It was true. The SS had by now metastasized, its growing number of combat field divisions just one part of its presence. The other, far darker manifestation of the SS came in the form of the notorious *Einsatzgruppen* of *Obergruppenfuehrer* Reinhard Heydrich. In four groups, roughly a thousand each, these killing teams had the job of executing communist cadres and Jews—most by shooting, some in public hangings—all of whom were to be considered "partisans." Over a million innocents were murdered this way, prior to the time when, per Andrew Roberts' apt phrasing, much "more industrialized processes were adopted."[20] But before the extermination camps were up and running, the worst *Einsatzgruppen* killings occurred at Ponary and Rumbula in the Baltics, where about 100,000 were executed, and at Babi Yar, near Kiev, where 33,000 died in two days of shooting at the end of September 1941. The *Heer* was ordered to provide logistical support to the murderous *Einsatzgruppen* and, as Roberts also observed, had awareness of the atrocities, to its "everlasting shame."[21] In all the annals of conflict, it is hard to find actions of such systematic, psychopathic brutality. But the evil manifested in these massacres was to prove highly counterproductive.

The mass killings of innocents in the East revealed a fatal strategic design flaw at the societal level. From publication of *Mein Kampf* on, Nazi ideology was driven by the twin beliefs in the need for eastern *Lebensraum* and that the justification for seizing territory there lay in the fact that these rich, fertile lands were populated by the *Untermensch*, who at best deserved only to be dominated by Germans. That so many in the coveted areas were Jews only fed the anti–Semitism that formed another of the pillars of Nazism—and made it even easier to slide from oppression to atrocity.

Heydrich eagerly seized the opportunity to kill innocents after he received a vaguely worded instruction from Goering on July 31, 1941, just a month after the invasion of Russia, to pursue a "final solution to the Jewish question." He and his men now began shooting Jews at will, and with a will. They did this despite the fact that Goering's instruction explicitly mentioned only "emigration and evacuation of the Jews."[22] Needless to say, many non–Jews were caught up in the killings, and news of these atrocities began to leak out soon, kindling rage and resistance—from partisans behind the lines as well as from Red Army soldiers who now had ultimate motivation to give their all to defend Mother Russia and its people. Thus did the Germans miss an opportunity to exploit to their advantage anti-communist sentiments that were widespread in the Ukraine and the Baltic countries.

In his *German Rule in Russia,* Alexander Dallin noted: "During the first weeks the Germans advanced through territory which, until 1939–40, had not been part of the U.S.S.R. It was natural that in the formerly Polish-held Western Ukraine and Western Belorussia, as well as in the Baltic States, the overwhelming majority of the people had remained bitterly hostile to Soviet rule."[23] Yet here were the sites of the mass shootings by the *Einsatztruppen* who trailed behind the advancing *Heer.* Dallin went on to observe that, even as the panzers struck deeper and the Germans "entered territories which had experienced an entire generation of Soviet rule ... [g]rievances against the Soviet regime were likewise widespread and intense." This led Dallin to conclude "there is little doubt that a skillful effort to win the population, civilian and military alike, to oppose the Soviet regime could have yielded substantial, and during the first six months of the war perhaps decisive, results."[24] But Nazi inhumanity sparked widespread resistance. In his study of this conflict, Alexander Werth—a journalist who was in-country during key periods of the war—affirmed that "[p]artisan (i.e., guerrilla) warfare in German-occupied territory held an important place in both government propaganda and actual military planning almost from the beginning of the war."[25]

Foolishly, the Germans allowed ideology to trump strategy, creating a problem that was nettlesome from the outset of the war in the East, and was to grow dangerously in magnitude and effect in the coming years. Needless to say, the Soviet media in Moscow and commissars on the front lines made considerable use of these German war crimes to instill a profound sense of duty and determination in the Red Army, as well as across Soviet society as a whole. One can only imagine how different the situation would have been had Hitler embraced rather than victimized these populations.

As to the situation at the front, after the resounding success in the Ukraine, Guderian and his panzers headed back to Army Group Center to spearhead the drive on Moscow. Initial results were once again remarkable, with some hundreds of thousands of Russian troops caught in yet another pincer movement. But the Red Army's resistance stiffened as the weather worsened, and with the appearance of Josef Stalin's "fireman general," Georgi Zhukov. His earlier command up at Leningrad—characterized by an unflinching willingness to suffer great casualties in order to halt German advances, and the massive use of the civilian population to dig defensive works—had saved the city from capture. Now he was brought to the central front to rescue Moscow, where he immediately told the tired, beaten troops, that had been retreating for months, to stand firm and fight.

They were soon reinforced by fresh divisions that came from Siberia and the Far East.

These troops arrived via the lone, long rail line that the Germans, lacking a wide-ranging strategic bombing capability, could not interdict. And they allowed Zhukov eventually to conduct the battle for Moscow on the tactical offensive, though he first had to blunt the edge of the German panzers. As at Leningrad, he mobilized large civilian masses to dig anti-tank ditches and improvise other field fortifications. They were also sent into battle, ill prepared and suffering massive casualties, including at Tula, where Guderian's panzers were held off. But in the end, Zhukov recalled in his memoirs, the real reason the German advance was halted early in December—within twenty kilometers of the Kremlin—was that, the enemy had "made mistakes in organizing their armored shock groups ... [which] were inadequately supplied with infantry. Experience should have shown that exclusive reliance on armored forces was insufficient."[26] An important lesson the panzer leaders learned in the campaign in France the previous year had been neglected. Tanks by themselves were vulnerable; accompanied by infantry, and with close air support, they were most potent.

At the end of the first week of December 1941, the Germans were completely stalled along virtually the whole Eastern Front in Russia, and the Red Army was preparing a series of counter-offensives that were destined to test Hitler and the *Heer* to the utmost. Guderian, who was brooding in his headquarters on the Tolstoy estate at Yasnaya Polyana, openly opposed the Fuehrer's "stand fast" order, favoring instead a planned retreat. Hitler, less and less able to brook dissent, sacked Guderian on the day after Christmas. Several other of his senior officers were relieved of command as well. Some were brought back later in the war—as was Guderian, who ultimately went on to play a major role in revitalizing Germany's armored forces.

Out in the Atlantic, the U-boat wolfpacks were encountering growing difficulties, particularly because the United States Navy was now waging an increasingly vigorous, though undeclared, war at sea against them. In North Africa, Erwin Rommel was fighting desperately in a complex and confusing armored duel with the British. In the end, on the verge of a great victory, he strove for too much. And on December 6 Rommel had to order the first of a series of skillful retreats that took his *Afrika Korps* back to the line from which he had launched his offensive back in March. The next day, Japanese forces attacked Pearl Harbor.

*     *     *

In the summer of 1941 the United States imposed an oil embargo on Japan, making war near-inevitable. With average annual oil consumption at 3.5 million tons—nearly two-thirds allocated to the Imperial Navy, the rest split between the other services and civilian needs—Japanese total reserves of 5.5 million tons left Tokyo with poor prospects lest new sources of supply were acquired. Reassured by their neutrality treaty with the Soviets, and knowing that Hitler's invasion of Russia occupied Stalin's attention fully— securing Japan's northern flank—Japan's leaders decided that it was time to strike southward to seize resource-rich British Malaya and the Dutch East Indies.

Yamamoto's belief that the Americans would not stand by idly in the face of such aggression had by now gained wide acceptance, though it took longer for the Japanese senior military leadership to approve mounting a major carrier strike at Pearl Harbor. Late in October, though, Yamamoto's plan was formally approved, in part because of the belief that the Americans would be forced to split their efforts, with much of their navy having to be diverted to assist Britain in its fight against the U-boat menace. Antony Beevor takes the view that "Japan would never have dared to attack the United States if Hitler had not started the war in Europe and the Atlantic."[27]

But dare Japan did. Yamamoto was aware of the incredibly high stakes—and stayed knowledgeable about American public opinion thanks to the *Life Magazine* subscription that he kept right up to the war's start. He wanted desperately to command the attack on Pearl Harbor in person. But he was considered too vital to the war effort to risk his life in this fashion, and the assignment was given instead to Admiral Chuichi Nagumo, a less daring, less imaginative officer.

The attack was prepared with typical Japanese concentration on details. Lessons from the British attack on the Italians at Taranto the previous year were fully absorbed; and the shallow-running torpedoes upon which success would depend

Isoroku Yamamoto at a navy planning meeting aboard *Nagato*, 1940 (public domain, Wikimedia Commons).

were tested and re-tested to make sure they worked at Pearl Harbor. But at the same time these preparations were being made, hope remained that war could be avoided. The Japanese strove hard to reach a peaceful resolution to the crisis caused by the American oil embargo and freezing of assets. As late as just ten days before the attack on December 7, there was still thought that diplomacy might work, as the American Secretary of State Cordell Hull passed a note to the Japanese indicating a willingness to end sanctions if the Imperial Army withdrew from "China." Hull had not intended this to mean "Manchuria" as well—where the Japanese had ruled, with wide international acquiescence, for over a decade—but that was how the word choice was interpreted by the Tokyo government, which was also asked to sign wide-ranging non-aggression pacts covering all countries with interests in East Asia and the Pacific. The Japanese were deeply offended by the expansive demand for withdrawal from "China." Clearer wording, as John Toland once observed, "might have enabled Foreign Minister [Heihachiro] Togo to persuade the militarists that negotiations should be continued." But now it seemed that "[a] war that need not have been fought seemed certain to begin."[28]

Despite good American intelligence about the coming war, Japanese operational security on this occasion proved to be excellent. Very few were in the know about the Pearl Harbor plan, and there were virtually no coded radio messages that mentioned it. Surprise was achieved only partly because of this good security. The other reason for success was that the link between warning provided by U.S. intelligence and the response by senior leaders was attenuated. This is not a criticism solely of the Americans, either, for Josef Stalin had had more than ample warning of the impending German invasion in June 1941. In the American case, surprise occurred because a Japanese attack was expected to fall primarily upon the Philippines; a strike on Pearl Harbor, more than three thousand miles from Japan's home islands, was considered unthinkable. In Stalin's case, he clearly *wanted* to believe that his German ally would continue to abide by the terms of the existing non-aggression pact.[29] He suffered from what psychologists call "motivated bias." The Americans, on the other hand, saw looming what they *expected* to see—known as an aspect of "cognitive bias." There was also a widely held belief that the Japanese simply were not this capable.

In the ensuing events, doubts about Japanese capabilities were swept away. As to the specific effects of the strike on Pearl Harbor, they were spectacular but not crippling. Per Yamamoto's operational design, the *Kido Butai* massed six carriers—a seaborne version of Guderian's notions about concentrating panzer divisions. The carrier force launched over 350 attack aircraft in two roughly equal-sized waves. They swiftly sank four American battleships outright, damaged another four in harbor, and sank or damaged several cruisers, destroyers, and smaller craft. Nearly two hundred aircraft were destroyed on the ground, dozens more as they rose to confront enemy raiders. Over 2,400 Americans died on December 7. Japanese losses were limited to 29 aircraft and five midget submarines—the latter, a seeming echo of Borghese's innovations in naval special warfare, performed execrably and might even have blown the whole surprise against more alert foes.

But the massive oil tank farm, the shipyard, and maintenance facilities were left relatively unscathed, as were the American aircraft carriers. The *Lexington* and *Enterprise* were out on plane-delivery missions to the U.S. garrisons on Midway and Wake Islands, respectively. *Enterprise* had been due back in Pearl Harbor on December 6, but Admiral William F. "Bull" Halsey, in command of this carrier task force, ordered reduced speed when heavy weather was encountered, delaying their scheduled return—saving *Enterprise* and its companion vessels.

Aside from the controversies and conspiracy theories about whether Franklin Delano Roosevelt had a hand in allowing the surprise attack to take place, perhaps the sharpest other debate is about whether Admiral Nagumo should have launched a third strike, knocking out the fuel and other shore facilities. Doing so would have crippled the American ability to pursue a counter-offensive in the Pacific, likely for years. Mitsuo Fuchida, the pilot who led the first wave, argued fiercely in favor of a third strike when he got back to the carrier *Akagi*. But Nagumo's view, as Fuchida reported it, was that the *Kido Butai* had already achieved its mission, that Japanese losses had more than doubled from the first to the second waves, and that radio intercepts indicated that over fifty American fighter planes were still able to rise and meet the next attack wave.[30] Beyond this, there was still a worrying question about where the American carriers were, and the Japanese were now short on fuel, with barely enough left to get home. Continuing combat action could fatally compromise the fuel situation. Chuichi Nagumo decided that caution was the better part of valor in this instance.

Though he supported Nagumo's decision officially—at least in the immediate wake of the attack—in private Yamamoto was from the first "sorely disappointed" with his colleague's timidity on the verge of a great victory that would have had lasting impact.[31] But in front of his senior staff—all of whom were sharply critical of Nagumo's failure to launch a third wave against Pearl Harbor—Yamamoto offered a metaphor to explain why the decision had been taken not to strike one more time: "It would be fine, of course, if it were successful. But even a burglar hesitates to go back for more."[32] Yamamoto was always solicitous of the feelings and reputations of his subordinates; but he was also a great poker player—a game he came to love during his years in the United States—and there can be little doubt that, had he led the attack as he had requested, the *Kido Butai* would have been "all in," and the potential of his daring strategic design fully realized.

Yamamoto's vision, carried out imperfectly in actual practice, had nevertheless prevented the Americans from being able to interdict Japanese forces that now launched their amphibious version of the German *Blitzkrieg* concept. Beyond the outer perimeter shield of fortified Pacific islands that the Japanese hoped to create by conquest, British and Dutch holdings in Southeast Asia came under their guns as well. Soon island after island fell to coordinated Japanese sea-air-land attacks—including the Philippines, but only after very bitter fighting there. The eminent military historian Allan Millett provided perhaps the clearest summary of these and other swift, stunning blows, and of the concept of operations that underpinned them:

> Japanese landing forces swept into Luzon, Hong Kong, Malaya, Guam, the Solomons, New Britain Island, and the Dutch East Indies and routed Allied defense forces without serious losses to their amphibious expeditionary forces and their supporting air and naval units…. [L]anding craft and barges brought the troops ashore at multiple, narrow landing sites distributed along long stretches of coastline…. The grand tactics of *infiltration and exploitation* worked well, especially in confounding a larger Commonwealth army in Malaya.[33]

The campaign in Malaya was indeed "especially confounding," as General Yamashita was assigned command of the invasion force, the 25th Army, just a few weeks before the war started. He was determined to use lessons he picked up during his sojourn in Germany, in particular the value of massed tanks and the importance of speed of movement, relative to the enemy's ability to react. Yamashita was wary of throwing too much force into the campaign, fearing this might slow him down; so, he gave back one of the four divisions the Imperial General Staff had assigned to him for this attack. And instead of the very conventional advance that characterized the plan when he took command, he envisioned something quite unorthodox.

What Yamashita saw was an opportunity to land on the Malayan peninsula simultaneously at three separated points—Singora and Patani in the north, and Kota Bharu far to the south—rather than to concentrate his force in one landing zone, as the General Staff preferred. From these sites his dispersed invasion force of not much more than 30,000 combat troops was to advance by all possible means, with infantry often relying on bicycles to traverse rough paths and small detachments on barges outflanking the British defenders—who numbered over 150,000 in all—with left and right "hooks" from the sea on either side of the peninsula. Yamashita also knew that enough of the terrain was "tankable," allowing his concentrated armor to operate in areas the British thought impassable. Thus, he achieved in the Malayan jungles the kind of armored surprise that Guderian's panzers had in the forests of the Ardennes in 1940.

The whole campaign in Malaya—especially the ability to hold the initiative with such a small invasion force—was made possible largely due to Japan's command of the sea and air supremacy, a state of affairs that was highlighted by the sinking of the battleship *Prince of Wales* and the battle cruiser *Repulse* by Japanese attack aircraft on December 10. The British idea had been to send these heavy ships—with their escorting destroyers, comprising "Force Z"—to the waters off Singora on the northeastern coast of Malaya, there to devastate the invasion fleet and the 25th Army's thin-skinned transports. In the event, though, these marvelous warships were swiftly and easily sunk. Admiral Phillips, the commander, knowing the great risks, had sent off his escorts when he went in for the attack, saving them from destruction. But the lesson to be drawn from of the loss of these capital ships to air attack was clear: "the annihilation of Force Z signaled the end of a maritime era."[34] The age of battleship dominance was over.

Interestingly, on the west side of the Malayan peninsula the Japanese were performing amazing feats where they shouldn't have been able to at all. They had virtually no naval capability beyond the barges and small boats—the former portaged overland to the west coast, the latter seized from the British then used against them—on which a portion of the invading troops moved and made their various landings. In a memorandum sent to the First Sea Lord, Admiral Dudley Pound, on January 22, 1942, Prime Minister Churchill sharply criticized British performance in this area, concluding "we have been absolutely outmaneuvered and apparently outfought on the west coast of Malaya by an enemy who has no warship in the neighborhood."[35]

How did this happen? In part—but only in part—it is a story of the invading force relying heavily upon close air support. But this was only one part of Yamashita's overall design. As his chief of staff Masanobu Tsuji described and assessed the overarching concept of operations, he reasoned that it succeeded *because of* its very unorthodoxy. It was "a different plan based on unorthodox tactics in which surprise attack and rapidity of movement were the principal elements."[36] Quite Rommel-like. Clearly, Yamashita had imbibed much of the spirit of *Blitzkrieg* during his sojourns in Germany—and added impressive flourishes of his own.

British Empire forces, vastly greater on the ground than the invading force, could never react quickly or effectively enough to stem the tide of the Japanese advance. And in just over two months the Malayan Peninsula was traversed down its entire length, the great fortress of Singapore besieged and put under bombardment. Its surrender followed quickly on February 15, in what Winston Churchill sadly described as "the worst disaster and largest capitulation of British history."[37] For beyond the 130,000 prisoners that Yamashita's men gathered in, there were other, just

Tomoyuki Yamashita won Japan's greatest victory at Singapore (public domain, Wikimedia Commons, http://news.cntv.cn/military/20110503/109697.shtml).

as dire, consequences. The British historian James Leasor summarized the larger situation this way:

> The fall of Malaya and Singapore led directly to the collapse of the Dutch East Indies. Burma was overrun within weeks and the Japanese tide swept on, up to the Indian frontier.... There was, too, the incalculable economic loss to the Allies. The rubber, tin and oil—large proportions of the world output—so badly needed, now went to the enemies of the Allies.[38]

The invasion of Burma featured another demonstration of the power of Yamashita's "infiltration and exploitation" methods—though without him, as Hideki Tojo, still jealous of his old rival, sent "the Tiger of Malaya" off to Manchuria, supposedly to guard against the Russians. Yamashita spent the next two years in this virtual "military exile," recalled only after Tojo's dismissal in the summer of 1944 and given the close-to-impossible task of defending the Philippines. The outstanding defense Yamashita designed there will be covered later. For now, the important point is that his methods were diffusing, and led to the next success in Southeast Asia—the conquest of Burma—that brought the Japanese Empire to the very gates of India.

Why invade Burma? There were two good reasons. First, doing so fit neatly into the Japanese "perimeter defense" design, shielding the resources won in Malaya and the Dutch East Indies from direct assault. But another important reason to conquer Burma was that doing so would sever the Allied link to the hard-pressed Chinese forces that existed via the "Burma Road." Thus, the prospect of achieving a final victory over Chiang Kai-Shek and his Kuomintang armies loomed ahead tantalizingly as well. There was also the very real prospect of being able to pursue this campaign with an economy of force, as there were many disaffected Burmese willing to fight on Japan's side against their "colonial oppressors." Indeed, the Burma Independence Army that formed up for this campaign soon reached nearly 20,000 fighters—a quite ample supplement to General Shojiro Iida's two divisions that were tasked with the conquest. One of the key Burmese commanders fighting alongside the Japanese was Aung San, father of the future Nobel Laureate Aung San Suu Kyi.

Perhaps the best account of this remarkable campaign, one of the finest of all military memoirs, is Field Marshal the Viscount Slim's memoir, *Defeat Into Victory*. Slim is most thorough in his description of the Japanese strategic design and unflinching in his judgments about Allied deficiencies. He found "the most distressing aspect of the whole disastrous campaign had been the contrast between our generalship and the enemy's. The Japanese leadership was confident, bold ... and so aggressive that never for one day did they lose the initiative." He also noted that, in the actual fighting, "we had been completely outclassed ... the tactical method on which all their successes were based was the 'hook' ... we, by reason of our complete dependence on motor transport and the un-handiness of our troops in the jungle, could not carry out [or even parry] these hooks successfully in any strength."[39] General Joseph W. Stilwell, who oversaw the Chinese forces defending northern Burma, was deeply impressed by the Japanese ability to operate in very rough terrain at such "unbelievable speed" and even more succinct than Slim in his self-criticism. At an impromptu news conference held after he was flown out of the combat zone to India, Stilwell memorably articulated the view that "We got a hell of a beating. We got run out of Burma and it is humiliating as hell. I think we ought to find out what caused it, go back and retake it."[40] A day was to come when Stilwell and Slim would, to use the latter's phrasing, "turn defeat into victory." But that day was years off, and their knowledge of Japanese operational designs—and how to defeat them—was to be gained only at heavy cost.

For the present though, in Burma, Malaya, the East Indies and across the extensive chain of islands that formed its defense perimeter, Japanese forces brought to life the larger strategic design that had been envisioned prior to the war. Zero fighters—light but swift and highly maneuverable—proved far superior in technical design to anything the Allies had at the time. Long Lance torpedoes passed their first major battle test in the Java Sea, where their range, speed, and accuracy ensured victory in the surface action there against an Allied fleet. But for all the validation of Japan's strategic design, unless a broad naval mastery could be sustained, the sheer size of the shield of empire—now encompassing a significant swath of the world—would offer a wide range of possible entry points for enemy counterattacks. This was the real tension in Japan's—and, for that matter Germany's—strategic designs: the more the Axis Powers conquered, the more they had to disperse their forces to protect the outer edges of their holdings, and the more flexibility of choice they gave the Allies. At its heart, then, this was a tension that Japan could only manage by maintaining mastery at sea—and in the skies above the seas. After Pearl Harbor, the Japanese had a very good chance to consolidate their naval superiority by destroying American carrier forces, first during the May 1942 Battle of the Coral Sea, then the following month at Midway.

But something happened. The Japanese plan to extend their perimeter by setting up an airbase at the eastern end of the Solomon Islands, followed by a landing at Port Moresby in New Guinea off Australia's northeast coast, fell victim to American code-breaking efforts. Forewarned of the dire threat—if Moresby fell to the Japanese, the line of communication from Hawaii to Australia would be effectively severed—Admiral Chester Nimitz, who had replaced the hapless Husband E. Kimmel after the debacle at Pearl Harbor, decided to take advantage of his "information edge" and block the Japanese move. He dispatched two carriers and supporting ships to confront similar-sized Japanese forces and, over a several-day battle early in May—history's first in which opposing ships never came within sight of each other, aircraft alone carrying the weight of battle—the Americans thwarted the invasion of Port Moresby for the loss of a carrier, an oiler, and a destroyer. Japanese losses were a bit less, with some small vessels being sunk off Tulagi in the Eastern Solomons, along with a light carrier in the Coral Sea. But this battle made clear that a new mode of war at sea had fully emerged, one in which, as an eloquent French naval officer with long experience living in Japan put it, "enemy fleets are as phantoms to each other."[41]

This fundamental "finder dynamic" now dominated naval warfare—in submarine campaigns as well as surface actions, since locating convoys had become a key challenge for German U-boats and American "pigboats," too. "Finding" was to play a crucial role in the next naval confrontation, which took place at Midway Island and surrounding waters in June. In the wake of the Coral Sea battle, and after the humiliation of allowing Jimmy Doolittle's air raid on Tokyo, Admiral Yamamoto felt a need to lure out the American carriers and destroy them—to make up for missing them at Pearl Harbor—thus consolidating Japan's naval mastery. But he failed to reckon with Navy code-breakers, who figured out where and when Japan was set to strike next. Nimitz, with far smaller forces, just three carriers, one of them *Yorktown* that was still undergoing repairs after the Coral Sea clash, nevertheless decided to take the offensive. The Japanese had four carriers at Midway, augmented by a massive fleet of surface warships. But the latter would count for little in a battle fought at the outer range of attack aircraft. In the event, they *did* count for little, and the American carriers were able to catch the Japanese by surprise. But the "incredible victory," to use Walter Lord's term[42]—all four Japanese carriers were sunk, the *Yorktown* the only big loss on the American side—still depended on the skill and self-sacrifice of the U.S. Navy pilots.

Midway had a profound psychological effect on Yamamoto and his colleagues. They soon engaged in self-criticism of the "victory disease" that allowed them to be caught off guard, and developed a deep pessimism about prospects for the future course of the war. Cooler heads saw that the disaster arose from correctable errors. Mitsuo Fuchida saw the first as "a failure to take adequate precautions for guarding the secrecy of our plans." The other mistake was that "planners indulged in one of their favorite, and in this case fatal, gambits—dispersion."[43] Given that Japan assigned eight (!) carriers to this campaign, and that Yamamoto pioneered the doctrine of massing them in battle, their dispersion on this occasion—two were sent far away to the Aleutians—was a grave error. Guilt ridden, Yamamoto fell into a deep funk, vowing to forgo taking further offensive action in June or July that aimed at crippling the American carrier capability. This despite the fact Japan still had the edge in carriers. Historian Ronald Spector put the situation this way:

> Unless Japan could inflict a shattering defeat on the U.S. early in the war, she would gradually be ground down by steadily growing American military power. The Japanese still had sufficient forces after Midway to again take the initiative for another try at the U.S. fleet. Instead they reverted to the defensive and allowed themselves to be drawn into a battle of attrition in the Solomons.[44]

Instead of mounting a new offensive, the Japanese now chose to rely simply on their overarching defensive perimeter design. Its success would depend heavily upon their ground forces' ability to defend the perimeter's dispersed bastions long enough for the surface fleet, submarines, and carriers—as well as for land-based attack aircraft from nearby islands—to come to the rescue. The Empire was stretched to its very limits by July 1942. As were Italian and German forces at the very same time, it turned out.

\*    \*    \*

By July of 1942 Erwin Rommel could look back on the previous six months with considerable pride in the accomplishments of his *Afrika Korps*. Early in the new year he had launched a surprise offensive that quickly drove the British back to a position just to the west of the great fortress of Tobruk—the strongpoint that had thwarted his advance the previous year. The British fortified a line of defensive "brigade boxes" running from the sea southward for fifty miles—the so-called Gazala Line. In the last week in May, Rommel launched the next phase in his offensive with a massed "right hook" around the southern end of the Line by his panzers, augmented yet once again by the skillful use of 88s in their anti-tank role.

There was bitter fighting for three weeks, but the *Afrika Korps* finally won through, taking Tobruk in a single day on June 21—a stroke enabled in part by the innovative use of *Stukas* to bomb the minefields protecting the fortress, rapidly clearing lanes for the advance. The haul at Tobruk was huge: 35,000 prisoners and, as Alan Moorehead assessed the situation, with captured supplies and transport in such abundance that "Rommel had here enough British vehicles, enough tanks and guns, enough petrol and fuel and enough ammunition to re-equip at once and drive straight on to Egypt."[45] Over the objections of some of his superiors and the Italians—but with Hitler's permission—he resumed the advance. By July he was just sixty miles from Alexandria. Rommel achieved all this with smaller numbers of troops and tanks because of his adherence to the key doctrinal principle in the design for armored warfare he and Guderian had done so much to create: *keep the panzers massed.* As Rommel said to one of the British generals his forces had captured, "Why should I bother about the superior number of British tanks when their commanders always use them in driblets? Against those driblets I am the stronger with my army."[46]

At the same time that Rommel was driving the British before him, German fortunes in Russia were looking up after a hard winter of defensive fighting. Several major Red Army counter-offensives had been defeated, largely because Josef Stalin rejected the advice of Zhukov and other senior military leaders, who by now had begun to absorb and understand the key elements of Guderian's design for armored warfare and argued for a single, massive thrust against just one portion of the invaders' long front. As the official German history of the war notes, Stalin's demands for immediate, broad action were not to be successfully opposed: "Against their own better judgment, Zhukov and the Western Front HQ passed on these demands to the armies under their command and called for ceaseless attacks, which, as was later admitted, 'only cost pointless casu-

alties.'"[47] All this because the Soviet dictator held so firmly to his belief that "the strained and exhausted German army could be sent reeling by hard and essentially simultaneous blows on all major segments of the front."[48] Stalin was wrong. Very wrong. The counter-offensives failed, at a near-ruinous cost, precisely *because* of the too-wide dispersion of the Russians' offensive striking power. It was an error Zhukov did his best to make sure would not be repeated in the future.

But for now, the Red Army's failures in the winter and spring of 1942 gave the Germans the chance to resume the offensive in the summer. With strength enough to strike on only one section of the long front, Hitler chose to send fifty divisions forward in the south, holding in place in the center and north. Much of the order of battle was comprised of allied units, especially from Romania, Hungary, and Italy— but even Spain sent its "Blue Division" to fight in the East. The twin goals of the summer campaign were to capture Stalingrad and advance into the Caucasus, seizing the Soviet oilfields there. Andrew Roberts's view is that "the desire to take the important industrial city of Stalingrad was perfectly

**Erwin Rommel understood the need to mass armor on the attack (Creative Commons, courtesy Bundesarchiv, Bild 146–1985–013–07/ CC-BY-SA 3.0).**

understandable. With its capture the oil terminal of Astrakhan would be within reach, and the Russians would be denied the use of the Volga for transportation. Furthermore, Army Group A in the Caucasus would be safe from another Soviet winter offensive."[49] By July 23, when Hitler declared in his Directive 45 that the goals of the offensive were "reached for the most part," his forces "had conquered a large and in part very rich area." Two days later, Rostov-on-Don was reached and taken, and the prospects for reaching the oilfields at Grozny and Baku seemed quite good.

But, as Gerhard Weinberg insightfully notes, "the capture of [just] between 100,000 and 200,000 prisoners in three encirclement battles showed that the great victory Hitler trumpeted to his officers ... was in part illusory."[50] Indeed, the results of the 1942 summer offensive pale in comparison with the massive numbers of prisoners taken—numbering in the millions—by the panzer armies in the cauldron battles of the previous year. Nevertheless, the German war in Russia was nearing its high tide at the end of July with the 6th Army taking Kalach, close by Stalingrad. And while the other parts of the front remained largely static, earlier that month Erich von Manstein captured Sevastopol in the Crimea after a long siege—a coup for which Hitler promoted him to the rank of *Feldmarschall*. He was then sent north to advance the siege of Leningrad, running into very stiff opposition there. But even farther north, on the sea route to Murmansk—a port through which Allied-provided supplies were now pouring in great amounts—the *Kriegsmarine* and *Luftwaffe* struck the hardest of hard blows against an Arctic convoy when they sank twenty-three out of the thirty-three merchant ships in PQ 17 in a running fight from late in June to early July.[51]

This success was due in large part to the concentration of the major German warships in northern waters—a shift of forces that included moving the *Scharnhorst, Gneisenau,* and *Prinz Eugen* from France by means of a daring "Channel dash" in February 1942. Hitler had ordered this movement based on his growing understanding that his great ships should not be used as raiders upon the wide ocean. The better employment of their capabilities would be in closer-in waters, where they could operate under air cover and, especially, imperil the Anglo-American lifeline of convoys plying the rough seas of the Murmansk Route. In the operation against Convoy PQ 17, the *Tirpitz*—ill-fated *Bismarck's* sister-ship—along with the *Kriegsmarine's* two remaining pocket battleships *Lützow* and *Scheer,* and the cruiser *Hipper,* provided the strategic threat that induced the Royal Navy to disperse the convoy, allowing it to fall prey to U-boats, light surface vessels, and attack aircraft. T.V. Tuleja summed up the role of the larger warships quite well: "Although the surface force did not fire a single shot, its presence at sea dispersed the 34-ship [*sic*] convoy, simplifying the task of German aircraft and submarines."[52] *This* was the correct strategic design for the use of the surface fleet that had been built by the Germans at such cost and effort.

At the same time, Hitler and his minions came to realize that the greater war at sea would hinge on the success or failure of the U-boats. And when Hitler declared war on the United States just days after Pearl Harbor, many in the *Kriegsmarine* were pleased that they would finally be able to strike back openly and vigorously at the Americans who had been waging an undeclared war at sea against them. Doenitz reacted quickly, sending a handful of U-boats to American waters where they struck powerfully. For over three months, mayors of coastal cities who feared losses to business refused even to dim their lights at night—much less to enact full blackouts—providing ample illumination of targets for the sea wolves. Samuel Eliot Morison labeled this as America's "most reprehensible failure…. The massacre enjoyed by the U-boats along our Atlantic coast in 1942 was as much a national disaster as if saboteurs had destroyed half a dozen of our biggest war plants." Morison's final judgment on American negligence was biting: "Ships were sunk and seamen drowned in order that the citizenry might enjoy pleasure as usual."[53] Over a period of roughly six months, the U-boats sank 2.5 million tons of shipping for the loss of just six submarines. It was, as one member of the U-boat service put it, "a veritable Eldorado."[54]

The commerce war neared its crescendo in the wider Atlantic at the same time. By July 1942 the average number of U-boats at sea was about one hundred, with new boat production almost double the loss rate. While the Germans didn't have a physical barrier of island fortresses like the one the Japanese had built in the Pacific, U-boats provided a virtual barrier that the Allies would have to overcome if they were to carry the war to liberate the lands the Nazis had conquered. But, like the Japanese, the Germans were at their point of maximum expansion and had a most extensive perimeter to defend. If not an outright design flaw, this was at least a vulnerability of each of the Axis Powers: they had too much area to defend. If the Allies gained naval supremacy in the Pacific and European theaters, they would be able to strike where and when they chose. The Germans also had the major problem of the massive ground war in the East; but here, as they learned in the winter battles of early 1942, they could trade a little space—when Hitler allowed it, as he sometimes did—and then catch the attacking Russians off-balance with counterstrokes. Erich von Manstein was to become the great master of this battle doctrine.

# 5. Turning Points

On August 7, 1942, the United States Marines began the American counter-offensive in the Pacific with landings in the Eastern Solomon Islands at Tulagi and Guadalcanal. They quickly dispersed small forces the Japanese had on each island, and looked forward to finishing the airfield the enemy had been building on Guadalcanal. This was the first serious challenge to the Japanese defensive perimeter, one that had to be met with decisive force if the overall strategic design was to be upheld. And so, on the second night after the landings, Admiral Gunichi Mikawa, commander of the Japanese Eighth Fleet, assembled a task force of seven cruisers and one destroyer to attack the transports landing the American troops. An Allied force of eight cruisers and fifteen destroyers blocked his way. The fight that followed bore out the superiority of Japan's Long Lance torpedoes and the night-fighting capabilities of Imperial Navy sailors which, it turned out, mattered more in this fight than the American edge in radar. Four Allied cruisers were sunk—three American, one Australian—at no loss to the Japanese. But Mikawa, worried about his vulnerability to air attack at daylight, withdrew his force rather than risk going after the transports. Admiral Yamamoto was unhappy with the retreat; but the battle's strategic effect was felt. For the time being, Allied ships ceded the waters around Guadalcanal to the Japanese.

This left the Marines in a most tenuous situation, subjected to nightly bombardments by Japanese ships sailing down "the Slot"—the long, narrow body of water between the rough lines formed by the parallel northern and southern chains of the Solomon Islands. Transports could still come during the daylight hours, under air cover, bringing in supplies and reinforcements. But the Japanese brought men and munitions to the fight for Guadalcanal as well, a struggle that now took on the character of a "battle of the buildup." A main difference between opposing forces was that, while the Americans kept at the business of gradually adding to their forces, improving the now-named "Henderson Field" for their aircraft and gradually expanding their territorial control of the island, the Japanese took the tactical offensive with forces too small for the task at hand. This led to one disaster after another, because the Marines, due to the compactness of their positions, held off such attacks—particularly the fierce, massed "Banzai!" frontal assaults—in ways that Allied defenders of Malaya, Burma, and even in the Philippines, had not over the course of the previous eight months. Indeed, at one battle along the Tenaru River, eyewitness journalist Richard Tregaskis noted, "There was bitter fighting…. Our own casualties, I found, were only twenty-eight killed … whereas … the actual count of [enemy] bodies was 871."[1]

In another critical fight, for "Edson's Ridge"—so named for the particularly valorous Marine, Lieutenant Colonel Merritt Edson, who was later awarded the Medal of Honor—the Japanese "charged face first into the ring of flame created by Marine weapons," as Richard Frank described the battle. The aftermath: "The bodies of over 500 Japanese lay like a carpet in places, sprawled in the hideous poses of death."[2] The strategic importance of the battle was that this successful defense ensured that the Americans would maintain their hold on Henderson Field, from which the "Cactus Air Force" was to make it far too risky for the Imperial Navy to operate in the Slot during daylight hours. In this way the duel for Guadalcanal highlighted the subtle interplay of sea, air, and land forces upon which the outcome of the campaign depended.

Saburo Sakai, now a veteran fighter ace with nearly forty kills claimed to his credit,[3] had by the summer of 1942 been transferred to Japan's major base at Rabaul, over 500 miles from Guadalcanal. Nevertheless, he was ordered to fly a long-range fighter mission to the contested island, joining other Japanese squadrons headed to the fight from a few airstrips on closer-by islands. Up until this time, the Japanese Zero had far outclassed Allied fighter aircraft, including American Aircobras.

But at Guadalcanal Sakai came up against the Grumman F4F Wildcat for the first time. Stubby, not sleek like a Zero, the Wildcat's design made it both maneuverable and rugged. In dogfights, the American fighter pilots pursued tactics based on diving upon Zeros, firing in one pass, then rolling away and down. This was one way to limit the Japanese planes' reduced, but still significant, edge in maneuverability. What impressed Sakai most was the sheer toughness of the aircraft itself. In a dogfight with a Wildcat, he gained the advantage over a skilled American pilot and poured hundreds of rounds into the enemy's fighter. But, as he recalled in his war memoir, "I could not believe what I saw; the Wildcat continued flying almost as if nothing had happened. A Zero which had taken that many bullets into its vital cockpit would have been a ball of fire by now."[4] The Americans had chosen not to imitate the Japanese aircraft design, but to counter the Zero's swift, sleek elegance by creating a rugged fighter that could stay in the fight long enough to exploit the Japanese plane's vulnerability to catching ablaze when hit. As the most skilled of Japan's fighter pilots were lost to attrition, replaced by those with less and less training and battle preparation, the edge to the Americans grew substantially over time.

Something similar was starting to happen at sea, too, where the Long Lance torpedo and Japanese skill at night-fighting were eventually overcome by improving American tactics and the increasingly effective employment of radar, even in narrow seas where the Japanese sometimes sought to reduce the risk of detection by masking themselves near or behind small islands. Perhaps the most

**Japanese ace Saburo Sakai, master of the sleek Zero fighter plane (public domain, Creative Commons).**

dramatic example of the technological edge afforded by radar was in the battleship duel on the night of November 14–15—the first of the Pacific War—in which the *Washington* sank the *Kirishima*. It was a savage action that saw much damage to the American destroyers and to the battleship *South Dakota* in Rear Admiral Willis Lee's small task force. But the *Washington* more than made up for this by destroying the *Kirishima* and putting the remainder of the Japanese battle squadron on the run. And at daybreak, American warplanes decimated the transports bringing supplies and reinforcements to the hard-pressed Japanese troops on Guadalcanal. Lee had no doubts about the cause of his victory: "We … realized then and it should not be forgotten now, that our entire superiority was due almost entirely to our possession of radar."[5]

Lee was right, and in the five major naval battles around Guadalcanal—there were several smaller actions as well—the U.S. Navy gradually began to get the better of the Imperial Fleet, in large part due to the edge it enjoyed with radar. But there was another component to the informational advantage enjoyed, comprised of the network of coastwatchers the Australians had put in place after World War I. These brave observers, often operating from occupied islands, radioed their reports of Japanese naval and air movements down the Slot, providing time for warships to get ready for battle, and for the planes of the Cactus Air Force to climb to an altitude from which they could dive down on enemy fighters and bombers.[6] This information edge was much needed, given Japanese skill and determination. Ultimately, the American ship losses in the Solomons were slightly greater than the Imperial Navy's, with twenty-five sunk to the enemy's twenty-four. The U.S. Navy's loss of two fleet carriers was offset somewhat by the sinking of one Japanese light carrier and two battleships. In the air, though, the American loss of 100 aircraft of all types was far less than the more than 160 Japanese planes that were brought down, with the Wildcats beating the Zeros 60–42.[7]

All this attrition affected the Japanese far more than the Americans, given the latter's greater productive capacity that guaranteed a larger flow of new ships and planes as the war dragged on. But that lay years ahead. Perhaps more important was the fact that the Wildcat had countered the Zero effectively at Guadalcanal with an improved tactical approach ("dive and roll"). American innovation would soon see further improvement to this stubby aircraft, as well as to production of other fighter designs: Lightnings, Hellcats and, later in the war, Corsairs and Mustangs. These planes, in varied ways—from ruggedness and power to range and maneuverability—met and in some areas exceeded the Zero's capabilities. Yet Mitsubishi kept with the Zero as its primary fighter throughout the war, making only minor changes. The company's Raiden ("Thunderbolt") fighter— a short-range, high-climbing aircraft designed to attack American B-29 Superfortresses— came into limited use late in the war, but without on-board radar it proved almost entirely useless as a night-fighter when the Americans switched their B-29s away from daylight bombing during the spring of 1945. The best fighter innovation Mitsubishi did have in development—starting well before Guadalcanal—was the Reppu ("Strong Gale"), intended as the successor to the Zero. But its progress was stunted by emphasis on the Raiden. Only a few Reppu were ever produced, late in the war. Far too late.

The Guadalcanal campaign lasted six months, ending in withdrawal of the last 10,000 or so surviving Japanese troops late in January and early in February of 1943. From a design perspective, there were many lessons learned during the fighting. The most positive affirmation of Japan's pre-war design choices was to be found in the performance of the Long Lance torpedo. But the lack of radar on Imperial Navy ships began to tell quite heavily as the campaign wore on. And in the air the technical superiority of the Zero had been effectively challenged by the durable Wildcat, whose tactics—along with the early warning system provided by Coastwatcher reports—proved most vexing for even the best Japanese fighter pilots. On the ground, neither small-unit infiltration techniques nor massed *banzai* attacks worked well against determined, well-armed troops defending stable perimeters. To sum up, this campaign highlighted both technological and doctrinal difficulties with Japan's designs for battle on land, at sea, and in the air. Yet the greatest problem may have been that Guadalcanal shone a light on the most fundamental flaw in the strategic design based on creation of the island barrier chain: overextension. The perimeter envisioned, then created, was all too vulnerable to being struck at points of Allied choosing.[8]

As to Admiral Yamamoto's role in shaping Japan's wartime strategic design, his continuing use of his forces in driblets during the six months' fight for Guadalcanal can only be viewed harshly. Before the war, and through Pearl Harbor, Yamamoto was the great advocate of the *massing* of fleet forces, especially of aircraft carriers. But at Midway he dispersed his forces widely, giving the Americans the opportunity to fight on roughly even terms there and win—though some blame for Japan's defeat must certainly fall on Admiral Nagumo's shoulders for his clumsy handling of the *Kido Butai*. At Guadalcanal Yamamoto continued this pattern of strategic design error at the doctrinal level, frittering away his ships and aircraft in piecemeal attacks. Too late, he seems to have re-learned his own lesson about the need to concentrate forces with the development of his "I Operation," a series of surprise mass air attacks by hundreds of bombers and fighters. Begun just a month after the loss of Guadalcanal, these attacks hit across a wide range of targets, from the Eastern Solomons to New Guinea. Ronald Spector viewed these raids as "an impressive demonstration of how the Japanese might have used their advantage of interior lines to great effect against the widely separated, loosely coordinated commands of Halsey and MacArthur."[9]

Douglas MacArthur, who had escaped the Philippines prior to the end there, was now commanding a second, western, line of advance in the U.S.-led campaign in the Pacific. His forces in New Guinea benefited much from the diversion of Japanese troops and other resources to Guadalcanal. But the fact that he was leading one major campaign and Admiral Chester Nimitz the other, the latter coming at the Japanese from due east, gave Yamamoto a chance to strike decisively at one or the other. This is what Ronald Spector meant when describing Japan's "interior lines." Yamamoto finally realized this, coming back to the right way to use air power; but he wasn't to live to oversee Japanese efforts much longer. On April 18, 1943, on approach to the base at Buin on the island of Bougainville, his flight was intercepted and attacked by several P-38 Lockheed Lightnings. The twin-boomed fighters dealt with his Zero escorts and made short work of Yamamoto's own plane. As was the case with the Battle of the Coral Sea, Midway, and on several occasions during the Guadalcanal campaign, the Americans once again were able to benefit from information gleaned from their code-breaking efforts. Five days before the visit, one of Yamamoto's aides had radioed an itinerary to Bougainville—in just a simple variant of the standard JN-25 code[10]—a message decrypted that enabled the success of the mission to kill him.

Similarly, American code-breakers were having an increasing impact on the submarine campaign against the Japanese. For the area involved was immense, with enemy merchant ships and naval combatants ranging the seas from the Strait of Malacca in the southwest to the Aleutian Islands in the northeast. By the spring of 1943, although U.S. Navy submarines operating across this broad battlespace numbered little more than seventy, they were, as Clay Blair has concluded, "beginning to inflict serious damage on the Japanese shipping services."[11] That so relatively few American submariners were able to create much mayhem was due to the informational advantage that the "Magic" team provided them—ever more often and ever more reliably. Ronald Lewin summed up the crucial role of code-breaking in the Pacific campaign, noting that

> the area of that ocean, compared with the little inland sea of the Mediterranean or even the wider swathe of the Atlantic routinely used by convoys, is gargantuan, and the variety of islands and channels offers endless scope for alternative routing. To ensure a high rate of effective strikes against the Japanese convoys without the sure guidance of signal intelligence would therefore have involved an astronomical number of submarines to supply constant standing patrols. Even air reconnaissance, on the most lavish scale, could not have brought much alleviation.[12]

For all this growing adversity, the Japanese maintained a fundamental faith in their coding system, in part because, like the Germans, they couldn't envision the kind of high-performance computing capability that the British and Americans possessed. So they clung to a deeply inadequate design for their communications—a flaw whose costly consequences had already been felt, from the Coral Sea to Midway, and on to Guadalcanal. The very grave wounds already being inflicted by the intelligence-enabled U.S. submarine campaign were only to worsen. Then there was the killing of Admiral Yamamoto, which clearly should have alerted the Japanese to their terrible vulnerability to having their communications intercepted and then decrypted. But even the death of their leading strategic designer failed to spark the necessary introspection. And as late as the fall of 1944, the Japanese were still using the same coding system with which they began the war.

Indeed, just five weeks before the American presidential election that year, Army Chief of Staff General George C. Marshall felt impelled to send a letter to Governor Thomas Dewey, the Republican Party candidate who, Marshall learned, intended to speak publicly about the U.S. code-breaking capabilities in place since before Pearl Harbor. Dewey wanted to use this information to accuse Roosevelt of gross negligence in the matter of the surprise attack there. In his letter, Marshall urged Dewey to maintain his silence on this matter, noting that Japanese communications were "still in the codes involved in the Pearl Harbor events."[13] Publicizing the fact that these codes were being routinely broken, Marshall wrote, would have grave effects on the war effort. Dewey kept silent—and lost the election.

By the time Marshall sent his letter to Dewey in September 1944, the U.S. Navy's submarine forces had become by far the principal beneficiaries of the Magic code-breaking system. What in April of 1943 was beginning to grow into a serious threat was to metastasize quickly, with submarine attacks ultimately accounting for the sinking of nearly four-fifths of total Japanese merchant vessels and about one-third of the Imperial Navy's warships. But where the American submarine campaign in the Pacific was just beginning to shift into higher gear by the spring of 1943, German U-boats had by this phase of the war been at their peak of performance for some time, with over *one million* tons of Allied shipping sunk just in the first three months of that year.[14] The outcome of the Battle of the Atlantic—and likely of the war in Europe—was hanging in the balance.

*     *     *

Admiral Karl Doenitz was increasingly pleased with the performance of his U-boat skippers and their crews from the late summer of 1942 to the early spring of 1943. They had brought to life the strategic design for war at sea that he had been contemplating since the end of the First World War. His "wolf pack" concept had by now more than proved itself in attacks against escorted merchant ships. It even seemed that the Allied convoy tactic that had defeated the U-boats in World War I was no longer working as, of those million tons sunk in the first months of 1943, three-fourths were accounted for by ships lost *while under escort*. By this time, Doenitz had also risen to overall command of the *Kriegsmarine*, due to Hitler having lost faith in Admiral Erich Raeder in January, after learning of the failure of the *Hipper* and *Lützow*, along with half a dozen destroyers, to interdict the Allied arctic convoy JW-51 on New Year's Eve in what came to be known as the Battle of the Barents Sea. The light Allied escorts heroically fought the heavier German forces until British cruisers turned up, drove off *Hipper* and *Lützow*, and then sank the destroyer *Friedrich Eckold* with the loss of all hands.[15]

Hitler's appointment of Doenitz to command of the *Kriegsmarine* reflected his growing sense that the U-boats were now his last, best chance of winning the war at sea. But the fatal design flaw of the pre-war "Z Plan" that had, with its call for major battleship construction, prevented the more appropriate concentration on submarines, was still having its deadly effects. For even at its height in the first quarter of 1943, the U-boat service couldn't sustain more than 100 submarines at sea at any given time. And this level of presence was against the loss of 40 U-boats during those same months. By May, the losses grew even higher, thanks in part to the increasing presence of escort aircraft carriers, starting with the American *Bogue*, which came on the scene at the end of March. Correlli Barnett saw this as heralding "the beginning of a new era in convoy warfare—continuous air cover even when shore-based VLR [very long range] aircraft could not be present."[16] These aircraft, fitted with look-down radar, posed a grave threat to the U-boats. As did Allied code-breaking which, by this time, often intercepted Doenitz's messages to his deadly minions, allowing, among other things, for convoys to be rerouted so as to avoid coming under attack in the first place.[17]

The turn of the tide in the Battle of the Atlantic coincided with the reversal of Allied fortunes in the sea fight for the Mediterranean as well. But only after overcoming daunting adversity. For *Don* Borghese's naval commandos, who had inflicted grave enough damage on the British to shift the balance of power in the Middle Sea during the first half of 1942, were continuing to harass the convoys bringing supplies to the fortress of Malta. Italian torpedo boats, complemented by *Regia Marina* warships, German U-boats—one of which sank the British carrier *Eagle*—Stukas and other attack aircraft were having their innings. June 1942 was the high-water mark for the Axis in the Mediterranean, when a quite large convoy from Alexandria to Malta was forced to turn back with heavy losses, and fully two-thirds of a convoy from Gibraltar to Malta was sunk. The weakening of Malta meant that supplies could flow more easily to Rommel, who was driving hard for the Nile at this very time. But in August, yet one more try to bring succor to Malta finally succeeded—again at great cost in ships lost—when a fatally wounded tanker, the *Ohio*, was towed the last miles into the Grand Harbor.[18] Malta survived. Its refueled planes were able now to resume their attacks on Italian supply convoys headed to North Africa. Rommel was to suffer for it.

There has always been a sharp critique of Axis strategy centered on the notion that Malta should have been invaded, not just suppressed. But the high cost of the conquest of Crete in 1941, along with the growing demand for resources imposed by the Russian campaign, caused Hitler to demur. He also had little faith in the Italian Navy staying to fight for Malta if the Royal Navy came to contest an invasion of that island. General Kurt Student, the architect of the Crete invasion, recalled Hitler saying, "If the British fleet appeared on the scene, all the Italian ships would bolt for their home ports—and leave the German airborne forces stranded."[19] Thus the key alternative strategy was two-fold: to maintain a blockade of the island with Borghese's light forces, augmented by extensive minefields, and to suppress the ability of Malta-based aircraft to attack the convoys supplying the *Afrika Korps.* Rommel's chief of staff, Major General Fritz Bayerlein, put the situation quite clearly: "So long as Malta remained in British hands, the delivery of adequate supplies to our African front must be [*sic*] an impossibility

Karl Doenitz (right), with Albert Speer, faced rising U-boat losses (Creative Commons, courtesy Bundesarchiv, Bild 146III-372/CC-BY-SA 3.0, ca. 1943/1944).

unless Kesselring's Air Force was reinforced."[20] Given that the renewed German offensive in Russia during the summer of 1942 demanded full support from the *Luftwaffe,* there was little ability to increase pressure on Malta.

The revitalization of Malta's own air capabilities, now made possible by the fuel from the *Ohio* and the Spitfires flown to the island from carriers—British *and* American at this point in the war—created an absolute crisis for the *Afrika Korps,* which was stalled at El Alamein. The attacks on the Axis convoys as they traversed their roughly 600-mile routes from Italy to Benghazi—Rommel's nearest functioning port in North Africa—were grave, and came at night as well as during the day, due to Allied aircraft being able to locate Italian ships in the dark with their look-down radar. What supplies *did* eventually make it to port then had to run another 600-mile gauntlet to the front, now by truck, vulnerable all the way both to air attack and behind-the-lines British commando raids. Despite these sharp difficulties, Rommel received enough reinforcement to renew his assault on the Alamein position. He had been checked in his first rush in July 1942—Ultra decrypts played a part in giving away his plans to the British—but with fuel, new tanks, and reinforcement in the form of an elite German parachute brigade now fighting as dismounted infantry, he struck yet once again at the very end of August. By this time, Winston Churchill had replaced General Claude Auchinleck with Bernard Montgomery, a veteran of the 1940 Battle of France, who was soon to demonstrate his mastery of the set-piece battle.

This was *the* crucial moment in the North African campaign, Liddell Hart compellingly argued, "as the strength of the two sides was nearer to an even balance than it was either before or later … [Rommel] still had a possibility of victory."[21] When Auchinleck stopped the *Afrika Korps* in July, Italo-German forces were severely depleted, at the very end of their tether. Months later, when Montgomery mounted his counter-offensive in October, the odds were heavily on the Allied side. But in late August either side could have prevailed. Rommel tried his patented "right hook" maneuver that had worked so many times before, hoping that a breakthrough could then be swiftly, deeply exploited. Montgomery, having none of this, stayed on the positional defensive instead of getting into a maneuver duel with Rommel. By doing so he gave the British Desert Air Force freedom of action to strike at virtually all of the moving targets in the battle area. Realizing the very serious difficulties he was in, Rommel halted the attack after just 72 hours. Montgomery tried to cut off some of the retreating *Afrika Korps,* but his counter-stroke was repulsed with heavy losses, bringing an end to the Battle of Alam Halfa, so named after a key ridge for which the Germans had been aiming.

Seven weeks were to pass before the British Eighth Army mounted its major offensive, but it was at Alam Halfa that the *Blitzkrieg* was blunted by a methodical strategic design based on the positional defensive of ground units that created a free-wheeling arena for what Montgomery called "the tremendous power of the air arm in close cooperation with the land battle." He went on further about this action in his memoirs: "I think that this battle has never received the interest or attention that it deserves. It was a vital action, because had we lost it, we might well have lost Egypt. In winning it we paved the way for success at El Alamein and the subsequent advance to Tunisia."[22] Commenting on the various assessments of Montgomery's fine effort to conceal 8th Army's dispositions and skillful defensive use of armor, Correlli Barnett observed that "many authorities consider Alam Halfa, with its uncharacteristic features of indirectness, deception and manoeuvre, to be Montgomery's cleverest battle."[23] This is an interesting insight, especially in light of Montgomery's later battles, virtually all of them stamped with the attrition-oriented processes of bombardment and battering. All, that is, save for his over-bold plan at Arnhem, a costly defeat. But that is a tale for later. For now, Alam Halfa opened "Monty's" career in high command superbly.

For his part, Rommel too understood the profound implications of Alam Halfa, noting that "[w]ith the failure of our offensive against the British Alamein line, a new phase opened which was eventually to lead to the final collapse of our North African front." Furthermore, he understood that the "fact of British air superiority threw to the winds all the tactical rules we had hitherto applied with such success." This boded ill for the future course of the war overall, Rommel foresaw, with the new imperative being, instead of fostering skillful maneuvers, "to try to resist the enemy in field positions which had to be constructed for defense against the most modern weapons of war."[24] Rommel's conversion from master of maneuver to a designer of effective defenses can be seen from this moment forward, as he prepared for the inevitable British offensive to come. Later, as we shall see, he was to apply his defensive design genius to shoring up Hitler's Atlantic Wall—which was to be Germany's last, best hope for avoiding utter defeat. But the present task in Egypt was to craft a defensive design able to blunt the British advantages in armor (6:1 by the start of Alamein, if counting only the 200 German tanks), planes and men (nearly 3:1 in both these categories).[25]

Two weeks after Alam Halfa, Rommel went on leave to report to Mussolini and Hitler, see his family, and take a rest cure at Semmering for a liver infection and low blood pressure. His stand-in was General Georg Stumme, an excellent tank tactician and something of a diplomat, as he was able to smooth and repair the tattered relations with the Italians that resulted from Rommel's increasing gruffness with them. Stumme continued with the preparations for the coming battle according to Rommel's defensive design, which called for creation of deep minefields covered by artillery and anti-tank guns, with the armor held back for counter-attacking purposes.

By the time Montgomery opened the battle on October 23, Rommel's "devil's gardens" featured roughly half a million mines planted along the forty-mile front that ran from the Mediterranean to the untankable Qattara Depression. On the second day of battle, Stumme died of a heart attack. Rommel returned the following day, taking over the defensive side of a World-War-I–style attritional struggle. In preparing for the battle, Bernard Montgomery had shown far more than just a penchant for conducting a mindless slugging match, as he had mounted an elaborate deception to convince Rommel that the main blow would come in the south. Instead, he struck in the north. Yet even with this deception, the fight was hard and bloody; British casualties in the first five days were in excess of 10,000.

At this point there was a lull in the battle as Montgomery regrouped and planned for his next blow. He knew that, ultimately, the Axis forces, critically low on fuel and whose air cover was close to non-existent, could be worn down. The situation was due to the naval war in the Mediterranean turning in favor of the Allies, given that the demands of the Russian front drained off *Luftwaffe* aircraft, allowing the Allies a much-needed respite. This reduction in air support spelled an Axis disaster in the making—at sea and on land. As David Irving noted in his biography of Rommel, "revival of Malta and consequent harassment of his supply lines had devastated the Panzer Army's logistics."[26] Quietly, Rommel began to plan a retreat. Hitler kept him in place a few days with his infamous "victory or death" order to stand fast, but retreat was ultimately authorized, then undertaken with great skill. It was a withdrawal made necessary, even without the Alamein fight, because of the Allied landings—Operation Torch—in Morocco and Algeria on November 8, 1942. Indeed, as Robert Leckie argued, "Eighth Army should not have wasted itself in those furious frontal attacks, staining the desert sand with the blood of its men and the oil of its ruined armor."[27]

In the wake of Alamein, Rommel's view was that North Africa should now be abandoned, reducing the southern defensive perimeter of the Axis and allowing for the redeployment of the more than 70,000 veteran soldiers—German *and* Italian—who had fought so very gallantly under increasingly difficult, near-impossible conditions. As Rommel told Fritz Bayerlein, these men "could still win battles in Sicily or the South of France, could save us from total defeat."[28] Hitler and those around him were having none of this, however, preferring instead to hold on to a strategic bastion in Tunisia. The Fuehrer's view was reinforced in a meeting with Field-Marshal Kesselring, Commander-in-Chief South—one of Germany's ablest military men—on January 12, 1943, when the latter said that he was "optimistic about future developments both in Tunis and as regards the sea supply situation." The deputy chief of operations of the *Oberkommando der Wehrmacht*, General Walter Warlimont, who was in the room, noted that Kesselring's briefing "had a considerable influence on Hitler's attitude."[29] Which meant, as Andrew Roberts has put it, that "Rommel's reasonable and strategically sound requests to extricate his forces from Africa" were curtly denied.[30]

Now, fresh Axis troops flowed to North Africa and the first onrush of the Allied forces toward Tunis—which had only been briefly slowed by mild resistance from Vichy French forces—was halted. While this was going on, Rommel continued his skillful retreat, eventually making his way to Tunisia and turning to stand and fight at the so-called Mareth Line. In February, he was even able to take the offensive for five days, delivering several stinging blows to American forces in the vicinity of the Kasserine Pass. The Allied commander, General Dwight D. Eisenhower, grew quite concerned, noting that, among the many problems with the deployment of the inexperienced American troops, "by far the most serious defect was the fact that the U.S. 1st Armored Division was still not properly concentrated to permit its employment as a unit."[31] But Rommel lacked the resources and logistical support to continue his offensive, and the initiative passed permanently to the Allies, with Eisenhower's forces pressing from the west, Montgomery pushing north once he penetrated the Mareth position. Rommel continued to argue for evacuation; Hitler sacked him for his "defeatism." Fighting raged on until early May, when nearly a quarter million German and Italian troops surrendered. It was a catastrophe on the scale of the loss of the 6th Army at Stalingrad just a few months earlier—another failure of strategic design.

*    *    *

Where the surrender in Tunisia was an unmitigated disaster, the German sacrifice at Stalingrad may have planted the seeds of recovery on the Eastern Front. Thanks to the 6th Army holding on until early February of 1943—it had first arrived at the city's edge in mid–August the previous year—a major new offensive by Georgi Zhukov was delayed. Zhukov aimed at trapping even larger German forces in the south, an entire army group that had been driving to the Caucasus, and beyond to the oilfields of southern Russia. The original German "Blue" operational plan had called for taking Stalingrad to provide cover for the southern offensive of Army Group A. In the event, it was only *keeping* the 6th Army at Stalingrad, even after its being surrounded by Zhukov's November counter-offensive, that averted a greater catastrophe. Erich von Manstein, perhaps the finest of the *Heer*'s strategists and the man Hitler called upon to save the situation, put the matter simply: "Every extra day Sixth Army could continue to tie down the enemy forces surrounding it was vital as far as the fate of the entire Eastern Front was concerned."[32]

Of the quarter-million troops Germany committed to the battle for Stalingrad, more than 100,000 died during the fighting, 90,000 went into captivity, the remainder were wounded soldiers evacuated while doing so was still possible. Soviet casualties exceeded 1,000,000—grievous losses, even when considering the Russians' vast pool of manpower.[33] The successful escape of Army Group A and the stabilization of the German defensive lines soon followed, but it must still be acknowledged that Stalingrad was a bitter Axis defeat. The most dominant explanations for the debacle focus on Adolf Hitler's foolishness in splitting the summer 1942 offensive into two thrusts and his stubborn intransigence about holding Stalingrad rather than allowing the retreat of the 6th Army. Prior to Zhukov's offensive, Franz Halder, the Chief of the Army General Staff until September 1942, had continually warned Hitler about the growing risk of a Russian counterattack; but his assessments were rejected. Then, once the Red Army surrounded the Germans in Stalingrad, Halder's successor Kurt Zeitzler pressed the Fuehrer to allow 6th Army to break out as, in his view, "it would certainly have got through…. Thus the final catastrophe would have been avoided."[34] But as Manstein was well aware, such a retreat would have led to an even greater catastrophe.

As one looks at the correlation of forces on both sides during the summer of 1942, it appears that the German decision to mount the ambitious "Blue" plan, undertaken with over fifty divisions, made good sense. But there were two key strategic design flaws. The first, overextension of the front and thinning out of *Axis* forces—Italian, Romanian and other allied troops formed a significant part of Blue—is well known, an object of much critical attention. Even so, the sheer number of Axis ground units and air squadrons devoted to the fight suggests anything but a catastrophe in the making. That is, until one considers the other serious flaw, which has to do with organizational design. Far less attention is given to the importance of the structural shift in German field units at this point on the Eastern Front, which saw more units created, but each with fewer troops and tanks. The impetus behind this redesign of the *Heer* was the advice Hitler received from his top generals that taking the offensive again in the East would require an addition of nearly a million fresh soldiers. But when Hitler went to his Minister of Armaments, Albert Speer—whose career had been launched as the Fuehrer's personal architect—for the manpower, the latter told him this was simply not possible if war production were to be kept up. For Hitler, this was a vexing dilemma that threatened his ability to hold the initiative at this critical point in the Russian campaign.

Speer went so far as to argue against sending off even a small number of his workers to the military at this point because, as he put it, "the war economy was short far more than one million workers."[35] As Speer did not yet have a sufficient flow of foreign laborers—more accurately described as slaves—much less skilled ones from the conquered countries, it seemed as if the only solution available was to redesign the field units themselves. So began the process of weakening the very structures that had enlivened the *Blitzkrieg* in the first place. Infantry divisions now saw their traditional nine battalions cut to seven, and the companies that comprised them were drawn down from 180 to 80 men. As to panzer divisions, two were added, but their numbers of tanks fell in uneven ways, depending on their rates of attrition. By the time of Operation Blue, Liddell Hart observed, "barely half of the twenty existing armored divisions were brought up to strength in tanks."[36] Compounding the problem of having more but weaker units on an ever-lengthening frontage was the decision to shift several divisions to the West, an apparent reaction to growing worries that an invasion of northern France was imminent. The Allied raid at Dieppe in August 1942, though bloodily repulsed, underscored the need to prepare for full-scale assault in the West.

Even with the withdrawal of some forces, including excellent ones like the *Grossdeutschland* Division, and the scaling-down of those units that remained in the East, Manstein was able to take quite full advantage of the blessing of time provided by the sacrifice of the 6th Army. First, he oversaw the successful extrication of Army Group A from the Caucasus, then used some of its forces to build a mobile reserve. Next, he developed a concept of defensive operations that not only blunted Zhukov's post–Stalingrad offensive, but also recaptured some ground that had been lost—including Kharkov, the second largest city of the Ukraine—while inflicting sharp new losses on the Russians. The method he employed was to exploit the Soviets' imitation of German *Blitzkrieg* methods by allowing their armor to penetrate, sealing off the front behind them with infantry then attacking the advancing Russian tank forces in flank with his own panzers. By these means, during a period of counter-strokes from February 19, 1943, to mid–March,

Hitler thanking Manstein (center) for stabilizing the Eastern Front (Creative Commons, courtesy Bundesarchiv, Bild 146III-372/CC-BY-SA 3.0, ca. 1943/1944 Bundesarchiv_Bild_146–1995–041–23A/CC-BY-SA 3.0, Photographer Heinrich Hoffmann, 10 March 1943).

Manstein defeated the enemy offensive and seized the initiative. Field-Marshal Lord Carver, in his assessment of Manstein, highly lauded his "resolution and skill in handling his forces … [and] his belief in the need to pursue a mobile strategy … so that a reserve could be formed for offensive use."[37]

Manstein was not to be alone in the effort to restore the war in the East to some sort of equilibrium. After the surrender of the 6th Army at Stalingrad, Hitler reached out once again to Guderian, bringing him back after more than a year out of the action as his Inspector-General of Armored Troops in February—just as Manstein's counter-attacks were beginning to bear fruit. Guderian's formal "assignment of duties" was wide-ranging and included an amazing catch-all that empowered him "to give instructions on matters with which he is concerned to all branches of the staffs of the Army. All branches are ordered to supply the Inspector-General of Armored Troops with *any* assistance that he may require."[38] Further buttressing the effort to revitalize the panzers was Hitler's January 22 memorandum, "To All Those Engaged in Tank Production," which gave broad powers to Albert Speer to step up both quality and output. The heavy new Tiger tank, with its thicker armor and "88" gun, the medium Panther, and the up-armoring of the work-horse Panzer IV were to be emphasized. Now, with Manstein overseeing a skillful strategic defensive—peppered with tactical offensive counter-strokes—Guderian shepherding the renewal of the panzer forces, and Speer guiding tank production, fresh hope arose for the continued war against the Russians.

These rising German hopes coincided with a deepening Russian concern about the future of the struggle on the Eastern Front. So much so that the possibility of a negotiated peace was explored during the spring of 1943. Despite the "unconditional surrender" declaration made by Franklin Delano Roosevelt at the Casablanca Conference in January 1943—which was quickly affirmed by Winston Churchill—the Russians' fears of being abandoned by the West and the alarming new turn of the war brought about by Manstein and the seemingly revitalized German field forces led Moscow to consider an armistice. As Gerhard Weinberg has observed, in addition to the million-plus killed in action or wounded in the bitter fight for Stalingrad, Manstein's masterful counter-strokes in February and March "exacted an enormous further toll in casualties ... [and] ended in a very serious setback at the front.... It is from this perspective that one should, I believe, view the soundings for a separate peace with Germany."[39] Liddell Hart, in talks with many Germans who had been involved in or aware of these negotiations, noted that they failed to achieve peace only because of the German desire to hold on to Ukraine, while Moscow demanded a return to the borders of June 1941.[40] Roosevelt's "unconditional surrender" call did *not* bind Stalin.

Actually, in some important respects, the declaration made at the Casablanca conference backfired, as Nazi Propaganda Minister Joseph Goebbels took it as an opportunity to declare "total war," which not only shored up civilian morale but gave German soldiers, sailors and airmen a sense of grim resolve to keep up the fight to the end. J.F.C. Fuller was scathing in his criticism of the Allies' "unconditional surrender" demand:

> What did these two words imply? First, that because no great power could with dignity or honor to itself, its history, its people and their posterity comply with them, the war must be fought to the point of annihilation.... Secondly, once victory had been won, the balance of power within Europe and between European nations would be irrevocably smashed. Russia would be left the greatest military power in Europe ... [replacing] Nazi tyranny by an even more barbaric despotism.[41]

Yet at the very moment when the Russians were so willing to contemplate breaking from their Western partners, Hitler saw, in Manstein's brilliant field successes and Guderian's revitalization of the panzers, what Weinberg has described as "the opportunity to shake off the doubts created by the Stalingrad disaster.... He and a large number of his military advisors simply blamed the great defeat on the failings of their allies—ignoring the central German role in the catastrophic 1942 campaign."[42]

The dispute over possession of Ukraine—the key sticking point in negotiations conducted in German-held Soviet territory[43] by the foreign ministers of the two sides, Joachim von Ribbentrop and Vyacheslav Molotov—ended the last chance for a separate peace between Germany and Russia. The war on the Eastern Front was destined to drag on, and in the summer of 1943 the Germans, with a favorable balance of forces, new tanks and the initiative, were to gamble once more on a major offensive. As to Ukraine and the other portions of the Soviet Union now under German control, due to the brutality with which the occupation was conducted they were to see a strong uptick in partisan operations that began to have serious consequences for the *Heer*'s overstretched logistical systems. Given the deleterious effects on the Eastern Front of partisan operations, and the growing pressure on Germany from the West, it would seem that, as a matter of grand strategic design, this was precisely the time at which negotiating the Russians out of the fight would have had a profoundly beneficial impact on the overall course of the war. But once again, Nazi ideology trumped sound strategy.

The only serious objection to German policy toward captive peoples in the East was raised by Dr. Otto Bräutigam. He was a senior official in the Ministry for the Occupied Eastern Territories. In a scathing thirteen-page critique dated October 25, 1942, Bräutigam began by noting that, from quite early on, the Russians "found out that for Germany the slogan 'Liberation from Bolshevism' was only a pretext to enslave the Eastern peoples." He went on to decry the fact that "hundreds of thousands of Russian prisoners of war have died of hunger or cold in our camps," and noted further that "[i]n the prevailing limitless abuse of the Slavic humanity, 'recruiting' methods were used which probably have their origin only in the blackest periods of the slave traffic." Bräutigam continued in a fatalistic tone: "Our policy has forced both Bolshevists and Russian nationalists into a common front against us. The Russian fights today with exceptional bravery and self-sacrifice for nothing more or less than recognition of his human dignity."[44] He concluded by calling for a complete change in German occupation policy along far more humane lines—a clear sign that he saw the importance of the social dimension of strategic design. But Dr. Bräutigam's views were ignored by his superiors in the Ministry.

The flaw here is at the level of design that John Heskett categorizes as having to do with a national social identity. This manifests itself in the "deliberate attempt by ... nations to create a particular image and meaning intended to shape, even pre-empt, what others perceive and understand."[45] In the case of the Germans, Nazism was clearly a very sharp divergence from the traditions of a country steeped in the ideas about ethical statecraft that Frederick the Great articulated in his critique of Machiavelli, that Kant elucidated in his essay "Eternal Peace," and that even Otto von Bismarck, the "Iron Chancellor," espoused in his decades-long devotion to European peace to be ensured by a balance of power abroad and tolerant, generous social policies at home, such as workers' compensation insurance and old-age pensions. Nazism, with its notions of racial superiority, exclusivity, and aggrieved entitlement, was an attempt to reroute the currents of Germany's history and culture by means of authoritarianism and relentless propaganda campaigns at home and ever-increasing aggression abroad. To be sure, Dr. Goebbels and his minions were experts at social design, and made much progress in their efforts to "rebrand" Germany. But there were many who remained faithful to the older ideal of their country, resisting such change.[46]

There were some Germans who were especially repelled by excesses in the East, where they saw, in the twin evils of the *Einsatzgruppen* death squads and the harsh treatment of the Russians in the occupied zones, good reason to form an opposition to the Hitler regime—and to take action. And while those who joined this internal resistance, or at least sympathized with it, came from elite civilian and military circles, it was in the armed forces that the most serious efforts to terminate Nazi rule flourished. Such views in the military had been evident long before the overall course of the war began to turn against Germany, driven by abhorrence to Nazi ideology and social goals, and fear that Hitler's hyper-aggressive foreign policy was, eventually, going to lead to disaster. Thus, there were incipient plots against Hitler in 1938 (the "Oster Conspiracy"), right before the invasion of Poland (the so-called "Halder Plot") and again prior to the attack on France and the Low Countries (the "Zossen Conspiracy").[47] Too few in the military were willing to act in opposition to the Nazis at these points, though, given the reasonable grievances sparked by the Versailles Treaty and the early run of victories.

But by March 1943, in the wake of the Stalingrad disaster and of Manstein's amazing "save" on the Eastern Front, a major assassination plot had gotten under way. The *Abwehr,* German military intelligence—headed by Admiral Wilhelm Canaris who opposed Hitler, and replete with resisters—passed the plotters a British-made time bomb retrieved from an Allied airdrop intended for the French Resistance. It was successfully planted on the plane Hitler used for a trip to and from the headquarters of Army Group Center on the Russian Front. But its detonator failed, and so did "Operation Flash." This unlucky break slowed the Opposition, but the Allied demand for unconditional surrender a few months earlier was causing hesitation as well. Hans Gisevius, who had traveled to Switzerland at this time to meet secretly with American spymaster Allen Dulles, noted in his memoir "the grave psychological effect it [the demand for unconditional surrender] was to have upon many groups within the Opposition."[48] This point struck William L. Shirer, too, who wrote of "these German resistance leaders who were so insistent on getting a favorable peace agreement."[49] But their reluctance simply to surrender is most understandable, given that, especially in the wake of the Manstein-led recovery in the East, the war was far from lost militarily at this point.

From the point of view of the social dimension of design, and how it played out strategically, there were two major flaws. The first had to do with the fact that Nazi ideology called for subjugation, and to some extent the elimination, of conquered peoples in the East—many who would have supported the war against the Soviets if treated well. But ideology trumped strategy, and widespread resistance arose. In addition to this curious social design flaw, self-inflicted by the Germans, ultimate failure of their efforts to dispose of Hitler was due less to bad luck—a faulty detonator—and more to the unwillingness of the German resistance simply to surrender without any terms. Ironically, the Allied demand for unconditional surrender actually shored up the Germans' fighting spirit. Oddly enough, the aerial bombing campaign that was ramping up during the period from the autumn of 1942 to the spring of 1943—and causing growing casualties among German civilians—was also having the effect of reinforcing the popular will to continue the struggle. So, it seems that the Allies were inadvertently pursuing diplomatic and military strategies that were actually having the unintended consequence of lengthening the war—and making it ever bloodier. For the Germans were disinclined to surrender without being granted terms, and the *Luftwaffe* was showing its ability to make the British and American air forces pay a heavy price for the bombing of Germany.

*   *   *

Sir Arthur Harris, Britain's most aggressive true believer in victory through air power, took over as head of the RAF's Bomber Command in February 1942. For all his zealotry, though, he understood that daylight bombing was too costly an enterprise, given the strength of German air defenses. The Me 109 had now been joined by the Focke-Wulf 190, and both fighter aircraft types were showing themselves to be highly effective in a more strategically defensive role. So Harris switched to night bombing, which kept his forces safer from fighter interception. And, true to his beliefs, he shifted from what had become a norm of individual and small-group raids distributed over wide areas to massive attacks on single target areas. He did this in part due to faith in the effects of massive destruction, but also because General Josef Kammhuber, his principal opponent, had created a defensive line of "cells," covered by ground radars, in which German nightfighters orbited. Once detected, enemy bombers were illuminated by a network of searchlights, making them easy prey for fighters. Later on, German fighters had airborne radar. But for now, Kammhuber's system worked well against small raids.

The success of the Kammhuber Line only confirmed to Harris the need to overwhelm it with the largest numbers of bombers he could muster. Three months after he took command, in May 1942, Harris gathered 1,000 aircraft for a massive raid on Cologne.

Kammhuber's system as originally designed could not cope with a focused attack on such a scale, and only 36 enemy bombers were shot down. But by June, in the next attack by 1,000 planes, this time on Bremen, 49 were shot down—a one-third increase in defensive effectiveness, thanks to flying greater numbers of night-fighters in designated cells, better intelligence about the bomber streams, and improved ground control. Even with these upgrades, the defenses were not to reach a point of forcing the RAF to give up night-bombing. But bombing this way was highly inaccurate—on average only a third of aircraft were able to drop their loads within three miles of aim points.[50] Instead, principal effects were visited upon German civilians who, Harris believed, would crumple under such terror. The Germans did not. Instead, the attacks kindled a rage against the enemy, and steadfast willingness to keep on supporting the war effort. Nevertheless, Harris persisted over the summer and fall of 1942, and in March 1943 opened an offensive focused on German industrial cities.

Harris's first major arms industry target aimed at the Krupp complex in the heart of the city of Essen in the Ruhr. Here only about 150 of an attack force of over 420 bombers dropped their payloads within three miles of the Krupp buildings.[51] German civilians were the principal victims. In April the loss rate in the mass raid over Pilsen exceeded 10 percent of the bomber force. Given the inaccuracy of the bombing, and Albert Speer's increasing creativity in decentralizing German war production wherever possible, Sir Arthur Harris simply reverted to the psychological goal of breaking the will of the enemy with "area attacks" that burnt out city after city. By June, the cities of Düsseldorf, Duisburg, Wuppertal, Bochum, Oberhausen and others were devastated—all this happened while German war production continued to increase. Only the American-led effort to strike more accurately, during the day, opened up the prospect of doing serious damage to key German war industries. And early indications were that the U.S. Army Air Forces would be able to conduct daylight bombing successfully, for on April 17, 1943, the American raid on Bremen was completed with only slight loss. This was largely due to the German fighters still being too widely distributed—under the Kammhuber concept—to muster more than two dozen interceptors to confront the daytime raiders, who in this case were escorted by P-38s.

Another problem for German air defenses was that the Me 109s and Fw 190s were in high demand by far-flung front-line forces, which kept the numbers available for defense of the Reich itself limited. To some extent, though, this problem was solved by the ingenuity of Albert Speer and Erhard Milch—the latter was Udet's successor—who raised fighter production to nearly a thousand per month during 1943, slightly more than half of the total aircraft being manufactured. American losses were soon to increase, as we shall see in the next chapter, to unacceptably high levels. The danger was clearly antic-ipated by General Ira Eaker, commander of the American 8th Air Force, who in the spring of 1943 identified the sites where German fighters were being produced as his key target. He lobbied for this targeting priority with his own superiors, saying that "if the growth of the German fighter strength is not arrested quickly, it may become literally impossible to carry out the destruction planned."[52] In the event, German fighter produc-tion was *not* "arrested quickly," and the American strategic design based on daylight bombing was to be put to the severest of tests. Indeed, in the coming months over the summer of 1943, German air defenses grew quite a bit stronger, as the *Luftwaffe* was able to muster fighters in the hundreds now to meet any massed daylight raid, inflicting loss rates on the attackers between 15–20 percent.

But from a design perspective, Goering and Milch had some serious choices to make. Should they emphasize continued production of the Me 109 and the Fw 190 with incremental upgrades to armament and the power of their engines? After all, both fighters were still quite capable of taking on Allied bombers and fighters on roughly even terms. Or should they place a big bet on the Me 209, the intended successor to the 109—though not to be confused with the first 209 design, which Willy Messerschmitt had come up with in the late 1930s strictly as an air racer. Last, there was the possibility of moving beyond piston-engine-driven fighter aircraft to jets, propelled by turbines compressing air in a chamber, injecting fuel into it and then igniting the mixture whose combustion created a forceful flow directed out through nozzles, propelling the plane forward. There was interest among scientists in jet propulsion as early as 1935, when the Volta Conference in Italy was focused on the subject. And in 1937 a young German physicist/engineer, Hans Joachim Pabst von Ohain, was able to produce a functioning turbojet engine in Ernst Heinkel's research and design laboratory. There were still many bugs to be worked out—high-volume fuel pumps rugged enough for jet propulsion were difficult to make—but by 1939 Heinkel was ready to move on to building an airframe for the jet engine. Which he then did.[53]

Within weeks of the conclusion of the Polish campaign in the fall of 1939 Heinkel had a functioning jet aircraft, the He 178, which he was able to demonstrate to Ernst Udet and Erhard Milch. Both were of a mind that the war would soon be over, and that this was not the time to award a contract for such a radically new kind of warplane. And just a few months later, in February 1940, these senior leaders recommended to Goering and Hitler the near-to-consensus view in the Technical Office to cease development "on all projects that have not reached the production stage within a year."[54] This was an exceptionally short-sighted decision, focusing on existing aircraft designs when it was entirely possible that a much longer war loomed ahead. And even if the conflict was to be short and swift, there was little reason to forgo development of the next generation of combat aircraft during the envisioned period of peace—which for the Nazis would simply have been an interlude between the end of one war and the launching of the next. Why wouldn't they want the most advanced warplane at the ready for the next time around? This seems to be one of those instances in which designers—in this case "strategic designers"—are unwilling to go well beyond their existing comfort zones, venturing into uncharted territory. Ernst Udet, in particular, bore much of the blame for this failure of vision.

Willy Messerschmitt doggedly pursued development of the jet (Creative Commons, courtesy Bundesarchiv, Bild 146–1969–169–19/CC-BY-SA 3.0, 1958).

That said, Heinkel continued to do research on a smaller scale, and other manufacturers got interested in jets as well—Willy Messerschmitt in particular. His jet, the Me 262, had its initial flight in the summer of 1942, but a crash in August set him back, and seemed to confirm to Milch and the other skeptics that their intention to remain focused on Me 109 and Fw 190 production was correct. Messerschmitt was undeterred by the development ban still in force and, on May 22, 1943, he was ready to demonstrate the Me 262 again. This time it was flown by the *Luftwaffe*'s General of Fighters, Adolf Galland, who was one of Germany's leading aces until his accession to a position of higher command. Galland was amazed by the jet's speed, about 520 mph, which was over a hundred miles per hour faster than any other aircraft in use by either side in the war. He was also deeply impressed by its smoothness in flight and ease of handling. When asked about the plane's performance after this test, Galland simply said, "It was as though angels were pushing." In a telegram Galland sent to Milch right after the flight he was less poetic, but just as enthusiastic: "The aircraft 262 is a very great hit. It will guarantee us an unbelievable advantage in ops…. This aircraft opens up completely new tactical possibilities."[55]

*     *     *

For the Germans, May 1943 was a time of mixed strategic appreciations. North Africa had been lost and Doenitz's U-boats were being mauled in the Battle of the Atlantic. But prospects for the defense of Italy were good, and the air defenses of the Reich were steadily improving. If the Me 262 were brought into major production, the air war might even turn in Germany's favor. As to the Eastern Front, the situation had been more than stabilized after Stalingrad; the correlation of forces, so neatly restored by Manstein's punishing counter-blows against the Red Army, now offered the possibility that the Germans might even resume the strategic offensive. And while Rommel had been somewhat shunted aside, having been dismissed from command in North Africa in the wake of the Kasserine battle due to what Hitler called his "defeatism" about prospects there, Guderian had been brought back in a position of authority to help rebuild the panzer forces with newly designed tanks and self-propelled guns. Another important redesign was of the Stuka, armed in the spring of 1943 with guns under its inverted gull wings so that it could better serve in an anti-tank role.

Still, there were fundamental strategic design flaws that dimmed the Nazis' prospects—beginning with the naval situation. The failure to focus on building submarines in the pre-war period meant that too few were at sea now, and too little progress had been made in advanced U-boat designs able to counter the Allies' improvements in detection and tracking. Of the large group of surface warships built, some had been squandered as individual raiders, while the others had not been put in proper position to interdict the Arctic convoys until Hitler ordered a major redeployment to Norway early in 1942. From there they were able to participate, along with the U-boats and attack aircraft, in an often-successful running fight in northern waters. But overall, the naval situation was poor because, as the summer of 1943 neared, the Allies could use their command of the sea to strike at a point, or points, of their choosing along the vast coastlines of Axis-controlled Europe. The great design challenge for Germany and Italy now was going to be to craft an ability to defeat amphibious landings. The repulse of the August 1942 raid at Dieppe did not relieve the Germans of their worries, and Hitler and his minions began, in its wake, a more serious attempt to fortify the coast from the northern border of Spain to the Netherlands—a strategic design that would come to be called *Festung Europa*.

Another questionable design arose out of the German decision to solve the problem of having insufficient infantry and armored divisions by *reducing the size* of their battalions and regiments, and of the number of tanks. This move gave the Germans more "units of action," more pins to stick on situation maps, but it created false confidence in their offensive capabilities. While these smaller units were supple enough to prevail in movement battles, such as those Guderian envisioned and Manstein had been carrying out on the strategic defensive—a posture that still left much room for tactically offensive counter-strokes—the higher attrition that came with major offensives against prepared defenders would run down these new smaller formations quickly. German organizational redesign would only make sense if the proper doctrine—strategic defensive, with tactical counter-strokes—were to be followed. Instead, as we shall see, in the summer of 1943 the panzers would try to replicate their previous *Blitzkrieg* successes.

Yet another strategic design flaw that bedeviled the Germans was their complacency about information security. Blind belief in the efficacy of the Enigma machine gave the Allies an amazing edge in the war, one that extended from the Battle of the Atlantic to the Eastern Front—intelligence gleaned from Ultra was shared with the Russians, protected by a "legend" that high-level defectors among the Germans were passing this information.

In naval affairs, the German design flaw was largely technological. In terms of land warfare, the problem had to do with organizational redesign that only made sense if a mobile strategic defensive doctrine were adopted. In the air, it was time to de-emphasize bombers and instead focus on fighters for the defense of the homeland, as well as forces in the field. And in the information realm, a willingness to accept that Enigma could be cracked was needed. But perhaps the most serious design flaw, now quite evident, was at the social level, where brutal German policies toward people in the occupied territories kindled broad, determined resistance. This was true throughout the Nazi imperium, but was of particular importance in the East. There the people, from the Baltic countries to the Ukraine, were poised to join in or to actively support the fight against the Soviets. But Nazi ideology, driven by mad racial theories, trumped good strategy. The mistreatment of millions of innocents, and the murder of millions more—Jews and others—should be seen as both a terrible crime against humanity and a fatally flawed strategic design. Some, like Dr. Otto Bräutigam, saw this evil for what it was and objected. But he was ignored. Others, including many in German civil society and in the military, identified the proper strategy for the situation: overthrow the Nazis and negotiate peace. They failed early, but kept trying.

In Italy, defeat in North Africa as well as in the battle for control of the Mediterranean had left the Mussolini regime in the most precarious of positions. And King Victor Emmanuel—the House of Savoy still formally ruled Italy—backed by major factions of the people, as well as business and religious leaders, was by the spring of 1943 readying to depose the dictator. How had this come to pass from the heady days in the late summer of 1942 when Italian land forces were knocking at the gates of Cairo, and the *Regia Marina* was holding its own—thanks in large part to Borghese's "sea devils"—in the fighting against the Royal Navy? The answer, in the simplest terms, goes back to flawed design choices made before the war. With regard to air power, Italo Balbo, for all his vision, made the grievous mistake of believing that biplane fighter aircraft could serve well in the coming war. The Italians did pursue development of more advanced monoplane fighters—like the FIAT G 55, the twin-engine Ro 58, and the Macchi C 200—but none were produced *en masse* or available in time to sway the course of the war in this theater. And air power was the absolute key here, as surface fleets could not operate safely without an "umbrella." Both sides had learned this, the Royal Navy much to its chagrin while the *Luftwaffe* was supporting the Italians. But when the German airmen were called away to Russia, the Italians were helpless. In the air. At sea. And on land.

As for the Japanese, their strategic designs were at risk of coming completely undone at this point. The six-month fight for Guadalcanal had seen Admiral Yamamoto repeatedly violate his own doctrinal design that called for using naval and air forces in massed attacks. Instead they were used in driblets in this campaign. Too late, Yamamoto came to realize that he had to mass as much force as possible in his blows. His "I Operation," that employed large numbers of aircraft in sequential attacks aimed at single target areas at a time, was very effective. One can speculate that this return to his own doctrinal concepts would have characterized future operations, allowing exploitation of the widely separated, hardly mutually supporting, efforts of Chester Nimitz and Douglas MacArthur. But this was not to be, given Japanese complacency—like the Germans—about the security of its coded communications. The American Magic made possible the killing of Yamamoto, and helped U.S. submarine forces locate and inflict increasingly debilitating losses on Japan's merchant fleets. At this time, the Japanese had still not developed an overall design for protecting these vulnerable yet vital ships. As to Japanese land forces, they were now largely bogged down in China and Burma. General Yamashita, the one remaining strategic designer of stature, was still somewhat exiled in Manchuria. Troubles were clearly coming the Empire's way—and to *all* the members of the Axis.

# 6. *The Brink of Catastrophe*

On June 5, 1943, Admiral Isoroku Yamamoto's formal state funeral was held near the Imperial Palace in Tokyo. His death had been kept secret for over a month—out of concern over the damaging effects on Japanese morale when word of this grievous loss got out—but now his passing was being observed in a most public national ceremony. Enormous crowds lined the roads along which his funeral procession passed, and over three million people showed up at or at least near the Tama Cemetery. There half his ashes—the other half were sent to Nagaoka to lie next to his adoptive father's grave—were buried beside those of Admiral Togo, hero of Japan's great victory over the Russian navy at Tsushima in 1905—where Yamamoto had first served in a major naval battle.[1] But all this posthumous honoring, including Emperor Hirohito's granting of the Grand Order of the Chrysanthemum, could not disguise the fact that, as Samuel Eliot Morison summed up the effects of the loss of this great hero on the Japanese, "this was equivalent to a major defeat, since there was 'only one Yamamoto.'"[2] Events soon to unfold across the vast sweep of Japan's defensive perimeter in the Pacific were to bear out the painful truth that the loss of Yamamoto was indeed grievous.

In the Solomons, the end of the Guadalcanal campaign marked the starting point for preparations for an American offensive aimed at advancing up the chain, perhaps by leapfrogging past some Japanese holdings, leaving them isolated—a process actually begun up in the Aleutians when the Navy swept past Kiska, striking instead much farther west at the Japanese on Attu. Thus "the Slot" continued to be the scene of bitter, hard-fought naval actions in which cruisers and destroyers were the principal participants. Japanese aims were to send supplies and reinforcements to their garrisons on islands they still held in this area via a continuation of something like the so-called "Tokyo Express" that had kept their forces in the Guadalcanal fight for so long. The U.S. Navy worked very hard at interdicting this lifeline, and in preparing for the amphibious landings to come. And at the very end of June the situation had matured sufficiently to allow troop landings on two islands in the New Georgia group, Rendova and Vangunu, posing grave threats to the Japanese forces on Munda and Kolombangara. The Imperial Navy rose to the challenge, though, with renewed runs of the "Express" and in repeated actions with U.S. and other Allied vessels. On the night of the 12th of July in the Kula Gulf, for example, one Japanese cruiser and five destroyers were able to outfight an Allied group of three cruisers and ten destroyers. Once again, Japan's better torpedoes—and tactics for their use—shone through.

Yet even this victory carried a drop of poison, as the cruiser *Jintsu* had foolishly turned on its searchlights—the Japanese were still operating almost completely without radar—quickly falling victim to massed enemy fire. The ensuing heroics of the Japanese crews of the five destroyers still engaged led to a resounding tactical victory over far superior forces, but the longer-term strategic consequences were ominous. The legendary Japanese destroyer skipper Tameichi Hara summed up this action in the Kula Gulf as one in which "the loss of that one cruiser was more costly to Japan than were the casualties *Yukikaze* and her colleagues inflicted on three cruisers and three destroyers of the Allies."[3] More troubling was the fact that the Americans had learned enough from these actions to shift the concept of operations for their own destroyers. It had taken a year—from the outset of the fighting for Guadalcanal to the first week of August 1943—for the U.S. Navy to free its destroyers from duty at the van and rear of the cruisers' line of battle. Now they were allowed to imitate the Japanese by making independent torpedo attacks. And in the Vella Gulf on the night of August 6–7, six American destroyers took on four Japanese counterparts, sinking three with no loss to themselves. Morison called this "one of the neatest victories of the war."[4]

The larger problem for the Japanese in this area of operations was that they were once again being sucked into an attritional struggle in which, even when they performed better tactically—at the margin—they were still being ground down, slowly but inexorably. The loss of destroyers in particular was going to have deleterious effects on the campaign against the growing submarine threat to the *marus,* as the convoys in which these merchant ships moved became less and less protected. In the air, the Zero had lost its early advantages as new American plane types appeared. Now Japanese fighter pilots had to engage an enemy on more equal terms—often at a disadvantage when one considers the "information edge" the Americans had, thanks to the excellent early warning system provided by the coastwatcher network in the Solomons and the Magic code-breaking capability. These advantages at sea, in the air, and in the realm of intelligence combined to support gains in both the Solomons as well as in MacArthur's area of responsibility further west. Japanese troops fought doggedly, but gave way slowly in the Solomons, and were forced back repeatedly by MacArthur's forces. And on Christmas Day 1943, the Allies completed the occupation of Bougainville, by which time much of northeastern New Guinea had been taken. On Boxing Day, they landed at Arawe in New Britain. The great Japanese base at Rabaul now came under sustained aerial attack from both the southeast and southwest.

As to the other major line of advance against the Japanese defensive perimeter in the wider Pacific—Admiral Nimitz's first major target was to be Tarawa in the Gilbert Islands—in this area too the Imperial Navy chose to engage with just lighter forces, and in relatively small numbers. The result was more attrition and the sweeping-away of these obstructions to American advances. At the doctrinal level of strategic design, the Japanese failed to seize upon Yamamoto's fundamental admonition to concentrate forces for decisive blows—as he had in the six months after Pearl Harbor, and was in the process of attempting with his "I Operation" before his death. Instead, senior Japanese naval leaders chose to disperse their ships and submarines widely, trying to slow the enemy advance in all areas, rather than massing the fleet against one or the other of the Allies' axes of advance. Indeed, the departure from Yamamoto's strategic design was stark. Captain Andrieu d'Albas, a French naval officer with long experience in Japan, summed up the stodgy reluctance of the Imperial Navy to concentrate to strike a major blow at the enemy this way: "After the battle of the Santa Cruz Islands [a hard-fought Japanese victory in the Solomons] on October 26, 1942, the principal units of the Japanese fleet do not actively appear on the scene until the Battle of the Philippine Sea."[5] This was a lapse of *nearly two years*.

The Japanese Army was left largely to its own devices in the island fighting during this period. There were some evacuations, like the one at the end of the Guadalcanal campaign, and from other islands up the Solomons chain. And in late July, under cover of fog, the Imperial Navy managed the skillful extraction of several thousand Japanese troops from Kiska in the Aleutian Islands, which the Americans had leapfrogged by striking at Attu in May. The Attu battle had been bloody. A Japanese garrison of about 2,500 fought almost to the last man—only 28 were alive to be captured at the end—inflicting 3,000 casualties on the invasion force of 15,000. Ronald Spector said of this battle, "In proportion to the forces engaged, the Attu invasion was one of the costliest island campaigns of the Second World War."[6] Here too Imperial warships were used in piecemeal fashion, mostly as escorts for convoys bringing supplies and reinforcements. This meant that, even when the Japanese won an engagement, they could not exploit it, as had been the case in the Battle of the Komandorski Islands in March 1943 when the U.S. Navy lost the gun duel, but the Japanese fled anyway—convoy and all.[7] And then shied completely away from confrontation over Kiska in August.

But evacuation was a concept alien to Japan's design for imposing unacceptable costs on the Allies wherever they might try to penetrate the Empire's defensive perimeter. And, in many settings, it was simply not a practical possibility. This was especially true of the Central Pacific, where the next American blows were fated to fall. Why there? Because, as the U.S. Joint Chiefs reasoned, the MacArthur-led campaign in New Guinea was moving too slowly, requiring too many ground troops, and the alternative—an island-hopping drive through the Central Pacific chains could advance farther and faster, ultimately severing Japan's links with its holdings in the south. MacArthur objected vehemently to this approach. Nevertheless, it became official Allied policy when Roosevelt, Churchill, and Chiang Kai-Shek met in Cairo to discuss the Pacific War in late November 1943. Stalin didn't attend—the Soviet Union was still neutral toward Japan. But he met a few days later with Roosevelt and Churchill in Tehran to discuss next steps in the war against Hitler. As for MacArthur, he kept lobbying for his axis of advance against Japan. In the end, he succeeded. As his biographer William Manchester put it, Douglas MacArthur "was determined not to be outshone. He wanted the world's attention focused on his own flashing sword."[8]

MacArthur's success in the bureaucratic knife-fights for resources, troops, and priority meant that the Allies were to continue a divided, two-pronged advance in the Pacific—offering the Japanese good chances for concentrating against one or the other. A key problem, though, was the sheer expanse of Japan's defensive perimeter, which in the Central Pacific in particular offered U.S. forces a range of choices about where to strike. Thus, in the absence of high-quality intelligence—recall that the American Magic code-breaking capability, along with excellent communications security, had achieved what we would today call complete "information dominance" over the Japanese—there would always be a significant lag between the onset of an American attack and the Imperial Fleet's response to it. Besides which, thanks to Magic, dispositions of Japanese warships were often unmasked. So, when Admiral Nimitz's initial blow landed in the Gilbert Island chain at Makin and Tarawa on November 20, 1943, the Japanese garrisons were left largely to their own devices. They fought with their usual fanatical courage, especially on Tarawa where Marine casualties exceeded three thousand in just three days. But their fate was sealed from the outset. Effective Imperial Navy support came solely in the form of a handful of submarines, one of which, the *I-175,* sank the carrier *Liscome Bay,* killing over 600 of its crew.[9]

Still, there was some solace Japanese military leaders could take from the battle in the Gilberts. Their fortifications—particularly the pillboxes and bunkers made of layers of heavy logs covered with several feet of dirt, and reinforced with some concrete and steel—had held up well under the severe bombardment. So much so that the landing on Tarawa had been vigorously contested and very nearly defeated on the first day of fighting. By dusk on D-day, over a third of the 5,000 Marines who landed were dead or wounded. Major General Julian Smith, commander of the Second Marine Division that assaulted Tarawa, believed "Shibasaki [the Japanese commander] made his greatest mistake by not counter-attacking the slim Marine beachhead during this [D-day] night. Never again was it so vulnerable."[10] Despite the bloody toll Tarawa exacted, lessons learned from this battle guided improvements in U.S. island-hopping warfare tremendously. Reconnaissance, logistics, fire support and communications improved and, "in the minds of most American military planners and strategists the cost of the capture of the Gilberts was justified both in terms of the strategic gains ... and the tactical lessons."[11]

The challenge for the Japanese in the island war was to figure out how to counter the improving American approach. Four months before Tarawa, in July 1943, Emperor Hirohito had expressed his "grave concern" about the seeming fragility of the Pacific island barrier design. He summoned Hideki Tojo to a private audience, during which he upbraided the prime minister: "You keep repeating that the Imperial Army is invulnerable, yet whenever the enemy lands you lose the battle. You've never been able to repulse an enemy landing. Can't you do it *somewhere?* How is this war going to turn out?"[12] One of the ways Tojo intended to rectify the situation was to step up aircraft production, and to increase the Navy share to half of the total run of nearly 50,000 over the coming year. And when the Navy—which bore the primary responsibility for the fighting in the Pacific—asked, in the wake of Tarawa, for an increase to 60 percent, Tojo willingly acquiesced. But when it came to the allocation of troops of the Imperial Japanese Army, Tojo was much less generous. Of the fifty divisions Japan formed in the war, forty were deployed against China, leaving far too few for the Pacific—a situation John Keegan called a "fundamentally unbalanced strategic position."[13]

If there was an area of field operations where things went well during this period—was "fundamentally balanced," to paraphrase John Keegan—while catastrophes loomed elsewhere, it was in Burma. British General Sir Harold Alexander and his American colleague, General Joseph Stilwell—the latter commanding/advising Chinese troops—had been soundly defeated in 1942. But in 1943 Allied forces regrouped, were reinforced, and British and Indian troops were able to undertake the so-called Arakan offensive along Burma's northwest coast. Yet it quickly unraveled in the face of a skillful Japanese defensive in the difficult jungle-and-ridge terrain. William Slim had to be called in to retrieve the situation and extract the endangered forces who in his view "were fought out and many of them could not be relied on to hold anything ... were untrained for the jungle and feared it."[14] Japanese forces also dealt effectively with the threat posed by Orde Wingate's first Chindit raiding force that operated deep behind the lines. One-third of the brigade-strength force failed to return, the damage done to communications and rail lines quickly repaired. The Chindits would come again in 1944 and do much greater harm; but for now, they were dealt with. And for their part, the Japanese saw in the Chindits' methods something that Imperial Army forces might imitate when taking the offensive once again, threatening India.

However, stability in Burma was far outweighed by the quagmire in China that sucked up most Japanese ground forces. A large proportion of Japan's aircraft went to China also, to oppose General Claire Chennault—of "Flying Tiger" fame—now commanding the 14th Air Force. And there was another grievous deficiency in Japanese strategic design: an inexcusable failure to prepare for or adjust to increasingly effective American submarine attacks. The second half of 1943 saw merchant ship losses rising sharply. By December, sinkings for the year exceeded 1,500,000 million tons—*more than double* the damage done during 1942. This led to a net reduction in non-tanker shipping to 4,000,000 tons, as the losses far exceeded Japanese replacement capacity. Tanker production, due to the critical need for fuel, was prioritized, so available capacity of these vessels grew by over 100,000 tons in 1943.[15] This only slightly mitigated a situation that was worsening, ever more swiftly and dangerously, particularly because the Americans had solved their torpedo problems—for the most part—and were replacing older, more cautious submarine skippers with aggressive men who averaged about a decade younger. Yet during the months when losses inflicted by these new skippers grew sharply, Japan still dawdled. An organization tasked with countering submarines wasn't formed until November 1943. Much too late.

*          *          *

While American submarines were hitting their stride, dealing the Japanese telling blows from which they would not recover, German U-boats were on the defensive after the disasters of "Black May" 1943. The great historian of submarine warfare, Clay Blair, referred to U-boat captains and their crews at this point in the war as "the hunted."[16] A combination of full trans–Atlantic air cover, increased escort vessels, radar, high-frequency direction-finding technology—and, of course, the continued breaking of the Enigma codes—made life dangerous for U-boats trying to attack convoys transiting the main shipping routes. Karl Doenitz, now overall head of the *Kriegsmarine,* knew he had to withdraw from a head-to-head fight at this point, so he redeployed his forces away from the North Atlantic, sending some as far as to the Indian Ocean in search of prey. The shift was needed, and reduced U-boat losses. But even remote areas of ocean were unsafe, as U-boats sent to rendezvous with *milch cows* to refuel were too often attacked. "On a suspiciously large number of occasions, enemy aircraft [appeared] at the very moment when the pipeline was stretched between the two boats and neither was able to dive."[17] Doenitz refused to see it; but his skippers knew Enigma was broken.

Nevertheless, Doenitz was well aware that his approach to the U-boat campaign was in dire need of redesign. He had two basic paths to pursue. One was to make incremental improvements to the workhorse Type VII U-boat by making it stealthier and improving its armament. The other was to seek a transformational change, making the U-boat truly a submarine that could move at speed while staying under for long periods. This latter option meant that the U-boat would be more than just a vessel that could submerge, but which spent most of its life on the surface of the sea. Such a boat would be able to transit the dangerous Bay of Biscay—where Allied hunter-killer groups were on now constant patrol—evade long-range detection systems, and allow for keeping up with, even getting ahead of convoys while staying submerged. Could such a boat exist? Yes. Hellmuth Walter, an innovative engineer, patented an air-independent submarine engine in *1925,* driven by hydrogen peroxide—obviating the need for an oxygen supply drawn from the atmosphere. In 1934, as Hitler was achieving total power over Germany and rejecting the restrictions of the Versailles Treaty, Walter submitted a proposal to build U-boats with these new engines—and highly streamlined hulls—to the *Kriegsmarine.* It was rejected as being too radical. But Walter kept at it, designing, testing, improving. And as the war at sea got harder for the U-boats, Doenitz finally, in February 1942, let some contracts to Walter.

Once again, as in other key areas of strategic design, the problem was that the right solution was adopted too late. Walter's brilliant U-boat design for a vessel that could make better than 25 knots while submerged—over three times the underwater speed of the conventional Type VII—never came into use in combat. This was because, as Kenneth Macksey has observed, of "a U-boat building industry still divided within itself. Factions supporting competing concepts of power plant, hull, layout and performance vied for favor instead of being directed by a central agency to collaborate on one or two approved designs." Indeed, it wasn't until August 1943 that a pragmatic automotive engineer—one Otto Merker—was brought in to focus efforts and move toward mass production of the new types. Even then, he still had to grapple with overall policy set by Armaments Minister Albert Speer, whose "aim was merely to boost conventional production from 30 to 40 a month to replace current losses." However, Walter's Type XXIII, a smaller boat with traditional engines but featuring streamlined hull design, did see action late in the war.

**Hellmuth Walter's submarine designs were revolutionary (Wikipedia, courtesy Stadtarchiv Kiel Blue pencil.svg wikidata; Rights holder: Gesellschaft für Kieler Stadtgeschichte: Q28737428, CC BY-SA 3.0 DE).**

The XXIII made 14 knots submerged, and sank several vessels near the British coast in 1945—without the loss of single U-boat.[18] The first of the larger Walter boats was not deployed *until the last week of the war.*

Instead of successfully effecting transformational change in the U-boat service with Walter's radical redesign, Doenitz chose to emphasize incremental fixes. One early remedy, fitting U-boats with four 20mm anti-aircraft guns and calling upon them to fight it out on the surface when detected from the air, proved a disaster. U-boats in the Mediterranean and those transiting the Bay of Biscay from their submarine pens on the French coast, the latter sailing in groups to form "flak traps," enjoyed a brief period of success during June and July 1943. But the Allies soon adjusted their doctrine, eschewing immediate attack upon detection. Instead, the U-boats were shadowed until a number of aircraft could reach the scene and swarm the German subs. And by fall of 1943, when Beaufighters and other attack aircraft were equipped with rockets that allowed them to attack at stand-off range, losses mounted and Doenitz realized that "introduction of the rocket made it too dangerous for a U-boat to stay on the surface and invite air attack."[19] But delays in the production of Walter boats meant that his forces would be slowed terribly by the need to transit submerged, on batteries that allowed only very low speeds. For example, having to run submerged while crossing the Bay of Biscay to the wider Atlantic increased transit time *by several days,* yet another drag on U-boat combat effectiveness.

Another sort of fix was tried with the *Schnorchel,* a Dutch invention that the *Kriegsmarine* acquired when Holland was overrun in 1940. This device allowed a submarine to draw air from the atmosphere, and thus to run on its diesel engines while submerged. But even this incremental adaptation took time to incorporate into the U-boat force, and serious efforts to employ it didn't begin until after the "Black May" disasters—so it would not enter operational use until 1944. Besides, its "snout" could still be detected by Allied centimetric radar mounted on sub-hunting aircraft; and the U-boats' fields of vision were sharply restricted to periscope views when running on a *Schnorchel.* Once again, the superiority of the Walter design could be seen clearly, highlighting the risk of delaying the adoption of radical innovations.

Doenitz tried another incremental fix as well. In September 1943 he sent some U-boats back into the North Atlantic with a weapon that allowed them to strike from far greater range: the *Zaunkönig* acoustic torpedo that homed in on enemy ship noises. The "Gnat"—as the Allies called it—gave U-boats the ability to mount convoy attacks without having to approach so close that they would inevitably come under withering depth-charge attack from escort vessels. And if so attacked, U-boats had the *Pillenwerfer,* which released air bubbles concentrated so as to create a false sonar signature.

But just a few weeks after introduction of the Gnat, which Doenitz hoped could be used to target escorts as well as merchantmen, the Allies figured out what was happening and introduced noise-making "foxers" that drew the new weapon away from its intended targets.[20] Here was another example of an incremental adjustment by the Germans, countered swiftly and effectively by the Allies. As to radar detection from the air, so crucial to the outcome of the Battle of the Atlantic, it remained a mortal threat that could only be mitigated by the introduction of the Walter design. But that path had been forgone at several points, first during the interwar period of the 1930s, then again during the first three years of the war. Doenitz bore much of the responsibility for failure to shift to the Walter design in time for it to become the mainstay of the U-boat campaign. Instead, he opted for yet another small fix, the "Aphrodite"—a balloon with tinfoil streamers towed behind a U-boat steaming on the surface. This decoy helped limit surprise attacks on U-boats running on the surface, but it still allowed the Allied anti-submarine forces to get a fix on location and the time needed to "summon reinforcements in the form of surface vessels or aircraft that forced the U-boat to stay submerged while they plastered the area with depth charges."[21]

The fruitlessness of German efforts to solve the problems posed by the growing strength of the Allied anti-submarine campaign can be seen in a few statistics. U-boats sunk during the second half of 1943 *increased* 10 percent compared to the January–June period—from 113 to 124—despite the new technological fixes and the strategic choice Doenitz made to pull his boats from the North Atlantic after "Black May." The decline in U-boats at sea, on average, over the same period, was even sharper. The last six months of 1943 saw a drop of nearly *one-third* from the first half of the year—from about 100 to 70. The most alarming decrease was the amount of merchant tonnage sunk in the Atlantic, which fell almost *80 percent* during the last half of the year, to 340,000 tons from 1,600,000 tons sunk in the first half of 1943.[22] U-boats were entering a death spiral. The only way to counter the Allies now was to deploy a boat that could move at speed while submerged much of the time: the Walter. Without it, the brave crews of the U-boats—three-fourths of them died during the war—were stuck in their "iron coffins."[23]

But if the U-boats had by this time been effectively defeated, the German surface navy still mattered in the high north, where its efforts to interdict Allied convoys headed to Murmansk continued. The destruction of Convoy PQ-17 in the summer of 1942 had left the Allies leery of taking the Murmansk route during the months of long daylight. The very presence of *Tirpitz* and *Scharnhorst,* along with their supporting destroyers, deterred the Allies from sending even a single convoy to Russia by this route during the "white nights" of summer 1943. In the meantime, the Germans launched a raid in September on the Allied supply depot at Spitzbergen then returned to their lairs in the fiords of far northern Norway. Two weeks later, however, the British took a page out of Borghese's book by sending six midget subs to attack the *Tirpitz* in the Alten Fiord. Two foundered en route. Only two of the remaining four "X-craft" made it through the antisubmarine netting protecting *Tirpitz;* but they were able to plant explosives that went off to great effect. Cajus Bekker summed up the result: "The heavy damage thereby caused, though repaired *in situ,* immobilized the battleship for six months. Thus, of the 'fleet in being' only the *Scharnhorst* … was left to continue the standing threat to the Arctic convoys."[24]

*Scharnhorst* was hardly in a position to maintain this campaign against the arctic convoys on its own—the only *Kriegsmarine* capital ship still available for such duty. Of the two flotillas of destroyers that had been stationed in the high north, one was withdrawn in November, reducing the number of these vessels that could support *Scharnhorst* to five. Of the many U-boats that had been redeployed elsewhere during the summer lull, few had returned—and these were going to have significant difficulty locating enemy ships in the rough, stormy weather of the dark winter months in the arctic. The *Luftwaffe* presence had been sharply reduced as well, given the growing demands of other theaters of operations. Nevertheless, on December 19, one of its "weather reconnaissance" planes did spot a forty-ship convoy headed for Russia. This was Convoy JW-55B—the "A" had earlier slipped through unnoticed. *Scharnhorst* and five destroyers were sent off to intercept the convoy. In the action that followed, the destroyers were detached to hunt for the merchant ships while *Scharnhorst* remained at the ready to pounce when they were detected. But the Royal Navy escorts, including a battleship, were forewarned of looming action by intelligence and armed with radar that had an effective range of over forty kilometers. They detected and shadowed, then engaged and sank *Scharnhorst* in a sharp action on December 26.

Doenitz was to a great extent responsible for this naval disaster that cost the lives of nearly 2,000 German sailors—only thirty-six were rescued from the sea by the British after *Scharnhorst* went down. For the head of the *Kriegsmarine* had ordered his battleship to continue to search for the convoy even after being fully separated from its own destroyer flotilla. Thaddeus Tuleja assessed the gravity of the situation this way: "One blind German warship, pitting its strength against an unseen, unknown, lynx-eyed foe, presented only unacceptable odds."[25] Bekker's final judgment on this matter was that

the British took full advantage of the superior range and precision of their radar … the Germans often did not even utilize the equipment in their possession. Their application of the principle of "radio silence" to the use of radar indicates their failure to appreciate the true value of this method of reconnaissance.[26]

Why were the Germans generally forbidden to "ping" for the enemy with radar? By this point in the war, Doenitz had developed a deep concern that the active use of radar would allow the Allies to listen passively and detect his ships before his sailors could determine the location of hostile forces. In the tragic case of *Scharnhorst,* however, allowing use of radar—before it was disabled—would have given the ship a fighting chance to detect the onrushing enemy and either prepare a warm welcome or make a run for it.

*　*　*

The disabling of *Tirpitz* and the sinking of *Scharnhorst,* along with the many improvements in anti-submarine warfare meant that air attack was the only way left to strike effectively at the arctic convoys. But here as well German capacities had been crippled, with most aircraft being drawn from Norway to serve on more active fronts and, increasingly, to join in the fight against the bomber streams pounding the homeland. Ironically, Josef Kammhuber, the man who had done so much to craft German air defenses, was sacked from command of the XII Air Corps, and later from his position as General of Night-Fighters, then sent off in November 1943 to Norway. As *Scharnhorst* was sinking, Kammhuber was in that theater of action, but overseeing only negligible forces, unable to do more than stand by and watch disaster unfold. He lost favor in the wake of having briefed Hitler in June about the need to increase sharply the number of fighter aircraft defending Axis-controlled territory in the West, an argument buttressed by his assertion that the United States was now producing 5,000 bombers each month. Hitler thought this assertion ridiculous, and determined to demote and transfer Kammhuber.[27]

However, there *was* another reason to seek out new leadership and methods with which to conduct the air defense of Germany. Kammhuber's Line was just that: a line that, once pierced, allowed enemy night bombers to pass on to their distant targets against relatively light resistance. And the piercing of this line was made easier by the British introduction of Window, a counter-measure against ground radar that consisted of millions of strips of metal foil dropped by the bomber streams, creating a virtually impenetrable "cloud" through which the Germans could not see. Another possible effect of Window was the creation of many false radar contacts. This was a major innovation introduced by leading British defense scientist R.V. Jones and his colleague Joan Curran, and formed a key element in the electronic "wizard war" waged by both sides.[28] It made detection and tracking of the incoming bombers far more difficult, especially as the searchlights and radars of the German interior were widely dispersed—fighter airfields, too. But there *were* areas where illumination and flak batteries were highly concentrated: around cities. The problem was that German night-fighters had never taken after the bombers once the enemy came under fire from flak. This seemed a hard rule that could never be violated—until a thoughtful pilot, Major Hajo Herrmann, came along with a highly innovative design for better air defense.

Herrmann's idea was to concentrate fighter formations over the very cities that were coming under bombardment. Because illumination from the cities' searchlight defenses was so good, Herrmann reasoned, day-fighters that didn't have any sort of radar could be employed, and ground control was much simplified. This latter point was very important, as the German ground control capabilities were hardly as good as those of British Fighter Command had been in 1940. Indeed, General of Fighters Adolf Galland was so critical of *Luftwaffe* battle management of night operations that, during one of his visits to a ground command during an action, he commented that the confusing flurry of skittering images across myriad radar screens was "like a lot of water fleas in an aquarium."[29] Herrmann's concept of night-fighting operations didn't require much control; in fact, so little direction that the forces he led to attack the bomber streams came to be called the *Wilde Sau* ("Wild Boars"). Many, including Galland, were skeptical of this defensive design, in part because the fighters would have to operate in flak zones over cities, putting themselves at great risk. But Herrmann mitigated this risk by arranging to coordinate the altitude at which the flak was set to go off with the level at which the "Boars" would operate—somewhat above the flak. They would descend only when necessary to hit the enemy.

Herrmann's design was radical, calling as it did for willingness to lose some fighters to friendly fire from flak. Goering was reluctant to authorize creation of such units, but his—and others'—attitudes changed in the wake of the week of night raids on Hamburg that began in the last week of July 1943. The Allies called these raids "Operation Gomorrah"—quite apt, considering the firestorms that rose from incendiary bombs and favoring weather conditions. Jones's Window chaff completely outfoxed German radars, keeping losses on the first Hamburg raid to less than 2 percent of the 800 bombers the RAF employed in this attack. Over the course of the next raids during the week of "Gomorrah," over 40,000 German civilians were killed—most in the firestorm kicked up by the bombing, which burned down half the buildings in the city as well. This catastrophe proved to be the catalyst for change, and on August 1 Goering formally authorized a shift in emphasis to the "Wild Boar" concept. Three weeks later, when the British struck Berlin with 700 bombers, the *Wilde Sau* were ready, bringing down most of the 56 RAF aircraft lost—8 percent of forces used, a *quadrupling* of the enemy attrition rate over Hamburg! Window had been countered. *Luftwaffe* General Joseph "Beppo" Schmid, summed up target-area night-fighting (*Objektnachtjagd*) as "most primitive," but also "the most effective kind of night-fighting."[30]

To counter the Wild Boars, the British relied on deception, sending a few dozen Pathfinder aircraft to illuminate one city, drawing the Boars to it, while the main force struck elsewhere. This worked some of the time, but not often enough. The RAF next resorted to bombing in bad weather when the Boars would not be able to see them. This remedy made the British effort even less accurate than before, with RAF bomb drops now routinely being miles off from their intended aim points. It was a situation that put much pressure on American daylight bombers. The U.S. Army Air Corps began its major period of involvement in the bombing of Germany during the summer of 1943 with the firm belief that its aircraft, flying in tight formations and in broad daylight—so as to improve accuracy—would be able to fight off any *Luftwaffe* squadrons sent to interdict them. From early on, it seemed clear that this strategic design, based on the belief that their bombers' defensive firepower enabled them to operate beyond the range of fighter cover, was fundamentally flawed. On August 1, as Hamburg was burning, 180 American bombers flew from North Africa to strike at the Ploesti oil refineries in Romania. Almost fifty were shot down, an equal number seriously damaged. On August 17, just under 400 American bombers attacked Schweinfurt and Regensburg. Sixty were shot down.

These were unacceptable losses, in terms of material damage to the U.S. Army Air Forces and with regard to the morale of aircrews. These airmen may have slept on clean sheets before and after their missions; but knowing their expected lifespan was sharply limited posed a serious problem that required the higher command to set a policy of rotating airmen out after twenty-five bomb runs. During the second half of 1943, this policy hardly mitigated the dilemma; only a small percentage of the U.S. aircrews made it to this milestone. Yet they fought on, as Gerhard Weinberg has noted, with "steady determination in the face of very low odds on survival."[31] In return for their sacrifice, they did inflict some damage on German industry; but Albert Speer, by means of clever decentralization of manufacturing sites, was actually able to *increase* the production of aircraft and other weapons systems during this period. And when one considers the overall results of the Allied bombing offensive during the second half of 1943, John Ellis's assessment seems very much on point: "American operations had been indecisive, those of [the British] Bomber Command had been downright disappointing."[32] One positive thing that can be said of the Allied effort at this point is that it drew German fighters away from other fighting fronts.

From the perspective of strategic design, German defensive success in the fight against the Allied bombers had the dire, unintended consequence of driving leadership—Hitler and others, with Goering soon cowed into falling in line with them—to see an opportunity to resume the air offensive against the British. Weinberg observed that the "Germans were so confident that they were winning in the skies over German-controlled Europe that they again accentuated plans and production projects for bombers, not fighters."[33] To General of Fighters Adolf Galland this was absurd. He was fully aware of Allied production capabilities, and knew that improved Allied long-range fighter escorts—the one in use, the P-38 Lightning, was no match for the Me 109s and Fw 190s—would inevitably come on line. Even the idea of having drop-tanks to increase fighter range was well known. *Kondor Legion* pilots had experimented with them in air operations during the Spanish Civil War. Galland, who took up the mantle of "strategic designer" of the *Luftwaffe* after Ernst Udet's suicide, emphasized that fighter production and standing on the defensive were urgent needs. He argued that "it was senseless and harmful to try and continue the fiction of offensive activity."[34]

But Galland lost this argument, and considerable German production effort was diverted from defensive fighters to developing an offensive air capability. Awareness of the high attrition manned bombers would surely suffer led Hitler to emphasize development of guided missiles. The V-1 ("V" for *Vergeltungswaffen,* "retaliatory weapons") was a pulse-jet-powered flying bomb—or what we today call a cruise missile. The V-2 was a rocket-powered ballistic missile, a particular favorite of Hitler's ever since a July 1943 briefing during which chief scientist Wernher von Braun showed him a short film of a rocket launch. The V-3 was to be a "super gun." All three were under development during this period, but only the V-1 and V-2 ever saw use, and then just in the last year of the war. Opportunity costs imposed by the varied "V" initiatives were staggeringly high, as "resources that went to developing them could, according to the American Bombing Survey, have produced an additional 24,000 aircraft." Besides this cost, as Richard Overy noted, "Neither rockets nor flying bombs were war winners. The technology was immature."[35] Worst of all, though, Galland's beloved jets were hijacked by Hitler and other senior leaders—including Goering, who went along with the Fuehrer's preference. Now, instead of being produced as air defense fighters, jets were to be redesigned as *bombers.* A truly fatal decision.

*     *     *

**Adolf Galland (right) often clashed with Hermann Goering (center) (Creative Commons, courtesy Bundesarchiv, Bild 101I-343–0674–16 / CC-BY-SA 3.0, September 1940).**

While jet technology was being diverted to the mission of creating bombers capable of striking England once again, Albert Speer was also producing large numbers of conventional ground attack aircraft that, in conjunction with the revival of armor that Heinz Guderian was overseeing, could sustain the restored balance of forces on the Eastern Front. Despite the increasing pressure imposed by the Allied strategic bombing of Germany during the second half of 1943, production grew, so much so that by the end of the year nearly 20,000 combat aircraft had been manufactured—nearly a doubling of the production level from 1942.[36] Along with this, German armored forces saw great improvements as well, quantitative and qualitative—but especially the latter, as the heavy Henschel/Krupp Tiger and the medium Daimler-Benz Panther tanks came on line in increasing numbers in May and June of 1943. Guderian made sure that the workhorse Panzer IVs were being up-armored as well. And Ferdinand Porsche introduced the eponymous "Ferdinand" tank destroyer at this time as well, designed to engage Soviet T-34s at a range of over three kilometers. The situation was looking up in the East.

The question for the Germans now was about what to do in the wake of the successful counter-punching strategy Manstein had employed to stop the Russian offensives after Stalingrad. The enemy had been bloodied badly by Manstein, but once the fighting died down there was still a sizeable bulge in the German line in the vicinity of Kursk that could be used as a launching pad for future offensives in a number of directions. Given the restoration of the balance of forces, and assumed German tactical and technical advantages over the Red Army, many on the General Staff began to think in terms of a fresh offensive that would eliminate the threatening bulge and at the same time allow for the "writing down" of Russian forces through attrition in such a battle. One of the principal proponents of a continued offensive strategy in the East in the summer of 1943 was Field-Marshal Wilhelm Keitel, who had been serving as the Chief of the Armed Forces High Command, the OKW, (*Oberkommando der Wehrmacht*) since the start of the war. He was joined in this view by Colonel-General Kurt Zeitzler, Franz Halder's successor as Army Chief of Staff. Zeitzler, it seems, played on what historian Alan Clark referred to as "Hitler's pathological aversion to withdrawal" to gain and sustain the Fuehrer's support for the offensive.[37] Guderian argued against the attack; Manstein waffled. Hitler, with great misgivings, authorized it.

What followed, on July 5, 1943, was the beginning of the greatest tank battle in history. The Russians fielded 5,000 while the Germans—thanks to Guderian and Speer— had 3,000, many of better quality, especially the 250 Panthers and 200 Tigers. The *Luftwaffe* had recovered somewhat from its losses over Stalingrad—which it had so gallantly striven to supply—and in the months after, entering the new battle with roughly 2,000 combat aircraft. The Red Air Force had double that number engaged. And in terms of manpower, the 800,000 Germans faced nearly 2,000,000 Russians. But German pilots, tankers, and infantrymen were still superior, tactically. The only glaring deficiencies the attackers had were in guns, where the Russians' 25,000 greatly outnumbered the Germans' 10,000, and in the area of tactical intelligence, where the "Lucy" spy ring operated by German expatriate Rudolf Roessler[38]—whose network included some senior leaders of the *Wehrmacht*—fed Moscow exact details of the attack. The intelligence from Roessler had been supplemented for some time by Ultra intercepts that the British decided to share with Stalin. But these German disadvantages pale when viewed with a strategic design sensitivity to the cost of offensives against prepared foes, and the vastly greater Russian replacement capacity.

From the outset, it was clear the Germans failed to achieve surprise, and there was never a decisive breakthrough, as in past *Blitzkrieg* operations. Russian artillery let loose a thundering barrage on the attacking forces, and since they were fighting against an onrushing enemy more guns could be in use more of the time. To be sure, the Germans got the better of the fighting at the tactical level, both in the initial attack and during the massive Russian counter-offensive. The *Heer* may have lost nearly 800 tanks—over a fourth of the panzers engaged—but Russian armored losses were *five times* that number. The Germans lost 500 aircraft; the Red Air Force twice as many. And where the Germans suffered over 50,000 killed in action and 135,000 wounded, Russian casualties exceeded 700,000.[39] But Russian manpower reserves—including women, who were beginning to provide a significant presence in combat units—remained great, and Soviet armored production capacity was outpacing the Germans. Allied convoys, now arriving with little obstruction from the *Kriegsmarine* and *Luftwaffe,* brought hundreds of thousands of trucks—perhaps their most important contribution to the war on the Eastern Front, as they ensured the increasing advantage in mobility that the Red Army would have for the rest of the war.

Thus, the failure of Operation Citadel, as the German plan was called, was strategic, not tactical. Or rather, the tactical consequences were not to be immediately felt, as the Russians needed a month and more to retool and replenish their forces. But once they did so, Stalin and his Red Army would absolutely control the pace and direction of the fighting. Heinz Guderian—the loudest voice among those opposed to the offensive, who had argued instead for the kind of mobile counter-attacking concept of operations that

Manstein had employed so well in the months before Kursk—summed up the situation in the wake of the great battle:

> By the failure of *Citadel* we had suffered a decisive defeat. The armored formations, reformed and re-equipped with so much effort, had lost heavily both in men and in equipment and would now be unemployable for a long time to come. It was problematical whether they could be rehabilitated in time to defend the Eastern Front; as for being able to use them in defense of the Western Front against the Allied landings that threatened for next spring, this was even more questionable. Needless to say the Russians exploited their victory to the full. There were to be no more periods of quiet on the Eastern Front. From now on the enemy was in undisputed possession of the initiative.[40]

Guderian's analysis was penetrating, and seems to have gotten through to Hitler, who reacted quickly to news of Allied landings in Sicily, just five days after the start of *Citadel*, by calling off the offensive. Now, in addition to the impending debacle in the East, the Fuehrer faced immediate danger on his southern flank—which also posed a mortal threat to his ally Mussolini.

*   *   *

The Allied invasion of Sicily caught the Germans somewhat by surprise, due in part to the elaborate deception plan the Allies concocted—planting papers on a corpse that was floated ashore in Axis-friendly Spain[41]—to convince Hitler that the real targets were Greece and/or Sardinia. Even in the absence of such melodramatics, though, the Germans had to disperse their forces widely from Sardinia to southern Greece, because the Allies by now had virtually complete command of the Mediterranean Sea. That is, they *could* strike in force at any of these points. In this regard, the attack on Sicily was, as Royal Navy officer Donald Macintyre saw the matter, "a classic example of the successful use of sea power to attack a land power at a weak point of one's own choosing." Macintyre—who early in the war sank the *U-99* and captured its skipper, the "ace" Otto Kretschmer—also noted that, despite vigorous efforts by German and Italian submarines and Axis aircraft to thwart the landings, they went ahead with the loss of only twenty-five ships out of the massive armada that brought nearly 500,000 troops to bear.[42]

Against this juggernaut there were just 30,000 Germans on the island, augmented by well over 200,000 Italians—the latter in coastal defense units comprised of low-quality reservists and four "regular" divisions that had very poor transport and little artillery. The *Regia Marina* still possessed six battleships, seven cruisers, and seventy-five destroyers, but lack of fuel, no radar, and sparse air cover kept it in port. This left the naval fighting mostly to submarines, but Italian light forces more than lived up to the potential that Borghese and his colleagues believed in. And in many actions they mounted hit-and-run attacks and landed commandos behind the lines to disrupt the Allied advance. Along with these efforts, German ground forces provided leavening for the more competent Italian formations and, despite an early counterattack beaten back by naval gunfire, mounted a very skillful defense of the island that inflicted heavy casualties on the invaders. Thus, it took nearly forty days to conquer the island, even with the Allies' two best field generals—Bernard Montgomery and George Patton—in command. In the end, all remaining Germans and 75,000 Italians still willing to fight on—large numbers of the latter had simply surrendered—made it across the Strait of Messina to the mainland with their weapons. As Hanson Baldwin put it, "the Germans had sold space for time at a high price in Allied blood."[43]

In strictly military terms, the excellent German performance on the defensive led the eminent historian Martin Blumenson to go so far as to raise a question about who really won this campaign.[44] But there can be no doubt that the invasion landed (no pun) a profound political blow to the Axis. For just two weeks into this campaign Benito Mussolini's own "Fascist Grand Council" voted to grant greater governing powers to the king, who promptly dismissed the dictator and ordered his arrest. Mussolini's downfall was first greeted with shock in Germany. Propaganda Minister Goebbels expressed his dismay: "To think that ... a revolutionary movement that has been in power for twenty-one years could be [so easily] liquidated."[45] Goebbels' reaction aside, Hitler and his minions were well prepared for Mussolini's fall. Erwin Rommel, who had been on a "rest cure" after being brought back from Africa, was chosen to lead Operation Alaric—the occupation of Italy in the event that the new government in Rome made a separate peace with the Allies. Rommel handled the preparations exceedingly well, Alaric unfolded smoothly and, when the Italian surrender on September 8, 1943, was publicly announced, Alaric was succeeded by "Axis," the plan to disarm and capture Italian troops that sided with their new government's separate peace.

In the aftermath of the Italian *volte face*—a separate peace negotiated with the Allies that clearly contradicted their declaratory policy demanding unconditional surrender—Rommel in the north of Italy and Kesselring in the south swiftly disarmed nearly a million Italian soldiers, a quarter of whom were soon put on trains bound for Germany where they were to join Speer's slave laborers. The problem of what to do about the Italian armed forces solved, there was now the question of strategic design for defense of Italy. Rommel favored a relatively swift retreat up the peninsula, holding at a line north of Rome. Kesselring, who had earlier urged the Fuehrer to hold out in Tunisia rather than accept Rommel's plan for evacuation—a move that had led to an epic disaster—argued in favor of fighting for every inch of Italy. Hitler ruled in Kesselring's favor, as he had in North Africa; and this time Kesselring was right. Italy's mountainous terrain and rivers that ran lateral to the Allied line of advance made for ideal defensive fighting. Montgomery's initial landing at the very toe Italy, in Calabria on September 3, played right into Kesselring's vision—it was not at all what Rommel, who feared Allied landings far to the north, had expected. And when the Allies did make an amphibious "end run" at nearby Salerno a week later, they were quickly put on the defensive in very hard fighting.[46]

In fact, in the German counter-attack against Salerno, it was only Rommel's "debilitating squabbles" with Kesselring—to use David Irving's phrasing—that led the former to hold back two vital panzer divisions that "might well have tilted the balance against the enemy."[47] Hitler very soon realized that having both Rommel and Kesselring each commanding half of the forces in Italy was a bad idea—so he sacked Rommel. Kesselring went on to mount a highly skilled defensive campaign over the next year-and-a-half, what Dominick Graham and Shelford Bidwell called a "tug of war," one of the most searing episodes of which was the long struggle to drive German forces from the Benedictine abbey at Monte Cassino.[48] As to Mussolini, the location where he was being kept in "protective custody" high up in the Apennines was found, and on September 12 a raid composed of paratroopers and some SS, delivered by gliders and led by Otto Skorzeny, rescued him. Mussolini then assumed rule of the Salò Republic in northern Italy, which remained loyal to the Axis cause until the end of the war.

By December 1943 the Allied advance had been held up well south of Rome. The bitter fighting and slow progress have led some to criticize the underlying logic of the

Italian campaign. J.F.C. Fuller first articulated this view fully, arguing that the fighting here was "tactically the most absurd and strategically the most senseless campaign of the whole war," as it turned what Churchill called Europe's "'soft underbelly' into a crocodile's back; prolonged the war; wrecked Italy; and wasted thousands of American and British lives."[49] Victor Davis Hanson acknowledges that invading Sicily was a "needed warmup for the anticipated invasion of France in spring 1944," but is still critical of the long fight for the mainland. He sums the matter up: "The bitter Allied experience in Italy would be plagued by almost continual command mistakes and catastrophes until the end of the war in 1945."[50] For the Allies in Italy, New Year's Eve 1943 was a time filled with foreboding. On that day Eisenhower and Montgomery departed the theater, leaving forces that had, over the past three-plus months, seen a loss of 10 percent of American combat power, double that for the British.[51]

*    *    *

The second half of 1943 saw the Axis on the absolute brink of catastrophe in several theaters of operations. For Japan, still in possession of most of its Pacific "defensive perimeter," the most serious problem was the threat to its seagoing commerce. U.S. submarines now possessed torpedoes that worked reliably, and Nimitz had shown wisdom in replacing his many too-cautious older skippers with younger, more aggressive men. Continued decoding of Japanese radio traffic accelerated the submarine campaign, vectoring U.S. subs to their targets with timely accuracy. Against this, only in November did Japan form a command specifically tasked with countering the threat to its merchant fleet, its *marus.* Another problem at the command level was more strategic in nature; in the wake of Yamamoto's death no one emerged to champion his notion of concentrating major force against just one of the American thrusts. So MacArthur and Nimitz were able to continue their campaigns against too-dispersed Japanese opposition, wearing down both the ships of the Imperial Fleet and the Zeros by sheer, unrelenting attrition. All the while, the Army remained over-committed to the Asian mainland, where General Yamashita still languished in a kind of "command exile."

By December 1943 Italy had been well and truly broken in half, with some of its ground forces now fighting on the Allied side on the peninsula, and other units in Yugoslavia deserting the Axis to join the insurgent forces of Josip Broz "Tito." The major units of the *Regia Marina* had sailed off to Malta to surrender themselves to the Allies. But *Don* Borghese, "The Black Prince," and his men fought on alongside the Germans, as did the Italian submariners based at Bordeaux. Also, many other Italians in the army and air forces, who had formed strong bonds of loyalty and friendship with the Germans, made a similar choice. This was true of 10,000 Italians serving in Greece who stayed on with their German allies. And on October 16, 1943, the so-called Rastenburg Protocol was signed between the Reich and the Salò Republic, authorizing the Italians to form four infantry divisions to support Kesselring's forces. They fought with distinction, sometimes even throwing back Allied forces in one sector of the front or another. And the Italian pilots of Salò, now in the cockpits of better aircraft, shot down more Allied aircraft than they themselves lost—even after their German comrades had been called home. For all this, however, there is no denying that Italy had entered World War II with three fatal design flaws: Balbo's mistaken faith in biplanes, poor tanks, and a lack of radar on *Regia Marina* warships.

As to Germany's surface fleet, with the crippling of the *Tirpitz,* and then in December loss of the *Scharnhorst,* there was no longer any way to interdict convoys bringing hundreds of thousands of trucks and the many tanks, planes, and other supplies that now made Russia near-unstoppable. U-boats and the few *Luftwaffe* attack aircraft left in the high north could only harass, not halt, this flow of aid that plied the shortest of the three routes to Russia—the Persian Gulf and the Far East were the other two. The U-boats themselves were by now almost entirely on the defensive, thanks to Allied technical advances and German failure to have emphasized development of air-independent-propulsion submarines in earlier years. A similar critique can be leveled at the *Luftwaffe,* which missed the opportunity to exploit its edge in jets—an error compounded by a ridiculous debate about redesigning Messerschmitt's amazing aircraft *as a bomber* when the critical need was for a fighter aircraft able to deal with the long-range escorts now accompanying the B-17s and other bombers attacking Germany with increasing impu-

Valerio Borghese, "The Black Prince," who led Italy's sea raiders.

nity in daylight. But the greatest disaster during the second half of 1943 ensued when a strategic ground offensive was mounted in Russia early in July. Manstein's counter-punching strategy, fortified by Guderian's efforts to revitalize the panzers, should have been followed. Instead, as the Germans found out, too late and at high cost, *Blitzkrieg's* heyday had passed.

# 7. Last Chances

WHILE THE SITUATION on the Italian front at the turn of the year was stable, the position of Axis troops in the East was increasingly precarious. Soon after Kursk, Soviet forces were replenished and launched offensives at several points along an extended front against depleted, weary Axis soldiers. By now the Italians were long gone, and Romanian and Hungarian units had been terribly ground down in the constant fighting. As to the *Heer,* there was little chance of it continuing to practice the counter-punching battle doctrine Manstein had crafted. The Germans were too widely stretched, too lacking in transport and, due to the need to send *Luftwaffe* squadrons home to defend the Reich, had weak air cover. These deficiencies made it possible for the Soviets to exploit the mobility advantage that hundreds of thousands of Studebaker trucks sent from America gave them over the Germans. The Russians also had designed a way to ford rivers quite swiftly—overcoming this last major German defensive advantage—by means of prefabricated, mass-produced bridge parts that allowed assembly within 3–5 hours, and which could support loads of up to 80 tons. By January of 1944, there were nearly 130 battalions of engineers erecting these at many points.[1]

Thus it was no surprise that the months after Kursk saw extensive Russian advances, including the crossing of the Dnieper River north of Kiev, the great city of the Ukraine being liberated early in November 1943. In the wake of this defeat, it was all Manstein could do to prevent loss of his entire Army Group. By January 1944 his mobile reserves were severely depleted. He had to switch what remained constantly, from sector to sector, to master each new crisis. With the clear goal of wearing down Manstein's dwindling reaction forces, the following months saw the Soviets mounting multiple attacks on different portions of the front rather than focusing on one section in the hope of achieving a massive breakthrough at a single point. As Paul Carell assessed this doctrine of launching smaller-scale attacks on widely separated areas along the front in rapid succession, "the Soviet High Command had developed this pattern to a fine art…. As soon as a sector of the German front had crumbled the Russians swiftly aimed an attack with strong striking formations against another."[2] Even the rainy spring of 1944 gave the Germans no respite because, as Manstein noted, "Soviet tanks were more mobile than ours in snow and mud, thanks to their wider tracks."[3]

Under these trying circumstances—superior Soviet numbers, the Red Army's better mobility in messy weather and its clever doctrine of dispersed offensives—the Germans needed something of a near-miraculous nature to prevent the complete collapse of Manstein's Army Group South. In this instance, relief came in the form of the repurposed *Stuka,* now

armed with two 37mm cannons under its wings. As a high-angle dive-bomber, the *Stuka*
had previously had little success when trying to hit individual tanks. But, cannon-armed,
it could come in much lower-angled, with a much higher probability of hitting a moving
Russian tank. First used in number in the Kursk attack, where it had less effect operating
in areas dense with anti-aircraft guns, the Ju 87G provided a highly mobile anti-tank
capability that played a big role in preventing the defensive operations on the Eastern
Front from becoming a rout. For the pilots, it was highly dangerous duty. *Stuka* ace Hans
Ulrich Rudel—who personally destroyed over 500 Russian tanks—recalled in his memoir
being "in the air from dawn until dusk ... [but] our efforts are successful in preventing
any decisive breach of our front."[4] Rudel's recollection is correct. By March 1944 the situation was secure enough for Manstein to craft a remarkable maneuver that, while a
retreat, nevertheless struck hard blows, inflicting costly losses on Zhukov's forces.

Yet Hitler, tired of retreats, sacked Manstein. The firing was done in person, at a
fateful meeting that took place between the Fuehrer and his best field commander at
Berchtesgaden on March 30, 1944. Manstein was there awarded the Swords to the Knight's
Cross. Then, in a rebuke to Manstein's maneuver-based strategic design—that had repeatedly saved the situation in the East—Hitler told him, "The time for operating is over.
What I need now is men who stand firm."[5] Replacing Manstein was Walter Model, who
had risen to *Generalfeldmarschall* rank just weeks before his predecessor was dismissed.
Model had come to the Fuehrer's very close attention during the defensive fighting in
the East over the winter of 1941-42, due in no small part to the fact that his devotion to
standing fast and fighting along a continuous front was so much in tune with Hitler's
own instincts. Model felt that the clumsiness of the Soviets' tactics, in particular their
penchant for massed frontal assaults, made resistance all along the areas under attack
optimal. This worked in the terrible first winter of the war on the Russian Front; but it
came at a great and growing cost in German casualties, given that every foot of front was
contested. Manstein's design, on the other hand, had kept hard-pressed German infantry
from too-heavy losses, while the panzers' superior tactics on the counter-attack regularly
destroyed the Russian spearheads.

Model was also a fanatical Nazi who took the Fuehrer's notion of a "scorched earth"
retreat very much to heart. Too much so. He embraced not only the burning of crops and
villages, but also the execution of thousands of innocents as well. Indeed, a full year before
he replaced Manstein, Model had been identified in an official Soviet report on atrocities
that the Germans had committed in the area west of Moscow—where he was in command
of the 9th Army—as having "personally ordered all this."[6] He was put at the top of the
list of German war criminals that the Russians compiled. Model was still heading that
list when he committed suicide in April 1945. He belonged on it, as he was responsible
for the expansion of atrocities in the East, increasingly bringing regular army troops into
these vile practices. Such acts did not cow the Russians in German-occupied zones into
quiet submission, though. Instead, the amount of guerrilla activity grew, to the point of
there being half a million partisans operating by the spring of 1944. They blew up trains,
mangled tracks, attacked remote posts and struck in the cities as well. They existed in sharp
contrast to the German efforts to create anti–Soviet Russian forces—"Vlasov's Army,"
named for the opposing general who switched sides after his capture—which proved so
unreliable that most units were sent far to the West, where they served indifferently.

\*   \*   \*

Manstein's parting gift, the plan that rescued over 200,000 troops of Army Group South from death or capture, ushered in a period of relative quiet on the Eastern Front that lasted through May 1944. In Italy, Kesselring was dealing ably with fresh challenges there. The Germans took every bit of advantage the terrain offered there, inflicting heavy casualties on the Allies as they strove to advance in a series of what J.F.C. Fuller, alluding to the stalemates of the Great War on the Western Front, called "Somme-Ypres battles." And when an amphibious "end run" was made at Anzio in January 1944, the landing force was contained for four long months. Fuller labeled this bold Allied operation a "dismal failure."[7] Credit for German defensive successes during this period belongs largely to Field-Marshal Kesselring, who more than justified Hitler's decision to keep him in charge in Italy and instead send Rommel packing. Kesselring, described by his biographer Kenneth Macksey as "a man of cool appreciation and high intellect,"[8] got on very well with Hitler, and agreed with him—insofar as the Italian Front was concerned—about holding ground by means of defensive positional warfare.

Rommel, long a master of mobile operations, was by this point in the war coming around to this point of view as well. And the defensive design that he had pioneered at Alamein was now to guide his thinking about how to prepare against the looming Allied invasion in the West. Appointed first in an inspection role—in part to keep him in the public eye—Rommel was soon given command of Army Group B, whose area of responsibility ran along the "Atlantic Wall" from Belgium to Brittany. These were the zones most likely to be chosen for amphibious landings by the Allies. The Biscay coast and the south of France fell under the authority of Army Group G. All told, the two army groups fielded sixty divisions. Nine were armored, one mechanized. All were commanded by sixty-eight-year-old Field-Marshal Gerd von Rundstedt. In an ironic twist, Rundstedt, who had been skeptical of the *Blitzkrieg* war-fighting design back in the 1930s, now felt the proper approach to defeating the Allies was to allow them ashore, then draw them into a maneuver battle with his panzers. Rommel preferred to engage the invaders immediately on whichever beaches they chose to land. He had seen too much of Allied air power in Africa to believe that the *Heer* was going to be able to outmaneuver the enemy. Guderian, drawn into the increasingly acrimonious argument between Rommel and Rundstedt—which ran on for months, pending Hitler's final decision—sided with the latter.

While the debate raged, though, Rommel kept fortifying the Atlantic Wall. He was as ingenious as in the days when he had designed the "devil's gardens" at Alamein. Reasoning that the Allies would land at high tide—to reduce exposure to fire that landing troops would face crossing open beaches—Rommel planted obstacles designed to disable landing craft. To cope with glider-borne assaults, he planted fields of stakes—his "asparagus"—at any space open enough to allow for air landings. Millions of landmines were planted. As to artillery, he wanted all batteries within range of naval gunfire to be sited in concrete bunkers—and for each to have a dummy site as well—with those placed inland well dispersed and camouflaged against air attack. Rommel was enthusiastic about the potential of new light weapons like the anti-tank *Panzerfaust,* a German version of the bazooka. He was also eager to field more *Nebelwerfer* teams, given the potential of these multiple-rocket launchers, whose "Screaming Mimi" projectiles packed a very considerable punch—and whose operators could survive for significant periods as long as they shifted position after every salvo (the rockets left telltale smoke trails, giving away their points of origin). Thus the "wall" that had been more of a propaganda tool of Joseph

Goebbels than a real impediment to invasion was now turning into a mortal threat to the Allied expeditionary forces.[9]

With nearly three-fourths of the total number of German divisions in the West under his command in Army Group B, Rommel began to feel some degree of optimism about the chances of pushing the invaders back into the sea. In a letter to his wife and son, written on March 17, 1944—just prior to an important meeting with Hitler at Berchtesgaden—Rommel said, "Here in the West we have every confidence that we can make it." Soon after, in a meeting with Hitler and *Generaloberst* Alfred Jodl, chief of the operations staff of the *Oberkommando der Wehrmacht,* Rommel told them why he was "confident of destroying the enemy [invasion] attempt: by the end of April virtually the entire coastline would be saturated with enough obstacles to inflict severe losses on the landingcraft." He vowed "the enemy's not going to succeed in setting foot on dry ground in these sectors."[10] This was just what Hitler needed to hear, as he saw Germany's last real chance of any kind of acceptable outcome of the war resting on the ability to defeat the Allied invasion in the West, which would then free up dozens of divisions for transfer to the East, adding usefully to the 160 fighting there at present, restoring stability to that vital front.

When Hitler outlined the grand strategic criticality of the task he had assigned Rommel, the latter came away with a new sense of purpose—and hope for the future.[11] But the debate with Rundstedt dragged on as winter gave way to spring and the time of invasion in the West neared. Rundstedt was strongly supported by *General der Panzertruppe* the Baron Geyr von Schweppenburg, who commanded all armored forces in the West. When he learned that Rommel's design was based on the notion of a linear defense on the beaches, positioning virtually all forces at the water's edge, "Geyr was appalled at the proposal to put everything in the shop window," as Chester Wilmot summed up his objection.[12] Rommel remained convinced of the importance of defeating the invasion swiftly, on the beaches, and argued in rebuttal that Geyr's central panzer reserve "would never be able to move in time against the bridgehead in the face of Allied air power." The whole matter was remanded to Hitler who, as Wilmot put it, "produced an illogical compromise … [dividing] control of the armored forces, with the result that there was neither a strong tactical reserve, nor a strong strategic reserve."[13] The panzers were dispersed behind prospective landing zones, *but held well back from the beaches.* A fateful compromise.

*    *    *

Rommel's concern about the ability of the Allied air forces to prevent the panzers from engaging in the kind of maneuver battle at which they excelled was well founded because, by early 1944, *Luftwaffe* fighter squadrons in ever-increasing numbers had been brought home to the direct defense of Germany itself. In January the Allies commenced an air battle over Berlin that was to last, with only brief interruptions, for nearly three months. Many other German cities came under night bombardment during these months as well, given that at this point in the war German B/C 53cm "Lichtenstein" radars were being routinely jammed, gravely impeding the *Luftwaffe's* night-fighting efforts. But a new airborne SN2 radar, operating on a 330cm wavelength that the Allies had no current ability to jam, came into wide use after the first of the new year. Its angle of search, at 120 degrees, was five times that of the B/C, and its range was nearly four miles. To this formidable improvement in the night-fighters' sensors was added a remarkable advance in weaponry: oblique armament that consisted of two 20mm machine guns fixed atop the night-fighters, behind their cockpits, at a seventy-two degree angle. Deadly, it was called *Schräge Musik* ("slanting music"). The high-risk *Wilde Sau,* who attacked while in flak zones, had been superseded.

These improvements in the *Luftwaffe's* ability to sense and shoot—that is, to locate bomber streams then to sneak up on them to strike from below—had immediate and powerful effects. RAF losses at the outset of the so-called "Battle of Berlin" exceeded 6 percent, and were above 7 percent in attacks on Stettin, Brunswick and Magdeburg. Later on, greater numbers of bombers were shot down over Berlin, which was subjected to many more raids. In the end, the RAF assault on the German capital was abandoned after the loss of 72 bombers on the night of March 24/5.[14] The official British history of the air war provided a sobering assessment of the situation at this time:

> Bomber Command was compelled, largely by the German night-fighter forces, to draw away from its primary target, Berlin, to disperse its effort and to pursue its operations by apparently less efficient means than hitherto.… The Battle of Berlin was more than a failure. It was a defeat.[15]

And Berlin was not the only target the RAF gave up on. A week after ceasing its raids on the capital, a force of 800 Halifax and Lancaster bombers struck Nuremberg. Twelve percent were lost another 9 percent seriously damaged. Britain's night air offensive was suspended.[16]

But during the day the story was different. P-38 Lightnings and P-47 Thunderbolts escorting the American bomber groups over Germany—with only modest success, as Me 109s and Fw 190s were a good match for them—were, beginning in earnest in 1944, succeeded by P-51 Mustangs that proved every bit as good, perhaps even better than *Luftwaffe* fighters. When "Big Week," the bomber offensive aimed at German aircraft factories, began on February 20, 1944, a thousand heavies had an escort of over 700 long-range Mustangs—and some Spitfires. *Luftwaffe* fighters had a most difficult time breaking through the escorts to strike at the bombers—a pattern that was to be repeated again and again in the next weeks and months. By early May, the thousand-bomber raids often had well over a thousand fighter escorts, opposed by ever fewer German squadrons, now terribly worn down through attrition. Adolf Galland tried some innovations aimed at retrieving the situation; none worked well enough to turn the tide. His "destroyers"—tasked with going straight at the bombers—had to be "escorted" themselves, with two fighters for every destroyer. This heavy escort need was slightly reduced by his introduction of "storm units"—up-armored Fw 190s with four cannons, flying in tight-packed formations at the bomber streams. But these concentrations limited the number of attack points, and American losses actually dropped as a percentage of bombers sent on each raid.

Over a thousand German day-fighters were lost in the first four months of 1944. In large part this was the result of the new commander of the 8th U.S Air Force, Major (later Lieutenant) General James Doolittle—of Tokyo Raid fame—shifting the focus to the destruction of the *Luftwaffe.* Even though the bombers continued to suffer high attrition through April, Galland saw his pilots dwindle in number, with just handfuls of experienced ones remaining. By May, fighter strength left for defense of Germany fell below 300—from the 1,500 available in January. Doolittle's "Pointblank" plan worked, for the most part due to the superiority of the P-51.[17] So now Allied fighters and bombers in the thousands were at last fully free to roam wherever they wished in daylight. The incremental changes that Galland introduced—destroyers and storm units—had not been able to reverse the long odds the defenders faced. Galland went to Goering to argue for pulling a third of the remaining pilots out of combat, hoping to rest them and build a reserve that, when returned to action, could strike at the enemy in a single, massive blow. Galland convinced Goering of the "appalling seriousness of the situation in the air."[18] The *Luftwaffe* chief assented to the plan.

But by this point in the air war the only sensible answer was to pursue a transformational change—from propeller-driven aircraft to jets. From a purely technical design perspective, the Germans had, since before the war, enjoyed a very significant lead in this area. Yet, during those pre-war years, many senior leaders in the *Luftwaffe* saw a shift to this new technology as constituting too daring a leap. Then, when all was going well initially in the first years of the war, there seemed to be little need to pursue such a radical advance. Of course, from a "strategic design" perspective, the early run of German victories provided *precisely the time* during which to concentrate on making such breakthroughs. But the Germans squandered the initial, golden opportunity to focus on jets—for two long years. Even then it was not yet too late. If they had begun development and production in earnest in 1941, they would have had jets in sufficient numbers—and in time—to outclass the American P-51 Mustangs of 1944. Willy Messerschmitt, who despite official neglect had kept developing the Me 262 as a fighter, had his aircraft ready for short-range defensive purposes by mid–1942, he recalled. But Hitler, Goering, and other officials "were solely interested in long-range fighters and bombers. The jet fighter prototypes were therefore shelved and left to rot."[19] This was perhaps Germany's greatest strategic design error.

By May 1944, just as Galland was most desperate, the air attacks on Germany eased a bit. This slight reprieve went along with the quiet on the Eastern Front and the stability of the situation in Italy. But bombing in the West picked up, clearly preparatory to a coming invasion. There the debate between Rundstedt, Geyr and others on one side, and Rommel on the other, about disposition of the panzers had been resolved by Hitler unsatisfactorily, with German armor widely dispersed but kept well back from the beaches. It was the worst strategic design; yet Hitler in the end did lean more toward Rommel's views about mounting the stoutest defenses at the water's edge. The 7th Army in Normandy soon benefited from some serious reinforcing, as Hitler's intuition led him to worry about a landing there. Walter Warlimont, deputy chief of *Oberkommando der Wehrmacht*, recalled: "In April 1944 Hitler suddenly, and without apparent reason, included Normandy in his category of probable landing areas."[20] Besides ground forces, Doenitz was ordered to add U-boats to the defenses. Since the Battle of the Atlantic was by now lost, he created a flotilla, designating it the "Farmer Group," which was to attack the invasion armada when it appeared. The U-boats did on D-Day, with little success; Rommel's beach defenses were the only real hope.

*   *   *

While the U-boats had been defanged by 1944, increasingly victimized as they were by Allied code-breaking capabilities and technical advances like high-frequency direction-finding ("huff-duff") technology, their American counterparts were enjoying quite a heyday out in the Pacific. Where Ultra decrypts and "huff-duff" direction finders detected the U-boat dispositions, allowing most Allied convoys in the Atlantic to avoid Doenitz's wolfpacks—causing over an 80 percent drop in sinkings[21]—the American Magic code-breakers were regularly vectoring in U.S. Navy "pig boats" on Japan's increasingly vulnerable *marus*. The results were devastating, despite the concerted effort of the Imperial Fleet to emphasize convoy protection that had begun late in 1943. In the last five months of that year, American submarines had sunk 160 merchant ships totaling just over 700,000 tons. But the first five months of 1944 saw 216 *marus* sunk, amounting to more than a million tons of vital shipping gone—over a *40 percent increase* in both vessel and tonnage losses.[22]

And the American submarine campaign was aimed at more than just merchant shipping. As Clay Blair, the most eminent historian of submarine operations in World War II, noted, when Nimitz began operations against the Japanese in the Marshall Islands during the month of January 1944

> submarines were assigned many missions: (1) interception of Admiral Koga's major fleet units withdrawing from Truk to Palau and Japan; (2) interception of vessels attempting to support the Marshalls; (3) interception of vessels fleeing Truk, Saipan, and Palau during the air strikes; (4) photographic and other reconnaissance; and (5) lifeguarding.[23]

Needless to say, the U.S. Navy's submarine force was operating more than just in support of the advance into the Marshalls. It was also taking the fight deep into Empire-held waters, striking at oil tankers coming from the East Indies, venturing into China seas, even ranging near Japan's home islands. In overall effect, as Edwin Hoyt observed, "By the spring of 1944 ... the American submarines were steadily destroying Japan's ability to carry on the struggle ... [they] had become a blockading force."[24] The Imperial Japanese Navy's negligence in the matter of designing a strong capability for anti-submarine warfare, both before the war and during its first years, was a grievous blunder.

As to Japan's island defenses, the fundamental design based on creating a network of strongholds whose garrisons would be supported by attack aircraft coming from neighboring islands—and submarine and surface naval forces confronting the invaders—was already deeply compromised. The increasing air superiority of the U.S Navy made it possible to strike at several of these bastions nearly simultaneously, both weakening them and confusing the Japanese as to which was to be targeted next for a landing. Imperial Navy surface forces could hardly move to interdict the invaders in environments where the enemy controlled the skies above the sea. Only the I-boats could help, less in direct attack at this point, more in terms of moving supplies to the increasingly beleaguered garrisons. And while these troops continued to fight with fanatical bravery, their effectiveness diminished, as the Americans had learned important lessons from the bloody experience at Tarawa. Nimitz's next major move took U.S. forces into the Marshalls in the first week of February 1944 at Kwajalein, where the landing operations benefited from a longer preparatory bombardment, more tanks in the first waves ashore, and many tactical insights from Tarawa—for example, the advantage of using shotguns and flame-throwers against Japanese soldiers fighting from caves or pillboxes. The result: whereas the casualty rate at Tarawa had been 25 percent, at Kwajalein it was only 2 percent.

The Americans achieved similar results in their mid–February landing on Eniwetok, also in the Marshalls, where in five days of fighting the entire Japanese garrison of over 3,000 was wiped out—the fate of Imperial soldiers in virtually all the island fighting, where just handfuls of survivors were left to be taken prisoner—for a loss of just over 300 Americans killed in action. The capture of Eniwetok secured the Marshalls, as the remaining Japanese garrisons on Jaluit and Wotje could be left to "die on the vine." The "island hopping" strategy was evolving. Indeed, victories in the Marshalls made it possible not only to leap far, but enabled the Americans to choose among directions. Even as the Marshalls fell, Truk, a thousand miles away to the west in the Carolines, was being hit hard from the air. A week later Saipan, farther off to the northwest in the Marianas, was shelled from the sea. In the wake of these strikes in February 1944, Louis Snyder concluded, "the U.S. Navy could now roam at will through the Central Pacific."[25] All that was left for the Japanese at this point was to reconsider the manner in which they would conduct the tactical fights for their island strongholds. The important change they made was to stop trying to engage at the water's edge; instead, they would now defend in depth, from countless tunnels and caves, hoping to inflict heavy casualties. They would. They did.

But the American advances along two axes, one westward the other northerly—led by Nimitz and MacArthur, respectively—were inexorable. As Nimitz was hammering Truk into submission, MacArthur made his move on February 29, landing and annihilating the Japanese forces on Los Negros Island in the Admiralties, situated well to the east of the great Japanese base at Rabaul, which was itself now effectively surrounded. Admiral Mineichi Koga, who succeeded Yamamoto as commander-in-chief of the Combined Fleet after the latter's death, at this point strove to imitate the successful U.S. Navy "task force" design that embraced the carrier as the true capital ship of the Pacific War. For Koga, a battleship sailor, this was a big advance in his thinking. But for all his fresh insight, Koga still did not grasp the strategic opportunity that the widely separated American advances of Nimitz and MacArthur offered. The Imperial Fleet hadn't yet concentrated against one or the other; instead it continued to be parceled out, bit by bit, suffering further irretrievable losses to attrition. This was particularly true of the remaining carrier forces, whose pilots were now mostly untried young men who had been hurriedly trained, and whose first combat sorties were too often their last—partly due to their inexperience, but also because Japan had not significantly improved its aircraft designs while the Americans had.

U.S. task forces now ranged far and wide, reaching as far as Palau, less than 700 miles from the southern Philippines, where they shelled that island on March 29. Two days later Koga died when his plane crashed in a typhoon. His successor as head of the Combined Fleet was Admiral Soemu Toyoda. Like Yamamoto, Toyoda had strongly opposed the idea of going to war against the Americans. But like Yamamoto he gave all to the war effort, in particular arguing forcefully for more emphasis on aircraft production and pilot development. In this he showed an understanding of the way in which air power had transformed war at sea that exceeded his great predecessor's—Yamamoto, for all his insight, retained an affection for battleships that had been formed by his early experience as a junior officer under Admiral Togo at the Battle of Tsushima against the Russians in 1905. Toyoda made it his mission to rebuild the Imperial Fleet's aerial striking power over the spring months of 1944, in the hope that by summer he would be in a position, at long last, to concentrate in full strength against one of the prongs of the American advance across the Pacific. In this view, too, Toyoda was ahead of those who had preceded him. He saw that sending "packets" of forces, air and naval, to deal with the separate, but simultaneous Allied offensives was much inferior to massing fully against just one of them. He therefore advocated and began preparing for one mighty blow—a *Kantai Kessen*.

General Tojo and other high-level leaders in Tokyo were supportive of Toyoda's vision, but were well aware of the increasingly long odds that he faced in confronting the enemy in the Central Pacific. They understood fully that their own naval forces were declining while the Americans grew in strength and, as John Keegan observed, saw that "Nimitz's thrust was aimed like an arrow at the heart of Japan's central position."[26] They found the very deadly depredations of the American submarine forces alarming, too, and realized that the Empire was nearing a point at which the enemy "pig boats" could cripple all operations with their campaign to disrupt the flow of oil tankers coming from the East Indies. This dire situation led the land-power-minded Japanese junta to come up with a plan to shift almost the entire oil supply route to rail lines, with only a few short hops across still-controlled bodies of water. It was a bold strategic design whose success depended on being able to advance against improved Chinese forces now supported by a full-fledged air force of about 350 first-line combat aircraft commanded by Claire Chennault—who had come a long way from the desperate times he had overseen leading the "Flying Tigers" earlier in the war. The Ichi-Go offensive in China began in April, and made steady progress over the next few months. Hope stirred among the members of the junta in Tokyo.

There were positive signs coming from Burma as well. Instead of simply awaiting the next Allied offensive—recall that the Arakan attack had been beaten back by the Japanese in the spring of 1943—General Renya Mutaguchi, the new commander of the 15th Army, argued for and received permission to mount an invasion of India. Like Toyoda, Mutaguchi had aggressive instincts, realizing that, with the tide now running against Japan, only decisive rather than defensive action held hope of avoiding humiliating defeat. In the offensive he launched a month before Ichi-Go, Mutaguchi enjoyed the presence, in addition to his own troops, of a large contingent—more than 40,000 volunteers—from Subhas Chandra Bose's Indian National Army. In this respect, the Japanese did much better than the Germans in drawing recruits from among captured soldiers, for Indian resentment of continued British colonial control ran high and was exploitable. The 15th Army's invasion of India got off to a promising start, with much ground taken, though the British held on to their strongpoints in the Assam Hills, Imphal and Kohima, both of which were besieged. General William Slim, commander of the 14th Army trying to hold these positions, remembered, "The battle had not started well; at any time crisis might slip into disaster—and still might. We were in tactical difficulties everywhere."[27]

Overall, the Japanese strategic situation by May of 1944 was mixed. Nimitz's forces were advancing, seemingly inexorably; losses to submarine attack were rising precipitously; and Japan couldn't match the improvements the Americans were making to their warplanes. But much of the defensive perimeter in the Pacific was still in place, and Imperial Army forces were on the offensive in China. In Burma—and on the rough border with India—the 15th Army maintained the siege of Allied forces at Imphal and Kohima, and was striking elsewhere. But on this front the Allies demonstrated a robust capacity for keeping besieged troops supplied from the air—quite in contrast to the German failure to provide a similar sort of airlift to their doomed 6th Army at Stalingrad. On balance Japan's long-term outlook was grim, due to the inability thus far to halt the American advance across the Central Pacific. The energetic Admiral Toyoda saw that the only hope for stemming the tide of the enemy's leapfrogging advances was a major naval engagement. He believed that a *Kantai Kessen,* a decisive sea fight, was Japan's very best hope, and convinced the Imperial General Staff which, as Andrieu d'Albas noted, then "gave him directives according to which the air and naval forces were to prepare for a decisive action to take place at the end of May."[28]

The *Kantai Kessen* did not arise exactly in accordance with General Staff planning for battle at the end of May; but Admiral Toyoda had to wait only another few weeks. Nimitz's forces struck at Saipan in the Marianas in mid–June. Toyoda knew that this was *the* moment to strike back. And when the opposing fleets met on the 19th, main Japanese striking power consisted of nine carriers with just under 500 aircraft—nearly 300 land-based planes were able to join the fight as well. The Japanese also had a total of sixteen battleships and heavy cruisers, protected by twenty-eight destroyers and two-dozen I-boats. The U.S. Navy had fifteen carriers with a complement of over 900 aircraft, a total of fifteen battleships and heavy cruisers, seventy destroyers and twenty-eight submarines. It was the ultimate test of Japan's strategic design for carrier-based naval warfare, and this time the Americans wouldn't benefit from surprise—as they had at Midway two years earlier. In the event, Japan's design choice to forgo armoring their planes in favor of giving them an advantage in range over their American enemy proved a mistake. Japanese aircraft losses exceeded 600 in what came to be called "The Great Marianas Turkey Shoot." American losses were just one-fifth of Japan's, at 120, with eighty of these not shot down but rather having had to ditch for lack of fuel after making their strikes. The Imperial Navy lost three carriers—two sunk by submarine. The U.S. Navy suffered no sinkings.

Samuel Eliot Morison summed up this sea fight as "the greatest carrier battle of the war. Forces engaged were three to four times those in Midway, and victory was so complete that Japanese naval air could never again engage on any other terms than suicidal."[29] Why such a lop-sided result? Part of the answer is that it was a design error to rely heavily, as the Japanese did, on planes having longer range by not being armored. This was offset by U.S. radar capabilities, "Magic" code-breaking, and the resilience of American aircraft. Japanese planes easily turned into fireballs when hit. Vulnerability to U.S. fighters was matched in the realm of anti-aircraft fire, given American use of proximity fuses that allowed AA batteries to be very effective without actually hitting their targets. By 1944, American pilots also enjoyed the benefits of more training—and a greater chance of living long enough to gain vital combat experience. Japan's renowned destroyer captain, Tameichi Hara, summed up the defeat in the Philippine Sea this way: "[T]he strategy of this operation did not reckon sufficiently with the effectiveness of enemy radar and the enemy's increased pilot skill and plane capability; nor with the correlative decrease in the skill of Japanese pilots."[30]

\* \* \*

If utter disaster befell the Japanese in the Marianas in June 1944, it was a calamity more than matched by the series of reverses the Germans suffered beginning just a month earlier. These troubles began with a breakthrough on the main Italian front at Monte Cassino, where the Benedictine mountain monastery that had been heavily bombed but was still blocking the Allied advance after many months was finally taken, and continued with a final breakout from the Anzio beachhead. As Katharine Savage summed up the situation, "In May 1944 the front came to life. In Cassino a Polish brigade under General Anders stormed through the town and with matchless valor, in the face of deadly fire, charged repeatedly over the rubble and captured the commanding height…. The troops broke out from the Anzio beachhead to join the advancing armies … the Germans were in full retreat."[31] Albert Kesselring decided to avoid a fight for Rome that would surely destroy the Eternal City, choosing instead to withdraw his forces to a new defensive line to the north. On June 4, 1944, Allied troops entered what was now an "open city." Two days later came the invasion of occupied France at Normandy.

Long awaited, the landing still came as a tactical surprise, thanks to the "information edge" the Allies had with weather stations far west of any the Germans possessed. They knew a break in stormy weather was coming, providing an opportunity to strike when the Germans thought it impossible. Eisenhower, elevated to command of "Overlord," recalled the staff meeting on June 4, when his "little camp was shaking and shuddering under a wind of almost hurricane proportions," during which the Meteorologic Staff ruled out landing on the 5th. But then Group Captain Stagg made an "astonishing declaration, which was that by the following morning a period of relatively good weather, heretofore completely unexpected, would ensue, lasting probably thirty-six hours."[32] Eisenhower seized this opportunity to order the invasion to go ahead on the 6th, wrong-footing the Germans—Rommel in particular, as he took advantage of the bad weather to visit his wife on her birthday. Afterward, he intended to see Hitler at Berchtesgaden to get him, at long last, to endorse the notion of a "front line on the beaches," and to "reinforce the divisions in Northern France, if need be at the expense of garrisons in Norway, in Southern France, or the Channel Islands."[33]

The Germans did have *some* intelligence about how the invasion was to be launched, and when it might take place. With regard to the amphibious operations, German motor-torpedo E-boats sometimes shadowed the Allied practice exercises—this in addition to their often engaging in sharp battles with Channel convoys. And in the early hours of April 28, 1944, several E-boats, starting with two but rising to seven, caught sight of a major exercise with landing ships and smaller landing craft off the Devon coast at Slapton Sands. In the ensuing action, the Germans decimated the Allied convoy, torpedoing ships and knocking out landing craft with gunfire. Some 650 Allied soldiers and sailors died that night; the Germans gained invaluable intelligence.[34] Even more information about the impending landings came from the *Abwehr,* the German military intelligence service, which learned from an informant that the BBC would broadcast a poem by Paul Verlaine when the invasion was imminent—to serve as call to arms to the Resistance. Lines of the poem aired during the first days of June, noted by intelligence analysts and, "by 2215 hours on June 5 the High Command of the German Armed Forces, as well as Field-Marshal von Rundstedt, Naval Group headquarters in Paris, and Rommel's Army Group had been informed."[35]

The result: 15th Army in the Pas de Calais was forewarned—because that's where the invasion was thought most likely to occur. Inexcusably, the 7th Army in Normandy and Brittany was not put on full alert. Even so, the defenders fought hard at the water's edge, coped with the more than 20,000 Allied paratroopers who landed miles inland, and were generally well able to contain the initial lodgment. But their ability to throw the invaders back into the sea was crippled by the lack of heavy armored forces in the immediate vicinity. The strategic defensive design that Hitler had chosen—to spread out the panzers behind the various potential landing zones, but to hold them well inland—was a fatal compromise between Rundstedt's and Rommel's preferred views that ensured the success of the landing. And in the view of leading historians, *this* was the critical battle that determined the outcome of the war. Stephen Ambrose summed up the situation simply and very well, keying on the German need to free up forces for the continuing fight against the Russians by winning in the West: "Hitler had to persuade Stalin that the Wehrmacht was still capable of inflicting unacceptable casualties on the Red Army. To do that, Hitler needed more fighting men and machines. To get them, he had to strip his Western Front. To do that, he had to hurl the forthcoming invasion back into the sea."[36]

But as the battle unfolded in the days and weeks after the landing, the Allied armies only grew stronger, while the Germans were worn down in the hard fighting among the hedgerows that crisscrossed Normandy. They fell farther and farther behind in what became a "battle of the buildup" (Chester Wilmot's phrase), in part because continuing concern about a second landing—fed by elaborate Allied deception operations—delayed the movement of reinforcements from the 15th Army in the Pas de Calais. Still, the battle was hard-fought; the Allies made few advances in the early going. British and Canadian forces in particular, under Montgomery's command, were stymied. Alexander McKee summed up the scene by mid–June, "There was deadlock in Normandy. Only substantial reinforcements, on one side or the other, could break it."[37] In the end, though, even with some fresh forces joining the beleaguered 7th Army, Rommel knew he would lose; the Allies would break out. In a letter to his wife written June 23, Rommel said, "Militarily things aren't at all good. The enemy air force is dealing extremely heavily with our supplies and at the moment is completely strangling them. If a decisive battle develops, we'll be without ammunition."[38]

As to interdicting Allied supplies to the beachheads, by this point in the war the *Kriegsmarine* and *Luftwaffe* had very little striking power left. German E-boats did sink several ships in hit-and-run attacks; in addition, Borghese's manned torpedo concept of operations seems to have taken hold amongst the Germans, as they put fifty of them into action, sinking three more ships. The *Kriegsmarine* also introduced the first version of what we would today call a "naval drone" and, as Samuel Eliot Morison noted, these "remote-controlled explosive motor boats were employed with some effect." Still, he concluded, "All these 'secret weapons' were mere fleabites."[39] The one technological advance that could have made a difference was the first of the "vengeance weapons" (*Vergeltungswaffen*). The V-1s were early cruise missiles, introduced one week after D-Day. But instead of employing them in salvoes against beaches in Normandy or ports in southern England, Hitler ordered them used as terror weapons against London. Nine thousand V-1s were soon launched against that city—half were shot down, given their relatively slow speed—killing more civilians than had died in the first Blitz. Louis Snyder keyed on the V-1s, observing, "Why Hitler did not use the V-1 … to smash the build-up … remains one of the great mysteries of the war."[40]

While the Normandy battle raged, on June 22, the third anniversary of the German invasion of Russia, Josef Stalin launched Operation Bagration—named after the heroic general mortally wounded in the most bitter fighting against Napoleon's invading *Grande Armée* at the 1812 Battle of Borodino. Deploying over 2,500,000 million soldiers, nearly 8,000 attack aircraft, and 6,000 tanks, the Russians enjoyed a massive material advantage over the Germans—who had to fight an increasingly desperate battle in the West at the same time. But "Bagration" was not successful simply because of the numerical advantage the Russians enjoyed, or due to the crisis in Normandy; partisan forces performed a critical function from the outset that crippled the Germans. Alexander Werth summed up their contribution this way:

> There was close coordination between the Red Army Command and the partisans who succeeded, between June 20 and 23, in putting practically all the Belorussian railways out of action—precisely what the Red Army needed to paralyze the movement of German supplies and troops.[41]

It did not take long for the Russians to tear a nearly 250-mile-wide gap in the German front in fighting that cost the *Heer* nearly 400,000 soldiers—the total killed in action, wounded, missing and taken prisoner. Russian losses were nearly double, as their tactics remained less supple than their German foes; but the Red Army could still afford to suffer such an "exchange ratio."

If their battle tactics remained a bit balky, at the wider operational level the Russians were now waging mobile warfare much as the Germans had in earlier years—a kind of *Blitzkrieg* payback visited upon the designers of the doctrine best suited to the coordinated action of tank and plane. The *Heer* and *Luftwaffe* could no longer operate in this way, as Germany's best tanks—Tigers and Panthers—were relatively slow and heavy, better suited now for more deliberate-paced, positional battles. Thus, the strengths of the new German heavy tanks in armor and armament were offset by the fact that they were ill prepared to conduct the kind of mobile maneuver operations that had now diffused to the Allies. This was an important design flaw that manifested itself at the doctrinal level, and the consequences were felt all too soon. By July 18, 1944, Russian armored spearheads had advanced all the way beyond the pre-war Polish border. Just two days later the plotters who hoped to rid Germany of Hitler and work toward an armistice set off their bomb at his "Wolf's Lair" headquarters in East Prussia. Hitler survived the blast. Werth reported that "failure of the attempt was received in Russia with undisguised relief," as the Soviets feared the Fuehrer's death would be the catalyst for a separate peace between Germany and the Western Allies.[42]

The attempt on his life left Hitler deeply suspicious of his generals—it soon became apparent that many had supported the assassination attempt, or at least hoped for its success. But there was one senior officer who retained his confidence: Walter Model, who had taken command of two army groups in the East shortly before the *Attentat*. In Guderian's view, Model was "the best possible man to perform the fantastically difficult task of reconstructing a line in the center of the Eastern Front."[43] Over a few weeks, from the end of July through early August, Model stabilized the Eastern Front, thanks in part to his evolving notion of redesigning the remaining German forces away from standard divisional and regimental structures to more fluid, "informally organized combat and support units," as Carlo D'Este described Model's innovative thinking.[44] These small, flexible units—Model's variant of the earlier *Kampfgruppen* combined-arms concept—turned out to have quite a considerable punch and great maneuverability. Given the balky battle tactics that the Russians were still employing, Model's design matched up well, a major contributing factor in the Red Army's heavy losses—still just about double those of the Germans—during this period.

By mid–August, Hitler felt comfortable enough with the situation in the East that he sent Model to France to deal with what was now a collapsing situation there. Rundstedt had been relieved of overall command there on July 2, Rommel was badly wounded in a strafing run by a fighter-bomber on the 17th, and their successor Field-Marshal Gunther von Kluge had utterly lost Hitler's confidence by his apparent mishandling of the final stages of the Normandy battle—especially the risky counter-offensive that was mounted at Mortain in the first week of August. Hitler also worried, mistakenly, it seems, that Kluge had thought about surrendering to the Allies. Upon being sacked and called home, Kluge committed suicide, leaving behind a note that affirmed his loyalty to Hitler. The situation was bleak when Model went to France. It was a time when the Germans, aside from lacking wise leadership at the top, had lost nearly half a million troops killed, wounded, or captured in the West, with over a hundred thousand others still trapped in their isolated coastal fortresses now far behind the advancing Allies' lines. A "second front" had also opened up in France, as Operation Dragoon, the American-led landing on the Mediterranean coast— very actively supported by thousands of Resistance *Maquisards*—imperiled Army Group G. In the face of all these various difficulties, Model nevertheless asserted himself and, largely through force of will, began to restore the situation.

A key adjustment he made immediately was to create four fresh *Kampfgruppen*—each of from 1,200–1,300 fighting men with eight artillery batteries and just a slight leavening of armor—that soon reflected the value and fighting power of this organizational design. More significant panzer formations would be needed as well, and Hitler promised Model half a dozen armored brigades would be coming soon from Germany to give him a mobile reserve.[45] Model's impact on the campaign was immediate, and an amazing recovery soon stabilized the front in France. From the Channel coast through the Low Countries, veteran paratroops accustomed to fighting in small groups stiffened the will and helped restore the capa-

Walter Model (left), "the Fuehrer's fireman" in both East and West (Creative Commons, courtesy Bundesarchiv, Bild 183-J27784 / Adendorf, Peter / CC-BY-SA 3.0).

bilities of their comrades who had been demoralized by defeat and retreat. On the central portion of the front, Model's newly formed *Kampfgruppen* began to have a real impact on the advancing Allies, who were now beginning to suffer from fuel shortages and other logistical difficulties, and would soon be bumping up against the fortifications of the Siegfried Line. At the southern end of the front, most of Army Group G had made it to the Vosges Mountains, where they were now able to mount a stout defense. Omar Bradley, commanding the 12th Army Group, had no doubt who was responsible for the stiffening of the German defenses:

> In one of the enemy's more resourceful demonstrations of generalship, Model stemmed the rout of the Wehrmacht. He quieted the panic and reorganized the demoralized German forces into effective battlegroups. From Antwerp to Epinal, 260 miles south, Model had miraculously grafted a new backbone on the German army.[46]

Antwerp fell to the Allies on September 4, but its port would not be usable for some time, as German forces still controlled the Scheldt Estuary. It was the Allies' last big gain for a while. The next day Rundstedt accepted Hitler's request to return to duty as commander in the West. This allowed Model to concentrate on directing Army Group B, which faced dire threats from Montgomery's and Bradley's forces. What Model achieved in battle, Rundstedt accomplished at the staff level, quickly setting processes aright. As Martin Blumenson observed, "all the higher headquarters were for the most part intact and able to function…. The fabric of command, though stretched and worn, could be made serviceable."[47] Model and Rundstedt saved the Western front from collapse, and showed that the *Heer* still had hitting power. When Montgomery's ambitious "Market Garden" offensive—featuring 40,000 airborne troops aimed at seizing nine bridges—launched on September 17, the German response was swift. The attack failed.[48]

While Montgomery was being defeated at Arnhem, the other great Allied field commander, George S. Patton—whose 3rd Army had led the breakout from Normandy at Avranches and then swept across much of France—had been under a restrictive "shutdown," to use Bradley's term. Throughout September, and on into October, Patton "padded about his Army like a caged tiger."[49] This constraint on the 3rd Army arose out of continuing logistical difficulties, but also from Eisenhower's decision to pursue the next phase of the campaign along a broad front—which required frequent pausing by leading forces, so as to keep the advance "aligned." In the wake of the Arnhem debacle, the one major exception to a narrow-focused advance was in the area of General Courtney Hodges' 1st Army. His troops had been nibbling since September at Aachen, the much-bombed German city that had become part of the Siegfried Line defenses. Early in October, Hodges struck at the city. For three weeks his troops were mired in a bloody struggle for the city, finally winning out—but at great cost. The battles at Arnhem as well as at "Bloody Aachen" showed how hard it was going to be to pierce Germany's defenses in the West. Moreover, the bitter tactical fight at Aachen had the strategic effect of delaying the overall Allied advance.[50]

* * *

The summer offensives that had been launched against the Germans, coming at the Reich from across France and the Low Countries in the west, Italy in the south, and from several points in Eastern Europe, seemed to have run out of steam by October 1944, and a pause set in. But in the Pacific, this was hardly the case in the continuing campaigns against the Japanese. For in the wake of the "turkey shoot" in the Marianas Allied forces had been striking hard in several places, sometimes just raiding—either to "soften up" island defenses or to confuse the enemy—and sometimes landing on an important stepping stone along the way forward. At this point in the war, the Japanese were inferior everywhere across the Pacific, in numbers and in the quality of their aircraft—especially when compared to American fighter planes. One of the best examples of the hopelessness of the situation for the Japanese in the air during the summer of 1944 was the wild action in which their top ace, Saburo Sakai—still flying in combat despite loss of an eye—found himself when he was based at Iwo Jima. During one American raid, he rose up to confront the attackers, was separated from his squadron in the confusion of the ensuing dogfight, and ended up in the middle of a swarm of *fifteen* U.S. Navy Hellcats. He recalled the struggle to survive the *mêlée* this way:

> I rolled. Full throttle.
> Stick over to the left.
> Here comes another!
> Hard over. The sea and horizon spinning crazily.

*Skid!*
Another.
That was close!
Tracers. Bright. Shining. Flashing.
Always underneath the wing.
Stick over.
Keep your speed up!
Roll to the left.
Roll.
My arm! I can hardly feel it anymore![51]

Sakai and his supple Zero survived long enough for the Americans to run low on fuel and have to break off the action to return to their carriers. For days after, the enemy kept raiding Iwo Jima, then suddenly left. Sakai and his surviving colleagues—well over half the pilots in his unit were killed—were brought home for leave, then prepared for redeployment. As to the U.S. Navy, it didn't return to Iwo for nearly seven months, in mid–February 1945, when it faced a very stubborn defense. The reason for the departure of the force that had been softening up Iwo Jima was that the decision had been finally taken to merge the Nimitz- and MacArthur-led campaigns—a joining to occur in the Philippine Islands, the landing point roughly at their middle: Leyte. But before Nimitz could make it there, he felt a need to secure the Palau Islands, from which he would make the leap to meet with MacArthur.

On September 15, 1944, Marines landed on Peleliu in the Palaus, after a heavy preparatory bombardment. The Americans were confident that they had learned from Tarawa, and that the slight losses suffered in subsequent invasions confirmed this learning and augured well for this action. But they failed to reckon with the Japanese redesign of their defensive doctrine. Acknowledging failure of the "battle on the beaches" concept—and the absurdity of the *banzai* tactics—Japanese leaders now shifted to a defense-in-depth approach keeping their forces hunkered down during the enemy bombardment, allowing landing troops to come ashore in great numbers, only *then* subjecting them to sustained artillery and machine gun fire. This idea had been tried out to good effect in the defense of Biak, an island off the west coast of New Guinea, which lasted from May to mid–August. This new defensive design was well suited to Peleliu, as the island's hundreds of caves were soon connected by networks of tunnels. Hard fighting ensued, running into October, right up to invasion of the Philippines. And scattered resistance continued even after. In the end, almost all 11,000 Japanese defenders had died. Marine and Army casualties were close to 10,000. Robert Leckie said of this fighting, "In proportion of the number of men engaged, Peleliu was the fiercest, bloodiest battle of the Japanese war."[52]

The new defensive battle design was a great improvement in Imperial Army tactics, sharply raising the cost of American advances and lengthening the time required to capture an island. The value of these tactics would prove out in the hard fighting to come at Iwo Jima and Okinawa. Curiously, though, this advanced tactical thinking didn't seem to seep through to the strategic level when it came to the defense of the Philippines, where about a quarter-million Japanese troops awaited the invasion. They were strung out in peripheral defensive deployments, from Luzon in the north to Leyte in the center, and on to Mindanao in the south. Given the Allies' command of the sea and air superiority, they could invade at practically any point of their choosing; the Japanese defensive scheme virtually invited a landing at Leyte to split the enemy right in the middle. A strategic design in consonance with the new tactical doctrine wouldn't have spread out the defenders in this way; instead they would have been concentrated on the key main island of Luzon, which offered both positional battle prospects and much room for defending in depth. General Yamashita, long out of the major actions of the war, was finally brought back from Manchuria in the wake of Tojo's fall from power in the summer of 1944. Ten days before the invasion, which took place on October 20, 1944, Yamashita arrived to take command in the Philippines.

Yamashita wanted to conduct what Imperial General Headquarters called the "general decisive battle" on Luzon. Doing so offered much better prospects for his ground forces, and would give the Navy more room to maneuver than in the narrow, channelized sea passages in the central and southern Philippines. Headquarters went along with him, but only briefly. When the landings began at Leyte, it became apparent that MacArthur was striking there with massive force. In light of this, as Samuel Eliot Morison noted, "Imperial General Headquarters completely changed it strategy with respect to Leyte.... [I]t decided to make Leyte rather than Luzon the scene of the 'general decisive battle.'"[53] There was but one division on Leyte, the 16th, though hundreds of aircraft stood by to attack the invasion force, and the Navy was at the ready to put its *Sho* (Victory) plan into motion. The plan was unusually complex—even by Japanese standards—with its carriers feinting in the north to divert the Americans away from the landing zone, while warships, coming through narrow waters north and south of Leyte, were to shoot up the landing zone. As Andrieu d'Albas put the matter, "this immense outburst of energy, as the Japanese dashed to the rescue in one last supreme effort, had its touch of pathetic grandeur."[54]

The sea fight that followed on the 24th and 25th of October unfolded on a very grand scale. The four carriers that formed the heart of the northern diversion were all sunk; but, improbably, they succeeded in drawing "Bull" Halsey's carriers away from Leyte. This despite the fact that the "gambit tactics of using carriers as a decoy … [were] already known to United States Naval Intelligence"[55] and described in the *Seventh Fleet Intelligence Bulletin* disseminated on October 13, 1944—eleven days before the battle. Thus, with Halsey drawn away, the Japanese warships had a brief chance to strike at the landing zone; but poor coordination with the commander of the land-based aircraft that were to provide cover left them naked when they came under air attack en route to Leyte. And then, just as one of the striking forces was on the verge of breaking through to decimate the Allied transport vessels and bombard the crowded forces and supply depots ashore, a heroic, suicidal charge by a handful of destroyers and destroyer escorts, along with attacks by aircraft from half a dozen "jeep carriers" near to the landing zone, convinced Vice Admiral Takeo Kurita to break off his attack. In addition to the loss of four carriers, three battleships, ten cruisers and eleven destroyers went down. The Americans lost three carriers, two destroyers, and one destroyer escort, making it a most lop-sided victory for the U.S. Navy.

But one of the American carriers sunk was the victim of *kamikaze* suicide attack. From a design perspective, the *kamikaze* can best be described, in today's terms, as a cruise missile—albeit one with a human rather than a silicon-based guidance system. By this point in the war, the Japanese had far more planes than skilled pilots; it was logical to think in terms of providing just enough training so that individual operators would be able to fly to the attack site and crash into enemy vessels. Culturally, the Japanese were attuned to the notion of making ultimate personal sacrifices of this sort, and of the honor gained in taking such action—as it conformed to the strictures of *Bushido* (the "Way of the Warrior"). And strategically, the "Special Attack Corps" was more than simply a death cult; pilots were very sharply enjoined not just to die, but to make the most of their sacrifice. As *The First Order of the Kamikaze* stated, "Do not be in too much of a hurry to die. If you cannot find your target, turn back; next time you may find a more favorable opportunity. Choose a death which brings the maximum result."[56] Here we can see, in the fusing of pilot to plane, the classic point John Heskett makes about design as "used by people to construct a sense of who they are, to express their sense of identity."[57]

The Japanese *kamikaze* design was, in essence, a human-guided cruise missile that, as Victor Davis Hanson noted, had "greater range and vastly superior accuracy" than the German *Vergeltungswaffen* and, from October 1944 to the end of the war, accounted for *half* of all U.S. Navy losses.[58] The principal designer behind the *kamikaze* concept was Vice Admiral Takijiro Onishi, who had first partnered with Isoroku Yamamoto in building Japan's carrier strike forces, the *Kido Butai*. By the summer of 1944, Onishi was convinced that the only reasonable to chance to thwart the Allied advances was by means of striking their fleets by means of suicide attack squadrons. But his idea was so radical that, even among his *Samurai* colleagues, and at the High Command as well, there was much resistance. So much so that Onishi attempted an end run around his chain of command by asking for an audience with Emperor Hirohito. But when the emperor "learned from the duty courtier of the *Kunaicho* (Imperial Household Agency) why Onishi wanted the audience, it was refused."[59] It is important to note that the Imperial Army Air Service had advocates for suicide tactics as well, but the Army High Command squelched the idea successfully. For a time.

Onishi's breakthrough came in the wake of Japan's disastrous defeat in the Battle of the Philippine Sea, when senior leadership grew willing to try out even such an extreme innovation as was embodied in the *kamikaze* concept of operations. He won approval to employ suicide tactics in the looming battle for the Philippines; and there, in October, they enjoyed their first successes. In five-plane formations of Zeroes—three *kamikazes* with two acting as escorts, their small number thought to aid in avoiding detection and interception—Onishi's "special attack corps" had just four of these units in place, ready to participate in the fighting at Leyte. Their first success was in sinking the American escort carrier *St. Lo,* christened the *Midway,* but it was recently renamed in honor of the Norman town that was the scene of some hard fighting after D-Day. Several other ships were damaged by the *kamikazes.* For Onishi, the performance of his special attack corps at Leyte provided validation, sweeping away his opposition and preparing the way for significant expansion of this program. As to the U.S. Navy, as Morison noted, it "was confronted with a new problem of air defense. Nobody realized that this was the beginning of new and desperate tactics on the part of the Japanese, but the prospects were distinctly unpleasant."[60] Over the coming months these prospects became far more than just "unpleasant."

\*   \*   \*

The first ten months of 1944 offered the Axis Powers their last chances to avoid catastrophic defeat. For the Germans, the odds grew longer each day. Their U-boats had been decisively countered because of the failure to focus on the transformational change afforded by the air-independent propulsion technology that had been in the offing since the 1930s. Similarly, the air defense of the Reich had been shattered by the decision, first, to delay the production of jets, then by the ridiculous debate about producing them to serve primarily as bombers. As to the "V" weapons, the choice to employ them as terror weapons against British cities was a blunder; aiming them at logistical chokepoints in Normandy and at southern British ports would have had far greater effect on the course of the war. Last, the incomparable *Heer* was being driven back steadily during these months, on both the Russian and Italian fronts. In the West, the only real hope lay in Rommel's design for defeating the Allied landings on the beaches; but Rommel's squabbles with Rundstedt—and even Guderian—led Hitler to decide upon a compromise deployment of forces that prevented the Desert Fox from fully implementing his vision. Even so, the Normandy battle was a very near-run thing.

For Japan, this was the period in which their most serious design flaws became fully exposed. The failure to prepare against submarine attack on their vital sea lines of communication and supply led to a slaughter of the merchant fleets, and the loss of all too many warships as well. Just as grave was the exposure of the weakness of the aircraft design choice, made prior to the war, to emphasize long range and outstanding maneuverability at the cost of ruggedness. Japanese warplanes were simply too prone to becoming fireballs when suffering even modest damage; whereas American warplanes, though shorter-ranging, had more firepower, were armored, and eventually matched, even exceeded the maneuver capabilities of Japanese aircraft. One other key design flaw undermined Japan's armed forces: their Imperial Codes were not only "hacked," but these codes were kept in use throughout the war. The consequences were that American submarines were vectored in on juicy targets routinely, greatly increasing their effectiveness; and in the great carrier actions in the Pacific, the Americans often got the jump on the Japanese— at Midway and after. The Germans also showed too little sense of the importance of technical information security, and were complacent due to their faith in Enigma; but in relative terms it was the Japanese who suffered far more seriously for their poor design approach to keeping their sensitive communications safe from prying eyes and ears.

And what of the designers themselves? Of the original cast of leading designers, Balbo died early in the war, shot down by his own anti-aircraft gunners. Udet committed suicide. Yamamoto was killed when his plane was shot down in 1943—another victim of Japan's poor information security practices. Rommel, though likely innocent, was implicated by some of the plotters of the July 20 attempt on Hitler's life, but given a chance to commit suicide rather than suffer the humiliation of a public trial. He took poison on October 14. Guderian remained a chief architect of German field operations capabilities, though he never quite realized that the days of *Blitzkrieg* were long gone. As to Doenitz, he continued to enjoy Hitler's confidence, even as his U-boats became less relevant. Borghese was still in action on the Axis side, fighting hard for Mussolini's truncated puppet republic. But his great exploits at sea were over and done with, given the Allies' absolute command of the Mediterranean. He and his men now fought as raiders on land. Of all the Axis' leading strategic designers, though, Yamashita may have been the most tragic. The "Tiger of Malaya"—pioneer of very innovative operational concepts—was placed in "professional exile" by Tojo, for years after the capture of Singapore. Brought back into the fight just prior to the American invasion of the Philippines, he was forced to command in a campaign whose strategy had been set by others, and with which he disagreed vehemently.

After the first wave of Axis designers, a second followed—at least in some areas. Udet had done too little to advocate for jets; but Galland and Messerschmitt both lobbied hard for this quantum advance in air warfare and, by the fall of 1944, their efforts were on the verge of reaping dividends. Rommel and Guderian, master designers of *Blitzkrieg*, had been to a great extent superseded by two outstanding defensive fighters: Kesselring and Model. Kesselring pursued a military doctrine based on positional warfare and steady, deliberate retreats to prepared positions. Model, on the other hand, fought to hold ground, and during 1944 perfected his organizational redesign of *Heer* units around small, supple, battle groups that proved their worth both on the Eastern and Western Fronts. As to Japanese strategic design, Toyoda proved a worthy successor to Yamamoto, especially with his grasp of the notion of concentrating all force possible in a climactic *Kantai Kessen*. But the Japanese realized this was the right approach too late; by the summer of '44 the Allies were simply too far ahead, materially, to lose a clash of carriers. Thus Onishi's human-guided "cruise missiles," *kamikazes*, were absolutely necessary if Japan was to continue the war with any chance of stemming the Allied tide. The return of Yamashita to the war on land—a "second act" if not a second wave of strategic design— signaled an Imperial awareness of the high stakes now in play. A final play for both Axis powers.

# 8. Cataclysm

ON NOVEMBER 1, 1944—ALL SAINTS' DAY—the Allies began an important advance, attacking Walcheren Island, the last German bastion blocking the Scheldt Estuary that prevented the port of Antwerp from being used for the unloading of supplies. The Canadian 2nd Corps led this attack, but ran into stiff resistance from the German 70th Infantry Division, known as *Weissen Brot* ("White Bread") as it was comprised of men with stomach ailments who required a bland diet. Most were older, too, as Germany was now scraping the bottom of its manpower barrel. Yet the 70th fought hard, and the next day the Canadians needed help from the British 52nd Division. It took a week to clear the island; then the way from the sea to Antwerp—once free of mines and other obstructions—would be open. The value of this port stuck in Hitler's mind, and he began to think of ways to deny it to the Allies. This was when the first seeds of what became the Battle of the Bulge were planted. In the meantime, though, the *Heer* had to cope with still another looming threat from the further advance of American forces beyond Aachen toward the Roer River—only thirty miles from the Rhine. Americans had for some time been pushing slowly, yet very directly, through the Huertgen Forest toward the seven dams on the Roer that, if blown opportunely, could strand advanced units, leaving them prey to Model's battle groups.

On November 2, 1944, ten days after the conclusion of the battle for "Bloody Aachen," the U.S. 28th Infantry, the "Keystone Division"—so named as it was formed from elements of the Pennsylvania National Guard—opened a fresh phase in the advance into the Huertgen Forest. This was the shortest route to the dams, but clearly the toughest one. And in the days and weeks that followed, the American troops were tested to their limits. Even when more units were fed into the battle, especially the elite 1st Infantry Division—"the Big Red One"—progress was exceedingly slow in the heavy forest, measured sometimes in just yards gained per day. Chester Wilmot described the fighting this way: "resolute defense, repeated counter-attacks and recurrent rain reduced the battle to infantry slogging of the nastiest kind."[1] Model's performance in this battle was of the highest order, as he skillfully fed in additional forces as and when he deemed necessary. For the most part, though, he placed great reliance on the holding power of his small battle groups, an innovation in organizational design on the defensive side of the spectrum as important as the formation of the panzer division had been to the offensive. By the end of November, the American offensive petered out, the 1st Division losing 300 men in fighting on the 29th and 30th. Overall American casualties exceeded 50,000, the Germans little over half that.

Patton's 3rd Army, unleashed after the seemingly unending delays imposed by Eisenhower, was not idle while Hodges' 1st was slugging it out up north. Operating far to the south, Patton drove his soldiers relentlessly toward the Vosges Mountains, ultimately aiming at the Saar. But he also worked around the flanks of the main heights of the Vosges, leaving the Germans in what was dubbed the "Colmar Pocket." At this point, Patton successfully argued his army should break off its flank attack on the Pocket and strike instead to its north, right at the Saar. This left the hard task of attacking the Germans in the Pocket to the 7th U.S. and 1st French Armies. Yet when they struck, the German 19th Army—which had retreated in good order in the face of the Dragoon invasion of southern France—held their ground. Their retention of this important lodgment on the western bank of the Rhine, as General Eisenhower reflected on the matter, "later exerted a profound adverse effect on our operations."[2] Given slow progress all along the Allied front, on the 20th of November Eisenhower requested from the Combined Chiefs of Staff an easing of Allied unconditional surrender terms, for he saw "no signs of an early collapse of German morale in the west."[3]

Needless to say, this request was turned down and, in the face of such stiff German resistance—and the worsening weather—the situation in the West came to a near-standstill. The same held true in Italy where, between them, Kesselring and Mussolini retained sufficient forces to slow the Allied advance, which had broken through the "Gothic Line" north of Rome during September. In part the Allied advance was stalled by stout defenses; but the fact that some units of the 5th Army had been siphoned off for the Dragoon landings in southern France played a role as well. The balance of forces on each side was roughly equal; indeed, at least some of the time Allied armies in Italy were outnumbered, in terms of divisions—though German divisions were by this time in the war smaller than their adversaries' formations. The difference was more than made up, though, by the Allies' complete control of the air. Even so, the advance north was slow and difficult. The fighting spirit of the Axis troops remained high, and morale began to suffer among the Allied soldiers. Major-General W.G.F. Jackson recalled, "this 'end of war' psychosis appeared in the figures for desertions from Allied divisions which began to rise as winter approached … it was preferable to desert and survive rather than stand another winter in the mountains, taking part in hopeless attacks on strongly held German positions."[4]

While the situation in Italy ground to a halt, leading to what Jackson—who was wounded during the advance on Florence—called a "second winter of disappointment," Axis defenses on the Eastern Front were still benefiting from the fine work that Model had done to restore the situation there before heading West to stem the Allied advance after the breakout from Normandy. The massive Russian summer offensive seemed to have run out of steam in Poland by this time—though there is debate about the extent to which Stalin deliberately stalled here, to let the Germans bear the burden of stamping out General Tadeusz Bór-Komorowski's Polish Home Army so that the Soviet Red Army would not have to take on the task. In the event, Bór (the Polish word for "forest," one of his code names) led a spirited defense for over two months between August and October 1944—twice the length of the heroic Jewish defense of the Warsaw ghetto the previous year—before surrendering to superior *Waffen SS* forces. As evidence of Stalin's possible act of perfidy, Andrew Roberts argues: "Since the destruction of any future opposition to a Communist regime in Poland suited Stalin well, he refused the USAAF and RAF permission to land in Soviet-held territory, thus severely hampering their ability to drop supplies of food and arms to the Poles."[5]

But it is also possible that the Russian halt in Poland—which was to last into January 1945—resulted from a combination of factors. There was the improving German defense on the most direct Soviet route of advance to Berlin, for one thing. Another possibility was that Stalin wanted to knock the Germans' allies in the Balkans and central Europe out of the war, and then perhaps link up with Tito's partisans in Yugoslavia. Two of Germany's smaller allies in central Europe, for example, left the Axis while Bór and his army were keeping the Germans busy in Warsaw: Romania in August 1944 and Bulgaria in September. So, these important gains may have provided reason enough for the Soviet shift to a southern offensive. A larger political rationale for Stalin's southern advance was that, as Alan Clark argued:

> A direct march on Berlin before the Balkans had been overrun might mean that the war would be ended with a large area of Europe still under nominal German occupation. The governments of Hungary, Romania, and Bulgaria had all been in touch with Western agencies.... A sudden collapse of German resistance could be followed by a number of bourgeois "center" administrations that could appeal to the Allies for diplomatic support.[6]

However, in Yugoslavia, Tito carefully ensured that liberation of his country would be achieved by indigenous partisan forces—an accomplishment that was destined to limit Russian influence over Belgrade in the postwar period.

There is yet another explanation, of a military strategic nature, for continued Red Army thrusts well south of the front in Poland. Where strong German resistance could be expected on the direct northern line of approach to Berlin, an "indirect approach"—the term is B.H. Liddell Hart's—had far greater prospects for gaining a victory achievable at much lower cost in casualties. This was an increasingly important factor at the time, given the massive manpower losses the Russians had suffered over the past three-plus years of hard fighting. Beyond this consideration, though, was the Russians' knowledge that Hungary, though still a German ally, had gone "wobbly." Indeed, the Hungarian Regent Admiral Horthy had been intriguing to switch sides; the defection of Hungary would have led to the trapping of nearly a million German troops still deployed fighting in and south of the Carpathian Mountains. Only a miracle, it seemed, could save them. Yet disaster was staved off, and the Hungarians remained a German ally, their forces helping to repel the Soviet offensive in the fall of 1944 and keeping an escape route open for all those German soldiers who would otherwise have been cut off. All this happened thanks to another of Otto Skorzeny's "special missions," during which he kidnapped the Regent's son, forced Horthy's abdication, and installed a Berlin-friendly "prime minister," the Count Szalasi.[7]

By November 1944 the German situation had stabilized. In the West and in Italy, the forces on the ground were in rough balance. In the East the Germans were seriously outnumbered; but even here the Russians had halted their advance in Poland and the Red Army's attacks south of the Carpathians had been blunted. The Finns switched sides in September, but the damage they could do to the Germans was limited. There was still a lot of fight left in this war. Absent the Allied demand for unconditional surrender, this would have been a ripe time to pursue peace talks—as had been the case in November 1918. But in November 1944, the Germans had no prospect of starting negotiations, despite the fact that they still had nearly ten million soldiers in arms. To be sure, Doenitz's U-boats had been beaten, and Allied aircraft roamed the skies all over Germany. Yet there remained much blood to be shed on the ground, should the Allies insist on waging the war until Germany was finally engulfed. And fighting to the end seemed the Allies' intent, as news of the plan to de-industrialize a defeated Germany leaked out in September. The "Morgenthau Plan"—named for the American Treasury Secretary who sought to return Germany to its agrarian past—became a powerful propaganda tool in the hands of Joseph Goebbels, who used it to shore up the morale of a mass public by now deeply weary of the war.

Propaganda aside, the reality of the situation was that the Germans—and Mussolini's Salò Republic—had a final opportunity during this lull in November to think through the next, and surely final, steps in their strategic designs. Should they continue to pursue a stubborn defensive posture? Or was there still a chance to seize the initiative with a surprise offensive? To Hitler, a pure defensive ruled out virtually any chance of avoiding eventual, total defeat. Therefore, he committed himself to a last major offensive, by means of scraping together an attacking force some thirty divisions in size. On which front were they to strike? Robert Merriam, the "field historian" who compiled the U.S. Army's official five-volume account of the Battle of the Bulge, assessed the Germans' decision making this way:

> Where to attack? The Russian Front? No, the resources would be wasted in an attack which would have no decisive influence on the course of the war.... [E]ven a highly successful operation in the east could, at most, eliminate only twenty or thirty Russian divisions. While serious, such a loss would be only a drop in the huge Russian manpower barrel. Nor were there any grand strategic objectives which could probably be attained with such a striking force. Likewise, in Italy, supply, terrain, and weather precluded the possibility of a large-scale attack in this theater, and again the strategic objectives were minor.... In the west conditions appeared more favorable.[8]

Indeed, conditions were far more favorable in the West, as the Allies had only some sixty divisions there—the British had *no more troops* to commit to the war effort—all highly dependent on a few seaports for supplies.

Given that a successful offensive through the Ardennes—the scene of the *Heer's* great triumph in 1940—would cripple the Allied advance for a considerable time, allowing German formations to be shifted to the East for counterblows against the Russians, the timing of the attack was of crucial importance. Hitler wanted to strike in November, as this would allow for a shifting of forces east in time to thwart a looming Russian winter offensive. Guderian, who was made Army Chief of Staff the day after the July 20 attempt on Hitler's life, concurred with this view. However, Rundstedt and Model opposed the offensive aimed at Antwerp that Hitler had designed. Instead, they argued for a "small solution": a limited strike at the salient near Aachen, along the dividing line between British and American forces. Time was lost arguing over the plans—Hitler's prevailed— and it took until late November to muster the twenty-eight divisions needed to fill out the order of battle. In the event, the attack did not begin until mid–December. This delay greatly concerned Guderian. And it grew clear to him, just a week into the offensive, "that it could no longer result in a great success.... I decided to drive to Supreme Head-quarters and to request that the battle, which was causing us heavy casualties, be broken off and that all forces that could be spared be immediately transferred to the Eastern Front."[9]

Staffers at Headquarters took the opportunity to disparage Guderian, telling the Fuehrer that he was "ill informed and needlessly apprehensive." Worse, when Guderian persisted, pulling out intelligence reports reflecting the large number of Russian divisions massing in Poland, Hitler screamed at him, asking "Who's responsible for producing all this rubbish?" At dinner that evening (December 23), Jodl said that Guderian would receive no fresh divisions because "the Ardennes would be followed by another offensive in Alsace." Guderian's visit had proved a failure. Far from freeing up forces to defend against the impending Russian offensive north of the Carpathians, his arguments had resulted in OKW sending two panzer divisions, in reserve west of Warsaw, *to Hungary.* Undermined, but undaunted, Guderian went off to see Rundstedt, who appreciated his assessment of the situation and offered three of his divisions for redeployment to the East. Rundstedt went even further, identifying a fourth division currently in Italy that could be rerouted to the East. So armed, Guderian returned to Headquarters to restate his case. Jodl remained opposed to the troop movement. But when informed of Rundstedt's opinion, Hitler at last relented.[10] The divisions moved. And so, a glimmer of hope remained for avoiding utter catastrophe in the East.

Was Hitler's offensive in the West reasonable, even if desperate and unlikely to succeed? In July the preceding year, he had opted—with much support from his generals—to attack in the East at Kursk instead of keeping with Manstein's mobile defensive. But when his panzers were halted there, the initiative went permanently over to the Russians. The decision to attack at Kursk should be viewed as a basic failure of strategic design—mistaking a situation that demanded flexible defense for one that favored the offensive. Even so, by late 1944 Guderian had rebuilt the German armored forces, now able to provide a powerful reserve to plug any gaps the enemy's offensives might create. The difference with the prior year, though, was that Germany no longer had strategic depth; the Russians were in Poland, and Allied forces were pushing into the Po Valley in Italy and driving ever nearer to the Rhine in the West. An offensive made sense. And if the odds of success, as J.F.C. Fuller put them, "were probably in the neighborhood of ten to one," he still found the plan "imaginative and daring."[11] Indeed, it started very well, with surprise intact thanks to excellent communications security (at last!) and foul weather that limited Allied close air support. Also, Otto Skorzeny's behind-the-lines *Operation Greif,* featuring Germans posing as Americans, initially caused massive confusion during the opening days of the offensive.

The adversity that unraveled the December offensive consisted of both expected and surprise factors. When the weather cleared, the Germans knew they would be subject to relentless attack from the air; and they knew fuel would be a great and growing problem. A speedy advance, capturing some enemy fuel dumps intact, was critically important. But the unexpected plays a role in events, too. In this case it was the stubborn American defense in front of St. Vith, and at the critical road hub at Bastogne. The Germans didn't expect Patton's 3rd Army to pivot swiftly enough to make a major difference in the battle, either—though they should have anticipated this, given his lightning operations during and after the breakout from Normandy. Meeting with Eisenhower and Bradley at Verdun on December 19, Patton was asked how soon he could join the battle—a request entailing his having to turn the 3rd Army 90 degrees north. He promised to hit the Germans in "the Bulge" in four days with three divisions. Eisenhower and Bradley viewed this pledge skeptically. Yet, as Patton noted in his memoir, "the attack of the III Corps, with the 80th, 26th, and 4th Armored Divisions jumped off on the morning of December 22, *one day ahead of the time predicted.*"[12]

Patton's strike from the south soon relieved Bastogne, and defending forces firmed up on the western and northern edges of the Bulge as well. Air attacks contributed when the weather cleared up, not only hitting the Germans on the ground but also inflicting heavy losses on the carefully hoarded *Luftwaffe* reserves that had been allocated to the offensive. At the same time the Battle of the Bulge was going on, Mussolini thought it a most opportune moment to take the offensive in Italy. The day after Christmas he struck along the Serchio River, some twenty miles north of Pisa, with two Italian divisions and one German. They hit hard at the U.S. 92nd (African American) Division, which gave ground grudgingly until reinforced by three fresh divisions. By New Year's Eve, the offensive was called off. Soon all the ground gained by the Italo-German forces was retaken. The same held true in the Ardennes where, by the end of January, the Bulge had been fully reduced. Hitler and his supportive generals badly misplayed the ending of this battle, choosing to fight for the ground they had gained. Instead, as Omar Bradley observed, "Prompt withdrawal from the Bulge might yet have spared the enemy sufficient reserves for defense of the Rhine River … the finest defensive barrier in all western Europe…. [The] bid for a few more weeks delay in the Bulge was to end in the collapse of his Western front."[13]

German casualties in the Ardennes campaign—from initial offensive in mid–December to the last rearguard actions in January—amounted to more than 100,000, with American killed, wounded, captured and missing about three-fourths that number. Even more damaging, though, was the loss of over 800 panzers, roughly 40 percent of those in the attacking force. *Half* of the 2,000 attack aircraft that Adolf Galland had so carefully husbanded were lost as well. Galland's view had been that the ground and air forces employed in the Ardennes should all have been put at the ready to counter the Red Army offensive soon to come. His logic was compelling, based on his belief that the *Luftwaffe* still had technological parity with the Red Air Force. Galland assessed German fighter effectiveness simply: "They could have achieved quite different results against the enemy in the east than against the one in the west."[14] This kind of sharp-edged dissent rankled Goering, and even Heinrich Himmler, who helped engineer Galland's dismissal as General of Fighters on the 13th of January 1945—the day after the final Russian drive to Berlin began. Galland was put under house arrest—until Hitler found out, freed him and convinced him to take command of Germany's handful of jet fighters at the very end of the war. They performed exceptionally well; but at this point were far too few to influence the war in any meaningful way.

*   *   *

Nineteen forty-five opened badly for the Japanese as well. In the wake of the Imperial Navy's defeat at Leyte Gulf, the high command decided—against the wishes of General Yamashita—to double down on the defense of Leyte Island. As it was still the rainy season for several weeks after the great naval battle late in October, the high command ordered Yamashita to send reinforcements to Leyte while they could be ferried there under cover of foul weather. Often enough, though, there were breaks that cleared the skies for U.S. Navy fliers to search out the Japanese convoys. They caught one and destroyed it—at a cost of 10,000 Imperial Army troops drowned. Yamashita finally prevailed in curtailing further wastage of forces. Those that remained on Leyte fought to the end, but had too little room for maneuver, and too few troops to enjoy even a remote chance of success. As William Manchester summed up the sheer futility of the Japanese effort to hold the island, "Leyte had been a catastrophe. The Japanese had lost sixty-five thousand crack troops."[15] And by the first week in January 1945, an armada of a thousand ships with over a quarter million troops was steaming toward Luzon.

Yamashita was ready. He had almost as many troops as MacArthur, and on Luzon would have much room for maneuver. Yamashita was hardly of a mind to sacrifice troops in static, defenses—even like those of highly sophisticated design that had been evolving during the island fighting in 1944. For the "Tiger of Malaya," who had defeated British Empire forces three times his size back in the early months of 1942, maneuver was the most precious of the principles of war. Besides, he reasoned, trying to fight on the beaches of Luzon would expose his men to sustained, withering naval bombardment. A defensive design based primarily on trading space for time, defending far from the coast in rough terrain, had a more reasonable, if still remote, chance of success. Better to strike at the invasion fleet with *kamikazes* while it was en route to Luzon—which is what he did, with the suicide attackers sinking or damaging forty ships as they neared the landing zone in the Lingayen Gulf. Overall, during the whole Philippine campaign, the *kamikazes* sank two aircraft carriers, three destroyers, five transports and six smaller craft. They seriously damaged twenty-three carriers, five battleships, nine cruisers, twenty-three destroyers, five transports and six smaller craft. For a cost of just under 1,200 Army and Navy suicide pilots, over eighty enemy ships had been sunk or damaged, with very substantial loss of life.

Even after the suicide attacks in the Philippines ceased—by mid–January—there was worry about the future prospects for the use of this tactic as Allied forces moved nearer to Japan's home islands. Raymond Lamont-Brown summed up the reaction of senior American naval leadership well:

> Admirals King, Nimitz and Halsey continued to be concerned about *kamikaze* attacks. The truth was that more U.S. warships had been sunk by *kamikaze* attacks in three months of operations in the Philippines than had been lost or damaged in [all] the previous Pacific naval battles, including Pearl Harbor.[16]

Still, even this amount of damage did not impede the invasion of Luzon; and the lack of an immediate Japanese counter-attack on the ground gave the invaders the opportunity to launch skillful maneuvers of their own. And so, a strategic chess match developed between MacArthur and Yamashita over the following weeks, with the former mounting deep thrusts on land and sea-borne "hooks," opening up whole new lines of advance. Yamashita parried where he could, withdrew where he had to, and intended to leave Manila—which had little intrinsic strategic value—an open city. But there, in the capital, a Japanese admiral remained with over 15,000 sailors and marines. Sanji Iwabuchi was ordered to fight for the city and did, overseeing a bitter defense and causing Manila's destruction in a firestorm made worse by atrocities committed by his troops—who killed well over 100,000 civilians.

The battle for Manila went on through much of February 1945, and from November to this time Japan had been suffering steady, increasingly serious reverses elsewhere. In Burma, for example, Japanese forces worn down in the recent offensives at Imphal and Kohima proved inadequate to the task of holding that country when the Allies went over to the attack after the end of the monsoon season late in October. The Japanese, however, did conduct a skillful withdrawal from northern Burma between December 1944 and February 1945—employing a tactical design similar to Yamashita's in the Philippines, but with unit structures not unlike the small combat teams upon which Model had grown so reliant. For a while, the Japanese held on in the central region of Burma at points that kept control of the oilfields near Mandalay and Yenangyaung. General Hayotaro Kimura, commanding the Burma Area Army, managed to achieve much with little; though, as

B.H. Liddell Hart concluded, "the credit of the campaign largely went to the small Japanese rearguards."[17] Even so, the loss of northern Burma was significant, as a major portion of the Burma Road to China had been opened up—and would soon be completely cleared of Japanese. Furthermore, efforts to hold the central portion of Burma made Imperial Army forces there vulnerable to an amphibious "right hook" far to their south—which was now in the offing.

Amphibious "hooks," such as were mounted by MacArthur on Luzon and contemplated by William Slim in Burma—the latter operation given the name "Dracula"—were possible now because the Allies had achieved almost complete command of the air and the seas. This degree of control benefited naval task forces as well; they could now roam far and wide, mounting a raid with carrier aircraft here, bombarding a still-occupied island there. The only warriors who saw any slackening of intensity in their campaigning were the submariners. After reaching their high point in sinkings—with over 300,000 tons accounted for in October of 1944—their numbers fell off sharply. This was not due to any decrease in efficiency, but rather to the *lack* of remaining Japanese targets. The merchant *marus* had been massacred. Nearly a third of Imperial Navy warships sunk had been lost to submarine attack as well. All this damage was done by a force that never exceeded fifty boats as sea at any given time, widely dispersed over vast areas of ocean. The reason for their stunning successes can be summed up simply as growing from two Japanese design failures: first, to craft more secure codes, so the American subs could not be so easily sent to where the *marus* were moving; second, the unwillingness to focus organizationally and doctrinally on antisubmarine warfare and the escorted convoying of seaborne commerce. Max Hastings' critique of the Japanese on this point is telling:

> It is extraordinary that [Emperor] Hirohito's nation went to war knowing the importance and vulnerability of its merchant shipping, yet without seriously addressing convoy protection; the Tokyo regime built huge warships for the Combined Fleet, but grossly inadequate numbers of escorts. Japanese antisubmarine techniques lagged far behind those of other belligerents. Their radar and airborne antisubmarine capabilities were so feeble that American boats could often operate on the surface in daylight. While the Germans lost 781 U-boats and Japan 128, the Imperial Japanese Navy sank only 41 U.S. submarines.[18]

With few targets left for the "pig boats" to prey upon, what is it they were doing at the outset of 1945? One interesting task they were assigned was to begin stalking their counterparts in the Imperial Navy. At this point in the war, Japan's I-boats were often used as a primary means of keeping isolated island garrisons supplied—which the Americans knew and exploited to great advantage. Admiral Nimitz also assumed I-boats would deploy to protect the approaches to the next likely targets of invasion—providing yet another clue as to their likely whereabouts. Needless to say, decoded radio messages helped with this endeavor as well. So, when U.S. submarines were sent to hunt their counterparts, good intelligence helped achieve excellent results, greatly contributing to heavy submarine losses the Japanese suffered from January 1945 on. By the end of the war, "pig boats" would account for one-fifth of all Japanese subs lost. They sank two long-range U-boats as well![19]

Another important job American submariners took on was to provide photographic reconnaissance—very close in—of islands next on the list for amphibious attack. They did so in the case of Iwo Jima, one of the Volcanic Islands located 750 miles from Tokyo. This small, reverse-teardrop island—its land area just over eleven square miles—was important because friendly airstrips there would halve the flight times to and from Japan of the B-29s operating from Saipan and Tinian. Airfields on Iwo would allow P-51s with drop tanks to provide fighter escort, too. This was no mystery to Japanese leaders, who sent one of their finest officers, Lieutenant General Tadamichi Kuribayashi, to prepare the island's defenses. He arrived in June of 1944 and immediately put the garrison of 21,000 soldiers and marines to work digging bunkers, improving caves—there were 1,500— adding pillboxes and connecting everything by networks of tunnels. His work was truly the finest representation of the Japanese design for island defenses. High bluffs and cliffs added to the defenses, limiting landing zones to the east or west coasts on the south end of the island. In terms of his battle doctrine, Kuribayashi rejected *banzai* charges, emphasizing aimed fire instead. Pacific War veteran Robert Leckie said of this, "They were not marksmen equal to the Marines, but their commander had made them the best in the Empire."[20]

They were certainly good enough to give the three Marine divisions assigned to take Iwo Jima—some 60,000 troops—a thin time over the five weeks of fighting that began with initial landings on February 19, 1945, and continued until the bitter end on March 26. Marine casualties on the first day rose to 2,500, as the Japanese relied on firepower from hidden positions to strike at the troops coming ashore. The defenders learned to descend into deep tunnels during bombardments, then rush to fighting positions as soon as things quieted. For the Marines, progress was agonizingly slow, with hard fighting for every yard. And on the third day of battle, the U.S. naval forces supporting the invasion came under attack by a *kamikaze* group of 20 bombers escorted by a dozen fighters. They had taken off from their base at Katori in Chiba Prefecture, Japan, then refueled on Hachijo Jima before the final 600-mile run to Iwo Jima. The trek was worthwhile, as the *kamikazes* sank the escort carrier *Bismarck Sea,* severely damaged the *Saratoga,* struck escort carrier *Lunga Point,* and hit two tank landing ships and a cargo vessel as well. All the attackers perished, with most of the fighters choosing to ram American ships after protecting the bombers on the way to their targets.[21]

But this was the only serious *kamikaze* attack during the struggle for Iwo Jima. The island's distance from Japan was a big part of the problem in this case, though senior leaders in Tokyo were also interested in husbanding their suicide attack aircraft and pilots for the fighting as it grew nearer to the home islands. For by now the lesson drawn from *kamikaze* attacks mounted in the Philippines, and in the single action at Iwo Jima was clear enough: if the Allies strove to invade Okinawa, then to push on to Kyushu, they would have to run a gauntlet of suicide squadrons in numbers that would dwarf the previous actions. Given the heavy losses the Combined Fleet had suffered thus far in the war, and the growing superiority of better-trained American pilots and their improved aircraft, Ronald Spector concluded that, at this point, "[t]he only hope was to turn the planes into human missiles by crash-diving them into the American men-of-war."[22] The *kamikazes* can be seen as highly maneuverable cruise missiles—Germany's unmanned V-1s could only fly in a straight line to their targets. The difference with today's cruise missiles and their software-based guidance packages, of course, is that Japan's World War II versions were guided to their targets by human-brain "wetware."

However significantly *kamikazes* featured in the Imperial strategic design by the spring of 1945, Kuribayashi could not count on any further use of them on his behalf after their first attacks early in the fight for Iwo Jima. And while he waged a masterful tactical battle over the course of five weeks—his troops inflicted over 25,000 casualties on the invaders—the outcome of the battle was never in doubt after the opening days of hard fighting to gain a lodgment.[23] After two weeks of intense action, Kuribayashi sent a message to Tokyo: "I am not afraid of the fighting power of only three American divisions … *if* there are no bombardments from aircraft and warships." But on March 4, his request for air and naval support had a fatalistic tone: "Send me these things and I will hold the island. Without them I cannot hold."[24] Needless to say, such assistance was not forthcoming. Kuribayashi and his men fought on, demonstrating the value of the Japanese defensive design that had emerged over the years of the Pacific War. Three weeks after his desperate request for support, the island finally fell to the weary Marines. All but a relative handful of the Japanese defenders died. Soon American bombers and escort fighters were using the island regularly, and the Japanese homeland was quickly set ablaze in repeated fire bombings.

By the end of March 1945, Japan's situation had become extremely grim. Aside from the vulnerability of the home islands now to destruction from the air—Japanese fighter aircraft, except for a handful of experimental types, couldn't even reach the altitudes at which the B-29s were operating—the Combined Fleet was hardly a shadow of its former self. The merchant *marus* were virtually gone. Yet Imperial Army forces in Burma still held a line against Slim's offensive, even if they had been pushed out of Mandalay by mid–March. Yamashita, too, was conducting a skillful defense of Luzon; his forces would still be on their feet and fighting at the end of the war in August. And while the initiative in China was slipping from the Japanese, they still held significant swathes of territory there, and countless millions of Chinese remained at their mercy. But for all the hard fighting their troops in Burma, China and the Philippines were engaging in, they had simply no effect whatsoever on the ability of the Americans to continue on to the next stepping-stones to Japan in the Ryukyu Islands. On the last day of March, Kerama Retto in this chain fell—it had little more than 500 defenders—with the bonus that U.S. forces captured 350 *Kaiten* suicide manned torpedoes based there, intended for use against the invasion fleet. The next day, April 1, the Americans landed on Okinawa. The battle for this island was to be Japan's last opportunity to show it could defeat an amphibious invasion.

\*   \*   \*

That same April 1—Easter Sunday—after a month of disasters in the field, Adolf Hitler moved into a deep underground bunker behind his Chancellery building in Berlin. March had seen the barrier of the Rhine breached, first at Remagen on the 7th, then at a number of other points. German troops lost in the Battle of the Bulge, and in other efforts to hold territory to the west of the Rhine, had left the *Heer* with too few formations to prevent crossings. In a telephone call with Omar Bradley on the morning of March 23, George Patton told him of his advance across the Rhine the previous evening: "I sneaked a division over last night. But there are so few Krauts around there, they don't know it yet."[25] The situation had become quite hopeless, even before Patton's "quarterback sneak"; Guderian himself had urged Hitler to order an immediate surrender on March 21, a suggestion that soon after led the Fuehrer to sack him. Thus ended the career of perhaps the most creative of Germany's strategic designers. Another symbolic loss came on the 30th, when the great U-boat ace Heinrich Lehmann-Willenbrock, who had sunk 180,000 tons of Allied shipping, died in an air raid on Wilhelmshaven.

But even as the Western Allies' forces surged into Germany from the West, April 1945 was a time of utter disaster in the East. In bitter fighting in East Prussia, Poland and

Hungary, German forces, as Martin Gilbert put the matter, "however battered and weak-ened, were determined not to yield, but only to be annihilated."[26] The military situation in Italy was better only in relative terms; there secret negotiations were under way to arrange a separate peace—via talks between representatives of the Office of Strategic Services (OSS) and the SS in Bern, Switzerland—an undertaking that outraged the Rus-sians, who viewed it as "an attempted double-cross of the USSR."[27] This "secret surrender," which focused on ending the fighting in Italy, ensuring a smooth shift to Anglo-American occupation would take place, was reached on May 2—just five days before the general end of hostilities in Europe. It was nevertheless an action that was to feed Russia's mistrust of its Western allies, adding its weight to the antipathy that would ultimately lead to the open rupture of the Cold War. In these last days, Hitler kept up his hopes that the alliance against him would fall apart—much as Prussia's Frederick the Great had been saved at the last moment in the Seven Years' War by Russia's defection from its Western allies. Hitler had no such luck.

By now the soldiers of the Western Allies were growing directly aware of some of the worst depravities of the Nazi regime, as they came upon concentration camps. On April 11 Americans liberated Buchenwald—stark proof of the darkness from which they had helped save the world. The Russians had had direct evidence of this aspect of Nazi evil since July of the previous year, when their advancing troops discovered Majdanek. Late in January, the Red Army also liberated Auschwitz. The Nazis seemed of two minds, as the most damning evidence of their crimes against humanity was about to come to light. Some camps were obliterated pre-emptively, others speeded up their pace of exter-mination. But there was simply far too much evidence to cover up. The design for mass death developed at the Wannsee Conference in late January 1942 had been followed meticulously, resulting in the murders of millions. It was a clear case of twisted ideology trumping good strategy as, aside from its sheer barbarity, this grim machinery of death imposed great costs on the war-waging ability of the Germans. Victor Davis Hanson has summed up the Nazis' madness well:

> Ideology, of course, clouded military judgment. Tens of millions of man-hours were invested in the perpetration of the Holocaust and "re-ordering" of the East.... The slave and extermination camps diminished the free European workforce, alienated neutrals, increased hatred of Germany, and drew down manpower and machines from the fighting.... [It was] killing in service of crackpot ideas.[28]

As to the final weeks of fighting, when resistance was collapsing in the West, the strug-gle in the East continued unabated—in part because fear of the retributive fury of the Russians was well founded, resulting in heroic efforts to evacuate civilian populations from their path. The remaining ships of the *Kriegsmarine,* virtually crippled since losing the *Scharnhorst* and the *Tirpitz,* nevertheless kept up a hard fight in the Baltic, rescuing civil-ians—and redeploying some soldiers—by means of sealifts out of the isolated "Courland Pocket" and East Prussia. Cajus Bekker estimated the number moved at "no less than two million" between January and May 1945—making this, in his view "a rescue action without parallel in the annals of history."[29] Retreating German forces in the East held on, often to the point of being wiped out, in order to buy time for refugees to make their way west, out of the grasp of the Red Army. Guderian had a special admiration for the skill and valor of these rearguard actions, singling out the commanders of the 24th Panzer Corps and of *Gross-Deutschland,* praising how they

> engaged in mobile encirclement battles, continued steadfastly and valiantly to fight their way west-wards, picking up numerous smaller units on the way. Generals Nehring and von Saucken performed

feats of military virtuosity during these days that only the pen of a new Xenophon could adequately describe.[30]

While Nehring and von Saucken, even in these last days of the Third Reich, were still able to validate Guderian's concept of mobile maneuver warfare, it must be noted too that Hellmuth Walter's sleek new U-boats and Willy Messerschmitt's jets were demonstrating proof of concept at the same time. Walter's Type 21s, outfitted with improved batteries that allowed for submerged speeds in excess of seventeen knots, began to sortie and achieve sinkings—without loss to themselves from Allied anti-submarine operations. But there were just a few 21s; and the Type 26, with fully air-independent propulsion and a submerged speed of twenty-five knots, was completed too late to join the fight. For Samuel Eliot Morison, it was "[f]ortunate indeed that the war in Europe ended when it did; for a couple hundred U-boats of these new types might have ruptured Allied sea communications."[31] The Me 262 jet did appear in greater numbers, achieving some remarkable successes. A classified report about these jets—commissioned by Eisenhower while he was President—concluded that the 262s

> literally flew rings around our fighters and bored holes in our formations with complete impunity.... For example, 14 fighter groups escorted the 1,250 B-17 raid on Berlin March 18 [1945], almost a one-for-one escort ratio. They were set upon by a single squadron of Me 262s which knocked down 25 bombers and 5 fighters, although outnumbered roughly 100 to 1. The Germans lost not a single plane.[32]

The advances in submarines and jets came too late, because Germany had wasted its pre-war technological lead in both areas. There is more to be said in the next chapter about why these fatal delays occurred; for now, it is sufficient to say simply that such delays *did* occur, keeping two of the most promising weapons systems from being available in numbers when the war began to turn against Germany. There was yet a third weapons program that could have helped immeasurably: the quest for an atomic bomb. Without a retelling of the story of the ferment in the physics field during the 1930s, or of the Allied Manhattan Project, it should be said that the Germans were in the forefront of this research and had a robust development program under way. That the Nazis failed where the Allies succeeded is a very dramatic tale, replete with failed air attacks on the Norsk Hydro heavy-water plant—key to the German effort—and a successful commando action that sank a ferry as it attempted to move the vital heavy water to safety. This latter action was taken despite the fact that numerous Norwegian civilians were traveling on the ferry that was carrying the heavy water.[33]

But the Germans' failure also resulted from their own errors. A leader of the *Uranverein* (Uranium Club), Werner Heisenberg, through negligence let his heavy-water reactor explode on one critical occasion—a grievous setback. The consequences of this mishap were amplified and extended by Walther Bothe, who eventually went on to win the Nobel Prize in physics after the war in 1954, but who made the mistake of believing that graphite couldn't substitute for heavy water as a means of moderating neutron speed. Thus, thanks in large part to Werner Heisenberg's sloppy operational error and Walther Bothe's major theoretical miscue, the wartime German nuclear program failed. It should also be noted, though, that the "Uranium Club" was a widely distributed research effort conducted at nine major, separate locations that did not operate in the kind of unison required for such a great undertaking.[34] Needless to say, the scientists on the Manhattan Project reached a different conclusion from Bothe's about the utility of graphite—and achieved a far more effective, deadly result. Credit must also go to the intricate, neatly conjoined, organizational design of the Manhattan Project.

**The Type XVIIB Walter U-boat had outstanding submerged speed (public domain, Wikipedia).**

In the face of these major failures—being too late with advanced U-boats and jets and too limited in approach to building an atomic bomb, there was now absolutely no hope of any sort left for the thousand-year Reich's life. Nothing remained but despair and death. In the West, and in Italy, the end came with mass surrenders—and growing German shame as the camps were liberated and their horrors widely revealed. But in the East the final throes of Nazism proved extremely costly. Aside from the hard fighting that was undertaken to make time for refugees to flee from what would become the Russian occupation zone, the last battle, for Berlin, became one of the bloodiest of the war.

In the final weeks of fighting the Red Army suffered over 350,000 casualties in and around Berlin—just under 100,000 of them killed in action—and lost 2,000 tanks, great numbers of them to the German version of the bazooka, the *Panzerfaust*. But Berlin was seemingly the great prize of the war, an object of some contention between the Russians and the Western Allies. The latter relented, leaving Berlin to the Soviets; but was the honor of taking the enemy capital worth the cost? Antony Beevor thinks not, noting, "Stalin saw the capture of Berlin as the Soviet Union's rightful reward, but the yield was disappointing and the waste terrible."[35] Even so, the symbolic value of victory here resonated. Nazism was dead.

*   *   *

One of the last messages that Hitler received in his bunker came from Japan, wishing him well despite the hopelessness of the situation. And by the time the Red Army finally closed in on his bunker, the Fuehrer himself already reduced to ashes, the struggle for Okinawa was entering its second month—even though the invasion plan had called for the island to be fully subdued in thirty days, by the end of April. The fighting there was to persist for nearly two more months, into late June 1945; for Okinawa's defense featured both the very latest ideas about how to conduct the fight on the ground—mostly from networks of caves and other strongpoints—and a much-increased use of *kamikazes*. In the end, the commanding generals on both sides died in this bitter battle. American casualties extended to 13,000 killed directly in action—5,000 of them sailors killed by *kamikazes*—with over 5,000 more from all services dying soon after from their wounds. The number of those who were wounded and survived approached 50,000. All told, losses were nearly 30 percent of the more than a quarter-million combat forces engaged. And in material terms, the invaders lost 36 ships sunk, nearly 400 more damaged, and some 700 aircraft. This was an intense sea-air-land fight.

In many ways, the battle for Okinawa validated key elements of the strategic design that the Japanese had been refining ever since Tarawa. The defensive scheme for ground fighting worked well once again, as a force of roughly 70,000 Japanese held on for nearly three months against a massively superior force. In the air, the Japanese lost over 1,500 *kamikazes,* but their concept of operations proved its effectiveness. Indeed, given the very heavy losses suffered by Japan's other attack aircraft in this battle—for far too little damage done to the enemy—"the Japanese High Command saw ... that all available air units should [now] take part in suicide missions."[36] *Kamikazes* developed a pattern during the Okinawa campaign of often striking by night, even though they were still detected by radar picket ships; for doing so made them much less vulnerable to being decimated by enemy fighters before they could dive onto their targets. This tactical approach made life hard for the small, relatively isolated vessels on the "ping line," a dozen of which were sunk by *kamikazes*. But increased ability to get to their targets by striking at night was to some degree offset by the difficulty of maneuvering into attack position in the dark. Edward Stafford, a destroyer escort officer who had to fight the *kamikazes* in the waters off Okinawa—and whose ship survived a repeated series of such attacks—recalled, of a particularly dangerous time:

> To crash a warship which is maneuvering and fighting back at night takes more than courage and determination and self-sacrifice. It takes experience and proficiency as a pilot. *Abercrombie* survived that midwatch of the third of June because thanks to Midway and the Solomons and the Marianas "turkey shoot" and other actions, Japan was just about out of such pilots.[37]

Stafford neatly summed up the situation for the Japanese: while losses to the incomparable pilots with whom they began the war impelled the rise of the *kamikazes,* the lesser skills of those who formed the suicide squadrons hurt their effectiveness. The cloak of night may have given some protection from enemy fighters, but radar detection meant the enemy would be forewarned, ready to fire and maneuver. As for daylight attacks, as few as one in four of the *kamikazes* on these missions actually made it to their targets. Despite all these daunting difficulties, the suicide attackers persisted—and did serious damage. At home they were venerated; "some people [even] came to look upon them as gods." Rikihei Inoguchi and Tadashi Nakajima, both of whom helped form the Suicide Force, noted, "They were human beings, with all the emotions and feelings, faults and virtues, strengths and weaknesses of other human beings."[38] Max Hastings has affirmed this view thoughtfully:

> The image of Japan's *kamikazes* taking off to face death with exuberant enthusiasm is largely fallacious. Among the first wave of suicidalists in the autumn of 1944, there were many genuine volunteers. Thereafter, however, the supply of young fanatics dwindled: many subsequent recruits were driven to accept the role by moral pressure, and sometimes conscription…. Yet some young men professed that they went willingly.[39]

And some older men shared a willingness to practice self-immolation via suicide attack. The most astonishing—and wasteful—example of this Japanese cultural trait was on full display in the last sortie of the *Yamato,* the world's largest battleship at over 70,000 tons, and the best armed with its nine 18-inch guns. Fuel was so short by now that it was given only enough to reach Okinawa. All knew this was a *kamikaze* battleship mission. The *Yamato* had been at Leyte, but withdrew with the rest of the Imperial Fleet in the face of the heroic defense conducted by light American forces. *Yamato's* second attempt to contest an amphibious landing came at the end of the first week of fighting on Okinawa; but it was unable to reach the island, beset by attack aircraft that sank it far from the arena of action. *Yamato* is perhaps the best example of the flawed Japanese strategic design for naval power: this massive battleship and its sister *Musashi*—lost at Leyte—along with the eight other battleships Japan possessed in 1941, reflected a clear failure, of Yamamoto and others, to recognize the primacy of the aircraft carrier.

The 32nd Army fought with suicidal fury as well, right up to the end—with some isolated units struggling on from their caves even after Okinawa was declared "cleared"— though many chose instead to revert to the Army's old frontal *banzai* tactics after all hope was lost. As for Okinawan civilians, tens of thousands died in aerial, artillery, and naval gunfire bombardments. Many were also entangled and killed in close-up fighting on the ground. But very large numbers of civilians also took their own lives—often by jumping off cliffs in the last two weeks of the battle for the island. The total civilian toll, from all causes, has been the subject of some debate; George Feifer's very thoughtful assessment of the overall reporting from both sides puts the sad number at over 150,000—to which the loss of 10,000 Korean slave laborers brought to the island to help build its defenses must be added. It is a death toll that should be seen as comparable to the carnage caused by the atomic attacks on Hiroshima and Nagasaki.[40] On balance, it seems clear that the brutal cost of the fighting for Okinawa, and what it foreshadowed for an invasion of Kyushu—and beyond—weighed heavily upon President Harry S Truman's mind as he pondered whether to use the ultimate weapon whose development was authorized by his predecessor, Franklin Delano Roosevelt, who had died in office while the fighting on Okinawa was under way.

For Truman, the choice to drop atomic bombs on Japan was, in his view, a matter of taking some lives to save more lives by shocking Japan into surrender. In its own way, then, the trauma of high American casualties on Okinawa contributed to Truman's controversial decision.[41] Okinawa had weighed just as heavily upon Emperor Hirohito's mind, too. Until this battle he had vigorously supported continuing the war. He believed in victory via a *Ketsu-Go* ("final decisive battle"). But, as Richard Frank noted, his faith was shaken in June of 1945: "The Emperor was in fact a vigorous advocate of *Ketsu-Go* until inevitable defeat loomed on Okinawa."[42] After this loss, he briefly urged the Army to mount an offensive in China; but this was no longer possible. Japan was barely holding on there, and was in retreat from Burma and other Southeast Asian holdings. And American submarines had brought Japan to the point of near-starvation and industrial collapse. The "strange neutrality" with the Russians was soon to end with their entry into the war—all good reasons to make peace. But the demand for unconditional surrender impelled the beaten to fight on, even with the Navy destroyed and the protective chains of island fortresses all fallen or isolated.

Despite the Empire's catastrophic defeats, Japan's coasts still bristled with defenses, and there were 5,000 planes assigned to the *kamikaze* units, with another 10,000 "regular" combat aircraft available—cockpits all fillable by the 18,000 pilots that remained on the rosters of the Army and Navy air services.[43] Even so, the Emperor grew increasingly firm about the need to surrender, and demanded a cessation to all fighting after Hiroshima and Nagasaki were bombed. Hirohito was viewed as Japan's living god; but his decision to surrender sparked resistance, even an incipient coup. Per John Toland's account, it was "protective" of him, as the coup planners hoped to

> isolate the Emperor from those urging him to seek peace. Then they would enlist Anami [the War Minister] to advise the Emperor to continue the war. A hard-fought Decisive Battle on the mainland would inflict such losses on the Americans that an honorable peace might be arranged. If not, they would carry on the war as guerrillas in the mountains.[44]

Yet, the Emperor could neither be isolated from those who agreed with his call for peace nor persuaded to continue the fight. So, an even more desperate measure, a "palace coup" mounted by younger officers, flared up briefly, but was put down by wiser heads. Soon after, the Japanese mass public heard the voice of their Emperor over their radios—the first time he had spoken directly to them—declaring Japan's intent to surrender.

*   *   *

When Emperor Hirohito's surrender broadcast aired on August 15, 1945, Yamashita was still leading his troops on Luzon in prolonged defense of that island. After the cessation of hostilities, he went into captivity and was put on trial for war crimes. Douglas MacArthur wanted to see him die for the destruction wrought in Manila, even though Yamashita had called for it to be an "open city" and had had no hand in the fighting during which thousands of innocent Filipinos were killed. Yamashita was accused of having held "command responsibility" and was tried on this basis. In a swift, one-sided proceeding—including charges for earlier atrocities committed while he was still in Manchuria—Yamashita was found guilty and condemned to death. His case was appealed to the U.S. Supreme Court, which affirmed both the verdict and sentence 7–2. But dissents by Justices Frank Murphy and Wiley B. Rutledge were biting, viewing the trial as a "legalized lynching." Murphy also said that a "spirit of revenge and retribution, masked in formal legal procedure for purposes of dealing with a fallen enemy commander, can do more lasting harm than all of the atrocities giving rise to that spirit."[45]

The "Tiger of Malaya" was joined in death by Admiral Ohnishi, the godfather of the *kamikazes,* who chose to commit suicide as a matter of honor and expiation. Three of Japan's most important strategic designers were now dead—the third, Yamamoto, had been killed in the shootdown of his plane in 1943. Admiral Soemu Toyoda, who headed the Combined Fleet from May 1944 to the end of the war—and strove, albeit too late and with a by now blunted instrument, to strike massive blows against the Americans—survived the war. He was put on trial for war crimes that were "in violation of the customs of war," but was acquitted. Toyoda recognized the primacy of air power and need to mass forces rather than deal them out in driblets, as Yamamoto had done during the Guadalcanal campaign. What might have been had Toyoda commanded the Combined Fleet earlier, when it still had a fighting chance, numerically and technologically, against the Allies? But by the time he rose to this level, American planes were more numerous, as well as more rugged; and there were few pilots of the quality and experience of Saburo Sakai left in the ranks. Sakai was kept out of combat late in the war, relegated to testing the advanced *Reppu* fighter. As he recalled, *Reppu* was "a sensational airplane … with its tremendous speed, and its rate of climb was astounding."[46] But only seven were produced before war's end.

Sakai's experience with the *Reppu* sounds much like Adolf Galland's with the Me 262. Galland, too, survived the war, soon after which he moved to Argentina and helped develop its Air Force—which was later on to play a highly effective role in the 1982 Falklands War against the British. But by then Galland had long been back in Germany, running an "air consulting" business—despite having been banned from service in the air branch of the *Bundeswehr* because of his Nazi affiliations during World War II. He was just thirty-three when the war ended, and lived on until 1996.

As to another German strategic designer who made it through the war, Karl Doenitz was tried for the war crimes of planning and waging "wars of aggression" and violations of the laws of war, found guilty and imprisoned for ten years. Upon release, he lived in relative obscurity; but his memoir, *Ten Years and Twenty Days,* remains an exceptionally insightful account of the reasoning of a high-level naval officer before and during a major war. His interview in the famous British *World at War* television series reflected his creativity as a strategic designer as well—though neither the memoir nor interview adequately addresses his failure to win support for the advanced Walter U-boat designs in the pre-war years. Doenitz played no role in the postwar West German Navy, and died in 1980 at the age of eighty-nine.

Heinz Guderian, the major developer of the *Blitzkrieg* doctrine, also held positions of great responsibility as the war dragged on, had a heart condition and lived less than a decade after the great conflict's end. Time enough, though, for him to write *Panzer Leader,* the memoir of all military memoirs, covering a wide spectrum of action, from the front lines in critical campaigns to high-level shouting matches with Hitler, with whom he had a stormy relationship. The great value of this memoir is the glimpse it gives of a designer's mind—especially the ability to grasp the subtle interplay of technical details and the organizational and doctrinal potential they unleash. Guderian's colleague in designing the key principles of modern maneuver warfare, Erich von Manstein, was convicted of war crimes in 1949, though his initial sentence of eighteen years was reduced to twelve, of which he served only three. Liddell Hart and Winston Churchill were among those who argued for his release. Manstein went on to play an important role as a consultant during the formation of the West German *Bundeswehr*. Its ability to scale up quickly—thanks to a clockwork-like reserve mobilization system—was one of his conceptual contributions. His own memoir, *Lost Victories,* remains a classic firsthand account of armored maneuver warfare, from the incredible victory of his offensive plan against Anglo-French forces in 1940 to his counter-punching defensive design against the Russians in 1943.

Italy's *Don* Borghese, too, exposed the mind of a master designer in his deeply introspective memoir, *Sea Devils*—the original title of the book was the plain-sounding *Decima Flottiglia MAS,* in honor of the daring unit he commanded. Where Guderian and Manstein had focused on maneuver warfare in the clashes of massed armored forces, Borghese's instincts had led him to actualize the potential of light forces to achieve great destruction and disruption at sea. Like Guderian and Manstein, he saw his ideas put into practice during war, with much effect. A devoted Fascist, Borghese kept *Decima Flottiglia MAS* intact and in service to the Salò Republic even after the rest of Italy had made peace with the Allies in 1943. French Admiral Raymond de Belot gave Borghese and sailors of *Decima MAS* high marks for what they achieved during World War II, noting that they "remained faithful to Mussolini and fought bravely to the end both at sea and on land."[47] After the war, Borghese inspired and energized a very dangerous neo–Fascist movement, was accused with having fomented an abortive coup in 1970 and had to flee Italy afterward. He died in exile four years later. But his legacy lives on today in the form of what is now called "naval special warfare." Mostly associated with U.S. Navy SEALs, Italians still retain great aptitude for this mode of operations.

As to some of the non-military strategic designers of the Axis Powers, their fates were varied as well. Alfried Krupp was put on trial for having used slave laborers during the war and, like Manstein, spent just three years in prison out of a twelve-year sentence. After which his company was put back in his hands and continued to prosper. He died in 1967, but the Krupp firms went on fabricating steel and building high-speed trains, warships and many other products. In 1999, Krupp merged with Thyssen to form one of what is still one the world's most successful industrial enterprises. Professor Willy Messerschmitt spent two years in prison—also for using slave labor—and returned to prosperity as well. His company is now part of the European Aeronautic Defense and Space (EADS) branch of the Airbus conglomerate. He lived on until 1978, dying at eighty—not long after having been inducted into the International Air & Space Hall of Fame. The tank and automotive designer Ferdinand Porsche was honored in his field as well, being named Car Engineer of the Century—posthumously, as he died in 1951—at a convention in Las Vegas in 1999. Porsche won this honor over many other leading nominees like Henry Ford, Karl Benz, Rudolf Diesel, and Ettore Bugatti. Needless to say, Porsche's firm has prospered since World War II as well. So have leading firms in Italy and Japan, like FIAT and Mitsubishi.

How did all these firms rebound as well and as quickly as they did? Germany, Japan, and Italy all recovered fairly swiftly from the devastation wrought by the war because they benefited from the grand strategic design of the American general, and later secretary of state, George C. Marshall, whose counsel informed and guided the decision making of Presidents Franklin Delano Roosevelt and Harry S Truman. Marshall saw that, by rebuilding these former foes, a bulwark against communist expansionism could be created. This was to be the basic architecture of the Cold War "containment" strategy that lasted for forty years until the fall of the Berlin Wall in 1989 and the collapse of the Soviet Union just two years later. Yet, even with this aid, the recovery of the former Axis Powers seems miraculous—until one factors in the ingenuity of the Germans, Japanese, and Italians themselves. They made the absolute most of the opportunity to rebuild—to *redesign*—their societies. Indeed, this fresh flowering of design among the defeated should cause us to look once more, in a summary way in the next chapter, at how peoples so creative went so far astray during World War II.

# 9. Why the Axis Lost

BY LATE MAY OF 1942, thirty-three months after the Nazi invasion of Poland, the Axis Powers were close to reaching their maximum extent of territorial expansion. Most of mainland Europe was under German or Italian control. Panzers were driving hard in Russia, where they had just crushed a major Russian counter-offensive, opening up the rich oilfields of the Caucasus to conquest. In the North African desert, Rommel was on the attack once again and Tobruk was soon to fall, with Cairo next coming under his gaze. At sea, Doenitz's U-boats were still enjoying their "happy time" off the American coast, and Britain's vital Atlantic lifeline was gravely imperiled. In the Far East, Yamashita's stunning victory over greater British forces at Singapore was followed by the complete rout of Allied troops from Burma, driving them all the way to India. The Imperial Fleet was overseeing a kind of naval *Blitzkrieg,* with island after island falling under a rain of swift, hard blows. To be sure, the *Kido Butai* had finally suffered its first casualty—a light carrier—in the Battle of the Coral Sea in early May. Yet even this action was still a tactical victory, with one American fleet carrier sunk, another seriously damaged. And Yamamoto was already contemplating his next offensive, which would be undertaken with a better correlation of forces in Japan's favor than had been the case in the attack on Pearl Harbor.

Richard Overy summed up the situation at this time: "On the face of things, no rational man in early 1942 would have guessed at the eventual outcome of the war.... The situation for the Allies ... was desperate." He also questioned the idea that the war turned on "decisive events"—such as Midway, Alamein, or even Stalingrad—arguing, "chances of a single battle or decision seriously explaining its outcome are remote." He saw instead that the war was decided by the cumulative results of repeated actions: "For much of the war the chief campaigns were based on attrition, *for months or years on end*—in the Atlantic Battle, in the air war, on the eastern front, in the slow erosion of the German foothold in western and southern Europe, or the Japanese hold on the islands of the south Pacific."[1] Overy is in line with Paul Kennedy's view that one must "[resist] all efforts at reductionism, such as that winning the war can be explained solely by brute force, or by some wonder weapons, or by some magical decrypting system.... The Second World War was so infinitely more complex, and fought out across so many theaters and by so many different means, that the intelligent scholar simply has to go for a multicausal explanation as to why the Allies won."[2]

It is with this complexity in mind that I have undertaken a design approach to thinking through World War II. Though Axis reverses between June and November 1942 obviously loom large in any explanation of the ultimate outcome of World War II, it must be remembered that, as Ronald Spector has argued, "The Japanese still had sufficient forces after Midway to again take the initiative for another try at the U.S. fleet." And in the months after Midway the Americans went on to suffer several stinging naval defeats off Guadalcanal. As to the fighting on land in the war against Japan, it was to devolve into years of "long jungle slugging matches."[3] In a similar vein, the German debacle at Stalingrad was no worse than the many epic defeats the Red Army had suffered over the course of the first year of the Russo-German war—and then again in the late winter and early spring months of 1943, when Manstein's counterpunching concept of operations had not only restored the balance on the Eastern Front, but had returned the initiative to the Germans. As to the later Sicilian and Italian campaigns, both provide masterful examples of extended defensive operations. Only in the June 1944 invasion at Normandy was a mortal blow threatened—yet in its wake Model miraculously restored order and stability, winning an important battle at Arnhem and yet again making another counter-offensive effort possible.

The simple point here is that, if historians like Richard Overy, Paul Kennedy and Ronald Spector are right, then my exercise in "strategic design analysis" has provided a sensible alternative way to explore the complexities associated with World War II's outcome more fully. Rather than telling a story of the triumph of greater numbers, or of good fortune at critical times, the design approach allows us to consider systematically the course of the many campaigns that, as Overy has put it, went on "for months or years on end." To remind, what I mean by "strategic design" is something broader than the typical use of this phrasing in the business context—which tends to focus on organizational structure. There are some strategic design studies, though, that take broader views, noting that "[o]rganizations are increasingly adopting a design approach to define and implement their innovation strategies, using design to leverage organizational transformations, and even embracing design principles as the overarching philosophy that guides their entire organization."[4] It is this notion of the *entire organization* that informs my reconsideration of World War II from a design perspective, the idea of "entirety" extending beyond unit structures to technology acquisition, battle doctrine, and larger questions about how these factors influence strategy.

Despite this complexity, a design analysis of the conclusions to be drawn from the foregoing chapters may be fairly neatly broken down into three parts: the pre-war years; the period of Axis ascendancy from 1939 through 1942; and the path to decline and defeat that ran from 1943 to 1945. While one or another of the dimensions of strategic design came to the fore in each period—a very good example being that technology acquisition strategy was crucial on land, at sea, and in the air during the pre-war years—*all* of the design factors had important roles, from before the war to its end. What to invest in was surely a high priority in the years before the outbreak of war; but the manner in which these technologies were to be employed in battle, and the units of action that would best actualize their potential, were key as well. For example, it was not simply the Japanese decision to invest in more aircraft carriers that mattered most; it was Yamamoto's belief that they should be concentrated in a striking force—the *Kido Butai*—that gave them exceptional hitting power. Similarly, Guderian's insistence on creation of armor-heavy panzer divisions ensured that the right sort of unit structure would empower the tank— along with the combined-arms doctrine of having tank formations closely supported by ground attack aircraft. Japan's *Kido Butai* and the German panzer divisions were two of the most important innovations in organizational design introduced in the interwar period.

But there were gaps and errors as well—that is, serious design flaws—evident during those years before the war. In naval affairs, for example, the Japanese demonstrated an almost complete misunderstanding of the role that the submarine could play, focusing on its potential to influence fleet battles rather than its more proper use as a commerce raider. This "sub blindness" led to the Japanese failure to plan for protecting their own shipping; but also, to neglecting the opportunity to wage submarine warfare against what would necessarily be extended Allied sea lines of communication. Captain Andrieu d'Albas, a French naval officer who spent much time in Japan, summed this matter up most succinctly in his thoughtful analysis of the Pacific War:

> The Imperial Navy had committed grave fundamental errors in disdaining to protect its own shipping, and in neglecting to attack the enemy's lines of communication. Those of Japan should have been maintained at any cost, as both the existence of the Japanese homeland and the prosecution of the war depended almost entirely on imports from overseas. Similarly, the exceptional length of the enemy's lines of communication should have induced those responsible for the naval building programs to include large numbers of submarines.[5]

D'Albas' critique is telling, identifying a key Japanese design flaw, in terms of its approach to what was to be, at heart, a naval war. Given the near-victory achieved by the German U-boats in World War I, Japanese neglect of both the threats and opportunities of submarine warfare is most puzzling.

The same can be said—almost—of the lax German approach to the submarine. Even after the restrictions imposed by the Treaty of Versailles were thrown off by the Nazis subsequent to their rise to power, the U-boat remained a lesser included element in the *Kriegsmarine's* "Z Plan." Instead, the Plan called primarily for creation of "super battleships" like *Bismarck* and *Tirpitz,* and a range of smaller, yet still deadly, surface warships. The *Scharnhorst* and *Gneisenau* were of this latter sort, elegantly designed to give them nearly as much firepower as the best British battleships, but more speed and better defensive armor belts. Technically, the surface fleet built by Raeder and his minions during the interwar period was a thing of beauty; but the lessons of World War I at sea should have impelled an emphasis on U-boats. And not only those that improved incrementally on earlier designs; the revolutionary Walter concept was there for the taking during the 1930s. Instead, those U-boats that were built were only marginally improved—that is, they were very good "submersibles," but not true submarines capable of moving at speed for long periods submerged. And so the *Kriegsmarine* went to war in 1939 with only a few dozen ocean-going U-boats—scarcely any more than they had in 1914. As to how to use the surface fleet, Raeder and his "battleship club" came up with an enlarged replay of the idea of using their warships as raiders, the old *Kreuzerkrieg* concept from World War I.

The Italians, too, retained a battleship-centric mindset, and the designs that they developed during the interwar period were also impressive. They featured firepower equal to the best British battleships, but less defensive armor in return for having somewhat greater speed. Like the Germans, the Italians chose not to build aircraft carriers, relying instead on land-based air support of their surface warships. This made more sense in the Italian case, given that the strategic geography of the Mediterranean offered ample points from which to support the *Regia Marina.* But there were two fundamental problems with the Italian strategic design: lack of ship-borne radar and very inferior fighter aircraft. Like the Japanese, the Italians relied on human rather than electronic vision—but didn't train for night-fighting. As was the case with the Japanese, the Italian choice to forgo radar was to prove costly. And in the air, the Italians had nothing like the Zero; thanks to Marshal Italo Balbo's belief in the continued viability of the biplane fighter—a view supported by the designers at FIAT—the Italians went into World War II with a woefully inadequate air combat capability. The effect on the *Regia Marina* was profound, as Commander Marc' Antonio Bragadin observed: "the possibility of both offensive and defensive action by the Italian Navy was limited in a great number of cases by insufficient air cooperation."[6]

The one area in which the Italians built upon a highly innovative idea conceived during World War I had to do with what is today called "naval special warfare." During that war, the idea was to have swimmer teams haul mines up to warships, deploy them on a timer, then swim to safety. It was a notion introduced early in 1918 by two Italian naval lieutenants who thought this could be a way to attack Austrian warships in Pola harbor. Just ten days before the war ended, these two penetrated Pola's defenses and mined and sank the battleship *Viribus Unitis*—"Forces United," the Habsburg motto. The Italians remembered this success, and research into commando-style action became part of preparations for a future naval war against Britain or France. Borghese championed this concept, and during the 1930s the *maiale*—a small manned torpedo deployed from a submarine—was designed and developed. As has been noted earlier, three of these two-man *maiale* teams penetrated the Royal Navy defenses of Alexandria harbor the week before Christmas in 1941 and put two battleships and a tanker completely out of action. As Rear Admiral Raymond de Belot, an insightful French observer of the Anglo-Italian sea war noted, "Six determined men had completely changed the balance of naval power in the Mediterranean."[7]

Japan and Germany had less luck with this aspect of naval strategic design. The Imperial Navy did develop a midget submarine during the inter-war era, the two-man "HA," with a notion in mind quite similar to that of the Italians—covertly attacking large warships. The HA became part of the plan for the attack on Pearl Harbor. But in the event, the five midgets deployed were mostly detected on their approaches; all failed to torpedo any American ships. Still, the Japanese did not give up on the idea of this mode of attack, and by 1945 had built 400 *Kaiten* and 250 *Kairyu* manned torpedoes. In theory, crewmen manning them were to aim them, then hop off and swim away prior to impact. Practically, though, these were both *kamikaze*-style weapons. As mentioned previously, the U.S. Navy destroyed the main *Kaiten* base near Okinawa before that battle. *Kairyu* were intended to be deployed in defense of Japan's home islands against an Allied invasion; but the war ended before their use became necessary. As to the Germans, they too developed manned torpedo weapons; but these had little material effect, sinking just three minecraft in the fighting after D-Day. On the other hand, *Kriegsmarine* designers came up with radio-directed attack vessels and, as Samuel Eliot Morison admitted, these "remote-controlled explosive motor boats were employed with some effect."[8] The first surface naval drones!

In terms of pre-war designs for achieving and exploiting command of the air, the Italian strategist Giulio Douhet certainly developed the broadest vision, based on his belief in the war-winning potential of the bomber. His idea was to build swift, far-ranging aircraft capable of hitting distant enemy homelands—with poison gas bombs.[9] And when Italy invaded Ethiopia in 1935, chemical weapons were indeed dropped on Emperor Haile

Selassie's defending forces, and his innocent civilian subjects. But the Italians were less eager to use such tactics against opponents possessing similar retaliatory capabilities. Poison gas bombs were never again used by Mussolini's forces. As to the Germans, their emphasis was on building an air force designed to provide close support to advancing panzers. They achieved this goal, with much success; but pre-war debates about the "Ural bomber" reflected a real sensitivity to the need to build a strategic capability as well. Unfortunately, Ernst Udet rose to a high position and was able to ensure the triumph of his bias in favor of close-support attack aircraft over long-range bombers. This was to have quite profound consequences for the Germans, especially in the Battle of Britain. Japan, too, focused on tactical aircraft—on land and at sea—though in their geo-strategic situation, this made very good sense.

The strategic designs that emerged during the 1920s and 1930s among what were to be the three major Axis Powers did reflect great strengths in some areas. Perhaps the most important insight of each had to do with the decision to concentrate hitting power. In the German case, this took the form of creating the tank-heavy panzer division that energized *Blitzkrieg*; at sea, the Japanese *Kido Butai* massed aircraft carriers, enabling a range of swift, widespread naval and amphibious operations. And while Italian technology strategy lagged, at least in terms of the continued dedication to the by-now-outmoded biplane and the neglect of radar, the *Regia Marina's* warships were well designed. Also, Italian naval commando concepts were absolutely first-rate; and on land, even with the too-lightly-armored FIAT tanks, the army was, early on, ahead of the Germans—at least conceptually. This could be seen in some Italian operations during the Spanish Civil War that, as Hugh Thomas observed, after early reverses reflected the kind of deep penetration actions the Germans were to perfect just a few years later. Perhaps the best example of their mobile operations came during a drive toward Valencia when, per Thomas, even the "Italian infantry in five days advanced 100 kilometers, along a front 30 kilometers wide."[10] This was a quite remarkable early demonstration of modern maneuver warfare.

The chief weaknesses of Axis strategic designs during the interwar period were in the technological realm. As already mentioned, Italo Balbo bore much blame for the Italian adherence to the biplane fighter aircraft. German failure to emphasize not just U-boat construction, but development of the Walter-type submarines, was an even greater error. As was reluctance to embrace jet propulsion, in which German designers had a very significant lead during these years. A lead they would retain during the war—making it highly frustrating for Willy Messerschmitt and other designers and engineers to have to wait and hope for some sort of official decision to fund a major move ahead with this technology. As to the Japanese, their neglect of ship-borne radar cannot be excused. Even the best human vision could not offset longer-ranging radar "eyes." Not over time. As early as November 1942, the night duel between the Japanese *Kirishima* and the USS *Washington* off Guadalcanal proved the superiority of radar for detecting and targeting the enemy. *Kirishima* was hit by the *Washington's* opening salvo, repeatedly pummeled, and was sunk in this action.[11] Beyond the neglect of radar, the Japanese also paid too little attention to securing their codes—a cavalier attitude that was to have grave consequences during the war.

\* \* \*

When the Germans invaded Poland in September 1939, *Blitzkrieg* was still in its early stages of development. Nevertheless, the panzer division proved itself as the appropriate organizational design for mechanized warfare, and the doctrinal element of close coordination with tactical aircraft was equally well affirmed in action. That said, the campaign in Poland could hardly be viewed as a tough test of the new design for land warfare—especially since the Soviets struck from the east while Polish forces were defending against German thrusts from the north, west, and south. A more serious challenge awaited the Germans in the West, where large Anglo-Allied forces were deployed in greater numbers—including of tanks—and had several months to prepare for the upcoming battle. In the event, the Germans won a great victory in the 1940 Battle of France, due in no small part to the massing of their tanks in just a handful of concentrated divisions while the Allied armor was widely distributed across all their forces in the field. Nevertheless, the bold Manstein/Guderian concept was hugely risky, and was clearly seen as such even at the time. Erwin Lessner, an Austrian who escaped the Nazis in 1941 and later served with the Allies, saw *Blitzkrieg*'s vulnerability clearly:

> The situation of the *Wehrmacht* of World War II, ten days after the start of the great offensive, suddenly grew far more critical than that of the German Army in the late summer of 1914. Motorized troops and panzer divisions were streaming through the breach of Sedan—a powerful but by no means impenetrable screen for the main force which was following more slowly and turning to cut off the BEF, the French Northern Armies, and the Belgians.... [T]he BEF and French Northern Armies, then not greatly weakened by losses, applied pressure from the front.... From the Maginot Line and its reserves at least 20, probably 25 divisions could march north-northwest and take the Germans in the Givet-Charleroi sector in the rear.... The situation was indescribably confused, with good chances for the Allies if they woke up. The German armies operated utterly carelessly. They gambled at war, betting all they had on the continuance of the Allied paralysis.[12]

Hitler and Rundstedt, at least, were aware of the tremendous risks Guderian, Rommel and their colleagues in the field were taking; which led the former two to insist on a brief halt while other German forces came up to deal with any serious counterattack that might arise if the Allies did "wake up." This move reduced the chances of a successful Allied counter-pincer; but it also granted sufficient time for the Allied evacuation at Dunkirk to be carried off successfully. That said, Anglo-French failure to mount an early, double-angled counterattack doomed the forces south of the breakthrough. The key point from a strategic design perspective, though, is that victory was made possible by the organizational innovation of the panzer division and the *Luftwaffe* having been purpose-built for close support. Even so, for all this, *Blitzkrieg* was still a very chancy business. And would continue to be.

If the land and air forces of the Reich were proving the value of their organizational and doctrinal designs at this time, the *Kriegsmarine's* results were more mixed. On the positive side, the relative handful of ocean-going U-boats were able to inflict stinging blows on British shipping from the very outset; and the general lack of radar among convoy escort vessels meant that a doctrine of night surface attacks was optimal—and would remain so until this deficiency was rectified. By then, however, there were enough U-boats available to breathe life into Doenitz's wolfpack concept. But if prospects for submarine warfare in the early years of the conflict were good, the same cannot be said for the *Kriegsmarine's* surface warships. Artfully designed to combine speed, firepower and defensive armor, the problem was the lack of a proper battle doctrine for their best employment. Admiral Raeder took a fatalistic view, but nevertheless ordered his battleships out to sea, "to inflict maximum damage on the powerful enemy even at great risk to themselves." As to the likely result of such confrontations, Raeder was under no illusions. But he was determined that the surface fleet would not remain inactive, as had been the case for the High Sea Fleet throughout much of the First World War. Instead, the *Kriegsmarine* was to go out, and likely down, fighting. In Raeder's words, his sailors would "show that they could die with dignity!"[13]

Thus, *Graf Spee* was quickly lost, trapped while raiding in the South Atlantic. And even in successful operations during the invasion of Norway, the *Blücher* and many destroyers were sunk. *Scharnhorst* and *Gneisenau* had their innings, though, first in a successful raid in the North Atlantic in November 1939. Later, during the Norwegian campaign, the British carrier *Glorious* sank under their guns. After France fell, these fine ships, as well as other lighter warships, found homes in French ports. But the *Bismarck,* the crown jewel of the Z-Plan—"Z" for *Ziel,* "target"—had bad luck on its first raid in May 1941. Though it sank *Hood,* a sea chase mounted by the Royal Navy caught *Bismarck* before it could reach the safe haven of a German-occupied French port. By now, Hitler knew that Raeder's strategic doctrinal design, using warships as raiders, was a gross misuse of a major investment. In the campaign against merchant ships, the battle fleet of the *Kriegsmarine* sent slightly more than 250,000 tons of shipping to the bottom in the period from September 1939 through March 1941. During that same time, six light German raiders, the so-called "armed merchants" whose total development cost was a tiny fraction of that invested in the warships, sank 600,000 tons.[14] U-boats, meanwhile, sank tonnage amounting to the *millions* by this point.

Despite the losses suffered in the first two years of the war, much of the surface fleet remained. *Bismarck's* sister-ship *Tirpitz* was now launched, but was not to raid on open seas, then head for a French port. Indeed, after *Bismarck* went down, warships no longer raided commerce, spending most of their time in French ports—under regular British air attack. After months of this, Hitler reasoned it would be better to base his remaining warships in the north, in Norway in particular. This was an easy move for *Tirpitz.* But a "dash" up Channel by *Scharnhorst, Gneisenau,* and *Prinz Eugen*—the last of these had sortied with *Bismarck*—while quicker and less risky than trying to sail around the British Isles, was still a gamble. But the sheer audacity of such a move paid off when "Operation Cerberus" took place on the night of February 11, 1942. The three warships, well escorted by lighter vessels and fighters, made it. Now, with such hitting power repositioned, it was possible to put these ships to their very best use: interdicting aid convoys headed to Russia via the arctic route to Murmansk. The point may be made here that even a flaw in the technological dimension of design—in this case, a heavy investment in surface warships instead of U-boats—can be mitigated, if not fully rectified, by an adjustment in doctrinal design. Shifting warships from open-ocean commerce raiding to convoy interdiction in relatively narrow seas was a wise move—at a critical time in the land campaign in Russia.

By this point, early in 1942, German field armies in the East needed all the help that could be mustered. For all the successes of the panzers in the summer and fall of 1941, they were close to played out by the time the ultimate thrust at Moscow was made as winter neared. In the face of fierce Russian counter-attacks over the winter of 1941-2, German lines came close to breaking, barely holding. Hitler's judgment, to "stand fast," seemed to be borne out—though this defensive success served later on to feed his near-mania about holding ground, even when prudence called for retreat. And since this fighting proved costly—even if much costlier for the Russians—there was no way for the Germans to take the offensive in the summer of 1942 without substantial replacements. The

General Staff estimated 800,000 fresh troops were needed; but this was impractical, Albert Speer contended. He argued, "It was not possible to release such a number from the factories for service in the army." War production would be crippled. So, a fix was attempted via organizational redesign; infantry divisions shrank from nine to seven battalions, companies from 180 to 80 men. Two new panzer divisions were created, but the "increase of the German Army's tank strength was superficial rather than real ... barely half of the twenty existing armored divisions were brought up to strength in tanks," per Liddell Hart's account.[15]

It is clear to see the enormous risk this engendered on the Eastern Front in the 1942 campaign: the German drives to Stalingrad on the Volga and toward the oil resources in the Caucasus were undertaken with plenty of operational units—on paper—but they were smaller-sized. This meant that fewer troops would need to cover greater stretches of front, and that attrition, felt more deeply and swiftly by troops conducting attacks, would be keenly felt, rendering a division *hors de combat* too easily. Defeat was foreseeable for these much-watered-down forces, so widely overstretched as they were. Without doubt, the Italian and Romanian forces crushed in November 1942 when the Red Army launched its counterattack had lesser combat capability than German units, and played a role in the Stalingrad disaster. But so did the downsizing of the *Heer's* own combat units, which proved an even larger factor. Of Hitler's view of the causes of the Stalingrad debacle, Gerhard Weinberg noted, "He and a large number of his advisors simply blamed the great defeat on the failings of their allies—ignoring the central German role in the catastrophic 1942 campaign."[16] Blaming their allies while averting their gaze from their own failings was to have grave consequences for the Germans as the war in the East moved toward its true turning point in 1943.

The Italians had indeed sent a sizeable field army of ten divisions to support the Germans in Russia—well over 200,000 soldiers—along with sailors of their light coastal forces, who performed with distinction in the Black Sea, particularly during the siege of Sebastopol. This commitment to the Russian campaign was a serious drain on Italian material and manpower resources, which had been deployed to North Africa in even larger numbers. There, stinging defeats had been suffered until the Germans sent Rommel, at the head of a small panzer force, to their rescue in February 1941. But there was no Erwin Rommel, nor any German field forces, to rescue the 230,000 Italian troops in East Africa, all of which ended up—minus those killed in action—in captivity by May 1941. This signal disaster bore out the warning that Winston Churchill had conveyed in late September 1935, first in a public speech then in a private meeting with the Italian diplomat, Count Grandi, back when Mussolini's forces were just days away from invading Abyssinia. Churchill said, "To cast an army of nearly a quarter of a million men ... upon a barren shore two thousand miles from home ... without command of the sea ... is to give hostages to fortune unparalleled in all history."[17] This was Italy's grand strategic design flaw from the start: its aims were far too widespread, creating more vulnerability than opportunity.

In this deficiency Italy was not alone, as the tide of German conquests in the early years of the war compelled a dispersion of forces away from the vital Eastern Front. Occupation duty consisted of imposing German rule, chasing resistance fighters and, even from early on, preparing defenses along the Mediterranean and Atlantic coastlines against future Allied amphibious landings. All this ate up troops and planes much needed in the East, where the more than thousand-mile front was too thinly held. Sixty divisions were eventually assigned to France and the Low Countries; another fifty were needed to hold the Balkans and Italy after Axis forces were defeated at Alamein in November 1942, then trapped in Tunisia six months later. Thirty more divisions—twenty in Scandinavia, ten in Germany—were kept from active fronts. All this was out of a *Heer* of little more than three hundred under-strength divisions. Nearly half of all German land forces were pinned down in this manner, unable to help on the Eastern Front. Like the Italians, the Germans were too widely dispersed due to the vast territorial expanse of their conquests. John Steinbeck summed up the paradox of early German victories in his wartime novel of occupation and resistance, *The Moon Is Down,* in which an occupier admits, "the flies had conquered the flypaper."[18]

Overstretch proved a problem for the Japanese as well, constituting a fundamental flaw in their strategic design. They had been waging a draining war in China throughout the 1930s, in which the enemy, no matter the cost and number of defeats in the field, had a deep reservoir of manpower upon which to draw. As to the occupation of Chinese territory by Imperial Army forces, despite major advances, there remained an unconquered, seemingly endless hinterland that always lay well beyond reach. Compounding this problem, the Japanese conquests after the attack on Pearl Harbor hugely expanded the area that the Imperial Army, Navy, and their air components had to cover. If China was a quagmire—a situation recognized by many in Headquarters, and reinforced by the drubbing Zhukov gave the Army in the Nomonhan border war with the Russians in 1939—at least in the Pacific Japan possessed a more promising strategic design. It was comprised of the creation of a broad perimeter of theoretically interlocking island fortresses from which long-ranging aircraft were intended to prevent invasions, or to come to the aid of neighboring islands that found themselves under attack. This basic design was enhanced by the notion of having the aircraft carriers of the *Kido Butai*—and the rest of the Combined Fleet—play a "fireman" role, along with Japan's submarines, coming to the rescue of any embattled island. As John Keegan observed of the design:

> The perimeter strategy was rooted deeply in the psyche and history of the Japanese who, as an island people, had long been accustomed to using land and sea forces in concert to preserve the security of the archipelago they inhabit and extend national power into adjoining regions.[19]

With regard to land conquests in Southeast Asia, General Yamashita showed in the conquest of Malaya and Singapore that great victories could be won with far smaller forces than the enemy put in the field. Though he was quickly shipped off to North China—Hideki Tojo apparently did this to prevent Yamashita from eclipsing him in the eyes of their fellow military men, the public, and the Emperor—the Imperial Army continued to conduct swift, infiltrating advances in Burma, driving British Empire troops into a 900-mile retreat to India, and giving Chinese forces under General Joseph Stilwell's guidance "a hell of a beating," as he put it. And in the conquest of the Dutch East Indies, the Japanese demonstrated a high level of sea-air-land coordination, truly a winning doctrinal design that was greatly empowered by the primacy of the Zero fighter at this time, the big advantage in naval strength after Pearl Harbor, and the value of the Long Lance torpedo in surface naval engagements.

Nevertheless, even during this period of remarkable victories, a few disquieting indicators suggested that there were flaws in the overall Japanese strategic design that could be exploited. Aside from the significant problem of overstretch—the neutrality agreement with the Russians should be viewed as a diplomatic attempt to mitigate the degree of exposure Japan would have on its northern landward front—there was the piercing of the Imperial codes that had been going on throughout the inter-war years, but which now would have a most profound effect on the course of the fighting. Indeed, Admiral Nimitz was always willing to act when he had an "information edge." This enabled him to send an interception force to the Coral Sea in May 1942, and allowed him to seize the opportunity to ambush the *Kido Butai* at Midway a month later. Just as important, "Magic" made it possible to vector in U.S. Navy submarines on vulnerable Japanese shipping, despite the subs' small numbers, initially unreliable torpedoes, and the vastness of the Pacific Ocean areas in which they roamed. Intercepts, from early on, had what Ronald Lewin called a "priceless significance," providing a convoy's information that was "not simply the number of ships, and often their individual names and cargoes, and the character of the escort, but also the route it is to take and *the noon position for some or all the days of its voyage.*"[20]

The Japanese suffered from other strategic design flaws as well, each quite apparent even during the early period of triumphs. At the social level, unspeakable atrocities committed in China—especially the Rape of Nanking—and in harsh occupations elsewhere, served only to foster resistance.[21] It was a strategic blunder driven largely by Japanese nationalist chauvinism, a flaw not too dissimilar to the race-based Nazi ideology that led to the gross depredations perpetrated against the innocent in occupied zones. In China and Russia—elsewhere, too—these war crimes only served to harden the will to resist of those subjected to the conquerors' rule. The powerful effects of Russian partisans were covered in earlier chapters. As to behind-the-lines resistance to the Japanese in China, there were equally important initiatives as well, not least the Sino-American Cooperative Organization (SACO), in which small numbers of U.S. Navy sailors, Marines and others advised what became a major resistance effort. Eventually, Samuel Eliot Morison noted, "SACO held three seaports and about two hundred miles of the China coast."[22] SACO's exploits inspired the *Terry and the Pirates* comic strip.

Claire Chennault's "Flying Tigers" rose to fame in this theater as well, being among the first to fight the Japanese with some degree of success in the air. The Tigers exposed the fundamental design flaw in the Zero which, for all its range, speed, and maneuverability, lacked self-sealing fuel tanks and was, overall, highly vulnerable to battle damage. This was so because, in design, nothing comes free. The great strengths of the Zero came at the price of vulnerability. Claire Chennault understood this, and trained pilots under his command in a battle doctrine designed to avoid Japanese strengths and exploit the Zero's vulnerabilities. He usually had early warning of Zero raids—thanks to ground observer reports radioed in from occupied zones and nearby friendly villages—and got his unwieldy P-40 Tomahawk fighters in the air early. This enabled them to get above the incoming Japanese, dive down upon them at tremendous speed due to the Tomahawk's heavy weight, then get away. Chennault instructed his pilots "never to dog-fight or try to turn with a Japanese fighter. Use your speed and diving power to make a pass, shoot and break away."[23] The Marines of the Cactus Air Force used the same approach at Guadalcanal—aided by radar and Coastwatchers—and inflicted just as stinging blows on the Japanese in the last months of 1942.

The long, hard fight for Guadalcanal highlighted another design flaw of the Japanese: their consistent violation of the principle of massing forces to improve the chances of victory. Repeatedly, the Imperial Army and Navy—and their respective air forces—went into battle in driblets. This ensured the campaign would devolve into an attritional struggle the Americans were better suited to waging. It was the Army's first hard fight against American troops, and the failure to send larger forces to the island can to some extent be explained by an arrogant belief in the superiority of the Japanese soldier. But for the Navy—and for Yamamoto—there was by now no excuse for sending small task groups into battle. They won numerous encounters, and inflicted more damage than they suffered, but Japan's sea power was ground down. Before Guadalcanal, at Midway, the Fleet had advanced in scattered fashion. Mitsuo Fuchida, who led the attack on Pearl Harbor, described the Midway disaster this way: "Instead of massing what could easily have been the most formidable single task force ever seen, Combined Fleet chose to scatter its forces, reducing them thereby to comparative feebleness."[24] This doctrinal design flaw persisted, and played a role in Japan's ultimate defeat.

*   *   *

Nineteen forty-two may have been, as Captain Henry Adams put it, "the year that doomed the Axis."[25] By December there was surely no doubt that German, Italian, and Japanese dreams of conquest had been thwarted and that the initiative had, mostly, shifted to the Allies. But the absence of chances for outright victory did not have to mean that the sole remaining path was to utter defeat. To use a chess metaphor, the Axis could still "play for a draw." Admittedly, the Allied demand for unconditional surrender acted as a forcing function, compelling continued fighting. But Stalin had explored the possibility of a separate peace on more than one occasion. As Gerhard Weinberg noted, "The prospect first of a possible Soviet collapse and thereafter of a Soviet-German peace hung over the alignment of the three great powers from June 1941 until the end of 1944 ... [Stalin's] pact with Hitler in the first part of the Second World War was ever present in the thinking of the British and American leaders."[26] With Russia out, the situation in the Mediterranean would shift sharply in favor of Axis forces—and D-Day would simply not have been possible in the face of German troops redeployed to the West.

The Japanese, as Weinberg also observed, "very much wanted such a German-Soviet agreement,"[27] as this would lead to a massive improvement in the Nazis' strategic situation *and* cause a great diversion of Anglo-Allied manpower and resources—perhaps for years— away from Japan's empire. Newly freed-up Japanese forces would improve the military situation in the China-Burma-India theater. And the troops available for island campaigns would be sharply boosted as well. But even absent an outright peace deal between Hitler and Stalin, the two months after Stalingrad saw a remarkable recovery in the German situation on the Eastern Front. Subsequent to the sacrifice of the 6th Army—ultimately, a needed one if the whole southern part of the front was to avoid collapse[28]—Manstein developed a doctrinal design for defensive use of panzers that inflicted hard blows on the Russians. His concept was based on allowing Soviet spearheads to penetrate for some distance, then striking them in flank near the front line they initially pierced, cutting them off and subjecting them to defeat in detail. It was a blueprint for sustained defensive successes; a most practicable one as well, given that the Germans, still deep in Russia, could well allow penetrations of this sort.

But many senior German military men, led by Kurt Zeitzler, who in September of 1942 succeeded Franz Halder as Chief of the General Staff, opposed the idea of remaining strategically on the defensive, limited just to landing occasional counter-punches on the advancing enemy. Instead, they saw in Manstein's successes the seeds of a great new offensive that could be mounted to pinch off the massive Soviet forces in the big salient near Kursk. Needless to say, Manstein was opposed to such a violation of his defensive design—Model was as well. Guderian, too, opposed going over to offensive operations and, in a meeting with Hitler on May 10, 1943—three years to the day from the launch of the victorious Battle of France—got the Fuehrer to admit that the idea of attacking at Kursk made his "stomach turn over." To which Guderian said, "In that case your reaction to the problem is the correct one. Leave it alone!"[29] But Hitler was ultimately swayed by staff officers like Zeitzler and Keitel, whom he saw every day, and so the offensive went ahead in July 1943—ending in the disastrous attrition that his field generals had predicted. Hitler was in part persuaded to "go" by the arrival of the new Tiger and Panther tanks. He thought that they would provide an insuperable advantage. But both had serious teething problems, and in any event were much slower than the workhorse Panzer IV— and *Blitzkrieg* needed speed.

Kursk was not the only place where German forces took the offensive when they should not have. After the very skillful defensive fight in Sicily during July and August of 1943, which Hanson Baldwin labeled "a German moral victory,"[30] too profligate use of the panzers was made in the efforts to thwart landings on the Italian mainland—which having occurred, knocked most Italians out of the Axis. At Salerno in September, far too much armor, including Tiger tanks, was thrown at the beachhead—in the face of massive Allied air support and naval gunfire often delivered at point-blank range. The result, as Hugh Pond summarized, was that the

> Air Force ... struck at every conceivable static and moving target. Wherever the Germans thought they were safe, the airmen sought them out and pounded them.... But above all, it was naval shelling that was causing the enemy dismay. Wherever they moved, wherever they fired from, they were certain to get in return a salvo from the ships' guns.[31]

The Allied formula was repeated again in the later fighting at Anzio, where ground-attack aircraft and naval gunfire support decimated the Germans who were desperately trying to throw this amphibious end run back into the sea. The right strategic design, though— in both cases—was to wage a defensive campaign instead, counter-punching opportunistically and withdrawing as needed. In Italy, Kesselring eventually figured this out, and managed to hold on there until the last days of the war in 1945.

But in dealing with the threat of Allied invasion along the Atlantic coast, the same dreams of offensive armored operations wrought eventual catastrophe. In this case, the problem was one of "dueling designs." The great question was how to employ the nine panzer divisions—and the one panzer grenadier unit—that comprised the beating heart of German defenses in the West. The other fifty divisions, it was fully understood, had to deploy along and among the fortifications of the so-called "Atlantic Wall," due to their lack of mobility. Rundstedt and other armored warfare experts argued that the panzers should be held together for the most part, ready to engage the invaders in a mobile maneuver battle once they had advanced inland. Rommel, who had firsthand experience of the crushing effects of Allied close air support, believed that the heyday of the *Blitzkrieg* was completely over, and that as much strength as possible—including the panzers—needed to be concentrated in the coastal zones, so as to give the *Heer* its best chance of defeating the invasion from the outset. For once ashore, as experience in Italy had demonstrated, the Allies could not be dislodged. The vehement arguments on both sides of this debate made it hard for Hitler to decide which operational design to choose. So, he chose both— and neither. The panzers were placed well inland, per Rundstedt's view, but were widely dispersed throughout France, behind the various invasion zones.

Ironically, the Fuehrer's muddled deployment decision can in large part be blamed on Guderian—one of the best of his strategic designers. The "Panzer Leader" drew a conclusion from the Italian campaign opposite to Rommel's. So much so that, as David Irving reported, "Guderian insisted that all the tanks must be held well out of range of the enemy's warship artillery—all the landings in Italy had shown that. He reported to Hitler: 'We'll have to lay down a precise Stop Line, forward of which no panzer divisions may be moved.'"[32] Even an excellent strategic designer can be wrong, and Guderian was surely mistaken in this instance. For, as Victor Davis Hanson thoughtfully observed of the Normandy campaign:

> The counterassaults of the reserve Panzer units against the beaches were too fragmented and small, and under constant air attack. Within a week there was a nearly hundred-mile contiguous beachhead. Within a month, a million Allied troops had landed.... It no longer mattered whether Hitler's Panzer reserves were immediately deployed at the beachheads or sent in from the rear.[33]

It turned out that Rommel was right; the invasion had to be stopped from the outset. And when it wasn't, the high-level bias toward offensive action somehow persisted and reasserted itself—disastrously.

While on the defensive in Normandy, the German 7th Army fought skillfully for nearly two months in the hedgerow country there. And here, finally, the Tiger tanks showed at their best. Not in extensive mobile-type operations—they were too slow for this, and would have been picked off too easily by air attack—but rather in small engagements, working closely with infantry. Again and again, the Tigers proved superior to all Allied armored designs. Perhaps the best demonstration of the Tiger's capabilities came on the 13th of June, exactly one week after D-Day. Michel Wittman, a panzer company commander spotted an incipient crisis posed by the advancing 22nd Brigade of the British 7th Armoured Division—the famed "Desert Rats"—who were threatening to outflank the whole *Panzer Lehr* Division and break the German front south of Bayeux. Wittmann boldly confronted the enemy with just five of his nearby Tigers. He quickly lost one, but the other four wrought havoc. Still, they would eventually have been overrun were it not for the intervention of eight Tigers from a neighboring company. This was all the reinforcement needed to stop the advance. Paul Carell summed up the battle this way: "A dozen Tigers had won a battle."[34] For all the many small successes of this sort, though, the Allies kept grinding away, World War I–style, until George Patton finally broke out of Normandy on July 30.

At this point, the best the Germans could hope for was a fighting withdrawal across France to the "West Wall," ultimately to the Rhine. But by now Rommel had been severely wounded and was convalescing, while Rundstedt had been dismissed—for "defeatism." *Feldmarschall* Günther von Kluge, their successor, was pushed by Hitler and other rear-area staffers into launching a major offensive to cut off Patton's 3rd Army by striking to the coast at Avranches. A preference for massed armored attacks continued to plague German planners—and Hitler himself. In this case, the result was a near-catastrophe: Of more than 100,000 troops—and four panzer divisions—committed to the operation launched at the end of the first week of August, ten thousand were killed, another forty thousand taken prisoner as Patton and Montgomery sought to mount a joint northerly-southerly pincer move to trap the whole German attacking force. Roughly half the Germans got away through the "Falaise Gap," but with little of their heavy equipment. Kluge, whom Hitler now suspected of secretly talking peace with the Allies, took his own life on August

19. Hitler finally realized the immediate, urgent need to revert to the defensive, and brought Model, his "fireman," to the Western command. Model worked something of a miracle, shoring up defenses and morale, and then inflicted a sharp defeat on the Allies at Arnhem.[35]

Model's success, not only at Arnhem, but in and around Aachen and at other points along the Western Front as well, led Hitler and his senior staff advisers to dream up yet another plan for a major offensive. Rundstedt was called back to active service once more, to take command of the attack that would come to be known as the Battle of the Bulge. But by now, as Charles Messenger noted, *Blitzkrieg* was a spent force: "What had been possible in May 1940 was no longer the case four-and-a-half years later."[36] Indeed, this brilliant operational brainchild of Guderian, Rommel, and Manstein, even at its beginning and through its early successes, was a highly risky concept that was susceptible to cool-headed defenders from the outset, and much more vulnerable later on to enemy commanders who had learned from others' and their own experiences.[37] And so, in December of 1944, and on into January of 1945, a great armored battle raged once more, with much attrition and little else. The Bulge expanded and contracted, and the Germans lost over 100,000 men, 600 tanks and 1,600 aircraft. These losses enraged Adolf Galland, who had made the case for the *Luftwaffe*—and much of the panzers used in the West— to be redeployed to the East, where both would have had an immeasurably beneficial effect against the Russians.

Galland's sensible argument was to focus on bloodying the Red Army—by now suffering its own very serious manpower problems—while holding at the Rhine in the West. As he put the matter:

> Now that the Red Army was prepared to push open the door to the West, the German leaders should have had no other aim than to throw all their [available] forces against this enemy. If the German divisions were sent against the East instead of to the Ardennes, then it would still have been possible to stem the Red flood. If our fighters, about 4,000 strong, were not [due to being tasked to support the Western offensive] to be used for their intended task of regaining air superiority over the Reich, then they might as well be used to assist the army in the last great battle of the war. They could have achieved quite different results against the enemy in the East than against the one in the West.[38]

But Galland's pleas fell on deaf ears at Hitler's headquarters; and, even after the losses suffered in the Battle of the Bulge, the *Heer* was ordered to keep on fighting west of the Rhine. It held on bitterly there, until March 1945; though by then attrition had taken such a debilitating toll that General Omar Bradley noted, "As a consequence of that debacle west of the Rhine, enemy resistance on the east bank of that river was disorganized and uninspired."[39] The Allies were soon across the Rhine, driving on into Germany; and, bereft of forces used in the Ardennes offensive, the *Heer* was overrun in the East.

By this point, early 1945, the U-boats had been completely defeated by Ultra decrypts of Enigma-encoded message content, and direction-finding technology that located them. The Ultra intercepts gave advance warning of U-boat dispositions, so that the majority of convoys could be rerouted away from them, avoiding contact in the first place. Code-breaking and direction-finding also enabled Allied attacks on the U-boats when they rendezvoused with their "milch cows." While Doenitz stubbornly kept to Enigma codes, his skippers knew their communications were compromised. Harald Busch observed that "on a suspiciously large number of occasions, enemy aircraft had made their appearance at the very moment when the pipeline was stretched between two boats and neither was able to dive, with the result that many U-boats had been destroyed in the act of refueling."[40] It was a most demoralizing time for German submariners, three-fourths of whom died in action during the war. Herbert Werner wrote a searing firsthand memoir of the U-boat war, in which he described the final defeat this way: "Inadequate boats and inexperienced young officers and helpless crews were bombed and depth-charged to the bottom in a steady procession, like ignorant animals filing to the butcher's block."[41]

This catastrophe resulted from failure to adopt the advanced Walter boat designs—not just his streamlined hulls for greater speed, but his air-independent propulsion system that made the U-boat a true submarine, not just a submersible. This technology emerged in the mid–1930s; but it was a time when Raeder headed the German Navy, and he was fixated on building battleships. The Walter boat design was thus shelved. Even when Doenitz took command of the *Kriegsmarine* in January 1943—chosen because Hitler realized that U-boats were his last hope of winning the war at sea—he opted *not* to focus on this breakthrough technology. Why? Because, as Doenitz noted in his memoir, the *Schnorchel,* an incremental fix, met "demand for a 100% under-water vessel of high speed."[42] A fatal error, as Allied detection equipment was enhanced to be able to pick up the *Schnorchel.* So merchant ship losses fell from a high of over 1,000,000 tons in the period January–March 1943 to *less than 70,000 tons* in the October to November quarter of 1944. Interestingly, the months from January–March 1945 saw a sharp rise in the sinking of Allied merchantmen, to close to 200,000 tons, thanks to the few U-boats of Walter's advanced design that were finally deployed.[43]

The story of the air war over Germany from 1943 to 1945 is a similar tale of incremental rather than transformational design approaches. While the Allies were improving their ability to provide long-range fighter escorts for their "precision" daylight air raids—and the P-51 Mustang posed a most formidable challenge to the Me 109—the *Luftwaffe* focused on providing its now aging fighters with enhanced cannon and rocket-fired weaponry that let them shoot at the bombers from greater range. Basically, though, the goal was to increase production of existing designs—a futile aim given Allied production superiority. The Germans needed jets! Aside from incremental, numbers-based thinking, there *was* an innovative attempt to take advantage of the B-17s' close formations by arming German fighters with 500-lb. bombs, then having them climb 3,000 feet *above* the Americans. The fighters imitated directional movements of the enemy, to stay right above them. The fighters' bombs, set on timers, were then released to go off in the middle of the B-17 "boxes." Cajus Bekker summed up the results: "Bombing bombers with fighters was new … [and met with] striking success."[44] This was true, at least initially; and in one instance, a bomb dropped amid a group of B-17s knocked down three at once. But the Allies responded by loosening their formations to limit losses, and redoubled their attacks on German fighters.

Given that jet fighter production had been long delayed—before the war by conservatism in the *Luftwaffe,* since 1943 by Hitler insisting that jets be designed as bombers—all that was left by late 1944 were last-gasps. The damage done by Japanese *kamikazes* during initial phases of the Philippine campaign in the fall of 1944 was seized upon by some in German strategic circles and seen as worthy of emulation. This led to the idea of creating a force of *Selbstopfermänner* ("self-sacrifice men"). Their champion was Hajo Herrmann, creator of the highly successful "Wild Boar" night-fighters. He urged *kamikaze*-style attacks on the Allied bombers, and organized "ram commandos" prepared to engage in such operations. Werner Baumbach was by now in a command that had oversight of this initiative, and opposed the idea fiercely. He argued the concept was "foreign to our mentality … not even the best solution, to put it mildly." Yet it had supporters at high levels, and the matter was taken all the way to Hitler himself for adjudication. In the end, for all the Fuehrer's bloody-mindedness, he rejected the notion, emphasizing that German pilots "must have a chance, however small, to come through."[45] Aside from this humane reasoning, the problem was that this method would just trade plane for plane. The Allies would win such an attritional fight. Only jets, lots of jets, would have made a difference.

For Japan, on the other hand, the suicide attack ratio was not plane-for-plane, but rather plane—even many planes—for ship. If the Philippine campaign was a testing ground, Okinawa was the *kamikaze* proving ground, where they cost the invasion fleet two ships sunk or damaged every three days. One can speculate, if not extrapolate, about heavier losses that would have been inflicted—by thousands more *kamikazes*—if Japan were invaded. Thankfully, the war ended before *that* became necessary. Japan surrendered after losing two cities to atomic bombs, but the Empire had already been fatally pierced by the Allied ability to mount amphibious invasions against island after island. Although they were increasingly well defended, their fanatical garrisons had no hope of naval and air forces coming to their rescue. Amphibious invasions shattered Japan's shield; and the commerce raiding campaign—led by U.S., British, and Dutch submariners—bled it dry. Lack of a good design for defending the *marus* was terrible, and Japanese failure to mount a submarine offensive against Allied merchant ships was inexcusable. Charles Lockwood, who led the Allied undersea effort, viewed this Japanese shortcoming as the result of an unfocused sub design process:

> They had a dozen different types…. They frittered away their building facilities and steel in playing with these sideshows … instead of building long-range, fast combat submarines of 50–75 days endurance, with which to harass and disrupt our supply lines.[46]

Clearly, even in the absence of the atomic *deus ex machina* Japan was doomed. Aside from the near-total loss of resources from abroad needed to fuel industry and feed the people caused by Lockwood's raiders, bombing burned city after city. Imperial field forces on the Asian mainland were by now being routed. With the collapse of the Germans, Russia would soon be ready to end its "strange neutrality" and join the war against Japan. Like its German and Italian partners, the Japanese pursued a strategy of expansion that had made all three main Axis partners vulnerable to deft counter-strokes undertaken by their resolute adversaries—at selected points that *they* chose, *when* they chose. While Japan's forces were ultimately outnumbered, they were nevertheless able to keep the numerical imbalance within reasonable limits. Yamashita demonstrated just what a smaller, but sizeable, Japanese field army could do on the defensive, keeping his forces on their feet and fighting on Luzon to the last day of the war. In the European theater, forces in Italy were roughly equal on both sides right into 1945. And in June of 1944, Allied troops in Britain totaled just under fifty divisions; Rundstedt and Rommel had *sixty* under their command. The Russians *did* outnumber the Germans in the East, but fought far less well— on the ground and in the air. German defeat there had more to do with flaws in strategic design than with numbers. This is why the Axis forces, in *all* theaters, were beaten.

*   *   *

Is the defeat of the Axis Powers proof that they *had* to lose World War II? Hardly. Many histories note how close they came to victory, focusing on two main explanations for why they didn't prevail. One school of thought favors crucial contingencies, pointing to examples such as Hitler's brief halt of the panzers at Dunkirk, or the sacrifice of the American torpedo bombers at Midway that diverted Japanese fighters, allowing Navy dive bombers to decimate the *Kido Butai* in a few short minutes of furious action. The other main line of argument embraces a more deterministic view, one that keys on the material strength the Allies were able to bring to the fight: countless Liberty ships moving men and materials across the globe, among which were 400,000 Studebaker trucks that gave the Red Army its mobility; and armadas of ships, planes and troops striking at selected points with superior force. Still, the Axis Powers won many victories, and they nearly prevailed—despite occasional blunders and greater Allied numbers. Writing in 1945, historian Henry Steele Commager observed of Axis performance: "They had almost succeeded." He went on, presciently, "details of their failure will intrigue students of strategy and tactics for generations to come."[47]

In my view, World War II continues to be "intriguing" and, despite all the wonderful narrative histories written and analyses compiled, one can still frame this greatest of all armed conflicts in terms of the puzzle posed by its outcome. Neither contingent events nor sheer numbers have provided final answers. For the one makes war a matter of chance, the other an algorithm to be followed to an exact, inevitable solution. The German philosopher of war, Carl von Clausewitz, introduced in his *On War* the concepts of "fog" and "friction" that made conflict, as he put it, "a game of cards."[48] In *War and Peace*, Leo Tolstoy, took a more deterministic view, arguing that strong currents of history set the fates of nations and led, inevitably, to the outcome of any particular war. He put his argument simply and clearly: "What is the cause of historical events? Power. What is power? Power is the collective will."[49] Thus the greater the masses, the more collective power there will be—presuming constancy of "will," which the Germans and Japanese definitely had, the Italians definitely not. Given Axis depredations, Allied will was as firm as that on the opposing side. Since the Allied "collective" was greater in mass, Tolstoy would have seen in this instance that the strong currents of historical power would take Germany, Japan and Italy to certain defeat.

With awareness of and respect for the arguments about war outcomes that derive from belief in either the role of chance factors or the determinism of calculations of mass, I chose in this book to add a fresh view: World War II was decided by Axis design flaws. All three of the main Axis Powers had strategic designs built on notions of vast territorial expansion—which made all three highly vulnerable to selected counterblows by their opponents. In terms of technology, Japan and Italy both fell far behind in development of radar—so crucial to naval warfare—while Germany built the wrong type of navy and ended up unable to exploit fully the tremendous hitting power of the U-boat. Compounding this error, the Germans failed to emphasize the production of advanced submarine designs, an area in which they had a great advantage. The same was true for the Germans in the air, where their lead in jet technology was never properly exploited. Although, when compared to the Italian belief in biplanes, and the Japanese decision to design their fighter planes for speed and range at the cost of ruggedness, German aircraft design efforts look better. Perhaps the worst design flaws, however, hit both the Germans and Japanese hardest in the area of information security. Both stubbornly held on to their coding systems, despite evidence they had been "hacked" that even *Kaleuns* commanding U-boats detected and reported.

Grand strategic and technological design flaws aside, the Axis Powers also suffered from significant muddling in the realm of battle doctrine. The Italian Army was utterly unsuited to waging mobile warfare in the deserts of North Africa, yet invaded Egypt and was quickly routed by a much smaller body of British Empire troops. Similarly, the German *Kriegsmarine* surface warships, of high technical quality, were utterly misused on the offensive as raiders. The more proper doctrine for their employment should have been to interdict the northern sea lanes that British and American ships used to bring vital aid to the embattled Russians. And in Russia, the Germans kept to the offensive too long, when the proper doctrine by 1943 was clearly to adopt Manstein's clever counter-punching defensive concept of operations. But instead, adherence to offensive thinking led to disaster at Kursk, and to the totally debilitating debate about whether to deploy the panzers in the West in one great massed formation, or to spread them out along the coastline to help thwart an Allied landing. This massing issue affected the Japanese as well, though in the opposite way; they neglected the very first principle of modern naval warfare—massed attack—first at Midway, then again in the long, hard fight for Guadalcanal. The Imperial Navy had pioneered the right doctrinal design for fleet actions in World War II, but then went out and dispersed or parceled their forces in driblets, time after time. Even at Leyte.

These are but the main highlights, or rather lowlights, that illuminate from a design perspective the reasons for Axis defeat. In the next chapter, the insights derived from this design-based reconsideration of World War II will be plumbed for their possible usefulness in framing a similar approach to analyzing current and near-future military affairs. But first a final point should be addressed about the emergence of the atomic bomb in 1945. To some, Allied development of nuclear weapons made it impossible for the Axis Powers to win, or even achieve a stalemate—thus rendering most, if not all, strategic analysis moot. Andrew Roberts puts this view well, noting that the Axis "had no hope of winning the war anyway, because a nuclear bomb was being successfully developed in New Mexico."[50] Certainly this meant the Axis could not win. But imagine the course the war would have taken had Germany built Walter boats and jets early on, and had Manstein's doctrinal design been adhered to in the East. Or if Japan (and Germany) had been less smug about information security and avoided being "hacked" by Ultra and Magic. The situation by 1945 would have seen the Axis still in control of very large swathes of territory and some hundreds of millions of conquered peoples. Even if the Allies *were* able to break through to drop an atomic bomb, the Axis could take murderous reprisals, and threaten more.

Such a situation would require the Allies to develop forces sufficient to defeat the Axis at sea, in the air, and on land—much as they actually did. Design analysis suggests, however, that this would have proved difficult if the Axis embraced engineering breakthroughs in submarines and aircraft. Karl Doenitz noted in a June 1942 memo, "the Walter boat would instantly render all but wholly ineffective the enemy's defensive measures, which are designed to defeat the current type of submarine."[51] Adolf Galland argued in a similar way for the Me 262 jet, which he test flew in May 1943 and described this way: "It was as though angels were pushing."[52] In less poetic terms, the Germans had a high functioning fighter by the middle of the war—and could have had one much earlier—whose speed outmatched the best of Allied fighters by 175kph. As to land battles, all the Germans had to do was adopt Manstein's ideas and recognize that Enigma had been hacked—which affected the war at sea and in the air as well. But, as F.W. Winterbotham recalled, "neither Hitler nor his top generals ever gave any indication on Ultra that they had caught on to the fact that their ciphers were unsafe."[53] Had the Japanese "caught on" to Magic and varied their codes, Midway would not have happened, nor many of the other Allies' Pacific victories.

To be sure, the Axis path to outright victory narrowed, perhaps even crumbled, by the end of 1942. But utter defeat—with Berlin in ruins, Tokyo burned, Rome occupied—was not foreordained. In the European theater of operations, the Germans were, simply put, better fighters. Good enough to defeat or stalemate more numerous enemies. Andrew Roberts affirms this:

> However unpalatable it might be to admit it, the statistics allow no doubt: soldier for soldier the German fighting man and his generals outperformed Britons, Americans and Russians both offensively and defensively by a significant factor virtually throughout the Second World War.[54]

Even the Italians fought better when leavened by the Germans. They did quite well in North Africa when Rommel led them; and the *Regia Marina* had the advantage in the Mediterranean when given *Luftwaffe* support. As to the Japanese, when following Yamamoto's and Yamashita's designs they demonstrated real superiority in the fighting at sea, in the air, and on land in the early part of the war. Minus Midway and, later, submarine depredations—both hugely enabled by Magic decrypts—it is not very hard to see that the Empire had good chances for achieving a reasonable outcome. Yes, the Axis blundered at times. So did the Allies. No war is waged perfectly. But this greatest of all wars was not decided by a few critical mistakes in battle; its outcome was determined by major, persistent, design flaws.

In my view, future wars will be similarly decided—and World War II's lessons for strategic design can—and must—be drawn and employed to help in this era of rapid technological change and renewed competition among the leading powers.

# 10. How World War II
## Still Guides Strategic Design

THERE ARE MANY WAYS in which the legacies of the Second World War continue to manifest themselves. Perhaps the most obvious is the United Nations Security Council, where the permanent members—who wield veto power—are the nations that played key roles in defeating the Axis: Britain, China, France, Russia and the United States. The fact that Germany and Japan, two of the world's most advanced industrial countries, do not have nuclear weapons of their own is evidence that the long memories of 1939–1945 continue to impel constraints on these one-time aggressors' abilities to develop the full range of military capabilities. Also, the organizational cultures of the German and Japanese armed forces have undergone sharp redefinition along self-defensive lines, a clear result of their experiences in World War II. Interestingly, the Italians do seem to be a bit freer, in terms of military capabilities; a key example being that the *Marina Militare* retains first-rate expertise in "combat swimmer" operations—a true testament to the enduring value of Borghese's ideas about how quite small teams can achieve strategic effects. Even so, Italy too remains a non-nuclear-weapons state. None of the former principal Axis Powers seems to have regained full trust.

In terms of land warfare, the mobile armored operational design that Guderian and Rommel did so much to pioneer before and during World War II remains the centerpiece of most advanced military thought today. Tanks have diffused globally, their defenses improved by composite and explosive-reactive armor—and even depleted uranium armor in some militaries. Yet tanks today remain very much like their World War II progenitors in both form and function. Indeed, General Norman Schwarzkopf's famous "left hook" during Operation Desert Storm in 1991 looked much like Rommel's right hooks in North Africa fifty years earlier. The showy "thunder run" to Baghdad in 2003 could have come straight from Heinz Guderian's playbook. Beyond the United States, the Indo-Pakistani wars have featured tank battles on a grand scale—as occurred in the 1965 conflict—as well as Guderian-like armored penetration operations that the Indian Army brought to a high level of efficiency in its invasion of East Pakistan (now Bangladesh) in 1971. But it is somewhat ironic to note that perhaps the best practitioners of the mobile maneuver form of *Blitzkrieg* developed by the Germans during the 1930s have been the Israelis. As Charles Messenger has observed of Israel's early conventional wars, "the Israelis have fought four campaigns against their Arab neighbors, employing in each many of the principles of *Blitzkrieg*."[1]

Similar durability and diffusion can be seen in naval operations, too, where the aircraft carrier that established itself as dominant by 1942 remains the largely undisputed capital ship of the 21st century—though John Keegan presented a very powerful dissent in his view of the implications of the 1982 South Atlantic War. In that conflict, just two British submarines bottled up Argentina's carrier and its other warships, signifying that, as Keegan put it, "command of the sea in the future unquestionably lies beneath rather than upon the surface."[2] Even so, the U.S. Navy is set to spend over $100 billion on a new generation of aircraft carriers—that will operate much like their 1940s forebears. And other nations have or are in the process of building or otherwise acquiring carriers. China has one already, with two currently (2019) under construction—the same number the U.S. Navy has being built at present. However, the PLA Navy is making a bigger bet on the future value of light coastal forces, heavily armed with high-speed missiles and torpedoes, as well as on increasingly stealthy submarines. As to the world's other navies, six have a single carrier each, while the Italians, who never finished the *Aquila* during World War II, have two, with another building. Still, an American edge in carriers persists: the U.S. Navy has eleven—just over half—of the world's twenty carriers in service.

Needless to say, jets are flying from the decks of the world's carriers today. And more broadly, jet technology, which the Germans neglected to emphasize in the 1930s, and delayed development of even during the war years, has come to dominate *all* modern air forces. The concept of close support that the *Luftwaffe* developed to near-perfection in its day is now *de rigueur,* in conventional wars as well as in the irregular conflicts that have proliferated since the end of World War II. Interestingly, design of the U.S. Air Force's reliable close-support aircraft, the A-10, was greatly enhanced by advice from former *Stuka* ace Hans Ulrich Rudel.[3] Strategic bombing, which none of the Axis Powers developed to any degree of skill, but which was employed with abandon by the Allies, continues to excite high-level thinkers about the future of air power—despite the poor track record of such aerial campaigns over the past eight decades.[4] But if strategic bombing seems stale as a concept, despite protestations of its still-ardent supporters among the "shock and awe" school of thought,[5] the most radical innovation in air power design arising in World War II was the *kamikaze.*

Clearly, Japan's suicide attack concept had deep implications for the future of war at sea; the ship sinkings by *kamikazes,* from the Philippines to Okinawa during World War II, as naval experts Wayne Hughes and Robert Girrier have noted, "represent the start of the missile era"[6] that dominates naval combat today. In 1971, India's navy demonstrated the great striking power of missiles during the war against Pakistan when three Indian missile boats hit and sank two enemy destroyers and an ammunition ship off the port of Karachi. Then they targeted an oil tank farm ashore and blew it up, which created a major fuel crisis for the Pakistani Army. Aside from naval affairs, missiles have largely replaced machine guns and cannons in aerial combat, and they have a major role in land warfare—particularly in terms of anti-tank capabilities. Long-range ballistic missiles, the descendants of the V-2, are key to a strategic attack paradigm that still has adherents, although their value seems more vested in deterrence than actual use. Last, it is important to remember that the *kamikaze* concept, though prefiguring the silicon-based guidance system of the missile, still retains its original human element as well—so clearly evidenced by the prevalence and global diffusion of suicide attacks, large- and small-scale, committed by the terrorists of our time.

Terrorism has in fact emerged in the decades since World War II as a mode of warfare in its own right. Perhaps this is due in part to the deliberate targeting of the innocent that characterized so much of the air campaigns waged by all the combatants between 1939 and 1945, from the terror bombing of Warsaw during the Nazi invasion of Poland to the American nuclear attacks on Hiroshima and Nagasaki that brought an end to the war. The German and Japanese brutality toward conquered peoples—especially the former's death squads in the field and death camps in rear areas—also catalyzed widespread resistance that bore out Clausewitz's profound belief in the enduring power of the "passions of the people." After World War II, these passions led to countless anti-colonial resistance movements. Almost all of them succeeded in throwing off or wearing down the will of foreign rulers. Since none of these movements could fight toe-to-toe with advanced militaries, they chose to engage in irregular ways, including by rediscovering and repurposing the *kamikaze* concept. Palestinians, Tamils, and others pioneered a range of postwar suicide tactics; but it was al Qaeda's death-bent teams, who took over those three airliners in September 2001, that returned the *kamikazes* to the air, wreaking massive human, psychological, and economic damage. Truly, the *kamikaze* lives on as a weapon of the weak, perhaps the most easily adapted, cost-effective strategic design to emerge from World War II.

But the *kamikaze* was just one way to increase the odds that a target would be struck with great accuracy. Much of World War II at sea, and of the fighting on land and in the air, depended on machine systems to guide humans into battle. It was here that the Allies shone. Britain's radars and Ultra code-breaking capabilities, the American Magic and the emergence of high-frequency direction-finding, all these stepped up when most needed to win crucial victories: The Battle of Britain; the long struggle against the U-boats; the stunning successes of the Americans at Midway and in the deadly submarine campaign against the Japanese. And more. If I were to choose just one design flaw that cost the Axis the war, it would be their laxity in information security and their arrogance about the effectiveness of their own signals coding systems. They lost due to having been *hacked*. Intruding into enemy information systems became an ever more important aspect of military affairs after 1945. One highlight that can be mentioned is the U.S. submarine campaign to tap into Soviet communications systems via their underwater cables during the Cold War.[7] Today, the ubiquity of and dependence upon cyberspace have made potential gains from hacking an enemy more valuable than ever. Axis information security systems were key examples of *design failure* in this critical dimension of modern warfare.

Another crucial Axis design failure was evident in the inability to prevent or defeat a major amphibious landing—the Allied attack at Dieppe in August 1942, so bloodily repulsed, was just an exploratory raid designed to test German defenses, not a full-on invasion. From North Africa to Sicily, Italy, and on to Normandy, the Allies' landings in the Afro-European theater were never thrown back into the sea. The same held true in Asia and the Pacific. From the American island-hopping campaign to William Slim's successful "end run" around Japanese field forces at Rangoon in May 1945—his "Operation Dracula"—the enemy proved unable to repel such attacks from the sea. Just five years later, Douglas MacArthur turned the strategic situation in Korea on its head by making a similar sort of end run at Inchon, outflanking most of the North Korean army. It is ironic that the Allies in World War II, and soon after the United Nations forces in Korea, made such excellent use of amphibious operations of the end-run sort, as it was General Tomoyuki Yamashita who pioneered this method in his conquests of Malaya and Singapore. He achieved these most remarkable victories with slender resources, relying instead on swiftness and multidirectional thrusts. Allan Millett has called this "[t]he grand tactics of infiltration and exploitation."[8]

The Malayan campaign that Yamashita masterminded may offer up important clues to the future design of amphibious operations in. For instead of the much larger forces the Allies mustered—even for end runs like Anzio—Yamashita preferred to operate with many small detachments. Certainly, he was heavily reliant upon having air superiority; but he showed in his great campaign that forces far smaller than those opposed to them were able to outflank the enemy repeatedly, throwing prepared defenses into absolute disarray. In a future replete with a profusion of highly accurate, even hypersonic, missiles it may well be that the "Yamashita paradigm" provides a better, more applicable approach to amphibious operations than the larger-scale model developed by the U.S. Navy and Marines during the 1920s–30s. Indeed, Yamashita's "many-small" design may prove key to all manner of future operations. This was the case in Iraq during 2007–8, when Coalition forces shifted from massing troops on large operating bases to setting up platoon-sized outposts in threatened areas, creating a security network comprised of countless small nodes. From them, these little units responded to threats swiftly, worked together to converge on insurgent formations and built better social ties to the locals, who began to provide useful intelligence. The result: the many-small design reduced deaths of innocent Iraqis by about 90 percent within a year, while at the same time decimating al Qaeda in Iraq.

Today's terrorist networks have also moved toward a strategic design based on the many-small concept. Indeed, this was the explicit goal of al Qaeda's visionary strategic designer, Abu Mus'ab al-Suri, whose aim was to see small cells arising across the Muslim world, from Morocco to Mindanao—and in other key areas—each capable of independent action without central control, but in pursuit of common goals.[9] Further evidence of a movement toward the many-small approach can be clearly seen in the rise of various Shi'a militias, from Hezbollah in Lebanon—where its small forces held off the Israelis in the 2006 war there—to the Iranian "Quds" units that have played such major roles in the conflicts in Iraq and Syria. The Russians have also shown some real aptitude with small formations, especially in the operations of their "little green men" in the Crimea and Donetsk. At sea, China's 500 hundred missile and torpedo boats reflect acceptance of the notion that the future of sea power is destined to be driven by a many-small navy, not a "few-large" one. It seems that Yamashita's pioneering campaign design in Malaya planted the seeds of an approach to military—and naval—operations that is blossoming fully in our time. Which means that the classic military principle of "mass" may be eroding.

What Yamashita developed did not emerge entirely *sui generis*. An earlier glimpse of what became his "infiltration and exploitation" concept can be seen in the small *Stosstruppen* units who spearheaded the "Michael" offensive in March 1918 that very nearly led to German victory in World War I. Their suppleness was a rebuke to the mindless adherence to the idea of employing huge masses of forces in attempts to break the long stalemate that plagued the Western Front. It was an approach that hearkened to even earlier times. As Lynn Montross observed, the stormtroops of the Great War provided just the latest evidence of a doctrinal and organizational back-and-forth interplay that stretches to antiquity. He summed up the matter this way: "If the methods of infiltration have a vaguely recognizable aspect, it is because the principle goes back to classical warfare. Actually, the armies of 1918 were bringing up to date the ancient tactical duel between the legion and the phalanx!"[10] J.F.C. Fuller also focused on this pattern in his study of Julius Caesar, noting that the smaller components of the legions, the maniples ("handfuls"), were able to outmaneuver the great single mass of the phalanx. As Fuller put it, the legion had "both a stable and a mobile element, the combination of which is the tactical base of true generalship."[11]

Many campaigns of World War II—on land, at sea, as well as in the air—reflected, in some way or another, modern twists on this organizational and doctrinal contest between many-small and few-large. So, this "design debate" played out with an additional factor introduced—about the merit of concentration versus dispersion of forces. The outstanding example of sheer concentration of key forces can be seen in the *Blitzkrieg* design, which was fully energized by the creation of a relative handful of panzer divisions, in which the vast majority of German tanks were placed. In the 1940 Battle of France, Anglo-Allied forces chose, conversely, to distribute their thousands of tanks roughly equally among all their field forces. The result: absolute triumph for concentrated armor. While this was a good design for offensive breakthrough operations, and worked in various other settings for a while—in the Balkans, North Africa, and Russia—by late 1942 Allied field forces were able to demonstrate their ability to replicate the German approach. In the North African desert, for example, the British, whose tanks "too often were committed to battle piecemeal," shifted to a much greater concentration of armor, and stuck with this fresh organizational form. As John Strawson noted, the need "for a master plan and persistent design was clear, and this need was to be properly recognized and satisfied by Montgomery."[12]

Zhukov was a great advocate of adoption of a "persistent design" that emulated the German model, a shift that replaced Stalin's risky penchant for ordering attacks all along the Eastern Front with concentrated blows at very carefully selected weak points. Given German overextension, and the shift in the *Heer* toward more, but smaller, field units, Zhukov was able to show how the strengths of the Germans' "old" design could be replicated while the vulnerabilities of their new one could be exploited. The result: signal victory at Stalingrad. Yet Manstein found a way to use smaller, but more numerous, German units on the defensive, allowing penetrations and then outmaneuvering the Red Army tank columns. Later in the war, both in the East and the West, Model showed how units even smaller than those created in 1942 could be employed with success in purely defensive battles. The American Army Group commander Omar Bradley observed admiringly, of the late–1944 fighting in the West, how his opponent skillfully "reorganized the demoralized German forces into effective battle groups.... Model had miraculously grafted a new backbone on the German army."[13] For all the evil Model perpetrated against innocents in the East—he would likely have been tried and executed for war crimes had he not committed suicide at war's end—it must be said that he was an excellent strategic designer.

But what are we today to make of the performance and often-differing results of the varied types of organizational designs employed in World War II? From the foregoing, it is clear that massed tank formations when on the offensive are to be preferred; but smaller armored units excelled when on the defensive. The massed invasion force at Normandy succeeded; but so did the many-small design that Yamashita employed in Malaya. And when one considers the war at sea, the evidence is conflicting as well. At Midway, Yamamoto chose to approach with only a portion of his carrier forces and suffered a catastrophic defeat. Soon after, in the long fight for Guadalcanal, he doled out his naval forces in driblets, another recipe for disaster. Yet, on the Allied side, carrier task forces were regularly employed in "packets" at various points along the Japanese defensive perimeter of fortress islands. And in the submarine campaign against Japan, Nimitz and Lockwood almost never chose to mass their "pig boats" in packs, as Doenitz did. Instead, the Allied submarines were, for the most part, "lone sea wolves" that achieved stunning successes. Their German counterparts, on the other hand, became victims when the doctrine of mounting massed attacks on convoys fell afoul of Allied decryption, detection, and anti-submarine weapons capabilities. For the U-boats, wolfpack tactics proved ultimately suicidal—at least when mounted by Type VII subs. Walter boats would have fared much better.

Thus, in addition to the organizational design discourse about many-small versus few-large, choosing between dispersion and concentration of forces is yet another important concern. While the submarine campaigns in the Atlantic and Pacific offer insights into both views, it seems clear that the Allies had the advantage on the offensive in the Pacific—and later, on the defensive in the Atlantic—thanks to the "information edge" they enjoyed over the Axis. So, it may not be fair to try to judge between concentration and dispersion based on these cases. Another instance where this design debate emerged was in the German discourse on how to defend against an Allied invasion in the West. Guderian, Rundstedt, and many others of the *Blitzkrieg* school of thought believed it wise to keep panzers massed, ready for decisive action against the Allies once they were ashore. Rommel made the case for dispersion of armor along the "Atlantic Wall," as he believed this was the best chance—in his view, the *only* chance—that Germany had to defeat an invasion. Hitler was torn by these competing views and "never made a final decision on which method of defense he preferred," as Martin Blumenson observed, then concluded: "Neither course of action was firmly established, to the detriment of the measures taken against the invasion."[14]

In the air, it seems concentration and larger formations were the norm when mounting strategic offensives. But on defense in the Battle of Britain Hugh Dowding demonstrated that creating many small fighter wings, then dispersing them widely and feeding them into action selectively, was highly effective. Much more so than the "big wing" concept favored by others that had more "punch" but took too long to get aloft and in battle formation. Yet here, too, it is clear that the information dimension played a critical role in empowering Dowding's defensive design. Not only the twenty-plus "Chain Home" radar stations along the coast, but the thousand Observer Corps posts that provided Fighter Command with a reliable, close-to-real-time tracking capability. During the daylight bombing raids over the summer of 1940, the Observer Corps' tracking capability enabled Dowding to feed in his fighters in the very most timely, efficient manner. They did this, as Len Deighton put it well, from widely dispersed posts "equipped with only enthusiasm, binoculars, an aircraft recognition booklet, and a simple sighting device." Of the simplicity of the Observers' "kit," Winston Churchill said it was like "going from the middle of the twentieth century to the Stone Age."[15] Even so, in April 1941 the Observers were rewarded for their contributions to victory in the Battle of Britain by being renamed the *Royal* Observer Corps.

The Observers began something of a tradition of planespotting in the postwar years. Intended as a hobbyist activity, it occasionally came under scrutiny for seemingly strategic intrusions into other countries' proprietary military information. In Greece in November 2001, for example, twelve British planespotters were arrested for tracking Greek military aircraft. They were found guilty of violating Greek national security, but exonerated a year later. Other incidents of this sort followed, including arrest of two British planespotters in the United Arab Emirates in 2015 on similar charges. But perhaps the most important achievement of planespotters in the post–9/11 era was their "outing" of the secret CIA "rendition" flights to even more secret overseas prisons for suspected jihadists.[16] The planespotters' link to the "war on terror" should prompt us also to acknowledge how their practices have diffused to militant organizations, among whom the more successful movements have all developed their own versions of an Observer Corps—operating from dusty streets in Middle Eastern cities and villages to Europe, Africa, Asia, and the Americas. Churchill's point, that this low-cost mode of observing represents an effective "Stone Age" approach in a machine age, highlights a special appeal this design has for terrorists and insurgents.

The "repurposing" of the Observer Corps design, especially adoption of its networked form and real-time monitoring function by terrorists and other malign actors, has played a role in increasing the difficulties faced over the past two decades in the conduct of both counter-terrorist and counter-insurgent campaigns—much as the British Observers during World War II greatly complicated the *Luftwaffe's* tasks. But this phenomenon, the spread of "observer organizations," is more than just another example of a diffusion pattern of an innovation, like *Blitzkrieg's* organizational and doctrinal forms spreading to the Allies by the middle of World War II. "Observing" has also featured a significant change of primary function. What began as a means of monitoring aircraft movements is now used by insurgents and terrorists to spy, ambush ground patrols and, perhaps most importantly, to gain a clear picture of the composition and disposition of opposing forces. Observing offers a way to claw out an information advantage against far better armed adversaries. Not only in terms of helping to know more about the enemy, but also with regard to providing early warning of a hostile approach, so that the weaker force may disperse and remain well hidden. Indeed, as most of the world's conflicts have become irregular, the basic dynamic has shifted from the clash of massed forces to a tense and unending struggle between hiders and finders. This new dynamic may be "repurposing" war itself.

But at a less grand level, the design—or, more correctly, redesign—phenomenon of repurposing can be seen and should be thoroughly explored in other areas as well. During World War II, the emergence of *kamikazes* is perhaps the most startling example of repurposing, as it turned the Zero from fighter plane into highly accurate, human-guided cruise missile. But there were other important instances of repurposing as well. In the German case, for example, repurposing played a dramatic role in improving the ability to destroy enemy tanks. This was first manifested when anti-aircraft guns, the famous "88s," were fired level at opposing tank formations. The gun was designed to propel its shells at high velocity, so as to reach altitude quickly when shooting at aircraft. But this same velocity made the 88 perfect for penetrating armor. During the North African campaign, Rommel became particularly adept at feigning retreat with his panzers so as to draw enemy tanks into "88 traps." These were so deadly in the desert war that, as Paul Carell put it, "The miracle weapon, the 88mm, was to hold the stage."[17] Similarly, some of the *Stuka* fleet was repurposed by putting anti-tank guns under their wings in 1943. The result was an amazing new capability for an aircraft that had, by mid-war, lost virtually all its value as a bomber. This redesign opened the door for future anti-tank aircraft, like the A-10.

Some instances of repurposing can be seen, to a degree, in recent U.S. military developments. While it is a commonplace to hear reports of the use of remotely piloted "drones" to strike at today's enemies—from South Asia to Yemen, East Africa, and beyond—the unmanned aircraft had been around for decades prior to being "newly armed," as Bob Woodward described its repurposing during the 2001 invasion of Afghanistan.[18] Before Operation Enduring Freedom, as the campaign to overthrow the Taliban and go after Osama bin Laden was labeled, drone aircraft had been used primarily for reconnaissance purposes during the 1990s. But as early as 1973, the Israelis were already using drones as aerial targets to help train anti-aircraft gunners. These other-than-combat uses of drones arose despite the fact that, as early as 1940, radio and television pioneer Lee De Forest came up with the idea of designing an unmanned aircraft, attaching a transmission set that could send live video, and arming it with a bomb. He called it his "robot television bomber."[19] Needless to say, his idea drew no serious attention or support from senior American military leaders or defense industrial firms. The Germans, on the other hand, had a remote-controlled, explosive-laden small tank, the "Goliath," as well as some unmanned explosive boats that they employed, with effect, against the invasion fleet off Normandy.

Aside from the arming of drones since 2001, another major American effort to repurpose a significant Cold War–era weapon system has had to do with the fleet ballistic missile submarine. While many of these remain on duty today with their nuclear weapons, to maintain deterrence stability, some have been reconfigured so as to provide more traditional capabilities. For example, a converted "boomer" can hold an arsenal of up to 154 Tomahawk missiles, conventionally armed for land-attack missions. Given the stealthy ability of subs to come in close to an enemy shore without being detected, this kind of striking power could have an enormous effect on the course of a campaign under way on the ground. This might prove crucial in a place like the Korean Peninsula where, if a shooting war ever recurred, the small U.S. forces there—at this writing (2019) less than 30,000—would be in dire need of such fire support at the outset. Just a few "arsenal subs" of this sort could provide a winning advantage.[20] Another redesign for submarines— boomers but also smaller fast-attack boats—is to repurpose them to be able to deliver SEAL teams or Marines on raids, or to spearhead larger and more sustained incursions. This redevelopment is still in its early stages, but hearkens to the initial use of subs in this way during the Makin Raid of August 1942.[21]

* * *

The first part of this chapter has summarized the specific lessons that might be drawn from Axis decisional processes and practices prevalent during World War II. The issues considered in this last section concern whether—detailed instances and examples aside—analysis of the defeat of the Axis can help to identify enduring dynamics, or even some broader emergent "principles of strategic design." Given that in military affairs arms-racing and other preparations for war during "peacetime," and combat experiences during a conflict, reflect profound external influences on strategic designs, it seems that a primary area of dynamic tension consists of questions about the wisdom of either imitating the enemy's capabilities or innovating in search of a way around them. Throughout most of military history, the clashes of armed forces on land, at sea and, over the past century in the air, have often featured strong similarities between the combatants. What works well will diffuse broadly, so a great deal of imitation goes on. In World War II, the German panzer division design was soon replicated by the British, Russians and Americans.

But imitation is a process that can only arise in the wake of a preliminary spark of innovation—like the idea for the panzer division.

And within the rubric of innovation, there seem to be two fundamental forms that guide, yet impose fresh tensions on, strategic design: incremental versus transformational change. The former can be seen best in the case of the *Kriegsmarine,* which was largely imitative of the Royal Navy. The "Z Plan" called for building battleships capable of holding their own against those of the Royal Navy; but German designers made their warships a bit faster, with better defensive armor and still-great gun power. Incremental changes all, but still good enough to be employed with great effect—had the battle fleet been conserved for use as an interdiction force to close the arctic convoy route to Russia, rather than being frittered away in merchant raiding on wide-open seas, bereft of air cover. Even the area in which the Germans do at first seem innovative in their approach to the sea war—their submarine operations—reflects incremental design thinking. U-boats of World War II had better cruising range and more torpedoes than their predecessors in the Great War; but they were still slow when submerged, and generally forced onto the defensive when detected. The one development with potential to transform the submarine, Walter's design, was rejected in the 1930s as too radical, and deferred even in 1943 by Doenitz, who made a choice in favor of incremental solutions by trying, with the *Schnorchel,* to give his boats greater submerged speed and lesser chances of detection while on the prowl.

The Imperial Japanese Navy, for all Yamamoto's insights into the vast potential of the aircraft carrier, remained devoted to the surface warship as well. The Long Lance torpedo was an important incremental innovation that they hoped would convey an advantage in sea fights. And like the Germans, the Japanese went in for "giantism," with *Yamato* and *Musashi* even bigger and more heavily gunned than the *Bismarck* and *Tirpitz.* When Japan went to war against the Allies in December 1941, the Imperial Navy was clearly bifurcated, having ten battleships and ten aircraft carriers. This approach to strategic design hedges against the persistence of old systems, while at the same time exploiting, to some degree, the potential of new systems. In his thinking about future wars, Bevin Alexander described such an approach this way: "A policy of *broad preparation* will provide insurance in the event that a conflict develops which no one anticipated."[22] The U.S. Navy pursued a hedging naval strategy as well during the interwar period; though it was weighted more heavily toward the past, with seventeen battleships and just seven carriers. Thus, the early edge went to Japan, although the American innovation of a carrier "deck park" kept more planes on the flight deck, ready for launching more of the time. Japanese reliance on elevators to bring up planes from the hangar deck was a handicap, at and after Midway.

Italy's *Regia Marina* provided an interesting twist on the incremental-transformational spectrum of change. It was clearly a battleship navy, but one that had made incremental design improvements during the interwar years, like the decision to retain full gun power while increasing speed—at the cost of some decrease in defensive armor. But Italian designers stayed hard at work on remedying this weakness and came up with a breakthrough design that brought the *Littorio* and *Vittorio Veneto* into service in August 1940. They had all the gun power of their predecessors in the Italian fleet, but even greater speed—and featured armor better than that of the most modern British battleships. Marc' Antonio Bragadin made the point that "[t]hey were the splendid products of the Navy's best designers and of Italian master workmanship. At the time they were probably the best battleships in the world."[23] Unlike much of the rest of the Italian fleet, they had Gufo radar systems—good out to roughly 30 kilometers. The Italians hoped to make up for overall radar deficiencies with aerial reconnaissance, though they eschewed carriers due to the belief that the relative narrowness of the Mediterranean would allow extensive use of land-based aircraft for scouting and striking at the enemy. When the *Luftwaffe* was supporting the *Regia Marina*—Italian air power alone proved insufficient—this worked.

This brief exploration of the incremental-transformational dynamic as it played out in the respective navies before and during World War II carries with it some retrospective insights that help explain Axis defeat; but it also has implications for current and future naval affairs. Looking back, one can clearly see that the German Z Plan was a bust from the outset. The U-boat truly offered the *Kriegsmarine* its best chance for bringing Britain to heel via commerce raiding; and so submarine construction should have been the core of German naval strategic design. Needless to say, the Walter boat offered the best approach to making a "big bet" on submarines. Karl Doenitz knew this, and notes in his memoir that "it was the Walter U-boat alone, with its underwater speed of 25 knots, that would completely revolutionize maritime warfare."[24] As to Japan, rather than pursuing "broad preparation," its big bet should have been on a carrier-focused design approach, hedged just a bit by lighter surface warships (i.e., cruisers and destroyers) armed with their Long Lance torpedoes, and a submarine doctrine focused on commerce raiding rather than fleet engagements. For their part, the Italians' failures in naval design were due to a general lack of radar and Italo Balbo's mistaken belief in the continuing utility of biplanes. Too often, Italian sailors fought blind. Without viable air power, *Regia Marina* warships were sitting ducks.

What insights for today's navies does the foregoing analysis have? First, it seems clear that the U.S. Navy, the leading instrument of sea power at present, is wedded, with its "strike group" form of organization—the term echoes Yamamoto's *Kido Butai*—to a belief in the persistence of the aircraft carrier as *the* capital ship of the 21st century. Heavy investment in the *Ford*-class carrier, an incrementally improved version of its predecessors, affirms this belief. The U.S. Navy also retains a fleet of submarines—fifty "attack" and eighteen missile-firing boats—along with over sixty destroyers and nearly two-dozen cruisers that constitute its principal warships. So, the American design approach falls into the category of "broad preparation" for naval warfare. China's navy, on the other hand, is weighted toward missile and torpedo boats, of which it has over 500, and countless small robotic weapons—all designed primarily for engagement in coastal zones and narrow seas. China also has sixty-eight submarines armed with high-speed torpedoes. Much like Italy's *Regia Marina* in World War II, China's navy relies on land-based aircraft rather than carriers. As does the Russian navy, which has just one carrier, but over a hundred light surface warships and nearly seventy submarines. In a new era of great power competition, the U.S. Navy is still placing a big bet on carriers. It should think more about robots and high-speed missiles, as should the other American services.

Beyond China and Russia, others are shifting their emphasis in naval strategic design to missile- and torpedo-firing platforms. Both Iran and North Korea are depending on the guided missile—the descendant of the *kamikaze*—to dominate at sea in the future. Needless to say, missile fire is also the *sine qua non* of air power today, both in terms of dogfighting and with regard to ground attack. And even for armies, missile weapons are continuing to gain traction, though the retention of traditional artillery and tanks still reflects a "gun power" mentality much in line with World War II's "88s" and panzers. In the realm of strategic attack, sea- and air-launched missiles have now more than encroached upon the longstanding classical notion of the bomber aircraft dropping "iron on target." And when it comes to the potential for a nuclear exchange, the intercontinental ballistic missile is the clear weapon of choice. Sixty years ago, Bernard Brodie saw the rise of long-range missiles as forcing transformational change, noting that

> with truly cosmic forces harnessed to the machines of war, we have a situation for the first time in history where the opening event by which a great nation enters a war—an event which must reflect the preparations it has made or failed to make beforehand—can decide irretrievably whether or not it will continue to exist.[25]

The key, per Brodie, is preparation "beforehand"—the true realm of design.

The need for such preparation is the catalyst for arms-racing, modern variants of which we have seen from the Anglo-German naval rivalry prior to World War I to the Cold War nuclear build-up. In each, design factors played major roles. For the Kaiser and Admiral Tirpitz, the guiding design concept was to succeed with fewer ships—they could not outpace British shipbuilding—so they focused on a smaller fleet whose ships had better armor and water-tightness, along with improved optics for more accurate gunnery. During the Cold War, the United States built a nuclear arsenal of smaller mega-tonnage, but with missiles both more accurate and which were the first to be able to launch multiple warheads. Prior to World War II, German, Italian, and Japanese naval leaders strove to make up for numerical inferiority with better warship designs. The Italians almost did this. But for Germany and Japan the problem was not to overcome enemy quantity with incrementally improved quality in the same warship type; rather, the design challenge was to go *beyond* existing ideas about sea power. For Germany, this meant focusing on U-boats. For Japan, it meant forgoing visions of gun battles in favor of carrier warfare. Today, and tomorrow, it should mean more than a willingness to live with non-combatants held permanent hostage to threats of nuclear annihilation, mitigated only by the ethically repugnant notion of "mutual assured destruction" (MAD) that props up deterrence.

Ronald Reagan was the first world leader to take seriously the idea of defending against long-range nuclear missile attack—Lyndon Johnson had looked into the matter, but viewed missile defense as impractical. Edwin L. Meese—an artilleryman in his Army days, later Reagan's senior counselor—once told me that Reagan began asking him about how to defend against nuclear attack during his first term as California governor in the mid–1960s. Two decades later, now–President Reagan was still devoted to overturning the "immoral premise" upon which nuclear deterrence was based. He was intent upon reversing the arms race and replacing it with arms reductions. And on March 23, 1983, he gave his famous "Star Wars" speech about the need to design missile defenses: "I call upon the scientific community in our country, who gave us nuclear weapons, to turn their great talents now to the cause of peace, to give us the means to render those weapons obsolete." The Russians protested, saying missile defenses would undermine *their* deterrent; Reagan responded simply that research into missile defense should be shared globally, to rid the world of the threat of nuclear annihilation. Truly, he was thinking like a designer interested in effecting transformational change. His ideas were derided by many, at the time and after. But there has been good bipartisan support that has kept research going over the past four decades.[26]

And the missile defense design challenge *is* being chipped away at, with innovations like Israel's "Iron Dome" and the American "Terminal High Altitude Area Defense" (THAAD). The air defense network crafted by Dowding in the Battle of Britain, as well as the systems designed by Galland and Kammhuber for the protection of Germany, point out that there *are* indeed ways to design effective counters to threats posed by strategic aerial attack. But missile defense reflects not only a technical problem; it is also a sought-after design solution driven by broad ethical concern that innocents' lives should not be held in permanent peril in order to maintain deterrence stability. Nuclear strategy today, based on continuing to threaten innocent mass populations, violates a "just war" tenet, immunity of noncombatants, reflected across many cultures. See, for example, Thomist thought in the Christian canon and the insights shared by the Prophet Muhammad in the *Qur'an* and the *hadith*.[27] During World War II, the strategic bombardments conducted by all major combatants simply disregarded this important taboo—a violation that lives on in continued acceptance of MAD doctrine today.

But the Axis Powers, particularly Japan and Germany, went beyond just targeting civilian populations from the air; they heavily involved their ground troops in the mass killing of noncombatants—see the Japanese rape of Nanking and the German use of *Einsatzgruppen* on the Eastern Front, for example. The atrocities they committed reflect just a few salient points in an overarching design of cruelty toward conquered peoples that was destined to fatally undermine overall Axis grand strategy. It was a design that derived from poisonous ideologies, like the odd Nazi notion of "Aryan superiority" that seemingly allowed for the acceptability of even the worst treatment of the *Untermensch*—and which featured special hatred of the Jews at its core. Japanese chauvinism, although it didn't ultimately manifest in the form of death camps, did lead to dreadful policies in occupied lands, as well as brutal treatment of prisoners of war—at and beyond Bataan. These dark policies of inhumanity reflected not only evil; they also demonstrated an utter failure to appreciate the social factor in strategic design, sparking a determination to resist among the "conquered" that pinned down very significant numbers of Axis forces, keeping them from far better use on the various fighting fronts. But distraction of troops to occupation and suppression duties was just one cost of brutality; alienation of conquered peoples meant a lost opportunity to mobilize significant support among them for the Axis Powers' war efforts.

To be sure, there were small "successes" at co-opting some to switch sides, like the soldiers of Vlasov's Army in the European theater and Subhas Chandra Bose's Indian National Army in South Asia—the recruits for each being drawn from prisoners of war. But Vlasov's troops were found to be highly unreliable, and were generally deployed far from the Eastern Front. Bose's forces became a particular target of William Slim's counteroffensive in Burma. And they performed poorly. Indeed, at a key point in the British advance, as Slim recalled, "the 1st Division of the Indian National Army was encountered. It surrendered *en masse,* with its commander."[28] By way of contrast, resistance forces grew in strength in every area occupied by the Axis. In Russia and Yugoslavia, insurgents numbered in the hundreds of thousands. In Norway, resisters played a major role in tying down German forces and later in disrupting the production and shipment of heavy water for the Nazi nuclear project. In France, Maquis fighters greatly facilitated the Allied landings in Normandy, and the advance thereafter. One important French network was led by a woman, Marie-Madeleine Fourcade.[29] Japan too faced strong resistance, from the Asian mainland to the Philippines.

Axis brutality spawned all of these movements, a clear sign that the Fascists, East and West, had allowed their twisted ideologies to trump sound strategic design. German depredations committed against those in occupied Europe should be viewed as heavily ironic, too, given that the progenitor of modern strategic thought, Carl von Clausewitz, taught at the *Kriegsakademie* and, in his classic study *Vom Kriege,* cautioned against being careless about stirring up the "passions of the people." Fundamentally, he observed, "war deals with living and with moral forces." And in terms of the need to design military campaigns with humane values in mind, he made a strong case that "civilized nations do not put their prisoners to death or devastate cities and countries ... because intelligence has taught them more effective ways of using force than the crude expression of instinct."[30] Clearly, the Nazis either forgot or never read these passages from Clausewitz; although some officials sensed the catastrophic nature of the strategic design for a German "New Order" in Europe, especially as it was intended to be applied in the occupied areas of Soviet Russia. Dr. Otto Bräutigam, who served as deputy head of the Ministry for the Occupied Eastern Territories, reflected this sensibility in an October 1942 memo that, as William L. Shirer noted, "dared to pinpoint the Nazi mistakes in Russia":

> In the Soviet Union we found on our arrival a population weary of Bolshevism, which waited long-ingly for new slogans holding out the prospect of a better future for them. It was Germany's duty to find such slogans, but they remained unuttered. The population greeted us with joy as liberators and placed themselves at our disposal ... [but] the limitless abuse of Slavic humanity ... has forced both Bolshevists and Russian nationalists into a common front against us. The Russian fights today with exceptional bravery for nothing more or less than recognition of his human dignity.[31]

This problem, of the "liberator" morphing into "occupier," manifested repeatedly in the postwar years, spawning myriad anti-colonial movements. Virtually all emerged victorious politically, although some "lost" militarily. France's experience in Algeria provides a good example of how brutality in pursuit of pacification ruined the social design of colonialism, compelling France to relinquish its hold, despite having won the Battle of Algiers and other engagements. The design dynamic in the Algerian case demonstrated the strength of the social factor over purely military matters. About Algeria, Alistair Horne put the matter well: "While the armed rebellion might be seen to be 'withering away,' at the same time the political imprint of the revolution was imposing itself more and more indelibly on the population."[32] Against this resistance, and with public opinion in France—and around the world—turning against continued occupation, Algeria was set free.

A similar social-design dilemma bedeviled the Russian effort to hold on to countries that the Red Army "liberated." While not nearly as brutal as occupation practices of the Germans or Japanese, Russian rule was still quite harsh, spawning a mindset of resistance among the oppressed that, like in World War II and later in Algeria, "imposed itself more and more indelibly on the population," to use Alistair Horne's elegant phrasing. Once the label "occupier" can be attached to foreign forces, the structure of an intervening or invading power's strategic design begins to crumble. In the post–9/11 era, American involvements in Iraq and Afghanistan have both suffered from the disconnection of the military operational and social design factors. Clearly, American-led coalitions in both countries came with good intentions, and were reasonably attuned to issues of noncombatant immunity. But excessive use of air power and the inevitable collateral damage that comes with aerial bombing created deep resentments. Marquee events, like the sad display of mismanagement and malfeasance at Abu Ghraib prison in Iraq, also greatly harmed the intended social design: creating a Western-friendly, democratic Arab power in the

Middle East. Germany and Japan failed in their efforts to create a fascism-friendly consciousness in the areas that came under their military control because of their deeply flawed social designs. So, too, has ineptitude at the social level undermined American strategic design today.

Awareness of the social dimension of strategic design is the important first step in thinking through military interventions. Indeed, mapping "social terrain" is every bit as necessary as understanding physical terrain. This was no secret to Clausewitz, who had a great respect for and concern about social factors. He expressed his view of a people's natural social instincts—even their imperative—to resist foreign invasion and occupation in this way: "No matter how small and weak a state may be in comparison with its enemy, it must not forgo these last efforts [i.e., resistance] or one would conclude that its soul is dead."[33] Interestingly, one of Germany's top generals in World War II, Hermann Balck, keyed, in his late-life memoir *Ordnung im Chaos,* not on the mobile operations at which he was a grand master, but rather on this point about the rising importance of the social dimension in military strategy. As he put it, "we are now in a period of social wars … dynastic and national causes no longer resonate."[34] Balck's vision encompasses much of the spectrum of conflict today, from insurgencies to *intifadas,* and on to the seemingly noble-minded efforts at regime change in the name of democracy. Social aspects of strategic design mattered in World War II. They may be decisive now.

*   *   *

World War II did much to shape the contours of the international system as we know it today. The weapons types that matured during this conflict—tanks, planes, aircraft carriers, as well as a range of communications, sensing and computing systems—are still with us. As are the newer inventions like the jet aircraft and air-independent propulsion for submarines, neither of which was adopted early enough to make a real difference in World War II's outcome, thanks to German reluctance to embrace transformational change in these technological areas where the Nazis' lead over the Allies was great. Beyond such technological matters, the Axis also pioneered organizational designs that remain central to 21st century military affairs. The Germans' panzer division, the Japanese carrier *Kido Butai,* even Italy's innovations in "naval special warfare"; all these remain very relevant to present-day armed forces around the world. As does the *Blitzkrieg* doctrine—even if it is now referred to in such terms as "thunder runs"—and Yamashita's ideas about "infiltration and exploitation," phrasing that can also apply to the innovative concepts advanced by Guderian and Rommel. Needless to say, Japan's *kamikazes* can be seen as ushering in a human-guided missile age that their silicon-based successor systems will likely dominate for centuries to come.

The Axis Powers were not defeated by greater numbers, nor by a few mistakes at critical moments. In the greatest slugging matches the material balance was, most of the time, relatively even. This was so for the Germans at Kursk in 1943, in Normandy in 1944, and in Italy right up to the end of the war. For the Japanese, there was actually a quite significant material advantage at Midway—Guadalcanal as well—and there was a reasonable correlation of forces even at the outset of the invasion of the Philippines in late 1944. A key problem was that Axis strategic designs were too easily replicated by Allied armies (mobile tank divisions), navies (carrier groups) and air forces (close-support, in particular). Also, the Allies developed excellent sensing systems to detect U-boats in the Atlantic and Japanese Imperial Fleet movements in the Pacific—not to mention decoding (hacking) capabilities that exploited both German and Japanese complacency about information security, a truly cautionary example for this cyber age. As to Axis reluctance to embrace transformational change, this was perhaps fed by early successes, reinforcing high-level resistance to placing some "big bets" on breakthroughs like the jet and the Walter U-boat. Last, Axis failure to pursue humane social designs fed resistance among the occupied, fostered resolve among Allied liberators, and exposed a crucial design weakness: over-stretched imperiums that compelled a fatal dispersion of forces.

In the postwar era, the world's colonial powers came to realize that they were over-stretched; all retreated. The Soviet Union, too, succumbed to this, relinquishing its satel-lites in 1989 and, by the end of 1991, even going so far as to shed many of its constituent republics. The American response to all this was to declare, in the words of President George H.W. Bush, "a new world order" to be led by the United States—so recently the leader of the coalition that liberated Kuwait (with a World War II–style campaign). But this "order" soon lost its cohesion; and American attempts to use armed force to shore up and expand the areas of order have led to a reprise of the overstretch motif so promi-nent in the Second World War. The overstretch term itself is central to Paul Kennedy's magisterial analysis of world affairs over the past 500 years, *The Rise and Fall of the Great Powers*—suggesting that it is perhaps the most common flaw in strategic design. But the point of view advanced in the preceding chapters should make clear that a complete strategic design must incorporate and align technological, organizational, doctrinal, and social elements. A most daunting task. We can be grateful that design at this level is so difficult; otherwise the Axis would have won, ushering in a new dark age. They failed, not because of being outnumbered or unlucky, but due to their design flaws. The great hope now is to secure a better future for the world by becoming skillful strategic designers ourselves.

# Chapter Notes

## Chapter 1

1. J.F.C. Fuller, *Armament and History* (New York: Charles Scribner's Sons, 1945), v.

2. See Robert Cowley, ed., *What If?* (New York: G.P. Putnam's Sons, 1999), which has spawned several sequels.

3. MacKinlay Kantor, "If the South Had Won the Civil War," *Look Magazine*, November 22, 1960. Needless to say, the Civil War has proved highly fertile ground for ever more speculative alternate histories, with Harry Turtledove's time-travel-based *Guns of the South* among the most notable.

4. Victor Davis Hanson, *The Savior Generals: How Five Great Commanders Saved Wars That Were Lost* (New York: Bloomsbury Press, 2013).

5. Foote's comments are also cited in Geoffrey C. Ward, Ric Burns, and Ken Burns, *The Civil War* (New York: Alfred A. Knopf, 1990), 272. Other thoughtful studies of the outcome of this war include: R.E. Beringer, H. Hattaway, A. Jones and W.N. Still, *Why the South Lost the Civil War* (Athens, GA: University of Georgia Press, 1986); and G.S. Boritt, ed., *Why the Confederacy Lost* (Oxford: Oxford University Press, 1992).

6. Correlli Barnett, *The Swordbearers* (New York: New American Library, 1963), 15.

7. John Ellis, *Brute Force: Allied Strategy and Tactics in the Second World War* (New York: Viking, 1990), 30.

8. Walter Lord wrote two of the most dramatic, detailed, and contingency-affirming accounts of these crucial events: *The Miracle of Dunkirk* (New York: Viking Press, 1982); and *Incredible Victory: The Battle of Midway* (New York: HarperCollins, 1967).

9. The three most comprehensive accounts based on German senior officer critiques, largely of Hitler, are: B.H. Liddell Hart, *The German Generals Talk*—originally *The Other Side of the Hill*—(London: Cassell, 1948); Milton Shulman, *Defeat in the West* (London: Martin Secker and Warburg, 1947); and Seymour Freidin and William Richardson, editors, translated by Constantine Fitzgibbon, *The Fatal De-*cisions (New York: Berkley Publishing Company, 1956).

10. Alan Clark, *Barbarossa: The Russian-German Conflict, 1941–1945* (London: Cassell [1965] 2001), xx, 182. Another very balanced assessment of Hitler's generalship can be found in John Strawson, *Hitler as Military Commander* (London: B.T. Batsford Ltd, 1971). And for exposing the quiet "deal" apparently made by Liddell Hart—to focus in his work on blaming German defeat on Hitler in return for German generals crediting him as their inspiration for developing the *blitzkrieg* battle doctrine—see John Mearsheimer, *Liddell Hart and the Weight of History* (Ithaca: Cornell University Press, 1988).

11. Ronald Spector, *Eagle Against the Sun: The American War With Japan* (New York: The Free Press, 1985), 38.

12. Commander Marc' Antonio Bragadin, *The Italian Navy in World War II*, translated by Gale Hoffman (Annapolis: United States Naval Institute, 1957), 228.

13. Robert Leckie, *Delivered from Evil: The Saga of World War II* (New York: Harper Perennial, 1988), 627. Emphasis added.

14. J. Lee Ready, *The Forgotten Axis: Germany's Partners and Foreign Volunteers in World War II* (Jefferson, NC: McFarland, [1987] 2012) provides a most thorough view of the smaller nations who allied themselves with Hitler—and notes that nearly a fifth of those who served in Germany's own forces during the war were foreign volunteers.

15. Ernest R. May, *Strange Victory: Hitler's Conquest of France* (New York: Hill and Wang, 2000), 5. May's study in many ways complements Marc Bloch's magisterial *Strange Defeat* (Oxford: Oxford University Press, [1940] 1948).

16. Another classic study of this surprise attack is Roberta Wohlstetter's *Pearl Harbor: Warning and Decision* (Stanford: Stanford University Press, 1962). See also John Toland, *Infamy: Pearl Harbor and Its Aftermath* (Garden City, NY: Doubleday & Co., 1982), which provides an excellent overview of the official investigations into why American forces were caught so completely off guard.

17. Richard Overy, *Why the Allies Won* (New York: W.W. Norton & Co., 1995), 7, 17. Emphasis added.

18. Major General J.F.C. Fuller, *The Second World War, 1939–1945: A Strategical and Tactical History* (New York: Duell, Sloan and Pierce, [1948] 1952) revised, 402–3.

19. Martin van Creveld, *Technology and War* (London: Collier Macmillan Publishers, 1989), 229 notes that the defeat of the U-boats and the long-range escort of bombers were "two situations in World War II when technological superiority proved decisive."

20. Alan Moorehead, *The Desert War: The North African Campaign, 1940–1943* (London: Hamish Hamilton Ltd, 1965) is the classic eyewitness account, a central theme of which is the author's observation of how searing battle experiences against the Germans taught British tankers to mass their armor to avoid being defeated in detail by the panzers.

21. Dwight D. Eisenhower, *Crusade in Europe* (Garden City, NY: Doubleday & Co., 1948), 152. A similar, more recent assessment of the importance of the North African campaign to improving American military performance in the field can be found in Rick Atkinson, *An Army at Dawn: The War in North Africa, 1942–1943* (New York: Henry Holt & Co., 2002).

22. On the Burma campaign, see Field-Marshal Viscount William Slim, *Defeat Into Victory* (New York: David McKay Co., 1961). The best account of Tarawa is still Martin Russ's *Line of Departure: Tarawa* (Garden City, NY: Doubleday & Co., 1975).

23. Paul Kennedy, *Engineers of Victory: The Problem Solvers Who Turned the Tide in the Second World War* (New York: Random House, 2013), xv–xvi.

24. A thoughtful exploration of design concepts in general can be found in Harold Nelson and Erik Stolterman, *The Design Way: Intentional Change in an Unpredictable World* (Boston: The MIT Press, 2014), second edition. See also John Heskett's insightful views in his *Design: A Very Short Introduction* (Oxford: Oxford University Press, 2005).

25. Anna Meroni, "Strategic Design: Where Are We Now?" *Strategic Design Research Journal*, Vol. 1, No. 1 (July–December 2008), 31–38.

26. Cited in Hugh Thomas, *The Spanish Civil War* (New York: Harper & Brothers Publishers, 1961), 421.

27. Giulio Douhet, *Command of the Air*, translated by Dino Ferrari (New York: Coward-McCann, 1942). Douhet argued that attack with chemical weapons would be "so devastating that the physical and moral resistance of the people would collapse" (p. 24).

28. See, for example, Henry Petroski's classic *Invention By Design: How Engineers Get From Thought to Thing* (Cambridge: Harvard University Press, 1996).

29. Lynn Montross, *War Through the Ages* (New York: Harper & Row, 1960), 744–5. Revised and enlarged third edition. Emphasis in the original.

30. As Gordon Craig put it: "The most striking of all of Delbrück's military theories was that which held that all military strategy can be divided into [these] two basic forms." See Craig's "Delbrück," in Peter Paret, editor, *Makers of Modern Strategy* (Princeton: Princeton University Press, 1986), 341. A recent affirmation of Delbrück, but which makes the case for the primacy of attrition, can be found in Cathal J. Nolan, *The Allure of Battle: A History of How Wars Have Been Won and Lost* (Oxford: Oxford University Press, 2017).

31. A deeply thoughtful examination of German (and Allied) military doctrinal choices in the 1930s is Barry Posen's *The Sources of Military Doctrine: France, Britain, and Germany Between the World Wars* (Ithaca: Cornell University Press, 1984).

32. Lawrence H. Keeley, *War Before Civilization* (Oxford: Oxford University Press, 1996), 18 for the reference to fortification in Neolithic Britain. But see throughout.

33. Geoffrey Parker, *The Military Revolution: Military Innovation and the Rise of the West, 1500–1800*, second edition (Cambridge: Cambridge University Press, 1996), 13.

34. Heskett, *Design*, 84.

35. See John Edward Wiltz, "The Nye Committee Revisited," *The Historian*, Vol. 23, No. 2 (1961), 211–233.

36. Guderian wrote *Achtung—Panzer!* Rommel's study was entitled *Infanterie greift an (Infantry Attacks)*, a somewhat misleading title, given the book's true emphasis on mobile maneuver warfare. Both were published in Germany in 1937.

37. On this point, see Stuart Pugh, *Total Design: Integrated Methods for Successful Product Engineering* (Reading, MA: Addison-Wesley, 1991).

38. One of the best and clearest accounts of this first nuclear arms race is Steve Sheinkin's *Bomb: The Race to Build—and Steal—the World's Most Dangerous Weapon* (New York: Roaring Brook Press, 2012). It is written with young adults in mind, but speaks with authority to readers of any age or level of sophistication.

# Chapter 2

1. Two excellent accounts of Mitchell's influence, and ultimate fate, are Burke Davis, *The Billy Mitchell Affair* (New York: Random House, 1967) and Thomas Wildenberg, *Billy Mitchell's War with the Navy: The Interwar Rivalry over Air Power* (Annapolis: Naval Institute Press, 2013).

2. Adoptions were common among leading families lacking a son to carry on the name. The Yamamotos were distinguished, with *samurai* roots. Sadayoshi Takano, Isoroku's father, had fought on the shogun's side against the Meiji modernization plan. In defeat he wound up making just "a meager living as a swordmaker in Nagaoka Niigata, in the mountainous north of Honshu." See Edwin Hoyt, *Three Military Leaders* (Tokyo: Kodansha, 1993), 79. Adoption greatly improved Isoroku's professional prospects.

3. Hiroyuki Agawa, *The Reluctant Admiral: Yamamoto and the Imperial Navy*, translated by John Bester (Tokyo: Kodansha International Ltd., 1979), 72.

4. See the League of Nations, *World Economic Survey* (Geneva, 1945), Table III, 134.

5. Edwin O. Reischauer, *Japan: Past and Present* (New York: Alfred A. Knopf, 1964), third edition, 164.

6. Ronald H. Spector, *Eagle Against the Sun: The American War with Japan* (New York: The Free Press, 1985), 46. Emphasis in the original. The excellence of Japanese naval aviation is also affirmed from the British perspective in Arthur Marder, *Old Friends, New Enemies: The Royal Navy and the Imperial Japanese Navy* (Oxford: Oxford University Press, 1981), especially, 307–8.

7. Saburo Sakai, with Martin Caidin and Fred Saito, *Samurai!* (Garden City, NY: Nelson Doubleday, Inc., 1957), 55.

8. Hoyt, *Three Military Leaders*, 133.

9. Clay Blair, Jr., *Silent Victory: The U.S. Submarine War Against Japan* (Philadelphia: J.B. Lippincott Company, 1975), 91.

10. Atsushi Oi, "Why Japan's Antisubmarine Warfare Failed," in David C. Evans, editor and translator, *The Japanese Navy in World War II* (Annapolis: Naval Institute Press, [1969] 1986), second edition, 388.

11. For more detail, see David Kahn, *The Codebreakers*, revised and updated (New York: Scribner, [1967] 1996), 356.

12. John Prados, *Combined Fleet Decoded: The Secret History of American Intelligence and the Japanese Navy in World War II* (New York: Random House, 1995), 24. See also pp. 76–9 for his discussion of the abovementioned Red and Blue codes, and p. 82 for a description of the American intercept network.

13. Hoyt, *Three Military Leaders*, 100–1.

14. See Stuart D. Goldman, *Nomonhan, 1939: The Red Army's Victory that Shaped World War II* (Annapolis: Naval Institute Press, 2012).

15. Cited in Williamson Murray, "Versailles: the peace without a chance," in Williamson Murray and Jim Lacey, eds., *The Making of Peace: Rulers, States, and the Aftermath of War* (Cambridge: Cambridge University Press, 2009), 209.

16. Turkey, Austria, and Bulgaria were far gone financially and excused from reparations.

17. A.J.P. Taylor, *The Origins of the Second World War*, edition with new preface and introduction (New York: Atheneum, [1961] 1983), 189.

18. This is one of a number of keen insights to be found in Victor Davis Hanson, *The Second World Wars: How the First Global Conflict Was Fought and Won* (New York: Basic Books, 2017).

19. John Maynard Keynes, *The Economic Consequences of the Peace* (London: Macmillan & Co., 1919), 108.

20. B.H. Liddell Hart, *The German Generals Talk* (New York: William Morrow & Co., 1948), 14.

21. The degree to which Guderian was influenced by Liddell Hart, and the latter's actual influence on strategy in the 1930s, were sharply questioned in John Mearsheimer's *Liddell Hart and the Weight of History* (Ithaca: Cornell University Press, 1989).

22. Heinz Guderian, *Panzer Leader*, translated by Constantine Fitzgibbon (New York: E.P. Dutton & Co., Inc, 1952), 13.

23. Both quotes are from Williamson Murray, "Armored Warfare: The British, French, and German Experiences," in Murray and Allan R. Millett, editors, *Military Innovation in the Interwar Period* (Cambridge: Cambridge University Press, 1996), 40.

24. Desmond Young, *Rommel: The Desert Fox* (New York: Harper & Bros., 1950), 16.

25. Adolf Hitler, *Mein Kampf* (London: Hutchinson, [1925] 1972), 603.

26. See Norman Davies, *White Eagle, Red Star: The Polish-Soviet War 1919–1920 and the Miracle on the Vistula* (London: Random House UK, 2003).

27. Ernst Udet, *Ace of the Iron Cross*, translated by Richard K. Riehn (Garden City: Doubleday & Co., [1935] 1970), 88.

28. Herbert Molloy Mason, Jr., *The Rise of the Luftwaffe, 1918–1940* (New York: The Dial Press, 1973), 237.

29. Cajus Bekker, *The Luftwaffe War Diaries*, translated and edited by Frank Ziegler (Garden City, Doubleday & Co., 1968), 39.

30. Fritz Sternberg, *Germany and a Lightning War* (London: Faber & Faber, 1938).

31. Adolf Galland, *The First and the Last* (New York: Henry Holt & Co., 1954), 11.

32. See Mason, *Rise of the Luftwaffe*, especially pp. 185–6.

33. Bekker, *The Luftwaffe War Diaries*, 228.

34. Galland, *The First and the Last*, 12.

35. On this point, see Jonathan Steinberg, *Yesterday's Deterrent: Tirpitz and the Birth of the German Battle Fleet* (New York: The Macmillan Company, 1965).

36. The original limit in the agreement confined U-boat construction to three-fifths the number of British submarines, but a codicil allowed for expansion to numerical parity as required by "circumstances" the Germans were granted the right to deem "exceptional."

37. Cited in Winston S. Churchill, *The Second World War*, Vol. I, *The Gathering Storm* (Boston: Houghton Mifflin Company, 1948), 141.

38. Cited in G.H. Bennett and R. Bennett, *Hitler's Admirals* (Annapolis: Naval Institute Press, 2004), 35.

39. Edward P. Von der Porten, *The German Navy in World War II* (New York: Thomas Y. Crowell Company, 1969), 23.

40. Anthony Martienssen, *Hitler and His Admirals* (New York: E.P. Dutton & Co., 1949), 13.

41. Entry for September 3, 1939.

42. Von der Porten, *German Navy in World War II*, 18.

43. Kahn, *The Codebreakers*, 412.

44. These events are described in detail in David Kahn, *Seizing the Enigma: The Race to Break the German U-boat Codes* (Boston: Houghton Mifflin, 1991), 134–6, 205.

45. Italy declared war on Austria-Hungary that year, but not against Germany until 1916.

46. Churchill, *The Gathering Storm*, 173. In addition to his public speech, Churchill had a private conversation around the same time with the Italian ambassador to Britain, Count Dino Grandi, during which he made the same point.

47. Hugh Thomas, *The Spanish Civil War* (New York: Harper & Brothers, Publishers, 1961), 383.

48. Churchill, *The Gathering Storm*, 246.

49. Kahn, *The Codebreakers*, 473.

50. Telford Taylor, *Munich: The Price of Peace* (Garden City, New York: Doubleday & Co., 1979), 19.

51. Cited in Churchill, *The Gathering Storm*, 351.

## Chapter 3

1. T.V. Tuleja, *Twilight of the Sea Gods* (W.W. Norton & Co., 1958), 80.

2. Dudley Pope's *The Battle of the River Plate* (Annapolis: Naval Institute Press, 1956) remains the best and most detailed account of this naval battle.

3. For detailed figures of average numbers of U-boats on station and sinkings quarter by quarter throughout the war, see the statistical analysis in John Ellis, *Brute Force: Allied Strategy and Tactics in the Second World War* (New York: Viking, 1990), 548–9.

4. Friedrich Ruge, *Der Seekrieg*, translated by Commander M.G. Saunders, RN (Annapolis: United States Naval Institute, 1957), 52.

5. Willi Frischauer and Robert Jackson, *The Altmark Affair* (New York: The Macmillan Company, 1955) remains the authoritative account. Andrew Geer's novel, *The Sea Chase*—and the John Wayne/Lana Turner film that followed—were inspired by the hunt for another German freighter, the *Erlangen*, which tried to make it home to Germany from the South Pacific in the opening months of World War II.

6. Only 45 sailors from among the 1,474 total crew members on the three vessels survived.

7. Telford Taylor, *The March of Conquest* (New York: Simon & Schuster, 1958), 150.

8. Captain Donald Macintyre, RN, *Narvik* (New York: W.W. Norton & Co., 1959), 217.

9. March Bloch, *Strange Defeat*, translated by Gerard Hopkins (New York: W.W. Norton & Company [1940] 1968), quotes, respectively, from pp. 25, 37, 39.

10. General André Beaufre, *1940: The Fall of France*, translated by Desmond Fowler (New York: Alfred A. Knopf, 1968), quotes from pp. 212–3.

11. Alistair Horne, *To Lose a Battle: France 1940* (Boston: Little, Brown & Co., 1969), especially pp. 128–31.

12. Ernest R. May, *Strange Victory: Hitler's Conquest of France* (New York: Hill and Wang, 2000), 6–7. See also Book Four of William L. Shirer's monumental *Collapse of the Third Republic: An Inquiry into the Fall of France in 1940* (New York: Simon and Schuster, 1969).

13. Heinz Guderian, *Panzer Leader*, translated by Constantine Fitzgibbon (New York: E.P. Dutton & Co., Inc., 1952), 68–9.

14. Cajus Bekker, *The Luftwaffe War Diaries*, edited and translated by Frank Ziegler (Garden City, New York: Doubleday & Co., 1968), 118.

15. Cites from B.H. Liddell Hart, editor, *The Rommel Papers*, translated by Paul Findlay (New York: Harcourt, Brace & Co., 1953). Pp. 32–3.

16. May, *Strange Victory*, 442–3.

17. Beaufre, *1940*, 200.

18. May, *Strange Victory*, 452. See also Adolphe Goutard, *The Battle of France, 1940 (1940: La guerre des occasions perdus)*, translated by A.R. Burgess (London: Frederick Muller, 1958). This study makes a strong case that such a counter-offensive could well have worked, given the significant distance that separated the leading German armored elements from their infantry.

19. Both cites from Beaufre, *1940*, 190.

20. Andrew Roberts, *Storm of War: A New History of the Second World War* (New York: HarperCollins Publishers, 2011), 63.

21. Winston S. Churchill, *The Second World War*, Vol. I, *The Gathering Storm* (Boston: Houghton Mifflin, 1948), 657.

22. Correlli Barnett, *Engage the Enemy More Closely: The Royal Navy in the Second World War* (New York: W.W. Norton & Co., 1991), 188.

23. *Ibid.*, 195.

24. See Wolfgang Frank, *The Sea Wolves*, translated by Lieutenant Commander R.O.B. Long (New York: Rinehart & Co., 1955), 87.

25. Peter Fleming, *Operation Sea Lion* (New York: Simon and Schuster, 1957), 240.

26. For further details on these aircraft, and other types—including a few Italian models—that also appeared in the Battle of Britain, see Derek Wood and Derek Dempster, *The Narrow Margin* (London: McGraw-Hill Book Co., 1961), 433–452.

27. *Ibid.*, 444.

28. Bryan Cooper, *The Story of the Bomber* (London: Octopus Books, 1974), 96, 101.

29. Werner Baumbach, *Broken Swastika: The Defeat of the Luftwaffe*, translated by Frederick Holt (New York: Dorset Press, 1960), 79.

30. Adolf Galland, *The First and the Last*, translated by Mervyn Savill (New York: Henry Holt & Co., 1954), 31.

31. Richard Overy, *The Battle of Britain: The Myth and the Reality* (London: W.W. Norton & Co., 2000), 128.

32. Ellis, *Brute Force*, 26.

33. *Ibid.*, 543.

34. William L. Shirer, *The Rise and Fall of the*

*Third Reich* (New York: Simon and Schuster, 1960), 796.

35. Ruge, *Der Seekrieg*, 132. See also Martin van Creveld, *Hitler's Strategy, 1940–1941: The Balkan Clue* (London: Cambridge University Press, 1973), 29.

36. Leonard Mosley, *The Reich Marshal* (Garden City, NY: Doubleday & Co., 1974), 295.

37. See Milton Shulman, *Defeat in the West* (London: Cassell [1947] 2003), 68.

38. Cited in Paul Carell, *Hitler Moves East, 1941–1943*, translated by Ewald Osers (Boston: Little, Brown & Co., 1964), 13.

39. John Keegan, *The Second World War* (New York: Viking, 1990), 85.

40. Major General J.F.C. Fuller, *The Second World War: A Strategical and Tactical History* (New York: Duell, Sloan and Pearce, 1948), 92.

41. *Ibid.*, 94.

42. *The Ciano Diaries*, edited by Hugh Gibson (Garden City, NY: Doubleday & Co., 1946), 270–71.

43. Commander Marc' Antonio Bragadin, *The Italian Navy in World War II* (Annapolis: United States Naval Institute, 1957), 30.

44. Barnett, *Engage the Enemy More Closely*, 249.

45. Van Creveld, *Hitler's Strategy*, quotes and analysis from p. 32.

46. Gerhard Weinberg, *A World at Arms: A Global History of World War II* (Cambridge: Cambridge University Press, 1994), 210.

47. Alan Moorehead, *The Desert War* (London: Sphere Books, 1968), 42–3.

48. Van Creveld, *Hitler's Strategy*, 40–42. See also Charles Burdick, *Germany's Military Strategy and Spain in World War II* (Syracuse, NY: Syracuse University Press, 1968).

49. Joseph C. Harsch, *Pattern of Conquest* (Garden City, NY: Doubleday, Doran & Co., Inc., 1941), 239.

50. Cited in John Toland, *The Rising Sun: The Decline and Fall of the Japanese Empire, 1936–1945* (New York: Random House, 1970), 63.

51. *Ibid.*, 67.

52. Saburo Sakai, with Martin Caidin and Fred Saito, *Samurai!* (Garden City, NY: Nelson Doubleday, Inc., 1957), 42–3.

53. Ronald Spector, *Eagle Against the Sun: The American War with Japan* (New York: The Free Press, 1985), 544.

54. George Alexander Lensen, *The Strange Neutrality: Soviet-Japanese Relations During the Second World War* (Tallahassee, FL: The Diplomatic Press, 1972), 8–9.

55. Ruge, *Der Seekrieg*, 143.

56. Edwin Hoyt, *Three Military Leaders: Heihachiro Togo, Isoroku Yamamoto, Tomoyuki Yamashita* (Tokyo: Kodansha International, 1993), 105.

57. Gibson, ed., *The Ciano Diaries*, 296.

58. The "panzer division" terminology was actually introduced, and the concept was developed, by General Ludwig von Eimannsberger in his *Der*

*Kampfwagenberg* [Tank Warfare], second edition (München: Verlag J.F. Lehmann, [1934] 1938).

59. Major F.O. Miksche, *Attack: A Study of Blitzkrieg Tactics* (New York: Random House, 1942), 37.

60. Major F.W. von Mellenthin, *Panzer Battles: A Study of the Employment of Armor in the Second World War* (Norman, OK: University of Oklahoma Press, 1956), 20.

61. Roberts, *Storm of War*, 64.

# Chapter 4

1. John Keegan, *The Second World War* (New York: Viking, 1990), 156.

2. Admiral Franco Maugeri, *From the Ashes of Disgrace*, edited by Victor Rosen (New York: Reynal & Hitchcock, 1948), 26.

3. Marc' Antonio Bragadin, *The Italian Navy in World War II*, translated by Gale Hoffman (Annapolis: United States Naval Institute, 1957), 98.

4. J. Valerio Borghese, *Sea Devils: Italian Navy Commandos in World War II*, translated by James Cleugh (London: Andrew Melrose Ltd., 1952), 83.

5. Vice Admiral Friedrich Ruge, *Der Seekrieg*, translated by Commander M.G. Saunders, RN (Annapolis: United States Naval Institute, 1957), 243.

6. The high number of this U-boat was an attempt to deceive the Allies as to the actual number of German submarines—which was in reality far lower.

7. Correlli Barnett, *Engage the Enemy More Closely: The Royal Navy in the Second World War* (New York: W.W. Norton & Co., 1991), 376.

8. Thaddeus V. Tuleja, *Twilight of the Sea Gods* (New York: W.W. Norton & Co., 1958), 219. Emphasis in the original.

9. Two of the best accounts of this operation are the memoir by Baron Friedrich August von der Heydte, *Daedalus Returned: Crete 1941* (London: Hutchinson, 1958) and Alan Clark's *The Fall of Crete* (London: Anthony Blond Ltd, 1962).

10. Keegan, *The Second World War*, 172.

11. Von der Heydte, *Daedalus Returned*, 181.

12. Ludovic Kennedy, *Pursuit: The Chase and Sinking of the Battleship Bismarck* (New York: The Viking Press, 1974), 228. Other excellent accounts include: C.S. Forester, *The Last Nine Days of the Bismarck* (Boston: Little, Brown & Co., 1959); and William L. Shirer, *The Sinking of the Bismarck* (New York: Random House, 1962).

13. Cajus Bekker, *Hitler's Naval War* (Garden City, NY: Doubleday & Co., 1974), 70.

14. Victor Davis Hanson, *The Second World Wars: How the First Global Conflict Was Fought and Won* (New York: Basic Books, 2017), 89.

15. Cited in Cajus Bekker, *The Luftwaffe War Diaries*, translated and edited by Frank Ziegler (Garden City, NY: Doubleday & Co., 1968), 229. Emphasis in the original.

16. David Downing, *The Devil's Virtuosos: Ger-*

*man Generals at War, 1940–45* (New York: St. Martin's Press, 1977), 246.

17. William Manchester, *The Arms of Krupp, 1587–1968* (New York: Bantam Books, 1968), 458–9.

18. Heinz Guderian, *Panzer Leader*, translated by Constantine Fitzgibbon (New York: E.P. Dutton & Co., Inc., 1952), 161.

19. Gerhard Weinberg, *A World at Arms: A Global History of World War II* (Cambridge: Cambridge University Press, 1994), 269.

20. Andrew Roberts, *The Storm of War: A New History of the Second World War* (New York: Harper-Collins Publishers, 2011), 226.

21. *Ibid.*, 227.

22. Hannah Vogt, *The Burden of Guilt: A Short History of Germany, 1914–1945*, translated by Herbert Strauss (New York: Oxford University Press, 1964), 229.

23. Alexander Dallin, *German Rule in Russia, 1941–1945: A Study of Occupation Policies,* second, revised, edition (Boulder, CO: Westview Press, [1957] 1981), 64.

24. *Ibid.*, both quotes from p. 65.

25. Alexander Werth, *Russia at War 1941–1945* (New York: E.P. Dutton, 1964), 711.

26. Georgi K. Zhukov, with Harrison Salisbury, *Marshal Zhukov's Greatest Battles* (New York: Harper & Row, Publishers, 1969), 77.

27. Antony Beevor, *The Second World War* (Boston: Little, Brown & Co., 2012), 278.

28. John Toland, *Infamy: Pearl Harbor and Its Aftermath* (Garden City, NY: Doubleday & Co., Inc., 1982), quotes from pp. 275–76.

29. One of the best studies of surprise attack remains Roberta Wohlstetter's *Pearl Harbor: Warning and Decision* (Stanford: Stanford University Press, 1962). See also Gordon W. Prange, *At Dawn We Slept: The Untold Story of Pearl Harbor* (New York: McGraw-Hill, 1981). On Stalin having been taken completely by surprise by the Germans, see Barton Whaley, *Codeword Barbarossa* (Boston: The MIT Press, 1973).

30. Mitsuo Fuchida, "The Air Attack on Pearl Harbor," in David Evans, editor and translator, *The Japanese Navy in World War II*, second edition (Annapolis: Naval Institute Press, 1986), especially pp. 69–70.

31. See Edwin Hoyt, *Three Military Leaders: Heihachiro Togo, Isoroku Yamamoto, Tomoyuki Yamashita* (Tokyo: Kodansha International, 1993), 110.

32. Cited in Hiroyuki Agawa, *The Reluctant Admiral: Yamamoto and the Imperial Navy*, translated by John Bester (Tokyo: Kodansha International Ltd., 1979), 265.

33. Allan R. Millett, "Assault from the Sea," in Williamson Murray and Allan R. Millett, editors, *Military Innovation in the Interwar Period* (Cambridge: Cambridge University Press, 1998), 89. Emphasis added.

34. Richard Hough, *Death of the Battleship* (New York: Macmillan, 1963), 207.

35. The memo is cited in full in Winston S. Churchill, *The Second World War*, Vol. 4, *The Hinge of Fate* (Boston: Houghton Mifflin Company, 1950), 45.

36. Colonel Masanobu Tsuji, *Singapore: The Japanese Version*, translated by Margaret E. Lake (New York: St. Martin's Press, 1960), 54.

37. Churchill, *Hinge of Fate*, 92.

38. James Leasor, *Singapore: The Battle That Changed the World* (Garden City, NY: Doubleday & Co., 1968), 258. See also Noel Barber, *A Sinister Twilight: The Fall of Singapore 1942* (Boston: Houghton Mifflin Company, 1968).

39. Field Marshal Viscount William Slim, *Defeat Into Victory* (New York: David McKay Co., 1961), 95–7.

40. Quotes from Barbara W. Tuchman, *Stilwell and the American Experience in China, 1911–45* (New York: The Macmillan Company, 1970), 289, 300.

41. Captain Andrieu d'Albas, *Death of a Navy: Japanese Naval Action in World War II*, translated from the French by Anthony Rippon (New York: The Devin-Adair Company, 1957), 101.

42. Walter Lord, *Incredible Victory: The Battle of Midway* (New York: Harper, 1967).

43. Mitsuo Fuchida and Masatake Okumiya, *Midway: The Battle That Doomed Japan*, translated by Masataka Chihaya (Annapolis: U.S. Naval Institute, 1955), 269–70.

44. Ronald Spector, *Eagle Against the Sun: The American War with Japan* (New York: The Free Press, 1985), 177–8.

45. Alan Moorehead, *The Desert War: The North African Campaign, 1940–1943* (London: Sphere Books, Ltd, 1968), 194.

46. Cited in Paul Carell, *The Foxes of the Desert*, translated by Mervyn Savill (New York: E.P. Dutton & Co., 1961), 183.

47. See Joachim Hoffman, "The Conduct of the War Through Soviet Eyes," in *Germany and the Second World War*, Vol. 4, *The Attack on the Soviet Union*, edited by Horst Boog et al., Ewald Osers, translation editor (Oxford: Clarendon Press, 2009), 926.

48. Stalin's views at this time are detailed in Weinberg, *World at Arms*, 295.

49. Roberts, *Storm of War*, 317–8.

50. Weinberg, all quotes from *World at Arms*, 415.

51. The classic account of this disaster is David Irving's *The Destruction of Convoy PQ 17* (London: Cassell & Co, 1967). A later edition (New York: Richardson and Steirman, 1987) was published that included previously highly classified materials that made clear Irving's sharp critique of the Royal Navy was essentially in line with the facts.

52. Tuleja, *Twilight of the Sea Gods*, 223.

53. Samuel Eliot Morison, *The Two-Ocean War* (Boston: Little, Brown, 1963), 109.

54. Harald Busch, *U-Boats at War*, translated by L.P.R. Wilson (New York: Ballantine Books, Inc., 1955), 44.

# Chapter 5

1. Richard Tregaskis, *Guadalcanal Diary* (New York: Random House, 1943), 146–7.

2. Richard B. Frank, *Guadalcanal* (New York: Random House, 1990), 239–40.

3. Official Japanese records reflect full confirmation of only about half of these.

4. Saburo Sakai, with Martin Caidin and Fred Saito, *Samurai!* (Garden City, NY: Nelson Doubleday, Inc., [1957] 1978), 181.

5. Cited in Frank, *Guadalcanal*, 486. The most detailed account of this action can be found in Ivan Musicant, *Battleship at War: The Epic Story of the USS Washington* (New York: Harcourt Brace Jovanovich, 1986).

6. The liveliest account of Australia's Islands Coastwatching Service is Walter Lord's *Lonely Vigil: Coastwatchers of the Solomons* (New York: The Viking Press, 1977).

7. Further details of ships and aircraft lost during the campaign can be found in the tables in Frank, *Guadalcanal*, 601–2.

8. On this see Alvin Coox, "The Effectiveness of the Japanese Military Establishment in the Second World War," in Allan R. Millett and Williamson Murray, eds., *Military Effectiveness*, Vol. III, *The Second World War* (Boston: Allen & Unwin, 1988), 28.

9. Ronald Spector, *Eagle Against the Sun: The American War with Japan* (New York: The Free Press, 1985), 229.

10. John Prados, *Combined Fleet Decoded: The Secret History of American Intelligence and the Japanese Navy in World War II* (New York: Random House, 1995), 459. See also Carroll V. Glines, *Attack on Yamamoto* (New York: Crown Publishers, 1990).

11. Clay Blair, Jr., *Silent Victory: The U.S. Submarine War Against Japan* (Philadelphia: J.B. Lippincott Company, 1975), Vol. 1, 396–7.

12. Ronald Lewin, *The American Magic: Codes, Ciphers and the Defeat of Japan* (New York: Farrar Straus Giroux, 1982), 224–5.

13. General George C. Marshall to Governor Thomas E. Dewey, September 27, 1944.

14. This figure derived from: Wolfgang Frank, *The Sea Wolves: The Story of German U-Boats at War*, translated by Lieutenant Commander R.O.B. Long (New York: Rinehart & Co., 1955), 225–31; Correlli Barnett, *Engage the Enemy More Closely: The Royal Navy in the Second World War* (New York: W.W. Norton & Co., 1991), 580–5; and John Ellis, *Brute Force: Allied Strategy and Tactics in the Second World War* (New York: Viking, 1990), Table 38 on p. 549.

15. The most thorough account of this battle is Dudley Pope's *73 North: The Battle of the Barents Sea* (London: Wyman and Sons, 1958).

16. Barnett, *Engage the Enemy More Closely*, 600.

17. On the inflection point in the U-boat war, see Michael Gannon, *Black May* (New York: HarperCollins Publishers, Inc., 1998), and David Kahn, *Seizing the Enigma: The Race to Break the German U-Boat Codes, 1939–1943* (Boston: Houghton Mifflin, 1991).

18. See Peter Shankland and Anthony Hunter, *Malta Convoy* (New York: Ives Washburn, Inc., 1961), and Ernle Bradford, *Siege: Malta 1940–1943* (New York: William Morrow & Co., 1986).

19. Quoted in B.H. Liddell Hart, *The German Generals Talk* (New York: Quill, [1948] 1979), 161–2.

20. Fritz Bayerlein, "El Alamein," in Seymour Freidin and William Richardson, eds., trans. by Constantine Fitzgibbon, *Fatal Decisions: Six Decisive Battles of World War II from the Viewpoint of the Vanquished* (Mechanicsburg: Stackpole Books, [1956] 2013), 88.

21. B.H. Liddell Hart, *History of the Second World War* (New York: G.P. Putnam's Sons, 1970), 296.

22. Field-Marshal The Viscount Montgomery of Alamein, *El Alamein to the River Sangro* (London: Hutchinson & Co., Ltd., 1948). Both quotes are from p. 16.

23. Correlli Barnett, *The Desert Generals* (London: Allen & Unwin, 1960), 266.

24. *The Rommel Papers*, edited by B.H. Liddell Hart, translated by Paul Findlay (New York: Harcourt, Brace & Co., 1953). Quotes from pp. 286–7.

25. These relative strength ratios are derived from the Allied and Axis field returns compiled by the Historical Branch of the British War Office. See also: Fred Majdalany, *El Alamein: Fortress in the Sand* (Philadelphia: J.B. Lippincott Company, 1965), 78; and C.E. Lucas Phillips, *Alamein* (Boston: Little, Brown & Co., 1962), 123.

26. David Irving, *Trail of the Fox: The Life of Field-Marshal Erwin Rommel* (London: Weidenfeld and Nicolson, 1977), 201.

27. Robert Leckie, *Delivered From Evil: The Saga of World War II* (New York: Harper & Row, 1987), 392.

28. Cited in Paul Carell, *The Foxes of the Desert*, translated by Mervyn Savill (New York: E.P. Dutton & Co., 1961), 310.

29. Both quotes are from Walter Warlimont, *Inside Hitler's Headquarters, 1939–1945*, translated by R.H. Barry (London: Weidenfeld & Nicolson, 1964), 308.

30. Andrew Roberts, *The Storm of War* (New York: Harper, 2011), 314.

31. Dwight D. Eisenhower, *Crusade in Europe* (Garden City, NY: Doubleday & Co., 1948), 142.

32. Erich von Manstein, *Lost Victories*, translated by A.G. Powell (London: Methuen & Co., Ltd, 1958), 354.

33. Roberts, *Storm of War*, 343.

34. Kurt Zeitzler, "Stalingrad," in Freidin and Richardson, editors, *Fatal Decisions*, 150.

35. Albert Speer, *Inside the Third Reich*, translated by Richard and Clara Winston (New York: The Macmillan Company, 1970), 220.

36. Liddell Hart, *History of the Second World War*, 243. Discussion of the reductions in the numbers of infantry and tanks in German divisions at this time is on the same page.

37. Field-Marshal Lord Carver, "Manstein," in Correlli Barnett, ed., *Hitler's Generals* (New York: Grove Weidenfeld, 1989), 235.

38. Adolf Hitler, "Assignment of Duties to the Inspector-General of Armored Troops," February 28, 1943, Paragraph 7. Emphasis added.

39. Gerhard Weinberg, *A World at Arms: A Global History of World War II* (Cambridge: Cambridge University Press, 1994), 467.

40. See Liddell Hart, *History of the Second World War*, 488.

41. Major General J.F.C. Fuller, *The Second World War: A Strategical and Tactical History* (New York: Duell, Sloan and Pearce, 1948), 259.

42. Weinberg, *A World at Arms*, 463–4.

43. The senior German officers who told Liddell Hart about these talks placed them at Kirovograd. Drew Middleton, "British Book Says German and Soviet Officials Met in '43 to Discuss Peace," *The New York Times,* January 4, 1971 discusses Liddell Hart's claim and adds some additional detail, including the tantalizing point that the novelist James Gould Cozzens, in his Pulitzer-Prize–winner *Guard of Honor* (1948) includes a character who describes these talks as well. Cozzens served under very senior officers during the war who, it seems, had been made aware of the Ribbentrop-Molotov talks.

44. These cited passages and other selected portions of the memorandum can be found in William L. Shirer, *The Rise and Fall of the Third Reich: A History of Nazi Germany* (New York: Simon and Schuster, 1960), 940–1. The full report is in the Nuremberg Documents, *Nazi Conspiracy and Aggression*, Vol. III, 242–51.

45. John Heskett, *Design* (Oxford: Oxford University Press, 2002), 84.

46. On those who went along with Nazism, see Daniel Jonah Goldhagen, *Hitler's Willing Executioners* (New York: Vintage, 1997). On those in opposition, see Hans Mommsen, *Alternatives to Hitler: German Resistance Under the Third Reich* (Princeton: Princeton University Press, 2003).

47. See Terry Parssinen, *The Oster Conspiracy of 1938: The Unknown Story of the Military Plot to Kill Hitler and Avert World War II* (New York: HarperCollins Publishers, 2003). Hans Gisevius, *To the Bitter End: An Insider's Account of the Plot to Kill Hitler*, translated by Richard and Clara Winston (Boston: Houghton Mifflin, 1947) provides a firsthand account of German resistance to Hitler from 1933 on.

48. Gisevius, *To the Bitter End*, 467.

49. Shirer, *Rise and Fall of the Third Reich*, 1018.

50. See figures from Sir Charles Webster and Noble Frankland, *The Strategic Air Offensive Against Germany* (London: Her Majesty's Stationery Office, 1961), and Cajus Bekker, *The Luftwaffe War Diaries* (Garden City: Doubleday & Co. 1968), 301–7.

51. Bekker, *Luftwaffe War Diaries*, 309.

52. Quoted in Webster and Frankland, *The Strategic Air Offensive Against Germany*, Vol. 2, 20.

53. These early developments are well chronicled in Sterling Pavelec, *The Jet Race and the Second World War* (Annapolis: Naval Institute Press, 2007), especially pp. 20–25.

54. Bekker, *Luftwaffe War Diaries*, 327.

55. Both quotes are from Adolf Galland, *The First and the Last: The Rise and Fall of the German Figher Forces, 1938–1945*, translated by Mervyn Savill (New York: Henry Holt & Co., 1954), 255.

## Chapter 6

1. A most moving and thorough account of these proceedings can be found in Carroll V. Glines, *Attack on Yamamoto* (New York: Crown Publishers, Inc., 1990), 109–11.

2. Samuel Eliot Morison, *The Two-Ocean War: A Short History of the United States Navy in the Second World War* (Boston: Little, Brown & Co., 1963), 274.

3. Captain Tameichi Hara, with Fred Saito and Roger Pineau, *Japanese Destroyer Captain* (New York: Ballantine Books, Inc., 1961), 179.

4. Morison, *Two-Ocean War*, 282.

5. Andrieu d'Albas, *Death of a Navy: Japanese Naval Action in World War II*, translated by Anthony Rippon (New York: The Devin-Adair Company, 1957), 276.

6. Ronald Spector, *Eagle Against the Sun: The American War with Japan* (New York: The Free Press, 1985), 181–2.

7. On this action, see John A. Lorelli, *The Battle of the Komandorski Islands* (Annapolis: Naval Institute Press, 1984). On the overall campaign, see Brian Garfield, *The Thousand-Mile War: World War II in the Aleutians* (New York: Ballantine Books, 1969).

8. William Manchester, *American Caesar: Douglas MacArthur 1880–1964* (Boston: Little, Brown & Co., 1978), 339.

9. On this hard-fought campaign, two excellent accounts are: Martin Russ, *Line of Departure: Tarawa* (Garden City, NY: Doubleday & Co., 1975); and Edwin P. Hoyt, *Storm Over the Gilberts* (New York: Van Nostrand Reinhold Company, 1978).

10. Cited in Hanson W. Baldwin, *Battles Lost and Won: Great Campaigns of World War II* (New York: Konecky & Konecky, 1966), 468. See also the eyewitness account of the journalist Robert Sherrod, *Tarawa: The Story of a Battle* (New York: Duell, Sloan & Pearce, 1944).

11. Philip Crowl and Edmund Love, *Seizure of the Gilberts and Marshalls* (Washington: Office of the Chief of Military History, 1955), 156.

12. This is what Tojo related of the conversation to his trusted confidant, General Kenryu Sato, soon after the meeting. Cited in John Toland—who interviewed Sato after the war—*The Rising Sun: The Decline and Fall of the Japanese Empire, 1936–1945* (New York: Random House, 1970), 561. Emphasis in the original.

13. On the number and disposition of Japanese divisions, see John Keegan, *The Second World War* (New York: Viking, 1989), 546–7.

14. Field Marshal the Viscount Slim, *Defeat Into Victory* (New York: David McKay Co., 1961), 132.

15. Figures are from Clay Blair, Jr., *Silent Victory: The U.S. Submarine War Against Japan* (Philadelphia: J.B. Lippincott Company, 1975), 522.

16. Clay Blair, Jr., *Hitler's U-boat War: The Hunted* (New York: Random House, 1998).

17. Harald Busch, *U-boats at War* (New York: Ballantine Books, Inc., 1955), 138.

18. Both quotes, and information about Merker, Speer, and the Type XXIII U-boat can be found in Kenneth Macksey, *Military Errors of World War Two* (London: Cassell & Co., 1998), 144–5.

19. Cited in Busch, *U-boats at War*, 123.

20. Macksey, *Military Errors of World War Two*, 143, puts Allied response time at sixteen days.

21. A discussion of decoys and their limits can be found in Busch, *U-boats at War*, 87.

22. These three sets of statistics are derived from raw data provided in John Ellis, *Brute Force: Allied Strategy and Tactics in the Second World War* (New York: Viking, 1990), 548–9.

23. The term is from a U-boat skipper who survived the war, Herbert Werner. His memoir is entitled *Iron Coffins* (New York: Holt, Rinehart and Winston, 1969).

24. Cajus Bekker, *Hitler's Naval War*, translated and edited by Frank Ziegler (Garden City, NY: Doubleday & Co., Inc., 1974), 340. See also Thomas Gallagher, *The X-Craft Raid* (New York: Harcourt Brace Jovanovich, Inc., 1970).

25. T.V. Tuleja, *Twilight of the Sea Gods* (New York: W.W. Norton & Co., 1958), 245.

26. Bekker, *Hitler's Naval War*, 368.

27. On Kammhuber's fall, see Cajus Bekker, *The Luftwaffe War Diaries*, translated and edited by Frank Ziegler (Garden City: Doubleday & Co., 1968), 331–2.

28. For an account of this side of World War II, see R.V. Jones, *The Wizard War: British Scientific Intelligence, 1939–1945* (New York: Coward, McCann & Geoghegan, 1978).

29. Cited in Bekker, *Luftwaffe War Diaries*, 310.

30. Joseph Schmid, "German Nightfighting from June 1943 to May 1945," in David Isby, ed., *Fighting the Bombers: The Luftwaffe's Struggle Against the Allied Bomber Offensive as Seen by its Commanders* (London: Greenhill Books, [1946] 2003), 123.

31. Gerhard Weinberg, *A World at Arms: A Global History of World War II* (Cambridge: Cambridge University Press, 1994), 618.

32. Ellis, *Brute Force*, 174.

33. Weinberg, *A World at Arms*, 618.

34. Adolf Galland, *The First and the Last: The Rise and Fall of the German Fighter Forces, 1938–1945*, translated by Mervyn Savill (New York: Henry Holt & Co., Inc., 1954), 162.

35. Both quotes are from Richard Overy, *Why the Allies Won* (New York: W.W. Norton & Co., 1995), 240.

36. See Ellis, *Brute Force*, 551.

37. Alan Clark, *Barbarossa: The Russian-German Conflict, 1941–1945* (London: Cassell, 1965), 328.

38. The classic account of this spy ring is Pierre Accoce's *A Man Called Lucy, 1939–1945* (New York: Coward-McCann, 1967). "Lucy" was chosen as the codename because Roessler operated out of Lucerne—a risky choice, in my view, too "on the nose."

39. My figures are consistent with the approximate totals given by a variety of the leading sources on the battle, including: Lloyd Clark, *The Battle of the Tanks: Kursk 1943* (New York: Atlantic Monthly Press, 2011); David M. Glantz, *The Battle of Kursk* (Lawrence: University Press of Kansas, 2004); and John Erickson, *The Road to Berlin* (Boulder: Westview Press, 1983).

40. Heinz Guderian, *Panzer Leader*, translated by Constantine Fitzgibbon (New York: E.P. Dutton & Co., Inc., 1952), 312.

41. The classic memoir of the formulation and execution of this strategic deception is Ewen Montagu's *The Man Who Never Was* (Philadelphia: J.B. Lippincott Company, 1954). The most recent account of this matter can be found in Ben Macintyre, *Operation Mincemeat* (New York: Crown, 2010).

42. The quote and statistics are from Donald Macintyre, *The Naval War Against Hitler* (New York: Charles Scribner's Sons, 1971), 364.

43. Hanson W. Baldwin, *Battles Lost and Won: Great Campaigns of World War II* (New York: Konecky & Konecky, 1966), 225.

44. See Martin Blumenson, *Sicily: Whose Victory?* (New York: Ballantine, 1968).

45. This from Goebbels' diary entry for July 25, 1943, cited in Arthur Bryant, *The Turn of the Tide* (New York: Doubleday, 1957), 555.

46. On this battle, see Hugh Pond's *Salerno* (Boston: Little, Brown & Co., 1961).

47. David Irving, *Trail of the Fox: The Life of Field-Marshal Erwin Rommel* (London: Weidenfeld and Nicolson, 1977), 280.

48. See Dominick Graham and Shelford Bidwell, *Tug of War: The Battle for Italy, 1943–45* (New York: St. Martin's Press, 1986), and Major-General W.G.F. Jackson's excellent campaign analysis, *The Battle for Italy* (New York: Harper & Row, Publishers, 1967). Jackson served and was wounded in the Italian campaign. On the fight to take Monte Cassino there is no better account than Fred Majdalany's *Cassino: Portrait of a Battle* (London: Longman, Greens & Co., 1957), though Matthew Parker's *Monte Cassino: The Hardest-Fought Battle of World War II* (New York: Doubleday, 2004) is superb too.

49. Major General J.F.C. Fuller, *The Second World War, 1939–45: A Strategical and Tactical History* (New York: Duell, Sloan and Pearce, 1948), 265.

50. Victor Davis Hanson, *The Second World Wars* (New York: Basic Books, 2017), quotes from pp. 282, 284. A thoughtful assessment of the value of the battle for Italy—and the campaigns preceding it—is found in Douglas Porch, *The Path to Victory: The*

*Mediterranean Theater in World War II* (New York: Farrar, Straus and Giroux, 2004).

51. Rick Atkinson, *The Day of Battle: The War in Sicily and Italy, 1943–1944* (New York: Henry Holt & Co., 2007), 314.

## Chapter 7

1. On this design innovation, see Paul Kennedy, *Engineers of Victory: The Problem Solvers Who Turned the Tide in the Second World War* (New York: Random House, 2013), especially pp. 196–7.

2. Paul Carell, *Scorched Earth: The Russian-German War, 1943–1944*, translated by Ewald Osers (Boston: Little, Brown & Co., 1966), 295.

3. Erich von Manstein, *Lost Victories*, translated by Anthony G. Powell (London: Methuen & Co., Ltd., 1958), 524.

4. Hans Ulrich Rudel, *Stuka Pilot*, translated by Lynton Hudson (Dublin: Euphorion Books, 1952), 117.

5. Hitler's remarks are cited in Carell, *Scorched Earth*, 453.

6. Cited from the official report in Alexander Werth, *Russia at War, 1941–1945* (New York: E.P. Dutton & Co., Inc., 1964), 631.

7. Both quotes from Major-General J.F.C. Fuller, *The Second World War, 1939–45: A Strategical and Tactical History* (New York: Duell, Sloan and Pearce, 1948), 271. See also Carlo D'Este, *Fatal Decision: Anzio and the Battle for Rome* (New York: Harper-Collins, 1991).

8. Kenneth Macksey, *Kesselring* (New York: David McKay Co., Inc., 1978), 3.

9. Rommel's improvements to the Atlantic Wall and his state of mind are best described in great detail in Admiral Friedrich Ruge's *Rommel in Normandy*, translated by Ursula R. Moessner (London: Macdonald & Jane's, 1979).

10. The quotes are from David Irving, *The Trail of the Fox: The Life of Field-Marshal Erwin Rommel* (London: Weidenfeld and Nicolson, 1977), 305–6.

11. *Ibid.*, 306.

12. Chester Wilmot, *The Struggle for Europe* (New York: Harper & Brothers, Publishers, 1952), 193. A journalist of the highest personal courage, Wilmot parachuted into Normandy with the British 6th Airborne Division on D-Day.

13. *Ibid.*, 193 for both additional quotes.

14. For the statistics presented herein, and discussion of improvements to German airborne radars and armaments, see Cajus Bekker, *The Luftwaffe War Diaries*, translated and edited by Frank Ziegler (Garden City: Doubleday & Co., 1968), 337–39.

15. Sir Charles Webster and Noble Frankland, four vols. *The Strategic Air Offensive Against Germany* (London: Her Majesty's Stationery Office, 1961), Vol. III, 193, 206.

16. On this critical engagement, see Bekker, *Luftwaffe War Diaries*, 339–40.

17. For an excellent analysis of the air campaign over Germany during the first five months of 1944, including a discussion of the "Pointblank" plan, see Williamson Murray, *Strategy for Defeat: The Luftwaffe, 1933–1945* (London: Quantum Publishing, 2000), especially pp. 177–84.

18. Adolf Galland, *The First and the Last*, translated by Mervyn Savill (New York: Henry Holt & Co., 1954), 197.

19. Willy Messerschmitt, "The Me-262: Development, Experience, Success, and Prospects," in David C. Isby, editor, *Fighting the Bombers: The Luftwaffe's Struggle Against the Allied Bomber Offensive* (London: Greenhill Books, 2003), 187.

20. Walter Warlimont, *Inside Hitler's Headquarters*, translated by R.H. Barry (London: Weidenfeld and Nicolson, Ltd., 1964), 409.

21. David Kahn, *Seizing the Enigma: The Race to Break the German U-Boat Codes, 1939–1943* (Boston: Houghton Mifflin Company, 1991), 277.

22. Statistics for both periods include only merchant vessels of more than 500 gross tons, and are drawn from Theodore Roscoe, *Pig Boats*—the original title was: *United States Submarine Operations in World War II*, published by the United States Naval Institute in 1949—(New York: Bantam Books, 1982), 448.

23. Clay Blair, Jr., *Silent Victory: The U.S. Submarine War Against Japan* (Philadelphia: J.B. Lippincott Company, 1975), 534.

24. Edwin P. Hoyt, *War in the Deep: Pacific Submarine Action in World War II* (New York: G.P. Putnam's Sons, 1978), 133.

25. Louis L. Snyder, *The War: A Concise History* (New York: Julian Messner, Inc., 1960), 360.

26. John Keegan, *The Second World War* (New York: Viking, 1989), 548.

27. Field Marshal The Viscount Slim, *Defeat Into Victory* (New York: David McKay Co., 1961), 270.

28. Captain Andrieu d'Albas, *Death of a Navy: Japanese Naval Action in World War II*, trans. by Anthony Rippon (New York: The Devin-Adair Company, 1957), 285–6.

29. Samuel Eliot Morison, *The Two-Ocean War: A Short History of the United States Navy in the Second World War* (Boston: Little, Brown & Co., 1963), 342–3.

30. Captain Tameichi Hara, with Fred Saito and Roger Pineau, *Japanese Destroyer Captain* (New York: Ballantine Books, 1961), 263–4.

31. Katharine Savage, *The Story of the Second World War* (New York: Henry Z. Walck, 1958), 216. On the course and climax of the Cassino fighting, see Fred Majdalany, *Cassino: Portrait of a Battle* (London: Longmans, Green & Co., 1957).

32. Quotes from Dwight D. Eisenhower, *Crusade in Europe* (Garden City: Doubleday & Co., 1948), 250.

33. Paul Carell, *Invasion—They're Coming!* Translated by E. Osers (New York: E.P. Dutton & Co., Inc., 1963), 16–7.

34. Edwin P. Hoyt, *The Invasion Before Normandy:*

*The Secret Battle of Slapton Sands* (New York: Stein and Day Publishers, 1985) provides a detailed account of this action.

35. Carell, *Invasion—They're Coming!* p. 20.

36. Stephen E. Ambrose, *D-Day, June 6, 1944: The Climactic Battle of World War II* (New York: Simon & Schuster, 1994), 28.

37. Alexander McKee, *Last Round Against Rommel: Battle of the Normandy Beachhead* (New York: The New American Library, 1964), 121.

38. B.H. Liddell Hart, editor, *The Rommel Papers* (New York: Harcourt, Brace & Co., 1953), 492.

39. Both quotes from Morison, *The Two-Ocean War*, 406.

40. Snyder, *The War*, 375.

41. Alexander Werth, *Russia at War, 1941–45* (New York: E.P. Dutton & Co., Inc., 1964), 862.

42. *Ibid.*, 857.

43. Heinz Guderian, *Panzer Leader*, translated by Constantine Fitzgibbon (New York: E.P. Dutton & Co., Inc., 1952), 336.

44. Carlo D'Este, "Model," in Correlli Barnett, ed., *Hitler's Generals* (New York: Grove Weidenfeld, 1989), 324.

45. On Model's first moves, and their effectiveness, see Martin Blumenson, *The Duel for France, 1944* (New York: Perseus Books, [1963] 2000), 283–4.

46. Omar N. Bradley, *A Soldier's Story* (New York: Henry Holt & Co., 1951), 415–6.

47. Blumenson, *Duel for France*, 409.

48. Outstanding accounts of this battle include Christopher Hibbert, *Arnhem* (London: B.T. Batsford, Ltd, 1962), Cornelius Ryan, *A Bridge Too Far* (New York: Simon & Schuster, 1974), and Antony Beevor, *The Battle of Arnhem* (New York: Viking, 2018).

49. Bradley, *A Soldier's Story*, 427 for both quotes.

50. On this battle, see Charles Whiting, *Bloody Aachen* (New York: Stein and Day, 1976).

51. Saburo Sakai, with Martin Caidin and Fred Saito, *Samurai!* (Garden City, NY: Nelson Doubleday, Inc., 1957), 245.

52. Robert Leckie, *Delivered From Evil: The Saga of World War II* (New York: Harper & Row, Publishers, 1987), 780.

53. Samuel Eliot Morison, *History of United States Naval Operations in World War II*, Vol. 12, *Leyte* (Boston: Little, Brown & Co., 1958), 149.

54. D'Albas, *Death of a Navy*, 310.

55. Morison, *Leyte*, 160.

56. Cited in Raymond Lamont-Brown, *Kamikaze: Japan's Suicide Samurai* (London: Cassell, 1997), 21.

57. John Heskett, *Design* (Oxford: Oxford University Press, 2003), 84.

58. Victor Davis Hanson, *The Second World Wars: How the First Global Conflict Was Fought and Won* (New York: Basic Books, 2017), 122–3.

59. Lamont-Brown, *Kamikaze*, 31.

60. Morison, *Leyte*, 303.

# Chapter 8

1. Chester Wilmot, *The Struggle for Europe* (New York: Harper & Brothers, Publishers, 1952), 568.

2. General Dwight D. Eisenhower, *Report by the Supreme Commander to the Combined Chiefs of Staff on the Operations in Europe of the Allied Expeditionary Force 6 June 1944 to 8 May 1945* (London: His Majesty's Stationery Office, 1946), 90.

3. Cited in Wilmot, *Struggle for Europe*, 570.

4. Major-General W.G.F. Jackson, *The Battle for Italy* (New York: Harper & Row Publishers, 1967), 284.

5. Andrew Roberts, *The Storm of War: A New History of the Second World War* (New York: HarperCollins Publishers, Inc., 2011), 538.

6. Alan Clark, *Barbarossa: The Russian-German Conflict, 1941–1945* (London: Cassell, 1965), 402.

7. For a detailed account of this episode, see Charles Foley, *Commando Extraordinary* (New York: G.P. Putnam's Sons, 1955), 85–100.

8. Cited from Robert Merriam's single-volume condensation of the official history, *The Battle of the Bulge* (New York: Random House, [1947] 1957), 6.

9. Heinz Guderian, *Panzer Leader*, translated by Constantine Fitzgibbon (New York: E.P. Dutton & Co., Inc., 1952), 381.

10. These events, and all quotes, are from Clark, *Barbarossa*, 410–11.

11. Major-General J.F.C. Fuller, *The Second World War, 1939–1945: A Strategical and Tactical History* (New York: Duell, Sloan and Pearce, 1948), 346.

12. George S. Patton, Jr., *War as I Knew It*, annotated by Colonel Paul D. Harkins (Boston: Houghton Mifflin, 1947), 330. Emphasis added.

13. Omar Bradley, *A Soldier's Story* (New York: Henry Holt & Co., 1951), 490–1.

14. Adolf Galland, *The First and the Last*, translated by Mervyn Savill (New York: Henry Holt & Co., 1954), 242.

15. William Manchester, *American Caesar: Douglas MacArthur, 1880–1964* (Boston: Little, Brown & Co., 1978), 405.

16. Raymond Lamont-Brown, *Kamikaze: Japan's Suicide Samurai* (London: Cassell & Co., 1997), 82.

17. B.H. Liddell Hart, *History of the Second World War* (New York: G.P. Putnam's Sons, 1970), 634.

18. Max Hastings, *Inferno: The World at War, 1939–1945* (New York: Alfred A. Knopf, 2011), 540.

19. Theodore Roscoe, *Pig Boats* (originally titled *United States Submarine Operations in World War II* (Annapolis: United States Naval Institute, [1949] 1982), 394–5.

20. Robert Leckie, *Delivered from Evil: The Saga of World War II* (New York: Harper Perennial, 1988), 864.

21. For an account of this action, see Captain Rikihei Inoguchi, Commander Tadashi Nakajima, and Roger Pineau, *The Divine Wind: Japan's Kamikaze Force in World War II* (Annapolis: United States Naval Institute, 1958), especially pp. 122–4.

22. Ronald Spector, *Eagle Against the Sun: The American War With Japan* (New York: The Free Press, 1985), 440.

23. One of the finest accounts of this battle was written by the war correspondent Richard F. Newcomb, *Iwo Jima* (New York: Nelson Doubleday, Inc., 1983).

24. Both quotes are from Leckie, *Delivered from Evil*, 872. Emphasis added.

25. Cited in Martin Gilbert, *The Second World War: A Complete History* (New York: Henry Holt & Co., 1989), 651.

26. *Ibid.*, 654.

27. See Bradley F. Smith and Elena Agarossi, *Operation Sunrise: The Secret Surrender* (New York: Basic Books, Inc., Publishers, 1979), 186.

28. Victor Davis Hanson, *The Second World Wars: How the First Global Conflict Was Fought and Won* (New York: Basic Books, 2017), 510.

29. Cajus Bekker, *Hitler's Naval War*, translated and edited by Frank Ziegler (Garden City, NY: Doubleday & Co., 1974), 367. See also Vincent P. O'Hara, *The German Fleet at War, 1939–1945* (Annapolis: Naval Institute Press, 2004), 257–8.

30. Guderian, *Panzer Leader*, 398.

31. Samuel Eliot Morison, *The Two-Ocean War: A Short History of the United States Navy in the Second World War* (Boston: Little, Brown & Co., 1963), 561.

32. This is from the classified report by presidential aide Ralph Williams (1960), details of which seem to come, interestingly, directly from Galland, *The First and the Last*, 273.

33. For an overview of the attempts to sabotage the heavy-water production process, see Thomas Gallagher, *Assault in Norway: Sabotaging the Nazi Nuclear Program* (Guilford, CT: The Lyons Press, 1975), and Dan Kurzman, *Blood and Water: Sabotaging Hitler's Bomb* (New York: Henry Holt & Co., 1997). A great commando memoir is Knut Haukelid's *Skis Against the Atom* (Minot, ND: North American Heritage Press, 1989).

34. On the organizational difficulties and theoretical errors that plagued the German effort to build an atomic weapon, see Thomas Powers, *Heisenberg's War: The Secret History of the German Bomb* (Cambridge: Da Capo Press, 1993), and the fascinating arguments and deliberations of the German scientists, secretly recorded while they were in captivity soon after the war's end and chronicled in Jeremy Bernstein's *Hitler's Uranium Club: The Secret Recordings at Farm Hall* (New York: Copernicus Books, 1995).

35. Antony Beevor, *The Fall of Berlin, 1945* (New York: Viking, 2002), 406.

36. Lamont-Brown, *Kamikaze*, 174.

37. Commander Edward P. Stafford, USN (Ret.), *Little Ship, Big War: The Saga of DE343* (New York: William Morrow & Co., 1984), 286.

38. Both quotes are from Inoguchi et al., *The Divine Wind*, 152.

39. Max Hastings, *Inferno: The World at War,* *1939–1945* (New York: Alfred A. Knopf, 2011), 620–21.

40. George Feifer, *Tennozan: The Battle of Okinawa and the Atomic Bomb* (New York: Ticknor & Fields,1992), 532–33.

41. The best analysis of Truman's reasoning can be found in David McCullough, *Truman* (New York: Simon & Schuster, 1992), 436–44.

42. Richard B. Frank, *Downfall: The End of the Imperial Japanese Empire* (New York: Random House, 1999), 345.

43. Figures from *United States Strategic Bombing Survey*, Report No. 62, *Japanese Air Power* (Washington, DC: Government Printing Office, 1946), 24–5, 70.

44. John Toland, *The Rising Sun: The Decline and Fall of the Japanese Empire, 1936–1945* (New York: Random House, 1970), 1012.

45. Cited in Manchester, *American Caesar*, 487.

46. Saburo Sakai, with Martin Caidin and Fred Saito *Samurai!* (Garden City, NY: Nelson Doubleday, Inc., 1957), 310–11.

47. Raymond de Belot, *The Struggle for the Mediterranean, 1939–1945*, translated by James A. Field, Jr. (Princeton: Princeton University Press, 1951), 227.

## Chapter 9

1. Both quotes are from Richard Overy *Why the Allies Won* (New York: W.W. Norton & Co., 1995), 15, 17. Emphasis added.

2. Paul Kennedy, *Engineers of Victory: The Problem Solvers Who Turned the Tide in the Second World War* (New York: Random House, 2013), xv.

3. Both quotes are from Ronald Spector, *Eagle Against the Sun: The American War with Japan* (New York: The Free Press, 1985), 178, 218.

4. Giulia Calabretta, Gerda Gemser, and Ingo Karpen, *Strategic Design* (Amsterdam: BIS Publishers, 2016), 7.

5. Andrieu d'Albas, *Death of a Navy: Japanese Naval Action in World War II*, translated by Anthony Rippon (New York: The Devin-Adair Company, 1957), 348–9.

6. Marc' Antonio Bragadin, *The Italian Navy in World War II*, translated by Gale Hoffman (Annapolis: United States Naval Institute, 1957), 324.

7. Raymond de Belot, *The Struggle for the Mediterranean, 1939–1945*, translated by James A. Field, Jr. (Princeton: Princeton University Press, 1951), 149–50.

8. Samuel Eliot Morison, *The Two-Ocean War: A Short History of the United States Navy in the Second World War* (Boston: Little, Brown & Co., 1963), 406.

9. This is a central theme of Douhet's *Command of the Air*, translated by Dino Ferrari (New York: Coward-McCann, 1942).

10. Hugh Thomas, *The Spanish Civil War* (New York: Harper & Brothers, Publishers, 1961), 542.

11. See Ivan Musicant, *Battleship at War: The Epic Story of the* USS *Washington* (New York: Harcourt

Brace Jovanovich Publishers, 1986), 132–36 for a detailed account.

12. Major Erwin Lessner, *Blitzkrieg and Bluff: The Legend of Nazi Invincibility*, translated by A.B. Ashton (New York: G.P. Putnam's Sons, 1943), 171–72.

13. Both quotes from Cajus Bekker, *Hitler's Naval War*, translated by Frank Ziegler (Garden City, NY: Doubleday & Co., 1974), 24. Emphasis in Raeder's original memo.

14. *Ibid.*, 214.

15. Data and quotes from B.H. Liddell Hart, *History of the Second World War* (New York: G.P. Putnam's Sons, 1970), 243.

16. Gerhard Weinberg, *A World at Arms: A Global History of World War II* (Cambridge: Cambridge University Press, 1994), 463–64.

17. Winston S. Churchill, *The Second World War*, Vol. I, *The Gathering Storm* (Boston: Houghton Mifflin Company, 1948), 173.

18. John Steinbeck, *The Moon Is Down* (New York: P.F. Collier & Son Corporation, 1942), 185.

19. John Keegan, *The Second World War* (New York: Viking, 1990), 252.

20. Ronald Lewin, *The American Magic: Codes, Ciphers and the Defeat of Japan* (New York: Farrar Straus Giroux, 1982), 224. Emphasis in the original.

21. On these terrible, strategically counterproductive events, see: Iris Chang, *The Rape of Nanking: The Forgotten Holocaust of World War II* (New York: Basic Books, 1997); and Nicholas Tarling, *A Sudden Rampage: The Japanese Occupation of Southeast Asia, 1941–1945* (Honolulu: University of Hawaii Press, 2001).

22. Samuel Eliot Morison, *History of United States Naval Operations in World War II*, vol. 13, *The Liberation of the Philippines* (Boston: Little, Brown & Co., 1959), 301. See also the memoir of the SACO commander, Vice Admiral Milton Miles, *A Different Kind of War* (Garden City: Doubleday, 1967).

23. Cited in John Toland, *The Flying Tigers* (New York: Random House, 1963), 28.

24. Mitsuo Fuchida and Masatake Okumiya, *Midway: The Battle That Doomed Japan*, edited by Clarke H. Kawakami and Roger Pineau (Annapolis: Naval Institute Press, [1955] 1992), 270.

25. See his *1942: The Year That Doomed the Axis* (New York: David McKay Company, 1967), for a thoughtful, thorough exposition of this line of argument.

26. Weinberg, *A World at Arms*, 288–89.

27. *Ibid.*, 289.

28. Erich von Manstein, *Lost Victories*, ed. and trans. by A.G. Powell (London: Methuen & Co. Ltd, 1958), 354; Alan Clark, *Barbarossa: The Russian-German Conflict, 1941–1945* (London: Cassell, 1965), 255; Heinz Schröter, *Stalingrad*, trans. by Constantine Fitzgibbon (New York: Dutton, 1958), viii; and Antony Beevor, *Stalingrad: The Fateful Siege, 1942–1943* (New York: Viking, 1998), 310.

29. Heinz Guderian, *Panzer Leader*, translated by Constantine Fitzgibbon (New York: E.P. Dutton & Co., Inc., 1952), 309.

30. Hanson Baldwin, *Battles Lost and Won: Great Campaigns of World War II* (New York: Konecky & Konecky, 1966), 225.

31. Hugh Pond, *Salerno* (Boston: Little, Brown & Co., 1961), 203.

32. David Irving, *The Trail of the Fox: The Life of Field-Marshal Erwin Rommel* (London: Weidenfeld and Nicolson, 1977), 314.

33. Victor Davis Hanson, *The Second World Wars: How the First Global Conflict Was Fought and Won* (New York: Basic Books, 2017), 289.

34. Paul Carell, *Invasion—They're Coming!* Translated by E. Osers (New York: E.P. Dutton & Co., Inc., 1963), 157.

35. An authoritative recent account of this battle can be found in Antony Beevor, *The Battle of Arnhem* (New York: Viking, 2018).

36. Charles Messenger, *The Blitzkrieg Story* (New York: Charles Scribner's Sons, 1976), 214.

37. As to *Blitzkrieg* being a dodgy doctrine from its inception, see Lloyd Clark, *Blitzkrieg: Myth, Reality and Hitler's Lightning War* (New York: Atlantic Monthly Press, 2016).

38. Adolf Galland, *The First and the Last*, translated by Mervyn Savill (New York: Henry Holt & Co., 1954), 242.

39. Omar Bradley, *A Soldier's Story* (New York: Henry Holt & Co., 1951), 524. On the hard fighting west of the Rhine, see R.W. Thompson's classic *Battle for the Rhineland* (London: Hutchinson, 1958).

40. Harald Busch, *U-Boats at War*, translated by L.P.R. Wilson (New York: Ballantine Books, 1955), 138.

41. Herbert Werner, *Iron Coffins* (New York: Holt, Rinehart and Winston, 1969), 324.

42. Karl Doenitz, *Ten Years and Twenty Days*, trans. by R.H. Stevens (Cleveland: The World Publishing Company, 1959), 353.

43. Statistics are from Samuel Eliot Morison, *History of United States Naval Operations in World War II*, 15 vols. (Boston: Little, Brown & Co., 1947–1962), Vol. I, 410 and Vol. X, 365.

44. Cajus Bekker, *The Luftwaffe War Diaries*, trans. and ed. by Frank Ziegler (Garden City: Doubleday & Co., 1968), 317.

45. Werner Baumbach, *Broken Swastika: The Defeat of the Luftwaffe*, trans. by Frederick Holt (New York: Dorset Press, [1949] 1992), 186 for both quotes.

46. Vice Admiral Charles A. Lockwood, *Sink 'Em All: Submarine Warfare in the Pacific* (New York: E.P. Dutton & Co., Inc., 1951), 358.

47. Henry Steele Commager, *The Story of the Second World War* (Boston: Little, Brown & Co., 1945), 437.

48. Carl von Clausewitz, *On War*, edited and translated by Michael Howard and Peter Paret (Princeton: Princeton University Press, 1976), 86.

49. Leo Tolstoy, *War and Peace*, translated by Ann Dunnigan (New York: The New American Library, 1968), 1429.

50. Andrew Roberts, *The Storm of War: A New*

*History of the Second World War* (New York: Harper-Collins Publishers, 2011), 598.

51. Doenitz, *Ten Years and Twenty Days*, 236.

52. Galland, *The First and the Last*, 255.

53. F.W. Winterbotham, *The Ultra Secret* (New York: Harper & Row, 1974), 190.

54. Andrew Roberts, *Masters and Commanders: The Military Geniuses Who Led the West to Victory in World War II* (London: Penguin Books, 2008), 581.

## Chapter 10

1. Charles Messenger, *The Blitzkrieg Story* (New York: Scribner, 1976), 219.

2. John Keegan, *The Price of Admiralty: The Evolution of Naval Warfare* (New York: Viking, 1989), 272.

3. See Dave Majumdar, "American Warplane's Forgotten Nazi Past," *The Daily Beast*, October 12, 2014.

4. On the spotty results of strategic bombing campaigns, see Robert Pape, *Bombing to Win: Air Power and Coercion in War* (Ithaca: Cornell University Press, 1996).

5. A good example of which is Harlan Ullman and James Wade, *Shock and Awe: Achieving Rapid Dominance* (Washington, DC: National Defense University Press, 1996).

6. Captain Wayne P. Hughes, Jr., USN (Ret.) and Rear Admiral Robert P. Girrier, USN (Ret.), *Fleet Tactics and Naval Operations*, 3rd edition (Annapolis: Naval Institute Press, 2018), 162.

7. See Sherry Sontag, Christopher Drew and Annette Lawrence Drew, *Blindman's Bluff* (New York: Public Affairs, 1998).

8. A. R. Millett, "Assault from the Sea," in W. Murray and Millett, eds., *Military Innovation in the Interwar Period* (Cambridge: Cambridge University Press, 1996), 89.

9. Al Suri's *Global Islamic Resistance Call* is voluminous; but his ideas have been neatly summarized in Brynjar Lia, *Architect of Global Jihad: The Life of al Qaeda Strategist Abu Mus'ab al-Suri* (New York: Columbia University Press, 2008).

10. Lynn Montross, *War Through the Ages*, 3rd edition (New York: Harper & Row, Publishers, 1960), 744–5. Emphasis is in the original.

11. J.F.C. Fuller, *Julius Caesar* (London: Eyre & Spottiswoode, 1965), 74.

12. Brigadier John Strawson, *The Battle for North Africa* (New York: Grosset & Dunlap Company, 1969), 155 for both quotes.

13. Omar N. Bradley, *A Soldier's Story* (Henry Holt & Co., 1951), 415–6.

14. Martin Blumenson, *The Duel for France* (New York: Perseus, [1963] 2000), 7–8.

15. Len Deighton, *Fighter: The True Story of the Battle of Britain* (London: Jonathan Clowes, Ltd, 1979), p.96 for both quotes.

16. On these activities, see: Colin Blackstock, "Judges to decide today on plane-spotters," *The Guardian*, December 10, 2001; and Gerard Seenan and Giles Tremlett, "How planespotters turned into the scourge of the CIA," *The Guardian*, December 9, 2005.

17. Paul Carell, *The Foxes of the Desert*, translated from the German by Mervyn Savill (New York: E.P. Dutton & Co., 1961), 35.

18. Bob Woodward, *Bush at War* (New York: Simon & Schuster, 2002), 101.

19. Lee De Forest, "Robot Television Bomber," *Popular Mechanics*, June 1940.

20. See Sebastien Roblin, "The Navy has one submarine that could drop 154 Tomahawk missiles on North Korea," *The National Interest*, December 6, 2017.

21. G. Rottman, *Carlson's Marine Raiders: Makin Island 1942* (Oxford: Osprey, 2014).

22. Bevin Alexander, *The Future of Warfare* (New York: W.W. Norton, 1995), 51.

23. Commander Marc' Antonio Bragadin, *The Italian Navy in World War II* (Annapolis: United States Naval Institute, 1957), 32.

24. Admiral Karl Doenitz, *Memoirs: Ten Years and Twenty Days*, trans. by R.H. Stevens (New York: The World Publishing Company, 1959), 354.

25. Bernard Brodie, *Strategy in the Missile Age* (Princeton: Princeton University Press, 1959), 7.

26. The initial argument in favor of Star Wars was crafted by General Daniel Graham, *High Frontier: A Strategy for National Survival* (New York: Pinnacle Books, 1983). A more critical view was articulated by Frances FitzGerald, *Way Out There in the Blue: Reagan, Star Wars and the End of the Cold War* (New York: Simon & Schuster, 2000).

27. A classic exposition of the ethical principle of noncombatant immunity can be found in Michael Walzer, *Just and Unjust Wars: A Moral Argument with Historical Illustrations*, 5th Edition (New York: Basic Books, 2015).

28. Field Marshal the Viscount Slim, *Defeat Into Victory* (New York: David McKay Co., 1961), 412.

29. For an overview, see Trevor Nevitt Dupuy, *European Resistance Movements* (New York: Franklin Watts, Inc., 1965). On Mme. Fourcade, a recent detailed study is Lynne Olson's *Madame Fourcade's Secret War* (New York: Random House, 2019).

30. Carl von Clausewitz, *On War*, edited and translated by Michael Howard and Peter Paret (Princeton: Princeton University Press, 1976). Quotes are from pp. 76, 86.

31. Cited in William L. Shirer, *The Rise and Fall of the Third Reich: A History of Nazi Germany* (New York: Simon and Schuster, 1960), 940–41.

32. Alistair Horne, *A Savage War of Peace* (New York: The Viking Press, 1978), 400.

33. Clausewitz, *On War*, 483.

34. Hermann Balck, *Order in Chaos*, edited and translated by Major General David T. Zabecki and Lieutenant Colonel Dieter Biedekarken (Lexington: the University Press of Kentucky, [1981] 2017), 452.

# Works Cited

There is no way to pinpoint the exact number of books written about the Second World War. Amazon simply lists this category as "over 50,000." So what follows is necessarily a small slice of the total. My slice, the works that I have found very useful in my effort to provide a "design-based perspective" on that great conflict. Few of them are specifically focused upon design; but a great many of them can be mined for insight into how various technologies, organizational forms, and military doctrines were—or weren't—aligned. Several one-volume histories are among the works that reflect deep awareness of design issues, from J.F.C. Fuller's and Henry Steele Commager's studies soon after the war, to compelling analyses provided by Antony Beevor, Max Hastings, Victor Davis Hanson, and Andrew Roberts over the past decade. Earlier landmark accounts, by Martin Gilbert, B.H. Liddell Hart, John Keegan, Robert Leckie and Gerhard Weinberg have also proved of immense value to my work. But all the studies listed below have, in one important way or another, contributed to my understanding of the greatest of all wars that shaped, and whose lessons continue to influence, our world.

Accoce, Pierre (1967). *A Man Called Lucy, 1939–1945*, Coward McCann.

Adams, Henry (1967). *1942: The Year That Doomed the Axis*, David McKay Co.

Agawa, Hiroyuki (1979). *The Reluctant Admiral: Yamamoto and the Imperial Navy*, Kodansha.

Ambrose, Stephen E. (1994). *D-Day, June 6, 1944: The Climactic Battle of World War II*, Simon & Schuster.

Atkinson, Rick (2002). *An Army at Dawn: The War in North Africa, 1942–1944*.

_____ (2007). *The Day of Battle: The War in Sicily and Italy, 1943–1944*, both volumes published by Henry Holt & Co.

Balck, Hermann ([1981]2017). *Order in Chaos*, edited by David T. Zabecki and Dieter Biedekarken, The University Press of Kentucky.

Baldwin, Hanson (1966). *Battles Lost and Won: Great Campaigns of World War II*, Konecky & Konecky.

Barber, Noel (1968). *A Sinister Twilight: The Fall of Singapore, 1942*, Houghton.

Barnett, Correlli (1960). *The Desert Generals*, Allen & Unwin.

_____ (1963). *The Swordbearers*, New American Library.

_____ (1991). *Engage the Enemy More Closely: The Royal Navy in the Second World War*, W.W. Norton.

Baumbach, Werner (1960). *Broken Swastika: The Defeat of the Luftwaffe*, Dorset.

Bayerlein, Fritz ([1956]2013). "El Alamein," in Seymour Freidin and William Richardson, eds., *The Fatal Decisions: Six Decisive Battles of World War II from the Viewpoint of the Vanquished*, Stackpole Books.

Beaufre, Andre (1968). *1940: The Fall of France*, Alfred A. Knopf.

Beevor, Antony (1998). *Stalingrad: The Fateful Siege, 1942–1943*, Viking.

_____ (2002). *The Fall of Berlin, 1945*, Viking.

_____ (2012). *The Second World War*, Little, Brown.

_____ (2018). *The Battle of Arnhem*, Viking.

Bekker, Cajus (1968). *The Luftwaffe War Diaries*, Doubleday.

_____ (1974). *Hitler's Naval War*, Doubleday.

Belot, Raymond de (1951). *The Struggle for the Mediterranean, 1939–1945*, Princeton University Press.

Bennett, G.H., and R. Bennett (2004). *Hitler's Admirals*, Naval Institute.

Beringer, R.E. et al. (1986). *Why the South Lost the Civil War*, Georgia.

Bernstein, Jeremy (1995). *Hitler's Uranium Club: The Secret Recordings at Farm Hall*, Copernicus Books.

Blackstock, Colin (2001). "Judges to decide today on plane-spotters," *The Guardian*.

Blair, Clay (1975). *Silent Victory: The U.S. Submarine War Against Japan*, J.B. Lippincott Co.

_____ (1998). *Hitler's U-Boat War: The Hunted*, Random House.

Bloch, Marc ([1940]1968). *Strange Defeat*, W.W. Norton & Co., Inc.

Blumenson, Martin ([1963]2000). *The Duel for France, 1944*, Perseus Books.

_____ (1968). *Sicily: Whose Victory?* Ballantine Books.

Borghese, J. Valerio (1952). *Sea Devils: Italian Navy Commandos in World War II*, Andrew Melrose, Ltd.

Boritt, G.S., ed. (1992). *Why the Confederacy Lost*, Oxford University Press.

Bradford, Ernle (1986). *Siege: Malta 1940–1943*, William Morrow.

Bradley, Omar (1951). *A Soldier's Story*, Henry Holt & Co., Inc.

Bragadin, Marc' Antonio (1957). *The Italian Navy in World War II*, Naval Institute.

Brodie, Bernard (1959). *Strategy in the Missile Age*, Princeton University Press.

Bryant, Arthur (1957). *The Turn of the Tide*, Doubleday.

Burdick, Charles (1968). *Germany's Military Strategy and Spain in World War II*, Syracuse University.

Busch, Harald (1955). *U-Boats at War*, Ballantine Books.

Calabretta, Giulia, Gerda Gemser and Ingo Karpen (2016). *Strategic Design*, BIS Publishers.

Carell, Paul (1961). *The Foxes of the Desert*, E.P. Dutton & Co., Inc.

_____ (1963). *Invasion—They're Coming!* E.P. Dutton & Co., Inc.

_____ (1964). *Hitler Moves East, 1941–1943*, Little, Brown & Co.

_____ (1966). *Scorched Earth: The Russian-German War, 1943–1944*, Little, Brown.

Carver, Field-Marshal Lord Michael (1989). "Manstein," in *Hitler's Generals,* Correlli Barnett, ed., Grove Weidenfeld.

Chang, Iris (1997). *The Rape of Nanking: The Forgotten Holocaust of World War II*, Basic Books.

Churchill, Winston S. (1948). *The Second World War*, Vol. I, *The Gathering Storm*, Houghton Mifflin.

_____ (1950). *The Second World War*, Vol. IV, *The Hinge of Fate*, Houghton Mifflin.

Clark, Alan (1962). *The Fall of Crete*, Anthony Blond, Ltd.

_____ ([1965]2001). *Barbarossa: The Russian-German Conflict*, Cassell.

Clark, Lloyd (2011). *The Battle of the Tanks: Kursk 1943*, Atlantic Monthly Press.

_____ (2016). *Blitzkrieg: Myth, Reality, and Hitler's Lightning War*, Atlantic Monthly.

Clarke, Arthur C. (1951). "Superiority," in *The Magazine of Fantasy & Science Fiction*.

Clausewitz, Carl von (1976). *On War*, edited by Michael Howard and Peter Paret, Princeton University Press.

Commager, Henry Steele (1945). *The Story of the Second World War*, Little, Brown & Co.

Cooper, Bryan (1974). *The Story of the Bomber*, Octopus Books.

Coox, Alvin (1988). *Military Effectiveness*, Vol. III, *The Second World War*, Allan R. Millett and Williamson Murray, eds., Allen & Unwin.

Cowley, Robert, ed. (1999). *What If?* Putnam's.

Craig, Gordon (1986). "Delbrück," in Peter Paret, ed., *Makers of Modern Strategy*, Princeton University Press.

Creveld, Martin van (1973). *Hitler's Strategy, 1940–1941: The Balkan Clue*, Cambridge.

_____ (1989). *Technology and War*, Collier Macmillan.

Crowl, Philip, and Edmund Love (1955). *Seizure of the Gilberts and Marshalls*, Office of the Chief of Military History.

d'Albas, Andrieu (1957). *Death of a Navy: Japanese Naval Action in World War II*, Devin-Adair.

D'Este, Carlo (1989). "Model," in Correlli Barnett, ed., *Hitler's Generals*, Grove Weidenfeld.

_____ (1991). *Fatal Decision: Anzio and the Battle for Rome*, HarperCollins.

Dallin, Alexander ([1957]1981). *German Rule in Russia, 1941–1945: A Study of Occupation Policies*, Westview Press. Second, revised edition.

Davies, Norman (2003). *White Eagle, Red Star: The Polish-Soviet War 1919–1920 and the Miracle on the Vistula*, Random House UK.

Davis, Burke (1967). *The Billy Mitchell Affair*, Random House.

de Belot, Raymond (1951). *The Struggle for the Mediterranean, 1939–1945*, Princeton University Press.

De Forest, Lee (1940). "Robot Television Bomber," in *Popular Mechanics*.

de Gaulle, Charles (1932[2015]). *Le fil de l'épée*, Plon/[Tempus Perrin].

Deighton, Len (1979). *Fighter: The True Story of the Battle of Britain*, Jonathan Clowes, Ltd.

Delbrück, Hans ([1920]1990). *History of the Art of War*, four volumes, University of Nebraska Press.

Doenitz, Karl (1959). *Ten Years and Twenty Days*, World Publishing Co.

Douhet, Giulio (1942). *Command of the Air*, Coward-McCann.

Downing, David (1977). *The Devil's Virtuosos: German Generals at War, 1940–1945*, St. Martin's Press.

Dupuy, Trevor Nevitt (1965). *European Resistance Movements*, Franklin Watts.

Eimannsberger, Ludwig von (1934). *Der Kampfwagenberg*, J.F. Lehmann.

Eisenhower, Dwight D. (1946). *Report by the Supreme Commander to the Combined Chiefs of Staff on the Operations in Europe of the Allied Expeditionary*

*Force 6 June 1944 to 8 May 1945*, His Majesty's Stationery Office.

_____ (1948). *Crusade in Europe*, Doubleday & Co.

Ellis, John (1990). *Brute Force: Allied Strategy and Tactics in the Second World War*, Viking.

Erickson, John (1983). *The Road to Berlin*, Westview Press.

Feifer, George (1992). *Tennozan: The Battle of Okinawa and the Atomic Bomb*, Ticknor & Fields.

FitzGerald, Frances (2000). *Way Out There in the Blue: Reagan, Star Wars and the End of the Cold War*, Simon & Schuster.

Fleming, Peter (1957). *Operation Sea Lion*, Simon & Schuster.

Foley, Charles (1955). *Commando Extraordinary*, G.P. Putnam's Sons.

Forester, C.S. (1959). *The Last Nine Days of the Bismarck*, Little, Brown.

Frank, Richard (1990). *Guadalcanal*, Random House.

_____ (1999). *Downfall: The End of the Imperial Japanese Empire*, Random House.

Frank, Wolfgang (1955). *The Sea Wolves*, Rinehart.

Frischauer, Willi, and Robert Jackson (1955). *The Altmark Affair*, Macmillan.

Fuchida, Mitsuo (1986). "The Air Attack on Pearl Harbor," in David Evans, ed., *The Japanese Navy in World War II*, Naval Institute. Second edition.

_____ and Masatake Okumiya (1955). *Midway: The Battle That Doomed Japan*, Naval Institute.

Fuller, J.F.C. (1945). *Armament and History*, Scribner's.

_____ ([1948]1952). *The Second World War*, Duell, Sloan and Pierce.

_____ (1965). *Julius Caesar*, Eyre & Spottiswode.

Gallagher, Thomas (1970). *The X-Craft Raid*, Harcourt Brace Jovanovich.

_____ (1975). *Assault in Norway: Sabotaging the Nazi Nuclear Program*, The Lyons Press.

Galland, Adolf (1954). *The First and the Last: The Rise and Fall of the German Fighter Forces, 1938–1945*, Henry Holt & Co. Ballantine edition, 1957.

Gannon, Michael (1998). *Black May*, HarperCollins.

Garfield, Brian (1969). *The Thousand-Mile War: World War II in the Aleutians*, Ballantine Books.

Geer, Andrew (1948). *The Sea Chase*, Harper. Pocket Books edition, 1949.

Gibson, Hugh, ed. (1946). *The Ciano Diaries*, Doubleday & Co.

Gilbert, Martin (1989). *The Second World War: A Complete History*, Henry Holt & Co.

Gisevius, Hans (1947). *To the Bitter End: An Insider's Account of the Plot to Kill Hitler*, Houghton Mifflin.

Glantz, David M. (2004). *The Battle of Kursk*, University of Kansas Press.

Glines, Carroll V. (1990). *Attack on Yamamoto*, Crown Publishers.

Goldhagen, Daniel Jonah (1997). *Hitler's Willing Executioners*, Vintage.

Goldman, Stuart D. (2012). *Nomonhan: The Red Army's Victory that Shaped World War II*, Naval Institute.

Goutard, Adolphe (1956). *La guerre des occasions perdus*, Hachette.

Graham, Daniel (1983). *High Frontier, A Strategy for National Survival*, Pinnacle Books.

Graham, Dominick, and Shelford Bidwell (1986). *Tug of War: The Battle for Italy, 1943–45*, St. Martin's Press.

Guderian, Heinz ([1937]1999). *Achtung—Panzer!* Cassell.

_____ (1952). *Panzer Leader*, E.P. Dutton.

Hanson, Victor Davis (2013). *The Savior Generals*, Bloomsbury.

_____ (2017). *The Second World Wars: How the First Global Conflict Was Fought and Won*, Basic Books.

Hara, Tameichi (1961). *Japanese Destroyer Captain*, Ballantine Books.

Harsch, Joseph C. (1941). *Pattern of Conquest*, Doubleday, Doran.

Hastings, Max (2011). *Inferno: The World at War, 1939–1945*, Alfred A. Knopf.

Haukelid, Knut (1989). *Skis Against the Atom*, North American Heritage Press.

Heskett, John (2005). *Design: A Very Short Introduction*, Oxford University.

Heydte, Friedrich August von der (1958). *Daedalus Returned*, Hutchinson.

Hibbert, Christopher (1962). *Arnhem*, B.T. Batsford, Ltd.

Hitler, Adolf ([1925]1972). *Mein Kampf*, Hutchinson.

Hoffman, J. (2009). "Conduct of the War Through Soviet Eyes," in H. Boog, ed., *Germany and the Second World War*, IV, *Attack on the Soviet Union*, Clarendon.

Horne, Alistair (1969). *To Lose a Battle: France 1940*, Little, Brown.

_____ (1978). *A Savage War of Peace*, The Viking Press.

Hough, Richard (1963). *The Death of the Battleship*, Macmillan.

Hoyt, Edwin (1978). *Storm Over the Gilberts*, Van Nostrand Reinhold Co.

_____ (1978). *War in the Deep*, G.P. Putnam's Sons.

_____ (1985). *The Invasion Before Normandy: The Secret Battle of Slapton Sands*, Stein and Day Publishers.

_____ (1993). *Three Military Leaders: Heihachiro Togo, Isoroku Yamamoto, Tomoyuki Yamashita*, Kodansha.

Hughes, Wayne, and R.P. Girrier (2018). *Fleet Tactics and Naval Operations*, 3rd edition, Naval Institute.

Inoguchi, Rikihei, Tadashi Nakajima and Roger Pineau (1958). *The Divine Wind: Japan's Kamikaze Force in World War II*, Naval Institute.

Irving, David ([1967]1987). *The Destruction of Convoy PQ 17*, first edition Cassell, second, Richardson and Steirman.

_____ (1977). *Trail of the Fox: The Life of Field-Marshal Erwin Rommel*, Weidenfeld and Nicolson.

Jackson, W.G.F. (1967). *The Battle for Italy*, Harper & Row, Publishers.

Jones, R.V. (1978). *The Wizard War: British Scientific*

*Intelligence, 1939–1945*, Coward, McCann & Geoghegan.

Kahn, David ([1967]1996). *The Codebreakers*, Scribner. Revised and updated.

_____ (1991). *Seizing the Enigma: The Race to Break the German U-Boat Codes*, Houghton Mifflin.

Kantor, MacKinlay (1960). "If the South Had Won the Civil War," in *Look Magazine*.

Keegan, John (1989). *The Price of Admiralty: The Evolution of Naval Warfare*, Viking.

_____ (1990). *The Second World War*, Viking.

Keeley, Lawrence H. (1996). *War Before Civilization*, Oxford University Press.

Kennedy, Ludovic (1974). *Pursuit: The Chase and Sinking of the Battleship Bismarck*, Viking.

Kennedy, Paul (1988). *The Rise and Fall of the Great Powers*, Random House.

_____ (2013). *Engineers of Victory: The Problem Solvers Who Turned the Tide in the Second World War*, Random House.

Keynes, J.M. (1919). *The Economic Consequence of the Peace*, Macmillan.

Kurzman, Dan (1997). *Blood and Water: Sabotaging Hitler's Bomb*, Henry Holt & Co.

Lamont-Brown, Raymond (1997). *Kamikaze: Japan's Suicide Samurai*, Cassell.

League of Nations (1945). *World Economic Survey*, Geneva.

Leasor, James (1968). *Singapore: The Battle That Changed the World*, Doubleday.

Leckie, Robert (1988). *Delivered From Evil: The Saga of World War II*, Harper.

Lensen, George Alexander (1972). *The Strange Neutrality: Soviet-Japanese Relations During the Second World War*, Diplomatic Press.

Lessner, Erwin (1943). *Blitzkrieg and Bluff: The Legend of Nazi Invincibility*, G.P. Putnam's Sons.

Lewin, Ronald (1982). *The American Magic: Codes, Ciphers and the Defeat of Japan*, Farrar Straus Giroux.

Lia, Brynjar (2008). *Architect of Global Jihad: The Life of al Qaeda Strategist Abu Mus'ab al-Suri*, Columbia University Press.

Liddell Hart, B.H. (1948). *The Other Side of the Hill*, Cassell. Published in the United States as *The German Generals Talk*, William Morrow.

_____ (1953). *The Rommel Papers*, ed., Harcourt, Brace & Co.

_____ (1970). *History of the Second World War*, G.P. Putnam's Sons.

Lockwood, Charles A. (1951). *Sink 'Em All: Submarine Warfare in the Pacific*, E.P. Dutton & Co.

Lord, Walter (1967). *Incredible Victory: The Battle of Midway*, HarperCollins.

_____ (1977). *Lonely Vigil: Coastwatchers of the Solomons*, Viking.

_____ (1982). *The Miracle of Dunkirk*, Viking.

Lorelli, John A. (1984). *The Battle of the Komandorski Islands*, Naval Institute.

Macintyre, Ben (2010). *Operation Mincemeat*, Crown Publishers.

Macintyre, Donald (1959). *Narvik*, Norton & Co.

_____ (1971). *The Naval War Against Hitler*, Charles Scribner's Sons.

Macksey, Kenneth (1978). *Kesselring*, David McKay Co., Inc.

_____ (1998). *Military Errors of World War II*, Cassell & Co.

Majdalany, Fred (1957). *Cassino: Portrait of a Battle*, Longman, Greens & Co.

_____ (1965). *El Alamein: Fortress in the Sand*, J.B. Lippincott.

Majumdar (2014). "American Warplane's Forgotten Nazi Past," *The Daily Beast*.

Manchester, William (1968). *The Arms of Krupp, 1587–1968*, Bantam Books.

_____ (1978). *American Caesar: Douglas MacArthur 1880–1964*, Little, Brown & Co.

Manstein, Erich von (1958). *Lost Victories*, Methuen & Co., Ltd.

Marder, Arthur (1981). *Old Friends, New Enemies: The Royal Navy and the Imperial Japanese Navy*, Oxford University Press.

Martienssen, Anthony (1949). *Hitler and his Admirals*, E.P. Dutton & Co.

Mason, Herbert Molloy, Jr. (1973). *The Rise of the Luftwaffe, 1918–1940*, The Dial Press.

Maugeri, Franco (1948). *From the Ashes of Defeat*, Reynal & Hitchcock.

May, Ernest R. (2000). *Strange Victory: Hitler's Conquest of France*, Hill & Wang.

McCullough, David (1992). *Truman*, Simon & Schuster.

McKee, Alexander (1964). *Last Round Against Rommel: Battle of the Normandy Beachhead*, The New American Library.

Mearsheimer, John (1988). *Liddell Hart and the Weight of History*, Cornell University Press.

Mellenthin, F.W. von ([1956]1971). *Panzer Battles: A Study of the Employment of Armor in the Second World War*, University of Oklahoma Press/Ballantine.

Meroni, Anna (2008). "Strategic Design: Where Are We Now?" *Strategic Design Research Journal*.

Merriam, Robert ([1947]1957). *The Battle of the Bulge*, Random House.

Messenger, Charles (1976). *The Blitzkrieg Story*, Scribner.

Messerschmitt, Willi ([1946]2003). "The Me-262: Development, Experience, Success, and Prospects," in David Isby, editor, *Fighting the Bombers: The Luftwaffe's Struggle Against the Allied Bomber Offensive as Seen by its Commanders*, Greenhill Books.

Middleton, Drew (1971). "British Book Says German and Soviet Officials Met in '43 to Discuss Peace, *The New York Times*.

Miksche, F.O. (1942). *Attack: A Study of Blitzkrieg Tactics*, Random House.

Miles, Milton (1967). *A Different Kind of War*, Doubleday & Co.

Millett, Allan R. (1996). "Assault from the Sea," in

Williamson Murray and Millett, eds., *Military Innovation in the Interwar Period*, Cambridge.

Mommsen, Hans (2003). *Alternatives to Hitler*, Princeton University Press.

Montagu, Ewen (1954). *The Man Who Never Was*, J.B. Lippincott Co.

Montgomery, Field-Marshal the Viscount Bernard (1948). *El Alamein to the River Sangro*, Hutchinson & Co., Ltd.

Montross, Lynn (1960). *War Through the Ages*, Harper & Row. Third edition.

Moorehead, Alan (1965). *The Desert War*, Hamish Hamilton.

Morison, Samuel Eliot (1947–1962). *History of United States Naval Operations in World War II*, Little, Brown & Co.

_____ (1958). Vol. 12, *Leyte*.

_____ (1959). Vol. 13, *The Liberation of the Philippines*.

_____ (1963). *The Two-Ocean War: A Short History of the United States Navy in the Second World War*, Little, Brown.

Mosley, Leonard (1974). *The Reich Marshal*, Doubleday & Co.

Murray, Williamson (1996). "Armored Warfare: The British, French, and German Experiences," in Murray and A.R. Millett, eds., *Military Innovation in the Interwar Period*, Cambridge University Press.

_____ (2000). *Strategy for Defeat: The Luftwaffe, 1933–1945*, Quantam.

_____ (2009). "Versailles: the peace without a chance," in Murray and Jim Lacey, eds., *The Making of Peace: Rulers, States, and the Aftermath of War*, Cambridge University Press.

Musicant, Ivan (1986). *Battleship at War: The Epic Story of the USS Washington*, Harcourt Brace Jovanovich.

Nelson, Harold, and Erik Stolterman (2014). *The Design Way: Intentional Change in an Unpredictable World*, MIT. Second edition.

Newcomb, Richard F. (1983). *Iwo Jima*, Nelson Doubleday, Inc.

Nolan, Cathal J. (2017). *The Allure of Battle: A History of How Wars Have Been Won and Lost*, Oxford University Press.

O'Hara, Vincent P. (2004). *The German Fleet at War, 1939–1945*. Naval Institute.

Oi, Atsushi ([1969]1986). "Why Japan's Antisubmarine Warfare Failed," in David C. Evans, ed., *The Japanese Navy in World War II*, Naval Institute.

Olson, Lynne (2019). *Madame Fourcade's Secret War*, Random House.

Overy, Richard (1995). *Why the Allies Won*, W.W. Norton & Co.

_____ (2000). *The Battle of Britain: The Myth and the Reality*, Norton.

Pape, Robert (1996). *Bombing to Win: Air Power and Coercion in War*, Cornell University Press.

Parker, Geoffrey (1996). *The Military Revolution: Military Innovation and the Rise of the West, 1500–1800*, Cambridge University Press. Second edition.

Parker, Matthew (2004). *Monte Cassino: The Hardest-Fought Battle of World War II*, Doubleday.

Parssinen, Terry (2003). *The Oster Conspiracy of 1938: The Unknown Story of the Military Plot to Kill Hitler and Avert World War II*, HarperCollins.

Patton, George S. (1947). *War As I Knew It*, Houghton Mifflin Co.

Pavelec, Sterling (2007). *The Jet Race and the Second World War*, Naval Institute.

Petroski, Henry (1996). *Invention by Design: How Engineers Get From Thought to Thing*, Harvard.

Phillips, C.E. Lucas (1962). *Alamein*, Little, Brown & Co.

Pond, Hugh (1961). *Salerno*, Little, Brown & Co.

Pope, Dudley (1956). *The Battle of the River Plate*, Naval Institute.

_____ (1958). *73 North: The Battle of the Barents Sea*, Wyman and Sons.

Porch, Douglas (2004). *The Path to Victory: The Mediterranean Theater in World War II*, Farrar, Straus & Giroux.

Porten, E.P. von der (1969). *The German Navy in World War II*, Crowell Co.

Posen, Barry (1984). *The Sources of Military Doctrine: France, Britain, and Germany Between the World Wars*, Cornell University Press.

Powers, Thomas (1993). *Heisenberg's War: The Secret History of the German Bomb*, Da Capo Press.

Prados, John (1995). *Combined Fleet Decoded: The Secret History of American Intelligence and the Japanese Navy in World War II*, Random House.

Prange, Gordon W. (1981). *At Dawn We Slept: The Untold Story of Pearl Harbor*, McGraw-Hill.

Pugh, Stuart (1991). *Total Design: Integrated Methods for Successful Product Engineering*, Addison-Wesley.

Ready, J. Lee ([1987]2012). *The Forgotten Axis: Germany's Partners and Foreign Volunteers in World War II*, McFarland.

Reischauer, Edwin O. (1964). *Japan: Past and Present*, Knopf. Third edition.

Roberts, Andrew (2008). *Masters and Commanders: The Military Geniuses Who Led the West to Victory in World War II*, Penguin Books.

_____ (2011). *The Storm of War: A New History of the Second World War*, HarperCollins.

Roblin, Sebastien (2017). "The Navy has one submarine that could drop 154 Tomahawk missiles on North Korea," *The National Interest*.

Rommel, Erwin ([1937]1990). *Infanterie greift an* (*Attacks*), Fall River.

Roscoe, Theodore ([1949]1982). *United States Submarine Operations in World War II*, Naval Institute. Later edition, *Pig Boats*, published by Bantam Books.

Rottman, G. (2014). *Carlson's Marine Raiders: Makin Island 1942*, Osprey.

Rudel, Hans Ulrich (1952). *Stuka Pilot*, Euphorion Books.

Ruge, Friedrich (1957). *Der Seekrieg*, Naval Institute.

_____ (1979). *Rommel in Normandy*, Macdonald and Jane's.

Russ, Martin (1975). *Line of Departure: Tarawa*, Doubleday.

Ryan, Cornelius (1974). *A Bridge Too Far*, Simon & Schuster.

Sakai, Saburo, with Martin Caidin and Fred Saito (1957). *Samurai!* Doubleday.

Savage, Katharine (1958). *The Story of the Second World War*, Henry Z. Walck.

Schmid, Joseph ([1946]2003). "German Nightfighting from June 1943 to May 1945," in David Isby, ed., *Fighting the Bombers: The Luftwaffe's Struggle Against the Allied Bomber Offensive as Seen by its Commanders*, Greenhill Books.

Schröter, Heinz (1958). *Stalingrad*, E.P. Dutton & Co., Inc.

Seenan, Gerard, and Giles Tremlett (2005). "How plane-spotters turned into the scourge of the CIA," *The Guardian*.

Shankland, Peter, and Anthony Hunter (1961). *Malta Convoy*, Ives Washburn.

Sheinkin, Steve (2012). *Bomb: The Race to Build—and Steal—the World's Most Dangerous Weapon*, Roaring Brook.

Sherrod, Robert (1944). *Tarawa: The Story of a Battle*, Duell, Sloan & Pearce.

Shirer, William L. (1960). *The Rise and Fall of the Third Reich: A History of Nazi Germany*, Simon & Schuster.

_____ (1962). *The Sinking of the Bismarck*, Random House.

_____ (1969). *The Collapse of the Third Republic: An Inquiry into the Fall of France in 1940*, Simon & Schuster.

Shulman, Milton (1947). *Defeat in the West*, Secker and Warburg.

Slim, Field-Marshal Viscount William (1961). *Defeat Into Victory*, McKay.

Smith, Bradley F., and Elena Agarossi (1979). *Operation Sunrise: The Secret Surrender*, Basic Books, Inc.

Snyder, Louis L. (1960). *The War: A Concise History*, Julian Messner, Inc.

Sontag, Sherry, Christopher Drew and Annette Drew (1998). *Blindman's Bluff*, Public Affairs Press.

Spector, Ronald (1985). *Eagle Against the Sun: The American War with Japan*, Free Press.

Speer, Albert (1970). *Inside the Third Reich*, Macmillan.

Stafford, Edward P. (1984). *Little Ship, Big War: The Saga of DE343*, William Morrow & Co.

Steinbeck, John (1942). *The Moon Is Down*, P.F. Collier & Son Corporation.

Steinberg, Jonathan (1965). *Yesterday's Deterrent: Tirpitz and the Birth of the German Battle Fleet*, Macmillan.

Sternberg, Fritz (1938). *Germany and a Lightning War*, Faber & Faber.

Strawson, John (1969). *The Battle for North Africa*, Grosset & Dunlap Co.

_____ (1971). *Hitler as Military Commander*, Batsford, Ltd.

Tarling, Nicholas (2001). *A Sudden Rampage: The Japanese Occupation of Southeast Asia*, University of Hawaii Press.

Taylor, A.J.P. ([1961]1983). *The Origins of the Second World War*, Atheneum. With new preface and introduction.

Taylor, Telford (1958). *The March of Conquest*, Simon & Schuster.

_____ (1979). *Munich: The Price of Peace*, Doubleday.

Thomas, Hugh (1961). *The Spanish Civil War*, Harper & Brothers.

Thompson, R.W. (1958). *The Battle for the Rhineland*, Hutchinson.

Toland, John (1963). *The Flying Tigers*, Random House.

_____ (1970). *The Rising Sun: The Decline and Fall of the Japanese Empire*, Random House.

_____ (1982). *Infamy: Pearl Harbor and Its Aftermath*, Doubleday.

Tolstoy, Leo (1968). *War and Peace*, The New American Library edition.

Tregaskis, Richard (1943). *Guadalcanal Diary*, Random House.

Tsuji, Masanobu (1960). *Singapore: The Japanese Version*, St. Martin's.

Tuchman, Barbara W. (1970). *Stilwell and the American Experience in China, 1911–45*, Macmillan.

Tuleja, T.V. (1958). *Twilight of the Sea Gods*, W.W. Norton & Co.

Udet, Ernst ([1935]1970). *Ace of the Iron Cross*, Doubleday.

Ullman, Harlan, and James Wade (1996). *Shock and Awe: Achieving Rapid Dominance*, National Defense University Press.

United States Government (1946). *Strategic Bombing Survey*. Report No. 62, *Japanese Air Power*, Government Printing Office.

Vogt, Hannah (1964). *The Burden of Guilt: A Short History of Germany, 1914–1945*, Oxford University Press.

Walzer, Michael (2015). *Just and Unjust Wars: A Moral Argument with Historical Illustrations*, Basic Books, 5th edition.

Ward, Geoffrey C. et al. (1990). *The Civil War*, Alfred A. Knopf.

Warlimont, Walter (1964). *Inside Hitler's Headquarters, 1939–1945*, Weidenfeld and Nicolson, Ltd.

Webster, Sir Charles, and Noble Frankland (1961). *The Strategic Air Offensive Against Germany*, Her Majesty's Stationery Office.

Weinberg, Gerhard (1994). *A World at Arms: A Global History of World War II*, Cambridge University Press.

Wells, H.G. (1908). *The War in the Air*, George Bell & Sons.

Werner, Herbert (1969). *Iron Coffins*, Holt, Rinehart and Winston.

Werth, Alexander (1964). *Russia at War, 1941–1945*, E.P. Dutton.

Whaley, Barton (1973). *Codeword Barbarossa*, MIT.

Whiting, Charles (1976). *Bloody Aachen*, Stein and Day.

Wildenberg, Thomas (2013). *Billy Mitchell's War with the Navy: The Interwar Rivalry Over Air Power*, Naval Institute.

Wilmot, Chester (1952). *The Struggle for Europe*, Harper & Brothers, Publishers.

Wiltz, John Edward (1961). "The Nye Committee Revisited," *The Historian*.

Winterbotham, F.W. (1974). *The Ultra Secret*, Harper & Row.

Wohlstetter, Roberta (1962). *Pearl Harbor: Warning and Decision*, Stanford.

Wood, Derek, and Derek Dempster (1961). *The Narrow Margin*, McGraw-Hill.

Woodward, Bob (2002). *Bush at War*, Simon & Schuster.

Yardley, Herbert O. (1931). *The American Black Chamber*, The Bobbs-Merrill Co.

Young, Desmond (1950). *Rommel: The Desert Fox*, Harper & Bros.

Zeitzler, Kurt ([1956]2013). "Stalingrad," in S. Freidin and W. Richardson, eds., *The Fatal Decisions: Six Decisive Battles of World War II from the Viewpoint of the Vanquished*, Stackpole Books.

Zhukov, Georgi K., and Harrison Salisbury (1969). *Marshal Zhukov's Greatest Battles*, Harper & Row.

# *Index*

213